CW00801167

ATHEL JOHN

THE MUSTARD

SEED

The Transformation of the Anglo Saxons into the Christian English

www.atheljohn.com

© Athel John 2022

All rights reserved. No part of this publication may be reproduced, stored in a retrieval system, or transmitted in any form by any means, electronic, mechanical, photocopying, recording, scanning, or any other, without the prior permission of the author.

ISBN: 978-1-80227-322-9 (paperback)
ISBN: 978-1-80227-323-6 (ebook)

The author has asserted his rights under the Copyright, Designs and Patents Act, 1988, to be identified as the author of this work.

This book is for anyone of any background who has ever wondered what made the English.

Covering the periods 597 to 689 and 878 to 927, it recounts the epic transformation of the Anglo Saxons into the Christian English.

The perspective is unique, combining spiritual with secular, rediscovering lost or hidden things, reuniting the present with the past.

You will recover lost seeds from ancient times – people who laid foundations that endure to this day.

CONTENTS

1. Transformation 5

2. Introduction 6

3. Structure and Terminology 8

4. Preview of the Whole Book 13

5. Conception – Ethelbert and Bertha – 597 28

6. Gestation – 597 To 634 44

7. Trouble 71

8. Labour Pains 72

9. White Blade Returns 86

10. Birth – 634/5 87

11. Beneath the Lid 110

12. In the Nursery – 635 To 650 118

13. Precious Things 151

14. Open Heaven 152

15. Toddling – 650s to 663 180

16. Innocence Lost – 650s to 668 210

17. Cosmic Seed 237

18. Saint Martin of Tours (316-397) and His Spiritual Descendants 238

19. Charts of Martinian Christian Spiritual Descent 272

20. Off to School – Archbishop Theodore – 668 to 669 277

21. Postscript – King Oswy of Northumbria and His Sons 311

22. Graduation – The Nation of the English – 878 to 927 321

23. The Mustard Seed 373

24. Saint King Oswald of Northumbria 383

25. Index 386

CHAPTER 1.

Transformation

In the Dark Ages, a new Identity developed in the Anglo Saxon people groups.

Based on that new Identity, they gradually unified into one people group, the Early English.

It was a brand new and transformative Christian Identity that shaped them.

That was the foundation upon which they built their nationhood.

The backdrop was Dark.

The process was turbulent.

But into the Dark Ages, Light came.

It was an epic story. It has been all but lost to our history now.

This book rediscovers it.

Artwork: Ben Emet

CHAPTER 2.

Introduction

In a period of less than a hundred years from the year 597, a radical transformation of Identity came into the people group we now call the "Anglo Saxons" or "Early English". They took on a new Christian Identity. That gradually became the English-nation-uniting force for a number of related but fragmented Germanic people groups. And it bequeathed a sense of Christian Identity to their English descendants which lasted for more than a thousand years. It was birthed out of a momentous Christian Awakening which was amongst the greatest of all time.

That transformative Awakening has been all but lost to history. This book's purpose is to rediscover it. This book is different from most other books in that it combines secular history and political appraisal with Christian history and spiritual appraisal.

It is the fashion of Christian writers to write solely of Christian things and for fellow Christians, most often to disciple their readers. If a Christian writer tackles history, they mainly stick to the history of the Church or of Christian people. On the other hand, it is the fashion of secular writers to write histories focussed solely on the secular dimension of things, the politics of who did what to whom and when and for what gain. Where there is a Christian element in the history, it gets labelled "Religion" and is acknowledged. But little attempt is made to come to grips with the world-shaping effect of the spirituality of the Christian element. The two fashions write on either side of a great wall.

However, English history has intertwined the Christian Identity so completely with the National Identity that neither fashion, staying each on its own side of the wall, really tells the English what their spiritual roots are and how their Identity was founded upon those in their real world history.

So this book follows neither fashion. It takes the Christian and the secular together within real world history. It appraises how that combination first shaped the peoples who became the English and how "England" came to have "Christian Identity" from the earliest times.

This book is for anyone, Christian or not, English ethnic or not. If you come to this book from an ethnicity not traditionally thought of as English, well... the English were once not English. They were Germanic and became English through multi-ethnic Christian additions. If you come from a background that is not Christian, well... so too did the English.

This is not an academic book. There are no footnotes. I have taken trouble to research and try to be accurate, but my main focus is on interpretation and bringing lost or hidden things to light.

Neither is this book a Christian book. It shows how principles of Christian spirituality have shaped the real history of the English. But it is not full of Christian scripture quotes. Rather, I paraphrase a few of them or combine multiple threads of them to draw out the shaping spiritual principles.

Instead, this book is for anyone from any background who wants to understand how the ancient Christian spirituality got into English roots and shaped the sense of Identity.

CHAPTER 3.

Structure and Terminology

The Christian Awakening experienced by the Anglo Saxon people groups was amongst the most transformative of all time anywhere. The spiritual transformation led to political transformation. The fragmented Anglo Saxon people groups united around the new and shared Christian Identity. It was within that Christian Identity that they gradually became one people group: the Early English. England became the given name of their land.

This book is the story of the first three generations of the process. I am going to structure it around the natural cycle of Conception, Birth and Growing Up.

First, a map to position the various Kings who appear on the chart that follows it:

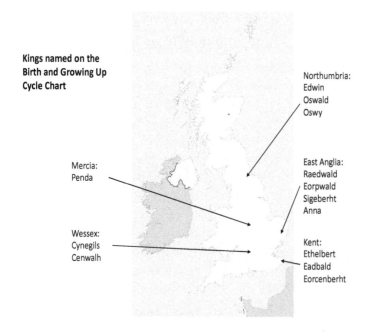

Kings named on the
Birth and Growing Up
Cycle Chart

Northumbria:
Edwin
Oswald
Oswy

Mercia:
Penda

East Anglia:
Raedwald
Eorpwald
Sigeberht
Anna

Wessex:
Cynegils
Cenwalh

Kent:
Ethelbert
Eadbald
Eorcenberht

Next, the chart below is a brief summary of the order that will be followed chapter by chapter. It is structured as a process from Conception via Gestation and Labour Pains to Birth, and after that through Nursery, Toddling and Loss of Innocence to Going Off to School.

Begin reading in the centre of the chart, at "Conception". Proto-Nation-Building events are shown in yellow.

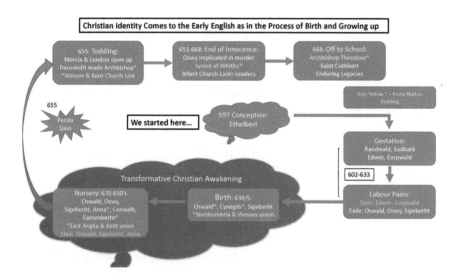

There will be one other chapter to add at the end:

Graduation: Alfred the Great and Family, 878 to 927. I treat them as the fuller-grown plant which developed out of the seed that the first three generations on the chart sowed.

Terminology

Before I begin the story, I should clarify some terminology that I use.

1. <u>Anglo Saxons.</u> Multiple Germanic people groups who invaded what we now call England before England existed. The process began as early as about 450 but got underway in earnest from about 540. This book commences from 597. In modern times, the phrase "Anglo Saxon" has

acquired latter-day "Imperialist" connotations. However, this book is set in the times when the peoples were barely emerging from their ancient Germanic roots. Applied to those times, I think it remains a time-honoured and succinct label to summarise many tribes. Therefore, I use it quite often to denote those Germanic people groups.

2. <u>Early English.</u> This phrase is a more modern replacement for "Anglo Saxon". I believe that it was coined with the intention to give less offence in post-Imperial times. "Anglo Saxon" in some understandings = "white and/or Anglo supremacist". However, I think that the term "Early English" is a more inclusive way of acknowledging the transformative Roman, Celtic and Frankish streams of Christian spirituality which permeated the Anglo Saxons from Roman, Celtic and Frankish sources. It was those that turned the Anglo Saxons into the Early English. And it was those that descended to shape "the English" and "England". Therefore, in this particular book, I use the phrase "Early English" when denoting the Germanic people groups which had those transformative spiritual forces at work within them.

   Summary: I use "Anglo Saxon" when denoting the Germanic people groups and "Early English" when denoting those same groups with the new Christian spirituality at work within them.

3. <u>Proto-English.</u> I sometimes use this phrase in place of "Early English", both to break the monotony and to convey the sense of Christian English Identity gradually morphing out of the older Anglo Saxon.

4. <u>Pagan.</u> In this book, the word normally means "the belief system preceding; not Christian".

There now follows a fuller guide to the Christian terminology I use.

I take care to distinguish between the streams of Christian Life encountered by the Anglo Saxons. There were four. All were contained within a Roman Catholic whole, but it is essential to discern each type within that.

- Roman Catholic: Representing the mainstream Church of Rome at the time.

- Britonnic: The main Christian way practised amongst the Britonnic Celts. It was acquired from the Old Roman Empire in the West between 177 and 407. This Christian way of the Britons had become isolated from Rome.

- Martinian and/or Gaelic Martinian: The Christian way that came to the Anglo Saxons from the Celtic Scots (a.k.a. Gaels) and Picts. It was descended from St Martin of Tours, hence "Martinian". Martin died in 397. His way of Christian spirituality spread posthumously and mainly after the fall of the Western Empire in 410. This Christian way of the Gaels had become culturally distinct from Rome.

- Romano Martinian: The Christian way that came to the Anglo Saxons from the Germanic Franks in Gaul. It, too, was descended from St Martin of Tours. The Franks, however, were more within the Roman Catholic cultural mainstream.

Although it may seem detailed, it is not possible to understand the spiritual and political dynamics of the period without the Christian distinctions. Neither is it possible to come to terms with the exact nature of the Christian spirituality which permeated the founding roots of the Early English.

Different mixtures of these streams impacted, in different ways, kingdom by kingdom. The two maps below represent the following:

i. The broad locations of the people groups who feature in this book.

ii. The broad locations of the Britonnic, Martinian and Romano Martinian Christian streams around and shortly after 597 when King Ethelbert of Kent first received the mission of St Augustine of Canterbury from Rome.

People Group Locations

Simplified for reference to the main narrative

Not every kingdom or tribe is on here

Britons, Picts and Scots, a.k.a. Gaels, were all "Celtic"

Franks were Germanic

The rest were the Anglo Saxons, also Germanic

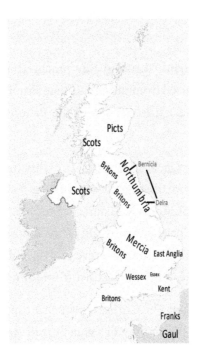

The most influential Christian streams on the Anglo Saxons would become the ones held to by the Scots, a.k.a. Gaels, and the Franks

3

Christian Identity up to 597

Anglo Saxons were going to embrace and be embraced by the Martinian and Romano Martinian Christian streams as they came from the Scots, a.k.a. Gaels, and the Franks.

They would for the most part reject and be rejected by the Britonnic Christian stream.

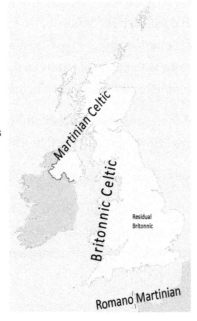

12

CHAPTER 4.

Preview of the Whole Book

Now that I have introduced you to the terminology I use, and to the structure of the book as covering a cycle from conception to growing up, here is a high-level overview of the whole period the book will cover from 597 to 689.

Christian Identity in the Early English took root in the period from 597 in a process that I liken to Conception, Gestation, Labour Pains, Birth, Nursery, Toddling, Loss of Innocence and Off to School.

It came to its Nation-Founding expression in a period that I liken to "Graduation". This was centuries later, in the time of King Alfred the Great of Wessex and family, broadly 878 to 927. I will add a Postscript chapter about that at the end of the book. A summary of that also follows within this high-level overview.

So, the story is broadly as follows:

Conception

Dates	Kings taking on Christian Identity and/or the Political Side of the Story	The Christian Influencers and/or the Christian Side of the Story
597 to 602	King Ethelbert of Kent. 602: First Canterbury Cathedral	Queen Bertha of Kent (Frankish). St Augustine of Canterbury (Latin Monk).

Gestation

Dates	Kings taking on Christian Identity and/or the Political Side of the Story	The Christian Influencers and/or the Christian Side of the Story
Before 616	King Raedwald of the East Angles, sympathetic but not wholly committed to Christian Identity.	Probably King Ethelbert of Kent.
616	Princes Oswald and Oswy of Bernicia flee into exile amongst the Gaelic Scots. Oswald later fully embraces the Gaelic version of the Martinian Christian Identity and so, too, in a more mixed way, does Oswy. They'll be back.	The Iona Community founded by St Columba. Gaelic Martinian Christian Life. St Columba passed away in 597, around the time St Augustine was starting out in Kent.
By 619	King Eadbald of Kent, son of Ethelbert, after a brief reversion to paganism.	Archbishop Laurence from Augustine's old team, and a phenomenon which put the Fear of God into Eadbald.
627	King Edwin of Northumbria, in mysterious circumstances, after many years thinking about it.	Queen Ethelburgha, Kentish daughter of Ethelbert and Bertha. And Paulinus, Latin Monk from Augustine's old team.
About 628	King Eorpwald of the East Angles, son of Raedwald.	King Edwin of Northumbria and Paulinus.

	However, Prince Sigeberht of the East Angles, younger son of Raedwald and brother of Eorpwald, has gone into exile amongst the Franks. Sigeberht later embraces their version of the Romano Martinian Christian Identity there. He'll be back	The Romano Martinian Christian stream of the Franks. The spirituality in the Franks had been reinforced by a Pictish Saint named Columbanus (not Columba) shortly before Augustine arrived at Canterbury. Their paths criss-crossed in Europe, but they never met.

Labour Pains

Dates	Kings taking on Christian Identity and/or the Political Side of the Story	The Christian Influencers and/or the Christian Side of the Story
By 630	Christian King Eorpwald of the East Angles murdered; the throne usurped.	Three years hiatus.
632	Christian King Edwin of Northumbria slain in battle with King Caedwalla of Gwynedd and King Penda of Mercia. Chaos ensues in the North.	Paulinus and Ethelburgha flee to Kent with royal children including Princess Eanflaed. She'll be back.

Birth – Transformative Christian Awakening on Multiple Fronts

Dates	Kings taking on Christian Identity and/or the Political Side of the Story	The Christian Influencers and/or the Christian Side of the Story
By 634		Bishop Birinus, Man of Mystery, arrives in Wessex. Sent from Rome. Frankish, probably of the Romano Martinian Christian Life reinforced by Columbanus.
	Returning from exile, Sigeberht takes over the East Anglian throne. Receives a dynamic community of monks out of what we now call Ireland. Also sends to Canterbury, seeking a Bishop from the Roman church.	Bishop Felix arrives at Canterbury, a Frank displaced by political upheaval in Burgundy. Definitely of the reinforced Romano Martinian Christian Life. Archbishop Honorius sends him on to the East Angles. He and Sigeberht, same spiritual background, hit it off.
By 635	St Columba, departed 597, appears to Prince Oswald, returning from exile, to strengthen him for the Turning Point Battle of Heavenfield.	St Columba still active, it would seem. Oswald, later Sainted, seems to have become a Fire-Starter in Christian terms.

Awakening of powerful Christian spirituality breaks out in multiple locations, encouraged and even sparked by Kings.	King Oswald takes the throne of all Northumbria. Sends to Iona for a Christian mission. Also reaches out to Wessex for a peace initiative to restrain King Penda of Mercia.	Iona, at second time of asking by Oswald, sends St Aidan. Hugely successful ministry, and in his wake comes a stream of ready-made and seasoned Gaelic Martinian Christian monks
	Nation Building Event 1: King Cynegils of Wessex takes on Christian Identity, godfathered by King Oswald.	Sponsored by Saint-King Oswald of Northumbria and Bishop Birinus.
	The Wessex royal house still had Saint-King Oswald at the heart of its culture three hundred years later when it created the Nation of the English. Queen Elizabeth II descends from that Wessex family. The Scottish line of descent to the English throne was chosen and anointed by St Columba.	Christian Turning Point 1. St Aidan, Bishop Birinus and Bishop Felix all powerfully influential at once across Northumbria, East Anglia and Wessex, all of them dynamic "imported" Martinian Gaelic or Frankish Christians. Kent, meanwhile, is making slow but steady progress in developing indigenous Roman Catholic Christian leaders from what was a zero base.

Nursery – like King Herod's of the Bible – Slaughter of the Innocents

Dates	Kings taking on Christian Identity and/or the Political Side of the Story	The Christian Influencers and/or the Christian Side of the Story
By 641	King Penda of Mercia slays Christian King Sigeberht of the East Angles. Christian King Anna takes the East Anglian throne.	Motivation of Penda: The Glory of Mercia. Penda also a resolute pagan. King Anna's family highly gifted in Christian terms, partaking of the spiritually reinforced Romano Martinian Frankish Christian stream, like Sigeberht. Anna more resistant to Penda than Sigeberht, as well.
642	King Oswald of Northumbria slain and dismembered by King Penda of Mercia. Prince Oswy succeeds to Bernicia as part of a now split-in-two Northumbrian throne.	King Penda to the Christian God: "That shows you!" But Northumbrian Christian Life increases and Oswald becomes a Saint-King. Oswy had also adopted Christian Identity at Iona in exile.
By 645	King Cenwalh of Wessex, son of Cynegils, after reversion to paganism, offends King Penda. Cenwalh escapes into exile at the court of King Anna.	Cenwalh persuaded into Christian Identity by King Anna during exile in East Anglia.

By 648	Cenwalh adopts Christian Identity, re-takes the throne of Wessex.	Infant Wessex church plods on.
Early 640s	King Eorcenberht, son of Eadbald, grandson of Ethelbert, succeeds to the Kentish throne. Nation Building Event 2: Marries Seaxburh, one of the daughters of King Anna of East Anglia.	Eorcenberht more committed to Christian Identity than his father, and Seaxburh inserts a Martinian rod in his Roman Catholic spine. Kent church still developing quietly. Kent and East Anglia together in developing educational and enlightenment standards.
Before 650	Eanflaed returns north. Oswy makes her his Queen. She was a child refugee in Kent with Paulinus and Ethelburgha after her father, King Edwin, was slain in battle with Penda.	Oswy committed to Gaelic Christian ways, Eanflaed to Roman ones. The Bernician part of Oswy's Northumbrian kingdom committed to Gaelic Christian ways, the Deiran part to Roman ones.

Toddling

Dates	Kings taking on Christian Identity and/or the Political Side of the Story	The Christian Influencers and/or the Christian Side of the Story
Early 650s	King Penda of Mercia harrying King Oswy of Northumbria, extracting tribute. King Oswy had children by a prior marriage before Eanflaed. Those children persuade one of King Penda's children, Prince Peada, to take on Christian Identity. Mercians possibly groaning by now for Christian Identity.	The Christian Great Awakening was moving into the consolidation phase by now.

Prince Peada of Mercia prefers outwardly Roman Catholic forms but is initiated into Christian Life with the Gaelic Martinian Christian spirituality. |
| 654 | King Penda corners and slays King Anna of East Anglia. Escalates hostility to King Oswy. | |
| 655 | Nation Building Event 3, much noted. Penda forces battle with Oswy at Winwaed. Oswy wins, to everyone's surprise, including his own. Penda slain. Proto-England sighs with relief. Mercians emerge to embrace Christian Identity. Peada made sub-king in Mercia under Oswy. Arrangement doesn't last, but the Christian Identity in Mercia does. | Oswy's revenge for years of bullying from Penda – sends the Gaelic Martinian Saints marching into Mercia.

Christian God to Penda, or so it would seem: "And that shows you!"

Mercia never had the same sweep of Great Awakening as broke out in 635. But it was to become resolute in adopting Roman Catholic forms, with |

		plentiful Gaelic Martinian Christian spirituality, and would embed this far and wide.
Also in 655	The King of Essex, another Sigeberht, adopts Christian Identity. Note: includes London.	Persuaded by King Oswy, who sends the Gaelic Martinian saints marching into Essex and London, as well as Mercia.
Also in 655	<u>Nation Building Event 4, little remarked.</u> A Wessex scholar named Deusdedit appointed Archbishop of Canterbury. Not a special career in itself, but the linkage of Kent and Wessex churches mattered very much.	First indigenous Archbishop, barely two generations after St Augustine of Canterbury began the process of building from a zero base. The effect of Wessex and Kent churches joining forces becomes a transformative foundation for nation building.

Loss of Innocence

Dates	Kings taking on Christian Identity and/or the Political Side of the Story	The Christian Influencers and/or the Christian Side of the Story
651	Oswy becomes King over the whole of divided Northumbria. In so doing, he engineers the murder of the Deiran King, Oswine.	Oswine at least as committed to Christian Identity as Oswy and much loved by St Aidan. Queen Eanflaed sorts things out in Religious terms, but it casts a dark shadow. Oswy later restored in Christian terms, when he refrains from vengeance over Mercia in 655.
Before 662	King Sigeberht of Essex and London murdered and his throne usurped.	East Anglia ultimately engineers baptism for the usurper, about 662, but not necessarily received willingly.
663	Deusdedit passes away.	Canterbury vacancy unfilled five years.
663/4	Nation Building Event 5: Synod of Whitby, in Northumbria. At this, King Oswy decides to build Northumbria as a Christian state on Romano Martinian church foundations rather than previous Gaelic Martinian church foundations. Still a strong inward Celtic culture, though. The effect	In that Northumbria after Whitby remains strongly Martinian in its Christian heritage from the Gaels, and in that the other kingdoms also have Martinian Christian heritage acquired via Frankish or Gaelic Christian sources, the Synod unifies the inward Christian Life of the many kingdoms. However, the human spirit within the Synod is

	is that Northumbria comes on board with the Romano Martinian Christian Identity developing in all the other kingdoms, so a further foundation for nationhood.	contentious and divided. It causes a fracture between Gaelic and Roman versions of outward Christian Identity. That descends into a more general and lasting sense of ethnic division. Unstable and fractious northern church appointments ensue after Whitby, especially regarding the Bishop of York.
By 668	King Cenwalh of Wessex falls out with Wine, the Bishop of Winchester. Wine departs and buys the bishopric of London from the King of Mercia, who is by now the over-king of London.	As at 668, the only pastoral leadership is from Bishop Wine in London and Bishop Chad in York. St Chad's ordination had been technically doubtful. Much contention in the North. Defeat about to be snatched from the jaws of victory?

Off to School – Archbishop Theodore

Dates	Kings taking on Christian Identity and/or the Political Side of the Story	The Christian Influencers and/or the Christian Side of the Story
668	Nation Building Event 6: Archbishop Theodore appointed to Canterbury.	Christian Turning Point 2: Archbishop Theodore appointed to Canterbury
By 673	Stable and gifted clerical appointments into many kingdoms, but complications in Northumbria Initiates a nationally structured way of governing church with political rulership participation. Improves underlying standards in church on multiple fronts and resolves infant conflicts.	Northumbrian Christian Identity comes into the grip of a Northern Church Colossus, Bishop Wilfrid. He (unintentionally) fosters a sense of North/South cultural divide Meanwhile St Cuthbert, a Colossus of Northern Christian Spirituality, leads a life of prayer on a tiny island. Becomes the hero saint of the North and, for centuries to come, of all proto-England.
679	Theodore brokers peace between Northumbria and Mercia.	Saint-King Oswald's bones get involved.

687 & 689		Cuthbert and Theodore pass away.
Legacies	The unifying Christian Identity that developed in Theodore's time, which integrated the political and the spiritual, endured more or less to the Great War, 1914-18, as did much of the church structure that he set up.	The potential in the English for the spirituality of a Cuthbert has never passed away. It is alive in our times and over much more of the world than Northumbria or England.
	English rulers first learned unifying ways of government from Theodore's ways of governing the church. Wessex later took them to the next level – proto-Parliament – in the nation-building times 250 years later.	And Cuthbert seems to have got involved in real world English history in 878 when Wessex began the nation-building. See the Postscript: Graduation.

PostScript – Graduation

Dates	Kings taking on Christian Identity and/or the Political Side of the Story	The Christian Influencers and/or the Christian Side of the Story
878	King Alfred of Wessex, Alfred the Great, wins the battle of Edington. The Turning Point battle with pagan Danish forces. It saved Christian Identity for the Early English. The Danish leader baptised in treaty after the battle.	St Cuthbert appears to Alfred to strengthen him for the Turning Point battle.

King Alfred's career bears a more general resemblance to that of King David of the Bible. |
| 910 | Alfred's highly gifted daughter, Aethelflaed of Wessex, a.k.a. the Lady of the Mercians, wins what is seen, with hindsight, to have been the ultimately decisive battle with the Danes at Tettenhall. | On Saint King Oswald's Day. The royal house of Wessex had treasured Saint-King Oswald ever since he had godfathered them into Christ in 635.

Oswald's bones had not long been laid in Aethelflaed's new church at Gloucester. |
| 927 | King Athelstan of Wessex, Alfred's grandson, becomes King of the English. | Alfred had been singled out by the Pope at age five. Athelstan was singled out by Alfred at age five and in many ways shaped by Aethelflaed. |
| By 1017 | King Canute, first Danish king of England, increases use of the title "Engla-Lond", | Canute's version of Christian Identity was far removed from the pristine Awakening |

	i.e. England, to denote distinction from his Danish territories. Canute had not long become a Christianised king.	spirituality of 635. But what a change. Just one pagan Danish leader first baptised via Alfred in 878. Five generations later, a Christianised Danish King of England.
597 to our own times	Alfred's family did not fight to establish England. They fought for the Christian Identity of a uniting people group which came to be called the English. Christian Identity was Conceived in them in 597 and Born in 635. You could say that the English were Christian before they were English, and it was Christian Identity that made the English.	The sense of Christian Identity within many of Theodore's structures endured to the Great War, 1914-18. As for the Martinian Christian spirituality, that broke out again in Protestants after the Reformation. It has been growing ever since and is now alive, worldwide and multi-ethnic.

CHAPTER 5.

Conception – Ethelbert and Bertha – 597

An epic tale lies ahead of us. Within three generations, what had been an almost entirely pagan culture was to become profoundly Christianised. It was one of the greatest Identity transformations in all human history. In the process, the Anglo Saxons were set on the path to becoming the English. Once the Christian flame had been lit in them, it spread like wildfire. It spread with the help of, rather than in spite of, many political leaders.

The story begins with the Conception of the Christian Identity in Kent in 597.

As seems fitting for a Conception, it arose out of one of history's lost love stories. I find that most heartening. It is very much the fashion to present early history as violence and sword. However, the English and their Christian Identity were conceived in love. Very unfashionable to present. But very consistent with the Christian God.

Ethelbert and Bertha

We begin at about the year 580 in Europe. Two young people were growing up in powerful families: a prince named Ethelbert, a princess named Bertha. The Roman Empire in the West had lost its power after 410. European territories were in flux. There were tribal migrations, and some tribes were building small kingdoms, often through warfare. The Christian church had survived in Rome itself and had wider influence beyond that. It was a stabilising and civilising force in the West. It knew no borders as we know them today.

Ethelbert and Bertha's respective tribes were related by common Germanic ancestry and similar Germanic language. Ethelbert's had remained pagan. Bertha's had adopted the ways of the Roman church.

The young Ethelbert grew up in Kent, to the southeast of what we now call England. He was of the invading people we later came to call the Anglo Saxons. A pagan. He had prestige as a near descendant of the earliest invaders of the land. In his home base, which we now call Canterbury, were the remains of Roman buildings greater than his own people could build. In later life, he was to become a noble and wise king, and thoughtful. We can reckon that as he grew up, he must have mused on the lost Roman civilisation whose buildings exceeded what his own people had achieved. He was destined to leave a Christian nation-seeding legacy.

The young Bertha was of the Germanic people called the Franks, from whom ultimately France derived its name. She grew up in what we now call France, of the powerful family we now know as the Merovingians. A Christian. Broadly what we would now call convent educated. Given that the next four generations of her female descendants were all to become Christians of notable devotion, we can reckon that she must have been more than a nominal Christian: most likely a devoted one. She would leave a legacy of strong Christian spirituality. She would also become the first catalyst for the spirituality of great Christian leaders to spark with the Anglo-Saxon world.

Their families were drawn together by cross-Channel trade, common tribal roots and ancient obligations. They wanted to build their alliance further by the custom of the times: marriage. Thus, it came to pass that in about the year 580, the young Ethelbert and Bertha were married. Bertha left home and family to settle in Kent.

They appear to have wanted to marry and to have loved one another. Bertha's family had also insisted that she be allowed to continue to practise her Christian faith. Ethelbert agreed. Because she was of a powerful family, Bertha was able to come over with her own Chaplain Bishop, Liudhard, and a team of about twenty monks.

The little team settled down in Canterbury. Outside the city there existed a small, brick-built Roman chapel, possibly a former Roman funeral shrine. It was made good and given to Bertha and her team for consecration for use in Christian worship.

The church was dedicated to St Martin of Tours. Tours is a city in the Loire Valley of France. We are going to encounter this Martin time and again as this book goes forward. Dying in 397, he left an enduring legacy of Christian spiritual greatness. He was one of the great Christians of all time by any standards. In this book, I call his Christian spirituality "Martinian". He was the spiritual example-hero of the Frankish people, and his life would have been a primary inspiration for the young Princess Bertha and her Chaplain, Liudhard.

The Martinian Christian spirituality was destined to transform the spirituality of the Anglo-Saxon peoples. It would also shape what became the nation of the English. From 410 onwards, it would even play a part in the rescue of Western civilisation, no less, after Rome fell.

You can still visit this little church of St Martin's. It is part of the World Heritage Site of Canterbury. And it is in use to this day, the oldest church in continuous use for Christian worship in the English-speaking world. As you walk into it, you go through a later-built extension. Through that and into the old heart of it, and you are in Bertha's original sanctuary. Stripped back to its old Roman brick, it is not much bigger than a living room. Considering all that was to come, it is tiny.

For many years after 580, Bertha and her team would process regularly from the city to the sanctuary to worship in it. We can assume that she prayed often for her husband. Ethelbert, however, remained pagan, although we can infer that he was sympathetic to Christian things. However, seventeen years elapsed with no change of Identity from pagan to Christian. Ethelbert became King of Kent and Bertha its Queen.

During that time, a Roman named Gregory was made Pope in Rome. Even detractors of the Papacy reckon him to have been the "most Christian" of all the Popes. He was destined to achieve greatness and become known as Pope Gregory the Great. He had strong gifts of Biblical understanding and seems to have had what modern Protestant Christians might call Life in the Holy Spirit of the Christian God. It was sometimes his practice, when circumstances made it feasible, to purchase freedom for slaves as they were brought to the slave market in Rome. He would also pay to have them educated.

Amongst those he freed and educated were young men of Anglo-Saxon origin. In the end, Gregory decided to sponsor a mission from the Roman Catholic Church to invite the Anglo-Saxon people into Christian Identity. In the year 596, he handpicked a Latin monk to lead it. The monk would become known as St Augustine of Canterbury. (Note: not St Augustine of Hippo; he was an earlier North African theologian). Augustine of Canterbury, like Gregory, can also be discerned to have known what it was to exercise significant powers of the Holy Spirit of the Christian God. So, knowing that in Queen Bertha and her team he had a Christian bridgehead in Kent, and that powerful Frankish families would help en route on Bertha's account, Gregory sent Augustine to begin the mission in Kent.

Augustine set off from Rome for Kent with his little team. It went through many dangers but not one was lost. It gradually swelled to about forty people by the time it arrived in 597, seventeen years after Bertha's even smaller team had first arrived there. Most of the team knew they would never see home, a warmer climate, better food and more ancient civilisation again. The mission was for life. Some of them were fellow monks. Others would have been freed slaves with trades and skills. They all owed loyalty to Gregory, either as a highly spiritual man with Christian authority or as someone to whom they owed their very lives.

The World that would Change

Here is another map.

The World that Would Change, 597

Simplified for reference to the main narrative

Not every kingdom or tribe is on here

Britons, Picts and Scots, a.k.a. Gaels, were all "Celtic"

Franks were Germanic

The rest were the Anglo Saxons, also Germanic

At around 597 Kent was the stable and enduring Anglo Saxon Kingdom.

To the North East, Bernicia was increasing in strength and coherence. Northumbria, i.e. the union of that with Deira, did not yet exist.

Mercia, destined to be strong, and Wessex, destined to found the Nation of the English, had little shape.

As at 597, there was no Britain, no Ireland, no Wales, no Scotland and no England. Nor was there any France.

Celtic Peoples

The various Celtic peoples, who had once been invaders themselves, now faced invasion from Germanic tribes coming from the East and South.

In the Celtic territories were multiple tribes of different traditions, languages and spirituality. The three main Celtic groups were:

i. Britons. As at 597, these were mainly in what we now call Wales and the Western side of what we now call England. Some were in what we now call Scotland. Some remained within the Anglo Saxon territories.

ii. <u>Picts</u>. As at 597, these were mainly in what we now call Scotland, but some were in what we now call Ireland. Their language was similar to that of the Britons. I think of the Britonnic language as similar to what we now call Welsh.

iii. <u>Gaels</u>, also known as <u>Scots</u>, from the Roman name for them, "Scoti". As at 597, most of these were in what we now call Ireland, but some were spreading into what we now call Scotland. Their language was quite different. It was what we now call Gaelic.

There was also a major difference by stream of Christian spirituality. This needs to be understood and will be returned to. It made the most profound difference to the history of the Anglo Saxons, the English and the various Celtic peoples.

a. The Britonnic people mainly had a Christian tradition developed in Roman Empire times, from 177 onwards. It was destined to make little headway with the Anglo-Saxon people groups. It seems to have become synthesised with their pagan ways in what we now call the Severn Valley and Lincolnshire. In general, however, it both rejected and was rejected by the Anglo Saxons. The Britonnic Christian way had also become cut off from the Roman Catholic mainstream. And events were to show that it was disinclined to engage with that.

b. The Picts and Gaelic Scots had the Christian spirituality that descended from St Martin of Tours after 410 when the Roman Empire lost its power. Theirs was a different branch of it to the Frankish one that was in Queen Bertha. I will trace it later in the book. The Gaels, in particular, were on fire with the Martinian spirituality, having the strongest Christian spirituality in Europe in those times. A key figure in its development had been St Columba, on Iona, an island off the west coast of what we now call Scotland. The Gaelic Martinian Christian spirituality of Iona was destined to embrace and be embraced by the Anglo Saxons to the North, just as the Romano/Frankish version of the Martinian spirituality would be to the South. The Gaels and Picts had developed different forms of outward expression of worship to the Roman Catholic mainstream, but they were strongly inclined to engage with it.

It would come to matter very much whether the differing Christian streams would engage with the Roman Catholic mainstream or not. The Anglo Saxons, as they developed into the Early English, would want vibrant Martinian Christian spirituality within prestigious Roman Catholic forms.

Now, St Columba died in 597, shortly after St Augustine first made landfall in Kent. The lamentations were still rising as Augustine's mission began. But Iona's time would come. Augustine was instrumental in the Conception of Christian Identity in the Anglo Saxons. Iona would complete its Birth.

I should add, for completeness, that there were many pockets of the Martinian spirituality amongst the Britons, notably in what we now call Wales. However, they seem not to have prevailed in the Britonnic culture as much as in the Gaelic.

Germanic Peoples

Amongst the Germanic peoples, we should start with the Franks. Occupying the Northern section of what we now call France, they had this in common with the Gaelic Celts: the Martinian Christian spirituality. However, with the Franks, this was subsumed to a greater extent into the mainstream of Roman Catholic outward forms of expression; hence I call it Romano Martinian. There were to be many corrupt bishops in the later history of the Franks, and they hog the attention of the history books. However, as at 597, some of the Frankish Christians were as on fire with the Martinian Christian spirituality as the Gaels. From this stream would come the Frankish bishops who would come to the Anglo Saxons.

As to the Anglo Saxons themselves, they mainly held to the old Germanic gods. They were divided into small kingdoms. As at 597, some of these were barely more than a warrior band. A strong kingdom was developing in the far North East, called Bernicia, close to the Picts and Scots. The most stable and continuous kingdom was Kent. Ethelbert was the King of Kent in 597. At that time, he also had influence over what we now call East Anglia, Essex and London. He was, more generally, the king with the most status out of all the kings.

The conventional history that has come down to us is of blanket ethnic hostility between Celt and Anglo Saxon. As we shall see, that was far from the case, especially when there was the Martinian Christian spirituality in common. There was hostility between some but not all Britonnic Celts and some but not all Anglo Saxons. The Britonnic Christian church seems to have partaken of the hostility to some extent.

In the Anglo Saxon territories in the East, South and Midlands of what we now call England, Christian spirituality was in trouble. The Romans had brought plenty of Christian life to the Britons in those territories before 407. However, it had declined in vibrancy by 597. It was not extinct. The Britonnic Christian way was tolerated. But it was little adopted; it barely impacted the Anglo Saxons at all. The newly dominating Germanic people groups almost entirely defined their Identity around the pagan gods of their Germanic ancestors. There was the tiniest Christian candle flame. But the candle was going out.

The Open Door

However, in the Anglo Saxon King Ethelbert of Kent, St Augustine turned out to be knocking on an open door. Pope Gregory had had the shrewdest of insights: not only had he handpicked the monk Augustine, who has been much underrated by history, but he had also sensed that King Ethelbert, who would not have taken on Christian Identity from the Britons, might be wide open to taking it on from Rome. For a number of reasons:

- Kent and the Franks had long been on terms, and Ethelbert knew the Franks, connected already to the Roman church, to be more powerful than any Anglo Saxon king and to have prestige in their Roman connection.

- Ethelbert could see in Canterbury the remains of a Roman civilisation greater than his own.

- We can infer that he must have been impressed by Bertha's Chaplain Bishop, Liudhard.

- Ethelbert seems to have loved his Christian wife. There can be no doubt that she prayed for him to convert. An existent letter from Pope Gregory reminds her of the call to do so. As at 597, King Ethelbert was possibly Europe's most prayed-over pagan.

- Through Bertha and Liudhard, Ethelbert had access to Frankish and Roman letters with their Christian ways of thinking.

- Bertha and Liudhard were of the Martinian Christian spirituality, the most dynamic in Europe as at 597. It was not a wet spirituality for a king from Anglo Saxon warrior culture to reject. Full of love, it was also a winsome one that a warrior could embrace.

Adding it all up, it seems likely that Ethelbert had some knowledge of and agreement with the coming of a mission from Rome. Some even say he might have sent for it. What we can say with certainty, however, is this. A time and season arose when political and spiritual realms of life converged to spark momentous change. In a balanced understanding, you could say that the time had come, under both God and man, for the Roman mission to arise. A great Pope had it close to his heart. A gifted expedition leader was available to him, one willing to sacrifice all. The connections were in place, political and spiritual. And there was love in the mix: natural love between King and Queen, and the love that arises from Christian spirituality.

So, the door was wide open. Christian Identity was about to be Conceived in the most influential Anglo Saxon king. We should note the composition of it – Romano Martinian Catholic – and position it on the map:

Christian Identity in the Early English

Conception, 597:

King Ethelbert of Kent

Early Influences:
Queen Bertha of Kent, Bishop Liudhard, both Frankish Romano Martinian Catholic Christians.

Decisive Influence:
St Augustine of Canterbury, Latin Monk, Roman Catholic.

Kent

Romano Martinian Catholic

Important: "Roman Catholic" back then was not like the latter-day post-Reformation Protestant caricature.

Pope Gregory the Great, sending Augustine, had in-depth Bible understanding equal to any celebrated Protestant scholar.

St Augustine of Canterbury had strong Christian spiritual gifts and has been much under-rated.

On his way through Frankish realms en route from Rome to Kent, St Augustine also seems to have sought out a portion of the spiritual mantle of that same St Martin of Tours as had already inspired the likes of Queen Bertha.

Augustine's Christian Message, Ethelbert's Response

Augustine first met King Ethelbert of Kent in about the Spring of 597, in the open air. Carrying a silver cross and picture of the Christ, he set out the Christian message of eternal salvation. Ethelbert's reception of the message was cautious. Augustine was completely upfront about the Christian God he represented. Ethelbert wanted time to think. It would be a major step to give up the old gods. The Sense of Identity of his people would be at stake. However, he immediately gave Augustine freedom to preach openly from a protected base at Canterbury.

Opinions vary as to how quickly Ethelbert went on to convert to Christian faith. Some say four years later, in 601. Others say quite soon, later on in 597. I will go for 597. By Christmas of that year, Augustine was able to conduct a mass baptism for up to 10,000 people. That was a significant proportion of the population of those days. It constituted what Protestant Christians of modern times would call a major "Awakening". It also implies a strong sweep of the power of the Holy Spirit of the Christian God, because, in a Christian understanding, it is impossible for any human being to convert another to

Christian faith. Only the Holy Spirit can accomplish that. The human task is to set out the Christian message. The Holy Spirit's task is to promote faith in it.

We should note here that the historian who recorded Ethelbert's own responses to the Christian message, Bede, stressed that Ethelbert never compelled others to accept it. Response to the Christ was voluntary. Therefore, many of the 10,000 would have been receiving the Christ for real, not currying favour with the King. However, I doubt that Augustine would have proceeded so boldly without the King included. So, let's place Ethelbert as a Christian by the time of that event: converted to Christian Identity in 597.

And let's weigh up Ethelbert's life from then on. It turned out to be generous, peaceable, noble, authoritative, and supportive of the onward spread of Christian spirituality. For example, his first response was to give, and he kept on giving. He gave land for Augustine's great Abbey in Canterbury and for the original Cathedral of Canterbury, which lasted from 602 to 1067. He used his extended influence in the sub-kingdom we now call Essex. In those days, it included what we now call London. Although the attempt to Christianise Essex was to be abortive until 655, Ethelbert sought to influence the people there to convert. He did not use force of sword. Instead, he used force of personal standing. It is reasonably well known that he gave the land that became Canterbury Cathedral. It is less well known that he influenced the giving of land for the first church of St Paul's in London. He also reached out to commend Christian Identity to the royal family of the East Angles, with moderate initial effect, as we shall see when we come to the "Gestation" chapter of the journey of the Anglo Saxons into Christian Identity.

Ethelbert's family seems to have been quite taken with Augustine, too. The royal family accompanied Augustine on his ministry travels within Kent, witnessing miracles in the process, as we shall touch on later. Ethelbert also arranged safe passage for Augustine to head West to meet with the leaders of the Britonnic church. That turned out abortive. We will look at that later, in the chapter about "Labour Pains".

It was most probably Ethelbert who caused Augustine to seek practical advice from the Pope back in Rome for the welfare of newly converted peoples: how to handle old pagan customs, for example. Pope Gregory replied with peaceable and wise advice.

As an honoured and senior figure amongst the many kings of the emerging small kingdoms, Ethelbert seems to have become an advocate for the new Christian spirituality. He sought political unity built around that. Given that the nation of the English slowly but surely arose out of political union based on commonly held Christian spirituality, that makes him the original seed-King of what created the English.

Ethelbert also went on to write the first law code for his people, written in what later developed into English. To our modern eyes, it is a difficult code. It spelt out monetary values for people when wronged, and aristocratic people were worth more than common people. The church was valued more highly, as well. That makes the modern mind snort. However, there might be no snorting from the Christian God of the Bible: "You set a high price on what you value, and if you set a high value on the things of Christ, then that is fine by me," would sum up one of the strands of the Christian God as revealed in his Bible. And anyway, the point is this. Just because the code was not perfect does not mean it was not a step forward by the standards of its times. It helped to end cycles of revenge and retribution. And it was quite something to accord value to the common people at all. The code took plenty of content from pre-Christian Germanic ideas. But I would say it was with Christian impetus that Ethelbert brought it forth for the improved wellbeing of his people.

In general, King Ethelbert of Kent, once he had become Christian, is widely credited as the first great founder of the more enlightened elements in Early English kingship, Christian and political life in positive union. This way of things would come to its ultimate expression centuries later in King Alfred the Great and his family as they founded the nation of the English. A final chapter of narrative in this book will look at that: Ethelbert the seed, Alfred the grown-up plant. For now, it's like this: once he had come into Christ, we find in Ethelbert the seed of what made the English.

It is instructive, then, to see how the fashion is developing these days in appraising Ethelbert's career. The fashion seems to be to leave out entirely the spiritual dimension of it. All, you might think, was for political gain. He wanted trading wealth with the Franks. He wanted interconnection with Roman prestige. He just happened to be a good egg as well: coincidence.

Well, none of the things he would have wanted politically are bad. But weighed up by the political dimension alone, it's a bit thin. Interconnection with Rome and the Franks did Ethelbert little good with his Anglo Saxon peer group of tough warrior kings. It was them he had to spend more time with. It would have made it harder, not easier, for him to sustain a position of honour and seniority if he was also advocating strange new ways.

And even if Ethelbert was by nature a good person, it leaves out the profundity of the Christian spirituality that can be discerned in him. Let's weigh him up against features that the Christian scriptures teach would be likely to develop in a ruler who has genuinely received the Christian God. Giving generously: tick. Noble character: tick. Seeker of unity: tick. Forceful but not domineering, using authority for good: tick. Committed to the spread of Christian witness and spirituality: tick. These were the values that developed in Ethelbert. What you find, if once you allow yourself to incorporate the spiritual dimension into history, is that Ethelbert's life manifested what you would expect to find if the Christian God has true influence in real life. Jesus Christ laid out a test in his lifetime: by their fruits you shall know them. Ethelbert's fruits were consistent with Christian spirituality.

And the point is this: the Christian spirituality in Ethelbert began to shape the real and political world in union with it. In him, the realms did not exist on either side of a great wall. He needs to be weighed up whole, with the incorporation of Christian understanding in the process. When you do that, seeing with two eyes as it were, King Ethelbert of Kent turns out to have been the genuine Christian article as well as a great founder-politician. Both dimensions of understanding history converged in him. And together, they made him the originating seed figure of Early English history because the English developed out of the same union, Christian and political in harmony, no great wall dividing the realms.

There is a statue of King Ethelbert, dating to 1450, which welcomes the visitor into the worship zone of the present Canterbury Cathedral. He is shown reaching out with a model of the original Cathedral in his left hand, as gifted by him in 602, and standing within a frieze of kings, having the pole position. It seems that the English of 1450 knew from whom and from what root they came.

Queen Bertha

Although younger than Ethelbert, Bertha passed away before him and little documentation of her has come down to us. She was brought up to manage a tough warrior king. She was also brought up as a Martinian Christian of deep devotion. And she was brought up to bring influence from the latter realm into the former. In character, she is largely thought to have been compliant and gentle.

What I like to do with Queen Bertha, however, is take a snapshot of her life as at 602. St Augustine's mission had succeeded, Ethelbert had converted, his people had followed suit, and Christian spirituality was laying down first roots in Kent. In that year, the first Cathedral of Canterbury was consecrated. By the standards of its time, it would have been a wonder of the age: enormous, and with an element of the old Roman building skills. I wonder how Bertha must have felt at the time of its consecration? For twenty-two years she had worshipped in the tiny sanctuary of St Martin's church. Now, this cavernous cathedral. Jesus Christ had taught this about the Christian faith: it would be like a mustard seed; the tiniest of all seeds, it would become the largest plant in the garden. What had Bertha's little team been in 580? A tiny seed. What were they about to become from 602? The largest plant in the garden.

Now, regarding a cathedral, such things have natural substance. They are not spiritual reality. However, they can be a sign in the natural world of realities in the spiritual world. So it was in this case, if you allow for a Christian understanding. Bertha was lifelong faithful to her Christian God. And I would see it that her God gave her a sign, in the size of the building, of what would follow on from her faithfulness. In the generations to come, her Christian faith would become the strongest spiritual dynamic by which the Anglo Saxon peoples would come to define themselves. A great plant did, indeed, emerge from Bertha's little mustard seed of faith.

There is one other key point to make about Queen Bertha of Kent: she and her little team became the first catalyst for spiritually empowered Christian leaders to spark with the Anglo Saxon peoples.

Queen Bertha – Catalyst

Now, I will explain more fully what makes for spiritual empowerment of a Christian leader as the book progresses. A chapter called "Beneath the Lid" will look at that. At this stage, I mainly want to develop the narrative of "Conception".

Three highly gifted Christian figures homed in on the Anglo Saxon peoples via the bridgehead of Queen Bertha and her little team. Pope Gregory was a true Christian Great. St Augustine of Canterbury has been much underrated. And further to note, in 601 Gregory sent a reinforcement to Augustine. He was called Paulinus. He would become the first Bishop of York and the first focal point for Christian Awakening in the North.

Above and beyond this, Bertha was the first conduit for the Christian spirituality which had once been in St Martin of Tours to come to the Anglo Saxon peoples. It was not to be underrated: more mysterious but also more transformative than Gregory, Augustine and Paulinus put together. For now, to lay down the marker: any modern Protestant Christian with Life in the Holy Spirit has spiritual kinship with St Martin. And St Augustine of Canterbury went out of his way, en route to Kent, to take on what had been in St Martin of Tours.

It was Queen Bertha and her little team that were the first catalyst to bring these strong spiritual Christian leaders and powers to bear.

In the Chapter House of the present Cathedral at Canterbury are twenty-one figures in stained glass, all significant within English history as it intertwined the Christian spiritual realm with the material world's political realm. The first three figures are Bertha, Augustine and Ethelbert. The Saint is sandwiched between the King and Queen because it was in their time he came and it was they who made his mission possible. The very first figure in the glass, in pole position, is Queen Bertha. The glass is Victorian, dating to about 1900. It seems that in 1900, the English knew from whom and what root they came.

Christian Identity in the English – Conception

It is often said that Christian Identity first came to the English in 597. I can understand why, but as you will see as the book goes forward, it was more complex than that. It took hundreds of years to fill out. And in its origin times, it followed a cycle comparable to Birth and Growing Up to the point of Going Off to School. Even that took three generations.

I think it would be more enlightening to say that, in 597, Christian Identity was Conceived in the English. It came to full-on Birth in 635. Between the two, as there are broadly 38 to 40 weeks in a natural human birth process, there were 38 years in the spiritual one. Those 38 years were a time of Gestation. They culminated in Labour Pains. There was difficulty and tumult. Bad seed was sown as well as good seed. The bad seed was to sprout bloodily during and after the Birth. The story becomes turbulent and, to use a phrase that was in use when I was growing up, for adults only.

We will proceed to it now.

But I must add that I just love the charming and true story, this lost love story, of King Ethelbert and Queen Bertha of Kent. The time of the Conception of Christian Identity was truly sweet in the Early English.

What a delight.

CHAPTER 6.

Gestation – 597 To 634

What happened next, after the Conception of Christian Identity for the Early English with King Ethelbert of Kent?

Er, not a lot, immediately. An epic tale was going to develop of bloody political setback versus irresistible spiritual momentum. Many a Christian mole was going to get whacked, but each time, a stronger Christian mole was going to pop up. But not just yet. That would come with Labour Pains as Christian Identity drew near to Birth; and then with slaughter once it was in the Nursery. But Ethelbert's reign was the Conception stage. Gestation was due next. And just as with Gestation, not an awful lot seemed to happen at first. Birth was thirty-eight years away. Before then, certain events took place in multiple locations, as shown on this map, during the Gestation period.

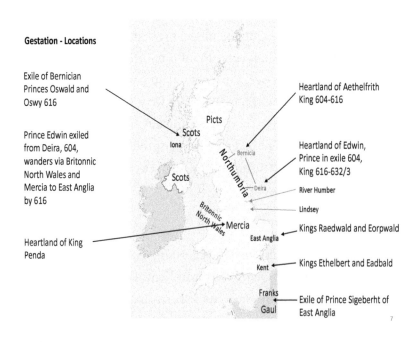

Gestation - Locations

Exile of Bernician Princes Oswald and Oswy 616

Prince Edwin exiled from Deira, 604, wanders via Britonnic North Wales and Mercia to East Anglia by 616

Heartland of King Penda

Picts

Scots

Iona

Scots

Northumbria

Bernicia

Deira

Britonnic North Wales

Mercia

East Anglia

Kent

Franks

Gaul

Heartland of Aethelfrith King 604-616

Heartland of Edwin, Prince in exile 604, King 616-632/3

River Humber

Lindsey

Kings Raedwald and Eorpwald

Kings Ethelbert and Eadbald

Exile of Prince Sigeberht of East Anglia

Now, the literal process of Gestation is complex in the extreme. And when you look at pictures of an embryo in the womb, it is fuzzy. It is a bit like that when you look at the Gestation period of Christian Identity in the Early English, too: fuzzy. This is by way of warning the reader that this chapter might be quite complex. However, I hope that the emerging baby of Christian Identity will come into focus out of the many details that have to be processed.

I will switch between South, North and East in this chapter, which will broadly follow a timeline from 597 to 628.

King Ethelbert and St Augustine in Kent – Challenges and Initiatives

I begin in the South at Canterbury.

As of late 597, St Augustine of Canterbury faced the classic dilemma of the Christian Revivalist of more modern times: OK, I've won 10,000 converts in year one. Now what? Jesus Christ had expressed what is known as the "Great Commission" – go and make disciples. He had not said, go and make converts. Whilst a Christian understanding would require conversion to be an essential first stage, the "Great Commission" requires pastoral structures for ongoing discipleship: lives founded on spiritual union with Christ; making a good finish and not just a good start.

Augustine's problem was this. His tiny team were all Roman imports. Indigenous Christian leadership would have to be developed from a zero base. And there, for now, we must leave Augustine and the small proto-church of Kent. It was going to go through a two-generations-long, quiet laying of foundations.

Except for one thing. In the short term, Pope Gregory sent reinforcements from Rome. In 601, there arrived in Kent another Latin monk, one Paulinus. Of him, nothing more will be heard for a further twenty-three years until he goes North. Bertha had to wait seventeen years for Ethelbert to adopt Christian

Identity, and five years more for Canterbury Cathedral to be founded, twenty-two years in all. Paulinus had to wait twenty-three years for his time to come.

King Ethelbert, meanwhile, did seek to take things forward. I will look shortly at the efforts he made.

Bernicia and Deira

Before that though, I must switch to the North East, to the territories on the map called Northumbria, comprising Bernicia and Deira. We need to reckon with two persons:

- King Aethelfrith of Bernicia. You can think of Bernicia as broadly what we now call Northumberland, from the River Tees northwards and including parts of what we now call the Scottish Borders.

- Prince Edwin of Deira. You can think of Deira as broadly what we now call Yorkshire and parts north of that to the River Tees.

As the two Angle-ish kingdoms became one, the name given to them was Northumbria, meaning "North of the River Humber". The first mover for the union was King Aethelfrith.

King Aethelfrith of Bernicia

King Aethelfrith of Bernicia was a lifelong pagan and a formidable warrior. Between 593 and 603, he grew powerful in the North East and in what we now call the Scottish Borders. He took much territory from Britonnic Celtic tribes. Soon, the Celtic Scots (a.k.a. Gaels) and Picts became concerned about the spread of the Bernician Angles. They joined forces in pre-emptive battle against Aethelfrith. However, Aethelfrith prevailed. By 604, the three people groups had come to terms in a peace treaty. As you will see later, few things in the history of the people who became the English were to become more important than the treaty that was made then between Scot and Angle. Those Gaelic Scots harboured in their midst the most dynamic version of the Martinian Christian Life to be found anywhere.

Next, as in 604, Aethelfrith was forcing a Northumbrian union of Bernicia and Deira. He had married into the Deiran royal family before that as part of the process. He set about becoming an over-king for the Northumbrian whole by a combination of force and marriage.

I might note in passing that the year 604 was momentous for this as well: Prince Oswald was born to Aethelfrith and his Deiran wife, Acha. Oswald was going to become the most remarkable Christian Saint-King in the history of the English and possibly the world.

To resume the narrative, however, in the process of forcing Bernician over-rule, around or soon after 604, King Aethelfrith dislodged a Deiran Prince into exile. This was Prince Edwin. I will spend a lot of time on his career shortly. He is the main figure in the Gestation period.

To summarise, as at about 604, in the North we find:

- Treaty of pagan Bernicia with the Martinian Christian Gaels.

- Prince Oswald of Bernicia born.

- Prince Edwin of Deira becomes a wandering exile.

Now, to keep roughly to a sequential timeline, I must take you back South again, to Kent, and King Ethelbert of Kent once more.

King Ethelbert of Kent – Christian Witness

Early in the 600s, King Ethelbert was taking his newfound Christian Identity seriously. Within Kent, a further Christian centre was established to the west, at Rochester. That mission endured.

Within London, which was then under his influence, the land for the first St Paul's was gifted. That mission foundered.

Ethelbert had also used his position of wider honour and seniority to secure safe passage for St Augustine of Canterbury to meet up with the Britonnic Christian bishops of the West. That had taken place before 604 and by about the time King Aethelfrith was coming to terms with the Scots. Augustine's mission to the Britonnic bishops foundered. We will look at that later, under "Labour Pains".

Now, I must switch eastwards, to what we now call East Anglia.

King Raedwald of the East Angles

Probably the most important effect of King Ethelbert's Christian testimony was with King Raedwald of the East Angles early in the 600s. His territory is now known as East Anglia. It is speculated that Raedwald is the king in the famous burial site at Sutton Hoo. Raedwald is thought to have visited Ethelbert in Kent. Ethelbert would have witnessed his newfound Christian faith to him. Raedwald seems to have responded in part.

If we compare the two Kings, Ethelbert was never noted as a great warrior. His prestige was based on three factors:

- As a descendant of the earliest invaders.

- Kent had been the most enduringly stable small Anglo Saxon nation. In the year 500, the mysterious Britonnic King Arthur had sent the Anglo Saxons packing back to Europe until 540. Except in Kent. There they had put down roots unbroken from 450.

- Kent had the most links to ancient Roman prestige. The Germanic peoples were surprisingly good at overthrowing Rome but even more surprisingly keen on adopting its ancient prestige upon doing so.

However, times were changing amongst the Anglo Saxons by Raedwald's day. To have prestige after Ethelbert, you had to be strong.

King Raedwald was strong. He was a powerful warrior. He had consolidated power in East Anglia. As Ethelbert aged, Raedwald supplanted him as the most prestigious of the small kingdom rulers. However, before that, he seems to have partially accepted Ethelbert's Christian witness. If he really is the king buried at Sutton Hoo, the treasures with him for the afterlife were mainly pagan but with a hint of Christian. However, we have to remember that the funeral arrangements were made by his wife. We have it from Bede that she was whole-heartedly pagan, whereas Raedwald, on the other hand, was half-heartedly Christian. He did not enter into the entire life and fulness of Christian faith. In his private sanctuary, he kept something symbolic of the Christian God alongside his idols of the other gods.

That would not satisfy the Christian God. The Christian God says he is jealous. For Raedwald, it was what you might call an "each-way bet". Who knew which god would show him favour? Keep on the good side of that Christian one, too. In his time, no great Christian mission was released into his territory to transform the identity of his people. It was Gestation time, not Birth.

Now, back to Kent.

King Ethelbert's Son – King Eadbald of Kent

There was another apparent stumble in Ethelbert's Christian witness, and in Queen Bertha's, too. Their son, Eadbald, was ambivalent towards Christian Identity.

At some point unknown before 616, Bertha passed away and Ethelbert took a new wife. When Ethelbert himself passed away in 616, his son Eadbald took that wife and bedded her. It had been a common custom for the pre-Christian tribes. However, in pastoral letters to Augustine, which would have been both prompted by and read out to King Ethelbert and taught to Eadbald, that was the sort of thing that Pope Gregory had expressly forbidden. In Gregory's version of Biblical understanding, by uncovering the wife with whom Ethelbert had been one flesh, Eadbald was also uncovering his father's nakedness. Strictly forbidden. And you can be sure that Eadbald knew it.

Around about 616, therefore, Eadbald had this policy: tolerate the presence of the Christian church but do not line up as a Christian yourself. However, at some time between then and 619, the late great Founder Apostle St Peter, no less, appeared in the night to the Archbishop of that time, Laurence, successor of Augustine. St Peter *scourged* the good Archbishop for vacillating over rebuking Eadbald's conduct with Ethelbert's wife. And when Eadbald saw the marks in the morning, the Fear of God so came upon him that he put that wife aside and took on Christian Identity himself.

We have this account from the first great historian of the Early English, Bede. In a later chapter, I will address it further, plus a few other Christian phenomena recorded in the Christian Awakening that turned the Anglo Saxons into the Early English. For now, I simply record it.

However, Eadbald never made a name for himself as a Christian dynamo. He has come down to us as shrewd and supporting quiet progress in the Kentish church. As can happen surprisingly often in Christian Life, or so you find from long experience of it anyway, the stronger Christian spirituality that we can infer to have been in Ethelbert was going to jump a generation to his grandson, Eorcenberht, Eadbald's son, from 640. Of that, more later.

Meanwhile, here is how it was for Christian Identity to the South and East as at 616: the new King of Kent was ambivalent about it, and its infant church was still building from a zero indigenous base. In East Anglia, the prestigious King Raedwald was, at most, semi-Christian. There was no Christian mission there. And the Christian mission in Essex and London had foundered.

And now, in 616, I must take you North again, for two highly significant events:

- Prince Edwin of Deira comes to power in Northumbria.

- Prince Oswald of Bernicia flees from Northumbria into exile with the Gaelic Scots.

Prince Edwin of Deira 604-616

I will pick up Edwin's career from 604 to 616 first.

When Bernician King Aethelfrith began forcing the Northumbrian union, Edwin, a rival Deiran prince, fled into exile. The date would be 604 or soon after. It is not clear where Edwin went between then and 616. There is one thing likely and two things certain, but in all of that, only one date is certain:

- Initially, Edwin was probably received into the Britonnic Celtic royal court of Gwynedd in what we would now call North Wales.

- Later, he spent time in the Anglo Saxon court of Midlands Mercia.

- By 616, he was in King Raedwald's court of the East Angles.

In Britonnic North Wales, Edwin would have been exposed to Britonnic Christian testimony. Some speculate that he may have been baptised there. However, even if he was, baptism is not Christian reality. Baptism is water. And water is… water. Baptism is meant to be a testimony of an inward spiritual change that has taken place upon receiving the Christ by means of a deposit within of the Holy Spirit of the Christian God. I am satisfied that, whether baptised or not, Edwin had not received the Christ in that way at this time. Like most other Anglo Saxons, the Britonnic Christian Identity was not for him. Prince Edwin was a pre-Christian semi-pagan wanderer, not a Christian one.

One thing does seem likely: there was a falling out in North Wales. He and a young Britonnic Christian Prince named Caedwalla came to enmity. We must remember this Caedwalla of Gwynedd.

At some point after that, Edwin definitely arrived in the Mercian court in the Midlands of what became England. In a later chapter, I will say more about the Mercians. Edwin was an Angle. Mercians were also Angles. However, they also had some element of alliance or familial mixing with the North Wales Britonnic Celts. Mercian Angles and Northern Angles, i.e. the likes of Edwin, were rivals. However, Edwin was tolerated at the Mercian court because, if ever he were to take the Northern throne, he would be beholden to the Mercians. Indeed, he married a royal Mercian princess, named Cwenburh. She had a young cousin. His name was Penda. It seems possible that at some point, in some way, Edwin fell out with Penda of Mercia as well as with Caedwalla.

Penda was to rise to become the warrior King of Mercia later in Edwin's life. Penda was also to be a lifelong pagan and restlessly warlike in spirit. He despised any Christian whose life was not as perfect as Christ's. This effectively means he despised any Christian. I have never seen this commented upon, but the likely Christian testimony that Penda despised would have been of the Britonnic Celtic, not the Martinian Celtic. Edwin had not taken to it; neither did Penda.

Now, we must remember this Penda, as well as Caedwalla. Penda was to become the unwitting tool of a primary principle in the Christian Bible: that the Christian God works all things for good for Christian Identity through those who are called in Christ, even if they go to the slaughter. That was going to get to work through Penda in real and bloody Early English history.

By 616, we can be certain that Edwin found himself in the court of King Raedwald of the East Angles. It would seem that he had never ceased to give up on a claim through his Deiran ancestry to the throne of at least that part of Northumbria. He had, therefore, become a focal point for intrigues. He also represented an existential threat to King Aethelfrith, the one who had first forced Northumbria into union in 604. So, by 616, Aethelfrith was hunting Edwin down. It is likely that the Mercian court found Edwin too hot to handle then, and that is why he had wandered on to East Anglia. However, Aethelfrith traced him to there and sent messengers to Raedwald. With threats and bribes, in 616, he demanded that Raedwald should surrender Edwin to the slaughter.

Aethelfrith was pagan, Edwin semi-pagan pre-Christian, Raedwald semi-pagan semi-Christian.

A root of bitterness planted

Before we describe what happened next, we must take note of something that King Aethelfrith had done prior to this. By 616, as he hunted for Edwin, Aethelfrith had brought forces into Britonnic North Wales. The peoples had come to battle. Aethelfrith's forces had prevailed and ravaged. Many Britonnic Christian monks had been called to the battle to pray for victory. Aethelfrith had slaughtered them first and later burned treasured records of the history and culture of those peoples.

A survivor of the battle and the cultural destruction was that same Caedwalla of Gwynedd, who had been at enmity with Edwin. He hated Northumbria now with a passion. And indeed, this event was one of a few that would give rise to the latter-day caricature that the period was defined by Anglo Saxon committing genocide on Celt.

There would have been an important spiritual consequence of this. The Christian Bible has the concept of a "root of bitterness". If that is permitted to grow up in someone who takes on Christian Identity, the Bible teaches that it will have harmful consequences. This Britonnic people group and Caedwalla held to Christian Identity. A root of bitterness had been sown in them. And for their future King, Caedwalla, there was already a personal rift with Prince Edwin. In later years it would widen.

I will now tackle Edwin's career as King of Northumbria in two periods, Edwin as pre-Christian semi-pagan, 616 to 627, then as firmly Christian, 627 to 633.

Edwin as King of Northumbria between 616 and 627

Now, to 616 again: King Aethelfrith of Northumbria had sent messengers to King Raedwald of East Anglia with threats and bribes seeking Prince Edwin's life. Raedwald was minded to hand Edwin over. His wholeheartedly pagan wife restrained him, stressing an obligation of honour.

Meanwhile, Prince Edwin had just had a dream. Bede's history recounts it. A stranger had appeared in the dream and promised restoration of what had been lost and expansion of power. However, Edwin was also told in the dream that the restoration was conditional. A stranger would come along one day and give him the following sign: he would place hands on Edwin's head. When that happened for real, Edwin was to obey what the stranger would say. Edwin never forgot the dream. The foretold restoration began very quickly from 616 onwards. The stranger did not come with the sign, however, until 627.

Listening to his wife, Raedwald decided not to hand Edwin over. But he also knew that Aethelfrith was a restless menace. He took pre-emptive action. He mustered forces and sped them north before Aethelfrith could gather forces, took him by surprise and slew him.

Raedwald then installed the friendly Edwin of Deira on the Northern throne.

What happened next was of world-history-shaping importance:

At that time, 616, Aethelfrith's Bernician sons fled for their lives. They went North. The oldest boy, Eanfrith, found shelter with the Picts. The two younger princes, Oswald, aged twelve, and Oswy, aged five, were received by the Scots for sanctuary. This was in honour of the treaty that had been made with their father Aethelfrith in 604. Amongst the Gaelic Scots, they would come under the influence of Martinian Christian Iona, a leading centre of Christian spiritual power in the western world at that time. It might not have had a tradition of grandeur, but it was on fire with the Holy Spirit of the Christian God. The two young Angle-ish Bernician princes would go on to receive Jesus Christ there. In doing so, the Gestation of Christian Identity in the Early English would make a great step forward. But many years were to pass before the consequences were Born into the real and political world through Oswald in 635.

Returning to Edwin, he was a warrior. In 616, all Northumbria lay before him and he took it. And he grew in might. By 627, Northumbria had become the main power amongst the small kingdoms. Edwin succeeded Raedwald as the most prestigious of the kings. According to Bede, he became both feared, suggesting an iron fist, and loved, suggesting a velvet glove. He made the roads secure for travellers, with refreshment points. He had a civilising influence, but you could not do that without force. There was a certain pride in him: a standard-bearer would precede him on his travels as if he were a Roman potentate. And there was a certain humility in him too: on the roads, he would often be on foot behind the standard in the midst of his people, not always on horseback.

In 627, Edwin was still pre-Christian. He had been exposed to Christian Identity but not yet adopted it in reality. By 627, Edwin had done three other things to note as well.

a) Like Aethelfrith before him, he had taken forces into Britonnic North Wales. And from there he had driven Caedwalla of Gwynedd into exile. That same Caedwalla with whom he had fallen out when once exiled himself in North Wales and whose youthful grudge had widened into more general bitterness towards the Northumbrian people after Aethelfrith had come slaughtering. Edwin had just made the grudge even more personal and embittered further Caedwalla's hatred of Edwin's Northumbria.

b) He had put aside his Mercian wife, Cwenburh, Penda's cousin. Penda would not have been one to let that lie.

c) He had survived an assassination attempt. This came from the royal family of the Germanic West Saxon people, soon to be known as Wessex. They wanted to roll back Northumbria's ever-increasing reach. Making semi-pagan promises to the Christian God, although not keeping them later, Edwin had responded to Wessex with a campaign that subdued them. In the battle that Edwin won, Wessex had had an ally: Penda of Mercia. He was still making his way in life at that point, not yet a king but very ambitious for Mercian dominion. It was a rare defeat for Penda. He would not have been one to let that lie, either. Especially since, as we shall see in a later chapter, there were ancient Germanic reasons for Mercian Angles to resent Northern Angles.

627 to 633 – Conversion: Christian Identity Adopted by King Edwin

So now we come to the year 627. A most mysterious piece of ministry by Paulinus led to Edwin and many of his people fully adopting Christian Identity. Not all of it was to endure – the change was part of the Gestation process, not yet the Birth – but it was spectacular in the time of its adoption.

Ethelbert and Bertha's daughter, Ethelburgha, played a significant part, along with St Augustine's reinforcement of 601, Paulinus. The map that follows shows the spread of Paulinus's Christian ministry from 624 to 628.

It includes further developments in East Anglia which followed hot on the heels of events in 627.

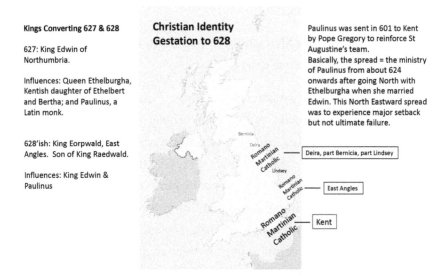

Kings Converting 627 & 628

627: King Edwin of Northumbria.

Influences: Queen Ethelburgha, Kentish daughter of Ethelbert and Bertha; and Paulinus, a Latin monk.

628'ish: King Eorpwald, East Angles. Son of King Raedwald.

Influences: King Edwin & Paulinus

Christian Identity Gestation to 628

Bernicia
Deira
Romano Martinian Catholic — Deira, part Bernicia, part Lindsey
Lindsey
Romano Martinian Catholic — East Angles
Romano Martinian Catholic — Kent

Paulinus was sent in 601 to Kent by Pope Gregory to reinforce St Augustine's team.
Basically, the spread = the ministry of Paulinus from about 624 onwards after going North with Ethelburgha when she married Edwin. This North Eastward spread was to experience major setback but not ultimate failure.

Although Edwin had possibly had exposure to Britonnic Celtic Christian witness when young, and possibly some sort of semi-pagan version of Christianity from King Raedwald's court by 616, it was around about 624 to 625 that his journey to Christian Identity really began. And it was a mysterious journey. It requires a little background in the Revelatory dimension of Christian spirituality to penetrate the mystery.

Bede's account of Paulinus's rather mysterious and highly spiritual Christian ministry to Edwin has been much misunderstood. I will try to recover it.

By 624, King Edwin was increasing in power and reach. The main communication routes between the small kingdoms were more by sea than land. Just as the main highway of the various Celtic peoples to the West was what we now call the Irish Sea, so the main highway of the Anglo Saxon kingdoms to the East was what we now call the North Sea. Northumbria, East Anglia and Kent engaged extensively by sea. So, in 624, King Edwin weighed up his options for increasing his reach. Although Northumbria had power, Kent had prestige. Time to use the North Sea to make a marriage alliance with Kent. King Edwin put aside Cwenburh, his Mercian wife, no doubt arousing Penda's anger, and made suit to Kent for a wife.

The Ethelbert and Bertha pattern was going to recur.

King Eadbald of Kent, Ethelbert's son, he whom the scourging of Archbishop Laurence by St Peter had shepherded into the Christian camp, agreed to Edwin's suit to marry Ethelburgha, his sister, Ethelbert and Bertha's daughter.

Queen Ethelburgha and Paulinus

Ethelburgha had her mother's Romano Martinian Catholic Christian spirituality. She also had a different character and experience to her mother. Bertha seems to have been compliant and grown up in a sheltered community. Ethelburgha had a family nickname, "Tate", meaning the lively one. She had grown up with the family's vivid memory of St Augustine's ministry. This had included miracles. We will recount in a later chapter a memorable one which we can infer she either witnessed or had taught to her from infancy. She also had the same sense of calling as Bertha with regard to a pagan husband: pray for him to become Christian. Just as a letter exists from Pope Gregory to call for that in Bertha, so a letter exists from Pope Boniface to Ethelburgha for the same.

King Eadbald, whether a wobbly Christian or not, insisted that Ethelburgha be allowed to keep practising her Christian faith. As Ethelbert had once done for Bertha, so Edwin now agreed for Ethelburgha, and she came North to marry in 624/5. Bertha had been accompanied by Bishop Liudhard. Ethelburgha came North with Paulinus, Augustine's reinforcement. Twenty-three years waiting, his time had come.

Paulinus seems to have been a potent mixture in spiritual terms. He had been sent in 601 to the highly gifted St Augustine of Canterbury by the highly gifted Pope Gregory. Gregory and Augustine both seem to have been familiar with the "Charismatic" realm of Gifts of the Holy Spirit of the Christian God. I explain "Charismatic" more as the book goes on. For now, it does not have the meaning in the modern idiom, with a small c, of "something attractive and compelling in a person". In the technical Christian sense, "Charismatic", with a large C, means someone using the Gifts of the Holy Spirit of the Christian God.

Paulinus seems to have been of the same mould. Whereas St Augustine is known to have exercised miraculous powers, Paulinus, as you will soon see, seems to have exercised revelatory ones. There are multiple "Charismata" which, as they work in combination, promote these two dimensions, the miraculous and the revelatory. These dimensions can become open to a Christian operating the "Charismatic" gifts if they also have significant "Anointing" from the Holy Spirit of the Christian God. That is another term I will explain as the book goes on, in the chapter called "Beneath the Lid". For now, it means "significantly empowered by the Christian God". It does not mean "rubbed with holy oil", in the way of the ancient Christian sacrament.

Given that Paulinus contained significant spiritual gifting within a Roman Catholic outer package, always prestigious to the Anglo Saxons, this made him a Christian Awakening waiting to happen.

And we must not forget Queen Ethelburgha's lively Romano Martinian Catholic Christian spirituality either. King Edwin was taking delivery of a potent combination.

King Edwin's Conversion

Paulinus got to work on King Edwin's understanding of the Christian message. I suspect there would have been prior misinformation to correct, so it was going to be a slow job. Meanwhile, Queen Ethelburgha, the lively one, we can be certain, got to work praying. And we must note the strong Christian spirituality of this Ethelburgha. Later in life, she was to experience much personal tragedy. She seems to have ridden through it all with such grace as to have been designated a Saint, capital S. So we can infer that there would have been a resilient Christian spirituality in her, now brought to bear upon King Edwin. He had more than he'd bargained for in this marriage.

Now, as to the mysterious means by which Paulinus led King Edwin into Christian Identity, I have yet to read a fair and reasonable modern secular appraisal of it. This is because the account was given by Bede, and Bede lived and breathed a different spiritual world to the modern one.

Bede was the first great historian of the Early English. His history was an "*Ecclesiastical*" one – a history of how the Early English first adopted Christian Identity. Since miraculous and revelatory powers were at work within that process – which is exactly what you would expect if the Christian God works consistently with his own Bible – and Bede was familiar with such powers, he included them. This is a great nuisance to the modern secular fashion of appraisal. At all costs, omit the Christian dimension; call it "Religion" and move smartly on. Recount who smote who and by whom they were smoten. But the foundational source of the studies of who smote who in this period, the compass and anchor point for them, is Bede: outright and profoundly Christian, with a sure, deft and authentically Christian spiritual touch. If you haven't got the same touch, you won't "get" Bede in his account of Paulinus. So, let's recover it, and in the process, Bede as well.

No-one doubts Bede's assiduous gathering of sources and general integrity with them. Sometimes he used a source which hindsight shows could have been better, but most of the time, no-one doubts the facts or his fairness with them. He was reliable and 1,300 years nearer to them than we are now. However, you encounter this attitude towards Bede: "Tut, tut, he will insist on interweaving the prophetic and the miraculous with his accounts. If only he would stick to the facts." This attitude spills over into appraising Paulinus.

Which is a problem. As you will see, Paulinus seems to have exercised the same revelatory powers as the Apostle Paul of the Christian Bible. As to Bede, he too had an unobtrusive but sure touch with the spiritual dimensions of Christian Life. And he lived in a culture in which the great Gaelic Martinian Christians had not long been at the height of their spiritual powers. His mentor, Benedict Biscop, had made a special point of seeking out a portion of the spiritual mantle of St Martin of Tours, just as St Augustine had once done, and from the same location: the island monastery off the French Riviera called Lerins. We will come to that in a chapter when we cover the life of St Martin more fully. Suffice for now to say that it was the place where his spirituality migrated after his death. It was also the seed point in 432 for the enormously powerful ministry of St Patrick, from whom, spiritually, the great Gaelic Martinian Christians who came out from the Scots into Northumbria descended.

Bede lived, breathed and worked within that same milieu. To adopt a modern Protestant English Christian term, Bede had what you would call Life in the Holy Spirit of the Christian God. The modern Protestant English have a muddly short-hand phrase for that, "Spirit-filled". Bede wrote from a "Spirit-filled" culture. And he knew how to recognize and document the "Spirit-filled" at work. For him, it was normal life. He might have considered an English Christianised culture of today that was devoid of the miraculous and the revelatory to be lacking. He would have wanted the likes of a St Cuthbert to walk into it and fill it: St Cuthbert, an Early English sublime expression of the Gaelic Martinian Christian spirituality, in which milieu Bede lived, and in whose spiritual lineage was his mentor, Benedict Biscop.

Put another way, Bede allowed himself to recount Christian English history with the second eye open, the Christian eye. Fair enough, given that "Christian" and "English" had a symbiotic relationship in real world history.

Paulinus and King Edwin

So now, to Bede's account of Paulinus and the conversion of King Edwin. It hinges on Edwin's dream in 616, when Aethelfrith sought his life and Raedwald was near to handing him over. A mysterious figure appeared to promise restoration but with a condition: when someone came to lay hands on Edwin's head, that would be the sign that he must do what the person said.

After coming North in 624/5, Paulinus found King Edwin a willing audience for Christian reasoning. No doubt he led with the message that St Augustine had brought to King Ethelbert in Kent: spiritual blessings in Christ. But Edwin did not respond to the message as Ethelbert had. He wanted a lot more time to think. And his political situation was not Ethelbert's. The neighbourhood was a lot more dangerous than Kent.

Edwin seems to have been a thinker, like Ethelbert of Kent before him. And to have cared for his people, too, like Ethelbert. But he was perhaps a more cautious man. And he had more inclination to war than Ethelbert had. Personal ambition in that, yes, but care for his people too: in that time and in that place, if the King were not the strongest warrior, his people might suffer for it.

The implication of Christian Identity for kingship in those times would not have been to forbid war. They were land-based times. Modern non-land-based wealth creation systems did not exist. You had to protect and prosper your people within the system. If you were weak, they were enslaved or dead. However, Christian Identity would have constrained how much and in what spirit war might be waged. Edwin would have had to think that through. Warrior culture was in the bones of the Northern Angles. It was not in the bones in Kent.

Edwin would also have had to think through the broader implications for his people. Their spiritual Identity was at stake. He would need to carry them with him through a revolutionary change of Identity from pagan to Christian. And the Northumbrian court was more volatile than the Kentish one. Could he carry it with him into a change to Christian Identity? Edwin had to consider political reality.

So, Edwin remained set in the old pagan ways for a while. Time went by. Ethelburgha bore their first child, a daughter, Eanflaed. This was on the same night as the assassination attempt was made on Edwin by Wessex. Before the campaign that followed it to subdue Wessex, Edwin made a promise to the Christian God: if he was given victory on campaign, he would renounce his idols and serve the Christ. He would also allow his infant daughter to be baptised as a Christian by Paulinus. Edwin won his campaign. Baby Eanflaed was baptised, plus another eleven members of Edwin's household. Edwin, however, held back. He refrained from idols, but also from the Christian God. He decided instead to submit to a lot more teaching from Paulinus.

It was now 627. Paulinus changed tack from reasoning. And now we must carefully heed the experienced "Spirit-filled" Christian life in Bede. And must also understand something of the revelatory dimension of Christian Life: messages in dreams and visions are normal, and being given insight into the dream of another can happen.

Bede records that, *as seemed most probable*, Paulinus was shown *in spirit* Edwin's old dream of 616 in the court of King Raedwald. Paulinus was shown what the stranger in the dream had said to Edwin. And he was shown that the dream had included something else: the stranger had laid a hand on Edwin's head and told him it was a sign; when someone came along and did the same, he was to obey that person's instructions. The promises in the dream, of restoration and increase of power, were conditional upon that.

Paulinus, shown in spirit the dream, and the words the stranger spoke in it, laid a hand on King Edwin's head. He asked whether Edwin had seen this sign before. He then summarised the words of the stranger in the dream. Bede records that at that moment, he sounded to Edwin *like* the stranger in his old dream. Edwin knew then that he must obey the Christian God.

Now, thus far, that is all consistent with the world of Christian revelatory experience. And that the dream was conditional is also consistent with the Christian God. God's dealings with his people are often, "If you will do this, then I will do that." And in his Bible, he works through dreams, especially when about to change real world history. As in the life of Jesus Christ's stepfather, Joseph, after the child had been conceived; and shortly after that in the warning to the Magi who visited the infant Christ. So it is consistent with methods which the Christian God is recorded to have used for interacting with real world history at defining moments.

Anyway, this is for certain. Edwin took on Christian Identity there and then. And with it, the sense of Identity of what was then the most powerful of the Anglo Saxon people groups began to change. As we shall see shortly, Paulinus in 627, like Augustine in 597, seems to have gone on to become a focal point for what Christians of more recent times would call a major Christian Awakening.

Paulinus and the "Treasure Hunt"

Before we go further, we should make a little more effort to validate Paulinus's mode of ministry to King Edwin. What had just happened shaped the secular and the political. Not by intellectual theory but by spiritual power. It matters to come to terms with it, therefore. Some think that Paulinus played mind games with Edwin. Others that Paulinus and Edwin must have met in 616; that Paulinus himself had been the person Edwin met in 616 and it had not been a dream at all. Or that somehow, eleven years later, Paulinus had rigged it. But Bede says clearly that it had been a dream in 616. And equally clearly that the person in the dream had vanished after speaking, proving, to Bede at least, because he says so, that it was a spiritual manifestation.

However, it *is* possible to relate the phenomenon to both modern Christian understanding and the Christian Bible. Here is the explanation.

As to the Bible, the Apostle Paul wrote much of the New Testament. He explained to Christian disciples how the Holy Spirit of the Christian God would work. To the church at Corinth, in Greece, he described how one particular "Charismatic" gift would work to impart Christian revelatory power when at its highest. The secrets of a person that no-one but God could know might, on occasion, be made open by someone with prophetic powers, and that person would come to faith in Jesus Christ on the spot. That was the type of power that Paul had once brought into ancient Greece. In Paulinus, that same type of power came from sunny Rome into chilly Yorkshire. Edwin's secret was opened, and he came to faith in Christ on the spot.

As to modern Christian understanding, certain pockets of the western church today teach a practice known as the "Treasure Hunt". The disciple of Christ goes on the streets seeking revelation about whom to speak to on behalf of Jesus Christ and on what subject. It may lead to an encounter with the Christian God for the person spoken to. Now, in Bede's account, we can see that Paulinus had just practised a related example of the modern "Treasure Hunt". It was in different outward clothing but of the same family of gifting. Both the "Treasure Hunt" and what Paulinus did rely upon revelatory enabling, in the way it is explained in the Bible by the Apostle Paul.

Interesting: a leading church of that sort of thing in modern times is a superpower of Christian spirituality in California. The Latin Monk Paulinus was of the same family of spirituality in Yorkshire in 627. Every form of the outward culture has changed. The underlying Christian spirituality has not. Well, it would not do, if the Christian Bible is any sort of reliable guide. I am with you in every generation to the end of the age, Jesus Christ and Peter between them had taught; yesterday, today, and forever the same, a writer to the Hebrews had amplified.

Now, if you make any sort of study of the history of Christian Awakenings, you find that it is quite normal for a sweep of Christian Awakening to accompany a leader with revelatory powers. Something transformative seems to follow the person around once they get their breakthrough. It seems to have become so for Paulinus. There are a few clues that something powerful started following him around. There were many conversions in Northumbria. A stronger Christian spirituality seems to have entered the East Anglian royal court. Renewal of older Christian ways came into Lindsey (Lincolnshire). And none of these things happened because King Edwin forced everyone to comply. As we shall see now, like Ethelbert of Kent, Edwin permitted freedom of response to Paulinus's Christian message. As exemplified by Bede in Coifi, Edwin's pagan priest.

Coifi, Pagan Priest

Edwin consulted with his leaders. He got Paulinus to address them. Edwin asked his chief pagan priest, one Coifi, what he thought of adopting Christian ways. Bede gives the account. Coifi's response was that he had concluded that the pagan gods that he had long served had been of no avail. However, he, Coifi, had long been a seeker after truth. In this presentation of Christ, he could see clearly that truth was in it, offering life, salvation and eternal happiness.

Now, there is a lot of debunking of Bede's account. However, he wrote as a Christian with Christian eyes. So now, pause here and consider what an open Christian eye would make of Coifi, pagan priest. Truth seeker.

Jesus Christ claimed to be the Truth, capital 'T'. It is normal, in Christian experience, for him to make himself known, during Christian witness, and by the agency of the Holy Spirit of the Christian God, to a truth seeker. And in Bede's account, here is what we see developing in Coifi as he speaks: hope. Now, when hope develops in a person during Christian witness, that is a sure sign that the Holy Spirit is at work. This is a clear principle in the New Testament of the Bible: Hope is the ignition sequence before the Holy Spirit lights up Faith in the Christ. As you read what Coifi said, you can see that he was experiencing what the Christian would discern to be the first hopeful effects of what Jesus Christ called the spiritual new birth. To use an old-fashioned Protestant Christian phrase, Coifi was getting "saved" – i.e. receiving the Christ by inward deposit of the Holy Spirit – as Paulinus spoke. If you have a background in this sort of thing, and then permit yourself to see it, that is what you can see in Coifi within Bede's account.

And he bore the fruits of it. There and then, Coifi took a spear, mounted a horse and rode off to destroy the idols in his pagan sanctuary. Then he set it on fire.

Phew.

I have read speculation about Coifi's background. I will throw in my pennyworth. He would have been lapsed Britonnic Celtic Christian synthesized with pagan, either from Edwin's younger days in exile or from a synthesis of Britonnic Christian and pagan in the region just south of the Humber called Lindsey, now called Lincolnshire. It would explain a lot, including why Paulinus would soon focus his ministry there, and the fact that Coifi's name, as I understand it, was not Anglo Saxon. What we are left with is not so much that Coifi heard the Christian message for the first time as that he heard Paulinus present it accurately for the first time.

To press on, it is important to register the spiritual vibrancy at work here with the priest Coifi. It is disrespectful to gloss over it, as in, "Religious, irrelevant to history." It helped to shape our history. Coifi had just set a transformative example for the people. They followed it.

We tend to think these days that all that would be at stake for a Christian conversion would be the intellectual adoption of one way of religious observance over another. Religion is seen as a political tool in our history and an optional lifestyle accessory. But Christian Life, on its own terms as its God sets them out, is neither religion, nor tool, nor lifestyle accessory. Christian Life, on its God's stated terms, is the Identity-transforming power of God. That is what came into English history. That is what was coming into Coifi. A latter-day secular appraisal of him might be, "One religious way was changed for another for reasons of compliance." What reasons of compliance? Edwin gave Coifi space for opinion and choice. He chose the Christian God. Vigorously. Coifi's choice, and Coifi's vigorous response, was to become typical of the times. And it shaped the politics. It was not the tool of politics.

Paulinus – Christian Awakening

The sweep of new Christian spirituality became a strong wave. Within Deira and parts of Bernicia, many people went on to adopt Christian Identity, flocking to Paulinus for baptism. Augustine had his 10,000 in Kent in 597; now Paulinus had his thousands in Northumbria 627. Interestingly, although he had been made the first Bishop of York (York was not formally an archbishopric until 735), Paulinus also spent a lot of time ministering south of the Humber, in Lindsey, now called Lincolnshire. I would speculate that he was following up with Coifi's people. Note: it was territory either in or hard by, and disputed with, Mercia. Paulinus was getting near to or onto Penda's patch. Not welcome. Not welcome at all.

628 – King Eorpwald and Prince Sigeberht of the East Angles

Because Paulinus would have taught him well, we can reckon that Edwin, whatever his intermingled warrior background, and despite his previous rather dark history, had become not a fake religious king using a new religion as a political tool but, instead, a starter-out in the development of his Christian understanding. Therefore, he went on to witness his new faith to King Eorpwald of the East Angles, one of Raedwald's sons. Ethelbert had witnessed to Raedwald; now Edwin did the same to Raedwald's son. Paulinus would have been involved as well. Edwin, we are told, *reasoned* with Eorpwald to give up idols. It is worth noting two points here:

a. King reasoned with King. The spread of Christian Identity was not through an Awakening of "Religion" as if walled off from "The State". Neither was it by force. It was a fusion of Christian reasoning and proto-statesmanship. The pattern of King reasoning with King to take on Christian Identity recurred time and again. That, more than the sword, was what unified them in the origin times of the Early English.

b. Edwin *reasoned*. Like Ethelbert, he did not use force of sword. I have seen it implied that he forced Eorpwald, just as I have seen it implied that Coifi would have converted because he knew what was good for his career. But

Edwin gave Coifi free choice, and Edwin also reasoned with Eorpwald. A stock-in-trade assumption in appraising Early English history is that it was all about force and the sword. Well, *Anglo Saxon* history may have been about force and the sword. But it was not so much force and the sword that made the *Early English* as it was the common Christian Identity – and freely chosen, at that. The enduring value of free choice passed into the most ancient English rootstock in these formative times, out of a Christian root.

Anyway, Eorpwald received the Christian Identity. With Paulinus in the mix, there would have been a movement of the Holy Spirit of the Christian God as well. The Christian flame was growing stronger in the East Angles than it had done in Raedwald's semi-pagan semi-Christian days.

However, Eorpwald is not the son of King Raedwald who should be brought most into focus here. We must take fuller note of his younger brother, named Sigeberht. What happened with him was a significant step forward in the Gestation of Christian Identity in the Early English.

Dates are not clear, nor the reasons, but before this, Prince Sigeberht of the East Angles had been obliged to go into exile. One infers a falling out with his father, Raedwald, or a quarrel with his more favoured brother, Eorpwald. Sigeberht made his way to Gaul, the homeland of the Germanic Franks. By the time Sigeberht went there, a new and reinforced stream of Romano Martinian Christian spirituality had entered parts of the Frankish church. It had been reinforced by a great Pictish Celtic Saint who came out of what we now call Ireland. His influence has been much overlooked in the history of the Early English. His name was St Columbanus. (Note: not Columba). We will look at Columbanus further in the later chapter about St Martin and his spiritual descendants. We noted earlier that St Augustine had started out in Kent just when St Columba had passed away and the lamentations were still rising. In a like manner, the paths of St Augustine and St Columbanus criss-crossed in Europe in 596/7, but they never met.

Anyway, to complete the picture, Eorpwald had received the Christ through the reasoning of Edwin and the ministry of Paulinus. Meanwhile, exiled with the Martinian Christian Franks, Sigeberht adopted Christian Identity too. And there was nothing nominal about it, as you will see later. He bore the fruits of having embraced the Romano Martinian Christian spirituality as reinforced by St Columbanus. It transformed him.

Sigeberht would soon make a hugely underestimated contribution to the Birth of Christian Identity in the Early English. His exile was to be almost as important as Oswald's with the Gaelic Scots. He would go on to channel the reinforced Frankish Romano Martinian Christian spirituality into East Anglia contemporarily with Oswald channelling the Gaelic Martinian Christian spirituality into the North.

King Raedwald – repaid one son with two

Now, in the process of defeating King Aethelfrith in 616 and installing Edwin in his place on the Northumbrian throne, Raedwald lost a son in the battle. In a beautiful twist of history, he was to be repaid two sons, in a way that would be unique to the Christian God. Here is how. And here we can uncover a hidden wonder of the Christian God beneath the surface of the history.

King Raedwald, for Edwin's sake, but quite possibly for the purposes of the Christian God as well, had lost a son. Well, the Christian God lost a Son as well once, his only and most treasured, he says. Raedwald was repaid in a most moving way. A way that has the imprint of the Christian God on it like a watermark in a banknote. The Christian Bible shows how God repaid a man called Job when he had once lost children for God's purposes. In the end, God paid him back double the number of children. It was similar for Raedwald. Because you see, in a Christian understanding, in Eorpwald and Sigeberht, once they had received the Christ, Raedwald now had two sons reborn to live forever.

What Could Possibly Go Wrong?

What had arisen between Edwin and Eorpwald was a dialogue of Christian reasoning between heads of state. Meanwhile, spiritual powers of Christian Awakening were following Paulinus around. As at about 628, with Eorpwald's conversion, the East Coast had now come into a loose union of Christian Identity: Kent, East Anglia and much of Northumbria were all taking first steps into the new Christian spirituality. And all would have been liaising by sea.

Above all, a Christian King now reigned in Northumbria, more powerful in military and territory than Ethelbert of Kent or Raedwald of the East Angles had ever been. A new and vibrant spirituality was under his protection and advocacy. A Christian one. Imparting light and a new spirit to a grim warrior people of gloomy gods.

It might be seen as an almost painless birth of Christian Identity in the Early English. But I call this the time of "Gestation" of the Christian Identity. It was not Birth. That is because we have yet to come to the Labour Pains.

They were going to be traumatic.

CHAPTER 7.

Trouble

By 628, Christian Identity for the Early English was nearing Birth.

But it was not yet certain. And it was a Dark Ages world.

The Nation-building Christian Identity would labour to be Born against the bloody background of that world.

By 633, Christian Identity would seem to have been put to flight.

But to adapt an old Christian verse, the light would continue to shine in the darkness. And the darkness would not put it out.

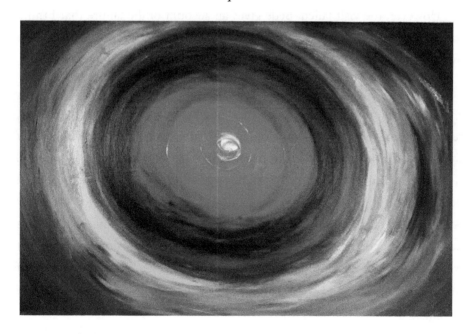

Artwork: Ben Emet

CHAPTER 8.

Labour Pains

Interlude – St Augustine and the Britonnic Bishops

Before we go on, I should make reference to a visit by St Augustine of Canterbury to the Britonnic Christian bishops in the West. It had taken place by 604 in two phases. The aim had been to unite the Britonnic Christian church with the new Roman Catholic mission and to bring it under Augustine's overall authority. He had written authority from Pope Gregory to validate that purpose. King Ethelbert used his influence to secure safe passage for Augustine via Anglo Saxon territories.

However, the visit failed. Bede gives an account of the failure that I think has been generally misunderstood so that St Augustine has been blamed for it by history (I think wrongly). I have therefore taken time out to look at this here, as an interlude, for completeness of picture.

The Britonnic Christian bishops, although supposed to honour the Pope, refused to unite with the new mission. Instead, after reluctant negotiations, they went away and sought an oracle from a hermit. The hermit set a test of humility. If Augustine did not stand when the bishops entered his presence to resume negotiations, it meant he was arrogant and should be spurned. Now, for Augustine to stand, within his own culture and understanding, would have been to subjugate the Pope, whom he represented, to the Britonnic bishops. It would have required him, therefore, to compromise his most innate sense of integrity. The Christian God does not set tests that require that. Nor would he subjugate the Pope to bishops.

Anyway, Augustine, having written authority from the Pope to confirm that the Britonnic bishops should line up with him, and having won a healing miracle contest to confirm his authority under the Christian God, and showing no fake humility, did not stand when the bishops entered his presence. And there the mission ended.

Augustine has been almost uniformly blamed for it by history. You have to wonder, however, at the level of maturity of the Britonnic bishops. You reject the Papal authority because he does not stand? You prefer a hermit who sets fake humility tests?

Augustine parted with a word of warning. If you do not join in with evangelising the Anglo Saxons, he said, you will perish at their hands. And indeed, King Aethelfrith of Northumbria, as we read earlier, would slaughter many Britonnic monks in 616. To read some appraisals of Augustine, you would think it had been some sort of prophetic curse. I would think, however, that it probably arose out of shrewd insider knowledge of the political climate.

There were consequences of the failure of Augustine's visit. I do not call them "Labour Pains" for the founding of Christian Identity in the Early English, but there were far-reaching consequences for the Britons, political and spiritual. There was an element of tragedy for them. That can be the case when a Christian body lets its people down.

i. Politically, they lost a potential advocate. Augustine regrouped to Canterbury. His focus and that of most of his successors became building Christian Identity from scratch amongst the Anglo Saxons. There would be no prestigious Roman church voice to intercede for the Britonnic peoples with Anglo Saxon rulers excepting, perhaps, that of Paulinus for Coifi's people a generation later. And then, ironically, a Britonnic Christian Celt would silence that voice.

ii. But that is just ahead of us. Spiritually, a Christian understanding can discern a Biblical pattern at work in the real world within what happened. The clue is in this: the Britonnic bishops can be understood to have rebuffed a last-ditch opportunity from the Christian God to renew their existing Christian way. From then on, the Holy Spirit of the Christian God was free, under Biblical patterns, to take the mantle of Christ to those who had not had the mantle before, the Anglo Saxons, its renewal having been rejected first by those who already had it, the Britons.

Now, the Christian Bible says that judgement begins in God's own house. Within that principle, Christian movements must either renew or lose their way. The Britonnic church, seeded from 177 in noble deeds, miracles and martyrs, seems to have become tired by 604. There is one thing I surmise about it and one thing which is certain. As to surmise, there seems to have been a certain synthesis with paganism in strands of it. The Holy Spirit of the Christian God will not co-operate with that. As to certainty, there had been two previous major missions from Rome to call the Britonnic church out of a heresy called Pelagianism.

In modern terminology, Pelagianism = self-righteousness, that is, striving for perfect righteousness in one's own strength, rather than God's. The Holy Spirit of the Christian God will depart from that if it goes too far. A Christian understanding would see moral codes as a helpful servant for the Christian, up until the Christian resurrection. But to be found righteous by the Christian God is a work of the Christ and the Holy Spirit from beginning to end. The Christian in whom Christ dwells expresses the goodness that the Holy Spirit prompts.

Now, within a Christian understanding, fake humility can be a symptom of self-righteousness. So I think that the hermit can be discerned to have been under Pelagian influence. Augustine's mission failed when the Britonnic bishops preferred his Pelagian oracle over the written authority of the Pope. That attitude would also have hindered them in fulfilling the Christian call to evangelise the Anglo Saxon invaders because, as I noted in previous chapters, the Anglo Saxons would turn out to be responsive to those who would co-operate with Rome. And I think there can be little doubt that the Britonnic church also harboured a certain hostility towards the Anglo Saxons. Understandable, in human terms. But that, too, would reduce its potential to evangelise. Even the Martinian pockets could tend to harshness, which was always a risk of the self-depriving lifestyle. St Martin and those most nearly in his spirituality were full of love, but harshness was always a possibility within the way of it, like a green apple not fully ripened.

So, tragedy: the Britonnic church had just had its third strike and was out. Hence, from 604 onwards, there ensued an exact replay of a basic pattern in the Christian Bible. A final opportunity to renew their way with the Christian God had been offered, via Augustine, to the Britonnic Christian way before the Christian message went out to the Anglo Saxons, except for Ethelbert of Kent. He, in the pattern of a Gentile Leader of the Old Testament, the likes of a Cyrus, secured passage for Augustine to the Britons via Anglo Saxon territories. But those invited first, the Britonnic church, did not discern the opportunity or the third-strike nature of it. After that, the new wave of Christian mission was to be for those who had never heard the Christian message but would receive it, the Early English. Those who had previously heard the Christian message but would not renew the way of it, the Britonnic Celtic church, were left to their own ways. That pattern is a backbone pattern within the Christian Bible. It played out in real world Roman history after Christ came. And it replayed within real world Britonnic and English history.

I cannot go deeper here into what became of the Britonnic church and people. I sorrow for the failure of Augustine's mission. It seems to me that the element of divisive bitterness which arose descends to us, culturally, to this day. However, this book is about how Christian Identity came to the Early English. The effect of the failure was that the Britonnic Celtic Christian church played little part in that. Amongst the Christian Celts, it passed mainly to the Martinian Gaels to give the message that would set the Anglo Saxon invaders on the road to Early English Christian Identity. This book deals with that.

Labour Pains

Therefore, to move on to the focus of this book: Christian Identity forming in the Early English.

King Edwin of Northumbria, King Eorpwald of East Anglia and King Eadbald of Kent were all in loose Christian union by about 628. Can we not take that to have been the birth of the Christian Identity that had first been conceived in Ethelbert in 597? And rather peaceful with it too?

Er, not quite. There were Labour Pains. And there was blood. The map gives an overview. It also includes the exiled princes whom we highlighted in the "Gestation" phase.

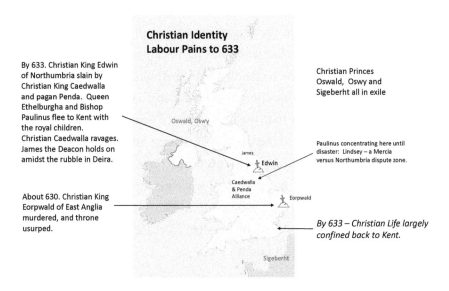

**Christian Identity
Labour Pains to 633**

By 633. Christian King Edwin of Northumbria slain by Christian King Caedwalla and pagan Penda. Queen Ethelburgha and Bishop Paulinus flee to Kent with the royal children. Christian Caedwalla ravages. James the Deacon holds on amidst the rubble in Deira.

About 630. Christian King Eorpwald of East Anglia murdered, and throne usurped.

Christian Princes Oswald, Oswy and Sigeberht all in exile

Paulinus concentrating here until disaster: Lindsey – a Mercia versus Northumbria dispute zone.

Oswald, Oswy

James

Edwin

Caedwalla & Penda Alliance

Eorpwald

By 633 – Christian Life largely confined back to Kent.

Sigeberht

Christian Identity had begun to spread under Edwin's banner. Northumbria was open to it. East Anglia was open to it. Paulinus was at the height of his powers of Christian spirituality. At York, in Deira, Paulinus had the help of a man known as "James the Deacon". James, who taught singing in church, was to become an unsung hero later. Paulinus himself, meanwhile, although bishop in York, was busy with Christian evangelisation to the south, in the Lindsey territory that we now call Lincolnshire. He may have been offering renewal of the Britonnic Celtic Christian way there. That seems to have become synthesized with Germanic pagan ways, and the two people groups seem to have co-existed. However, Lindsey was a zone of military dispute for the greater powers that bordered it, Mercia and Northumbria. Mercian Angles would have resented Paulinus's presence there; so too did the Germanic aristocratic element in Lindsey, which preferred Mercia. Paulinus's

Northumbria-sponsored ministry may even have strayed onto Mercian territory.

King Eorpwald Murdered

However, before events could blow up in the North, there was a very early setback to the East. Newly Christian King Eorpwald of the East Angles was murdered and his throne usurped. It was about the year 630.

His younger brother, remember, Prince Sigeberht, had found Martinian Christian Identity amongst the Franks. However, he was in exile. There was a hiatus of three years after Eorpwald was slain.

King Edwin Slain in Battle

Next up, a major setback befell the spread of Christian Identity amongst the Anglo Saxon people groups. Or so it would seem. King Edwin of Northumbria, guardian supreme of Christian messengers, was slain in battle with the Britonnic King Caedwalla of Gwynedd, part of what we now call North Wales, and the Angle-ish Penda of Mercia, soon to be King. It was probably late in the year 632.

The Root of Bitterness

The concept of the "bitter root" maturing to terrible effect is a Christian Biblical one. In 632, the bitter root that we noted to have been sown earlier in Caedwalla, King of Gwynedd, sprouted: out from the spiritual into political and military reality.

Caedwalla had scores to settle. Penda of Mercia, by now emerging as the resolutely pagan and pro-warfare soon-to-be King of the Anglo Saxon Mercians, joined forces with him. They had a target in view: Northumbria in general, and Edwin in person.

Christian Principles that played out

To understand all that was to follow, we must take note of four significant Christian teachings, the second of them below being foundational. They appear to have played out in the violent real world history.

i.   There is a clear instruction to Christians in the Bible: Christian must not make alliance with pagan. It is explicit. Caedwalla would have known it. His people group identified as Britonnic Christian. The Britonnic church may have been getting tired, but it knew its Bible. And its royals would have known that instruction. It was highly relevant in those times.

ii.   As spelt out by the Apostle Paul in the Biblical letter to the Romans, in all things God works for good for those who love him. This is a foundational principle of Christian understanding. We must note: (a) Paul does *not* say that God works all things for good. That is fatalism. He says God works all things for good for those *called within the purposes of the Christian God.* That is Christian. (b) Paul does *not* say that God works for the immediate good of the individual Christian at the time. In its context, the teaching includes that an individual Christian may succumb to the sword, but good will accrue to the Christian God's purposes. Those would include the spread of Christian Identity. Therefore, in all things, including when Christians are put to the sword, *Christian Identity* can overcome. As for the dead Christian, they are not lost. They go to be with the risen Christ pending their own resurrection.

iii.   The Christian God reveals in his Bible that he makes a distinction between those who take his name, i.e. call themselves Christian, and those who do not. He subjects those who take his name to strict judgement. Others, he weighs up by their lights. And he says he is very patient with them. This is relevant to Penda.

iv.   Revenge is a power reserved for the Christian God. Those who take his
       name may not abrogate the right to it. (Within the Christian God's
       Bible, authorities are expected to enforce law and order, uphold the
       security of their people – forcibly if need be – and are allowed to punish,
       within reason. But revenge is a dish off the menu). This is relevant to
       Caedwalla.

We are going to see all these Christian spiritual principles work out in the
violent real world history of Caedwalla and Penda.

Bringing Down King Edwin

First, however, to King Edwin and the politics. He represented Northumbria.
For Gwynedd in Britonnic North Wales, Edwin's violent predecessor
Aethelfrith had also represented Northumbria. And that older Northumbria
had sown a bitter root when it sacked North Wales. Edwin had added to it later
and made it personal, too, for Caedwalla when he drove him into exile.
Meanwhile, Mercia was coming to resent Northumbrian reach. Edwin had
subdued Wessex, married into Kent and was powerful in East Anglia by
peaceful contacts. Its Christian witness was not welcome in Lindsey, either.
Paulinus's Christian ministry in Lindsey was bearing fruit, but it was presuming
upon freedom of movement in a territory in which Mercia saw itself, with
political agreement within Lindsey, as top dog. Northumbria was getting above
itself. And besides all that, there was the nature of Mercia's emergent leader,
Penda: resolutely pagan; dedicated to the older Germanic culture of honour
through warfare; contemptuous of Christians. Edwin may have fallen out with
him when younger in the Mercian court and then later provoked him when he
set aside Cwenburh of Mercia for Ethelburgha of Kent.

Caedwalla and Penda joined forces to bring Edwin and Northumbria down.
Probably late in 632, certainly by 633, a combined force of Caedwalla and Penda
overcame Edwin's forces in battle. King Edwin was slain.

Penda returned to his homeland, honour satisfied for now. By his lights, he
had not done wrong. The Christian God, remember, reveals that he weighs the

likes of Penda by their lights. And is patient. Penda would have twenty-two more years and military dominion.

Caedwalla went on a murderous rampage, unchallenged throughout the north, in reprisals for what Aethelfrith had once done. The Christian King would have known that his Bible explicitly forbade alliance of Christian with pagan and that it reserved revenge for the Christian God. But his heart was bitter. Caedwalla's time was short.

The alliance of the powers, however, was to last until Penda's death. The unholy alliance, as a Christian appraisal of the history could reasonably call it, would become the lost secret of his military dominion. A more political appraisal might note that, contrary to caricature, military alliance with the Britonnic Celtic was to be very important for Penda's future Anglo Saxon military dominion. He was to be slain on the first day he lost the Britonnic support.

Ethelburgha, Paulinus and Eanflaed

In the chaos of early 633, most likely to protect the royal children born to Ethelburgha, Paulinus and Ethelburgha fled by sea back to Kent. Included was the young Princess Eanflaed. She had been that newborn daughter when Wessex had sought to assassinate Edwin. She had also been the first in Northumbria to be baptised in the days when Edwin was coming to terms with Christian Identity. As it turned out, she was not finished with the North East yet. Bertha's granddaughter, she was to have a key part to play in Northumbria's later Christian way forward. When she grew up, she became Queen Eanflaed of Northumbria. We come to that later.

Paulinus, meanwhile, ended his days as Bishop of Rochester in Kent. His ministry in Lindsey, which I would think was intended partly to renew the Britonnic Christian Celtic way, had been cut off. And here is the irony: it was Caedwalla, a Britonnic Christian Celt from the tradition that had rejected Augustine, cutting off the ministry of renewal of Christian ways to Britonnic

Christian Celts. That is the sort of irony that happens when those with Christian Identity nurture the root of bitterness.

All seems lost from a Christian perspective

Now, it seems fair to say that Paulinus had overstretched by 633. In Kent, after the early winning of converts, they had settled down to the boring stuff: pastoral structures, training the indigenous, cultivating discipleship. Paulinus made many converts further North. But pastoral structures were flimsy. There was most likely a great relapse once his personal presence had gone. Given that in those days, if the king fell, so too his state might also shatter, the loss of both Edwin and Paulinus was catastrophic for Christian Identity in the short term.

However, I think we can be too hard on Paulinus over the relapse. In post-Reformation times, there were two great British Christian contemporaries, John Wesley and George Whitefield. They led enormous Christian Awakenings, Wesley in parts of the UK and Whitefield in the young USA. Wesley founded a very Methodical church to retain his converts and disciple them. Whitefield did not. I have read that at the end of his life, he compared himself to Wesley and declared that he had made, by comparison, a rope of sand. However, the Christian Identity that George Whitefield helped to plant into the spiritual foundations of the USA, into its founding Sense of Identity, seems to be alive in its culture to this day. And I would discern a similar type of legacy from Paulinus. He seems to have been a sort of proto-Whitefield of Christian Awakening from 627 to 632 when disaster struck. The spiritual legacy would have endured in the foundations. Deiran York, his official seat, would go on to be hugely influential in the spread of its brand of Christian spirituality into the Early English. With Paulinus and James the Deacon, it was already a fusion of what was strong in Latin and Romano Martinian spirituality within prestigious Roman Catholic forms. It would soon get a dramatic infusion of Gaelic Martinian Christian spirituality too. That aggregate recipe would pretty much go on to make the English. Christian spirituality, when mediated by those who have strong gifting from the Holy Spirit of the Christian God, has a long-term way of rooting down, whatever happens on the surface. So it was with Paulinus, I would say.

However, as at 633, the Christianising superstructure collapsed everywhere except in Kent.

Remnants

Even so, keeping his head down in the Northern rubble, Paulinus's ally, James the Deacon, remained within the Deiran part of Northumbria. He survived the period and saw it through. Slowly but surely, pastoral structure was rebuilt. In 663, thirty years later, James would come to a Synod at Whitby, in the North East of what we now call England. A Synod is a gathering of Christian leaders. The elderly James attended with forceful new helpers and with the once-refugee Queen Eanflaed influencing things behind the scenes. That Synod at Whitby was to become a nation-shaping milestone in the process of transforming the Anglo Saxons into the Christian Early English. And within it, as you will see later, you might say, "James won."

As to Edwin, he was an immature Christian when death came, and all seemed lost when he died. Christian Identity was largely forced back into Kent.

There were three Christian Angle-ish princes, but all were in exile: Sigeberht with the Franks, and Oswald and Oswy with the Gaelic Scots.

But... when Edwin died, he had set course, since 627, for his life to come within the purposes of the Christian God. Therefore, his Christian Identity was going to overcome. His death would turn out to be the climax of Labour Pains for Christian Identity in the Early English. Birth was coming. What seemed lost would soon be stronger than ever.

Because Sigeberht, Oswald and Oswy were exiled amongst the *Martinian* Christians, the strongest spiritual force in the West. And from 634 to 635, they would all return at once. Oswald would become the lightning rod of the times. And the Pope in Rome, Honorius, had an additional Man of Mystery newly at his disposal. He was coming, too. The Dark Age of the Anglo Saxon people groups was coming to an end. The Early English were going to be Born.

Postscripts

Many people assume that the reason you would follow the Christian God is for all to go well for you. It is highly unlikely to be so, given that this same God gave up the one he called his only Son to crucifixion, and most of his early apostles died by violence too. But that is not what many people think. They think Christians follow the Christian God for what's in it for them. That is a religious form of thinking. It's fake. The Christian God's agenda is his Christ. He proved it with King Edwin. Because all did not go well for Edwin. He experienced more than a setback. Good was going to emerge out of it for Christian purposes but not for Edwin, in this life at least.

As to Queen Ethelburgha, Bertha's daughter, a refugee in Kent, she fetched up at a village called Lyminge. There she established a monastery which became noted in later years. Where she had it built is interesting. It provides corroboration of one of the miracles of St Augustine of Canterbury. The royal family of Ethelbert and Bertha would accompany Augustine on his travels, remember? The very young "Tate" may have had a formative memory of the great monk at work. She would certainly have been brought up on tales of his prowess. They included this one: the story goes that Augustine arrived at Lyminge as the villagers were packing up to leave it. The local spring of water had failed. Making like Moses, Augustine struck it with his staff. The waters flowed. The villagers received the Christ that he preached. The refugee Ethelburgha built her monastery next to the spring. It was to that place of treasured childhood Christian significance that she fled when her husband died.

Now, I don't see any good reason to doubt that St Augustine did this. It is a perfectly Biblical type of miracle. If you proclaim the God of the Bible, you can expect the God of the Bible, if he is really who he says he is, to act as he does in the Bible. There were other and more comfortable places Ethelburgha could have settled, ready-made ones by springs of water near her mother's old church in more civilised Canterbury. Pope Gregory had even warned Augustine not to get proud because of his many miracles. This does not mean that Augustine actually was proud. It was just a wise warning not to let it go to his head. During Christian history, the Christian God has given miraculous powers to Christians taking Life in the Holy Spirit of the Christian God to new and pagan frontiers. It has been a necessary part of their equipment for tackling the spiritual realm they would encounter there. In Bede, we see St Augustine take a sick man in front of western Celtic Britonnic bishops. The Christian God is recorded to have healed the man. It was in order to validate Augustine's authority under God, not just under Papal letters.

At this point, I just love the picture that emerges of those Latin monks. Since the Protestant Reformation, we have caricatured Latin monks: privileged elite; religious hypocrites defined by ritual; "dry as dust". Well, one of them, Augustine, took a leaf from Moses's playbook at Lyminge. The other, Paulinus, expressed in Deira the revelatory powers which had been in the Apostle Paul. In the Anglo Saxon real world. When the Christian rootstock was being planted.

King Penda holds dominion

Returning to the story, though, no-one knew in 633 that Christian life was about to become even stronger. Edwin had been the main shield and guarantor of Christian life. All must have seemed lost, or soon to be lost, outside of Kent. The political world appeared to have reshaped the spiritual world and put it back into an older and more violent mould. Penda of Mercia, now its King, was at the height of his energy and remained so for years to come.

As for King Caedwalla, he was on a follow-up campaign in the North that was so murderous as to be perceived by Prince Oswald, on his return to save the situation, to be genocidal. And Caedwalla having the label "Christian".

It was a time of the most terrible Labour Pains for the Christian Identity which would emerge in the Early English.

Prince Oswald Returns

But now, enter the young Bernician, Prince Oswald, Saint-King to be. White Blade. Fire Starter. Early England's Christ figure.

A most transformative Christian Identity is about to be Born.

CHAPTER 9.

White Blade Returns

Saint-King Oswald.

Lightning Rod.

Fire Starter.

Earth touching heaven.

And he's not alone.

The first Anglo Saxon step towards becoming the Early English is about to be made.

And like so many of the steps that would lead on to the Nation of the English, it proves to be a Christian step.

Artwork: Ben Emet

CHAPTER 10.

Birth – 634/5

Reminder

Before we go further, here is a reminder of basic terminology that I use. "Anglo Saxon" denotes the Germanic people groups. "Early English" denotes those same groups but with the new Christian spirituality at work within them. They gradually united around that.

Preview

In the years 634 and 635, three Anglo Saxon people groups embraced Christian Identity. These were East Anglia, Wessex and Northumbria. Kent, meanwhile, was maintaining and developing its post-597 Christian Life. This time around, there was to be no collapse of Christian Life in Northumbria. Neither was the new Christian King in East Anglia quickly murdered this time. He turned out to be deeply committed to Christian Life. And Wessex was to be so impressed with its conversion to Christian Identity that, after early failures, it went on to build first itself, and then later what became the Nation of the English, upon it.

These days, the fashion is to class the sort of thing that happened in 635 as "Religion" and present it as if the people had gone through some sort of politically calculated surface re-labelling exercise. However, if we allow ourselves to discover the spiritual dimension of history, something powerfully transforming can be discerned to have been loosed all at once into the spiritual world of the Anglo Saxon people groups. An enduring and shared Christian Identity came to Birth. The Anglo Saxons would embrace it with sincerity and grow up to become the Early English within it.

Preparations

At the heart of the transformation was Saint-King Oswald of Northumbria. Later generations called him "Bright Blade" or "White Blade". I think of him as lightning rod, fire starter.

But he was not alone. It was an epic time. We should start with spiritual foundations laid in the generations before.

In 563, a most dynamic and charismatic person of royal blood had emerged out of what we now call Ireland. He settled with a band of monks off the shore of what we now call Scotland. He was a Celt, of Gaelic or Scotic branch. The designations mean the same thing. Gael was the Celtic descriptor, Scot or Scoti the Latin one. This person's name has come down to us as St Columba. The site of the monastic settlement was the island of Iona. Set in what was then the seaborne main highway of the Celtic peoples, it was a leading Christian Light of its times.

A generation after that, a Pictish Celtic monk further emerged out of what we now call Ireland. He went into mainland Europe. The monk's name was St Columbanus.

There will be more about these two Celtic monks in the later chapter about St Martin of Tours and his spiritual descendants. Suffice for now to say that:

- St Columba's Scotic legacy to the Angle-ish was the Christian spirituality which became inherent in the life of Saint King Oswald of Northumbria. I call that spirituality Gaelic Martinian Christian. You could also add in "Catholic". I know that many imply otherwise, but it seems clear to me that the Gaelic Christians never saw themselves as a "Celtic Church" that was somehow separate from Rome. It was culturally distinct, but it engaged in full.

- St Columbanus reinforced the Martinian Christian spirituality of the Germanic Franks at a time when that was falling away. The Christian spirituality that came to the East Angles and to Wessex emerged from the

Frankish church as reinforced by Columbanus. I call that spirituality Romano Martinian Catholic Christian.

Both streams were within the Roman Catholic whole.

Locations

I begin with a map to locate the many names and locations.

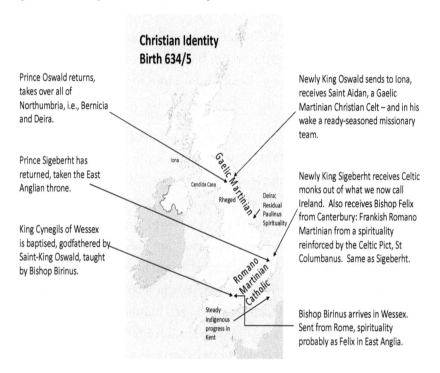

Christian Identity Birth 634/5

Prince Oswald returns, takes over all of Northumbria, i.e., Bernicia and Deira.

Prince Sigeberht has returned, taken the East Anglian throne.

King Cynegils of Wessex is baptised, godfathered by Saint-King Oswald, taught by Bishop Birinus.

Newly King Oswald sends to Iona, receives Saint Aidan, a Gaelic Martinian Christian Celt – and in his wake a ready-seasoned missionary team.

Newly King Sigeberht receives Celtic monks out of what we now call Ireland. Also receives Bishop Felix from Canterbury: Frankish Romano Martinian from a spirituality reinforced by the Celtic Pict, St Columbanus. Same as Sigeberht.

Bishop Birinus arrives in Wessex. Sent from Rome, spirituality probably as Felix in East Anglia.

Iona

Candida Casa

Rheged

Deira: Residual Paulinus Spirituality

Gaelic Martinian

Romano Martinian Catholic

Steady indigenous progress in Kent

Broad Sequence of Events

Bishop Birinus preceded Oswald into Wessex in about 634, and King Sigeberht may have been under way in East Anglia in 634 as well.

Saint King Oswald was under way in Northumbria from 635.

In Wessex, Saint King Oswald godfathered its royal house into Christian Identity in 635.

The Christian seed previously sown by Paulinus into Deira, which seemed to have become infertile as at 633, would soon be cultivated again, once St Aidan got to work after 635.

In East Anglia, what Paulinus had sown and seemed lost would also recover after 635.

Wessex and Bishop Birinus – Man of Mystery

Our re-construction begins at the bottom right of the map, with Bishop Birinus arriving in Wessex. Dates are uncertain, but it seems it was about 634. His origins are shrouded in mystery. Before we explore those further, we should look at Wessex.

Wessex originated as the territory of the people group called the West Saxons. It was to the South West of what we now call England, south of the Thames Valley, and excluding Devon and Cornwall. A warrior place, but in military Mercia's shadow. It had also held lands to the North of the Thames. However, those had recently been wrested from it by King Penda's Mercia. Its government was fragile, too. Kings struggled for power with under-kings. Furthermore, if you recall, the Wessex royal house had not long ago tried to assassinate King Edwin of Northumbria. Edwin had delivered a forceful humiliation, which weakened them. Having been humbled by one power, and lost lands to the other, Wessex was gaining lands from the Britons to the west by force. It was, perhaps, a rather desperate existence.

Of all the kingdoms, Wessex, the least likely, was ultimately to become the strongest. It would also be the one to establish the Nation of the English on a Christian foundation. We should look forward to that briefly now in order to get some perspective.

Wessex's defining Christian genius, two hundred and fifty years later, was to be King Alfred the Great. His family's hero was Saint King Oswald of Northumbria, who first godfathered the Wessex royals into Christian Identity in 635.

Alfred of Wessex, held by general consensus to have been Great, was the least likely of his family to become King. In that respect, his career was to be like that of King David in the Bible. He, too, was the least likely in his family. The life patterns of Alfred and David bore other resemblances, too. The English, it seems, came into defining national identity through the family of a Great Christian King from Wessex, whose life was not unlike that of King David of the Bible.

When the time came, 878 to 927, Alfred the Great's family set out deliberately to integrate Christian Life into the inmost fabric of the people who became the Nation of the English. During that period, however, they did not set out primarily to create a nation. Their focus was to save their Christian Identity. Emerging from much tumult to find they had done so, that was when they went on to call themselves "English".

I look forward to these things now so that you can get a perspective on how completely Wessex was going to be transformed by Christian Life once it had come and what it would finally do with it. And so that you can note that Saint King Oswald of Northumbria, who dominates this chapter, was its enduring hero throughout the later process that led to the founding of the Nation of the English.

I might note in passing, before going on, that it is a typical pattern of both the Christian Bible and Christian experience for the Christian God to use the unlikely or the least likely. And a timescale of two hundred and fifty years from sowing to reaping is sprightly for the Christian God, by the standards of his Bible.

So now, to Bishop Birinus, Man of Mystery.

Given the warfare between the people groups, and following the usual pattern in the Anglo Saxons, the Christian way that was in the Britonnic Celts was not received by Wessex. However – and would you call it coincidence or what? – Wessex did receive Christian mission out of the blue, or so it seems. It came from the European mainland. In about 634, Wessex received a visiting bishop commissioned directly by Pope Honorius of the Roman Catholic church. This visitor, Bishop Birinus, turned out to be exactly the right Christian leader in the right place at the right time. Wessex received his Christian message as warmly as King Ethelbert's Kent had received Augustine's in 597.

Now, maybe Birinus did come out of the blue. I am going to make a reasonable alternative surmise, however, the documentation being uncertain. Wessex wanted into this new-fangled Christian thing. But they did not want a Kent hand-me-down. They wanted the Wessex brand. As some think that King Ethelbert of Kent may have sent for the Augustinian mission, so Wessex may have put out feelers for one of their own.

Bishop Birinus's Christian roots are also uncertain. I am not alone in surmising that they were like those of Felix and Sigeberht in East Anglia: Romano Martinian Frankish from the monastic life strengthened by St Columbanus. Birinus was certainly the sparky power packet you would expect of that. However, there we must leave Birinus for the moment. He was a most gifted Christian teacher. The evidence is strong for that. His Christian mission was being well received in Wessex in about 634. The location given to him as a base is interesting. It was at Dorchester-on-Thames, hard by the disputed frontier with Mercia. A dangerous place in those days.

King Sigeberht and Bishop Felix, East Anglia

By that same year, 634, the exiled Prince Sigeberht, younger son of King Raedwald and brother of the murdered King Eorpwald of the East Angles, had been able to take the East Anglian throne. In exile with the Franks, he seems to have taken to Christian Identity with a passion. Later in life, he was to resign his kingly calling and swap it for a monk's.

We might note here in passing that the East Anglian court, in helping Sigeberht, seems to have wanted back the Christian spirituality which had previously been planted by Paulinus but then cut down by usurpation. It was still in the roots, just as it was in Deira.

Once made King, Sigeberht seems to have gone out of his way to seek Christian visitors to spread the Christian message in his kingdom. He received two key sources.

i. A dynamic company of monks came out of what we now call Ireland. Their ethnicity is uncertain to me, but I would think they would have been Martinian in their Christian spirituality. We must remember the name of one of these monks, Fursa. We will come to him again when we consider Christian spiritual phenomena which were recorded in the times of the Christian Awakening of the Early English. Think of him for now as a sort of Scotch bonnet chilli pepper received into the East Anglian spiritual stew.

ii. A Frankish Bishop named Felix, whose name means "Happy", had been displaced by political upheaval in Frankish Burgundy. His Christian spirituality was of the Romano Martinian stream that St Columbanus had reinforced in the Frankish church. I think we can be reasonably sure that King Sigeberht was a product of the same. Felix wandered seeking new opportunities. He came to Canterbury when it just so happened that Sigeberht had sent to Canterbury for a bishop. Archbishop Honorius sent him on to East Anglia. Felix and Sigeberht hit it off. Another Christian leader in just the right place at the right time. And Felix's ministry in East Anglia was to be as happy as his name.

King Sigeberht had a passion for education on Christian foundations many generations before Alfred the Great came along with the same. Bishop Felix shared that passion. Quite soon, Kentish and East Anglian royals, along with Kentish and East Anglian churches, would join up more completely and develop educational systems. Sigeberht and Felix in East Anglia were an early seed of the drive towards those. They were a profoundly Christian seed.

Saint King Oswald – and St Aidan Coming Soon

So, in 635, two gifted Christian clerics were the right people in the right place at the right time: Birinus in Wessex out of mysterious circumstances, Felix amongst the East Angles in more normal ones. A third was coming soon, to

Northumbria, possibly the most gifted of the lot: St Aidan, a.k.a. "the Apostle to English", another one destined to be the right person in the right place at the right time.

St Aidan would come in Christian love and transformative spirituality. It was that, not the sword, which seeded the golden civilisation in Northumbria which, within three generations, in Bede's time, would become a beacon of light to all of Europe. Before he could come, however, he had to be sent for. Which brings us to Saint King Oswald of Northumbria.

Or Prince Oswald, as he was in 634. He returned to Northumbria from sanctuary amongst the Scots about the year 634. He was to become a Saint-King, a cult, and the subject of sagas, and in European territories too. There are churches in England still dedicated to him.

Oswald overthrew the Britonnic Caedwalla. Reigned in Northumbria from 635 to 642. Embodied one of the most profound spiritual principles of the Christ and applied it into real world Anglo Saxon history. Laid the first foundation stone of Early English nation building. Sparked off Christian Awakening. Sent for St Aidan and team. Was slain and dismembered by King Penda of Mercia, after which, events replicated the full pattern of the cross and resurrection of Christ. And his bones, or what they represented, seem to have been active in two further nation-building episodes in 679 and 910.

The cultural dimension of his life was not easy for a modern mind to understand. The spiritual was Dramatic with a capital D. Oswald was a sort of Early England Christ figure, but a warrior king, not a cleric or a monk.

Oswald's Culture

There was Christian Integrity in those Gaelic Scots who brought up Oswald from age 12 onwards. When he was a refugee in their midst in 616, there would have been a calculation for them to make as to whether to receive him at all. Should they hand him back to new King Edwin of Northumbria? Or win favour with Edwin by killing Oswald, sending the boy's head, perhaps? Or receive

Oswald in the hope of one day having him in their debt if he were to take the Northumbrian throne?

Two hard-hearted choices with a certain outcome: the favour of King Edwin. One uncertain choice with an outcome that would possibly antagonise powerful Edwin.

They made the uncertain choice. They received Oswald. Why? I have read it was in order to curry favour with Oswald if he were to make it in the future. However, it seems obvious to me that they made their choice out of integrity: Christian Integrity. They honoured the treaty made with Oswald's father in 604. They received the son of the violent invader, Aethelfrith, who had bested them before the treaty. Within their culture, they would have done so in full knowledge of the culture of Jesus Christ: bless those who have maltreated you. It would have been in knowing obedience to that very challenging command of the Christ that the Gaels received Oswald.

As you will see later in the book, in the chapter about St Martin of Tours, a strong chain of transformative Christian grace of exactly this type – blessing the maltreaters – had descended in the past from St Patrick to St Columba. It was now extended in 616 to the young Prince Oswald. And in due course, the Gaels would do more than just receive Oswald. They would also lead him into the vibrant Martinian Christian spirituality that descended from Saints Patrick and Columba. Oswald grew up to embody it. And he would go on to embed the forgiving Christian grace which had once been extended to him into a Christian treaty with Wessex in 635.

Now, Oswald would have come to the Gaelic Scots as a young pagan brought up to be a Warrior like his warlike Angle-ish father. The Gaels were warlike as well. Oswald, already brought up to be a Warrior from early childhood amongst the Northern Angles, would have learned more of the same amongst the Gaelic Celts. Amongst these, it was normal to be both Christian and a Warrior. There would have been different ways of outworking between the pagan and the Christian. But Warrior was in the bones of each culture.

To combine "Christian" and "Warrior" may sound difficult to a post 1914-18 Great War modern mind. And since Medieval times, a thing called the Crusades has descended to corrupt the whole concept of "Christian Warrior". However, for the avoidance of doubt, the Crusades were an occult adventure. They were not a Christian one. There is a very easy clue. The recruitment message was, "Kill for Jesus in order to earn time off in Purgatory." That is an occult message. Given that the Crusades remain a hissing and a byword against Christian testimony from that day to this in some parts of the world, it shows you how serious a transgression it is to engage in occult activity in Christian clothing.

But that loss of integrity was many centuries after Oswald. Within the Gaelic culture which had received him from 616, St Columba had not been a monk behind a religious wall, separated from the secular. You can think of him instead as a proto-First Minister of the Gaelic Scots. He chose and anointed their kings. It was understood that there might be times when they would make war for the good of the people. They were hungry times and you needed land. Modern non-land-based wealth creation systems did not exist. There is no call in the Christian Bible to wanton violence. But neither is there a call to lie down like a doormat in a land-based system and die. And that could be the option back then if you were not strong in battle. If the King was a faint-heart, his people were dead or in slavery. Now, I understand that one of Columba's choices for king went too far in one particular campaign. But Columba would have expected him to show strength more nobly.

Oswald was of St Columba's time and culture. Within that, what greater hero of the Christian Bible than King David of the Old Testament and his warrior Psalms? King David's choices would have been to lead his people either into death and slavery or into life and freedom. And the Gaels would have seen it like this in Christian terms: how would Jesus Christ have come at all unless King David had fought his battles to secure the Messianic line?

Therefore, for Oswald when the time came, and Alfred the Great's family centuries later, there would be no call to lay down your Christian Identity on the doormat and let it die. An individual Christian might be called to give up life for Christ. But a Christian King would be called to preserve Christian Identity for his people even if that meant fighting for it.

We might even ask of ourselves in modern times, how would English civilisation have descended at all unless, from 878, Alfred the Great and family, who treasured the memory and culture of Saint-King Oswald, had made war like King David when it mattered? I will say it again, and will return to it again, that when they did fight, it was not to establish the Nation of the English. That was an after-product. They fought to save their Christian Identity from being overrun by an invading pagan one.

The point about Oswald for now, anyway, is this. His finishing school was in Columba's culture: Christian and Warrior. Full throttle in each. Very complex to appraise for the modern mind.

Prince Oswald Returns

Oswald returned in 634. I would assume he had a small force of Bernician warriors who had ridden North to seek his help against the ravaging Caedwalla. There would have been Scotic Gaels in his force, too, and his younger brother Oswy.

Each of the young Angle Princes had undergone conversion to Christian Identity. It is not certain quite when, but it is certain that they did. The location was most likely Celtic Iona. It is important to note here what the Christian Bible says about Christian Identity. It pertains to what was in Oswald. Christian Identity can be a fake thing, religious. Or it can be the transformative power of the Christian God: spiritual rebirth, no less. There can be little doubt that Prince Oswald was of the transformative Gaelic Martinian Christian way.

The Northumbria to which Oswald returned was in chaos. He had entitlement to the throne of the whole entity through his Bernician royal father, King Aethelfrith, and Deiran royal mother, Queen Acha. But there were new and separate kings in Bernicia and Deira. King Penda had returned to Mercia for the time being. However, the Britonnic King Caedwalla of Gwynedd remained, and his forces ravaged the North East. In 634 he killed the two new kings as well. That had the effect of making it winner-take-all-Northumbria if Oswald could defeat Caedwalla.

Now, we should have a look at Bede's take on events in the North in 634 before Oswald returned. It is his worldview I want to bring out, as well as the chaos. He wrote in the early 700s with the events still fresh in the memory. Deira's throne passed to Osric, a cousin of the slain Edwin. Osric, says Bede, was rash. He took on Caedwalla and was killed. Bernicia's throne passed to Oswald's older brother, Eanfrith. He had spent exile amongst the Picts north of the Firth of Forth during King Edwin's reign. Eanfrith, says Bede, was ill-advised. He came in peace to Caedwalla to make a treaty and was killed instead.

In political terms, Eanfrith's death would certainly have made a way for Oswald, older brother gone. Bede's less worldly appraisal, however, pays no attention to that. Bede had no doubt that each king had been handed over to Caedwalla for judgement under the Christian God. Each, when younger, had made a profession of Christian Identity. No sooner had they been made king than they renounced it and resumed the worship of idols. Perhaps it was to appease Penda. Or they reckoned Penda's gods had defeated the Christian God. However, the technical term for what they had done would be Apostasy. For Bede, the Old Testament Biblical analogy would have been the ten tribes of Israel handed over to the Assyrians because of Apostasy. He sees Caedwalla as the instrument of God's Judgement on the two kings. Bede records that so despised was their memory, they were written out of the records. The year 634 was credited to Oswald, even though he had yet to establish the throne.

I am not sure that I would be quite so forthright. My ways of understanding are more subtle. But I leave Bede's opinion to stand for you. Such was the black-and-white view of his world. Such was the chaos from which Oswald emerged. And such is the world that the Christian God says he has had to engage with throughout history.

One thing I think we can say with confidence. Oswald, with great boldness of Christian faith, was destined to take the first major step forward in uniting the fractious Anglo Saxon people groups. Kent and East Anglia were in the process of seeding the Christian educational contents of a civilised nation. But as we shall see, it was Oswald, in making Christian peace with Wessex, who would lay the first foundation stone on which was slowly built a unified nation to contain those contents. It was a Christian foundation stone that was laid, and during one of the most momentous Christian Awakenings of all history.

But the politics – really, with Oswald, who cares? We have to make the effort from the outset to work with the Christ-like spiritual dimension of Oswald's life. It shaped the real and political world. It is a matter of common decency and integrity to come to grips with it.

The Battle of Heavenfield

In 634, Caedwalla's army was terrorising in the North. Oswald clashed with his forces at the Battle of Heavenfield (!), most likely somewhere in the Tyne Valley. Caedwalla had stronger forces, and they were more battle-hardened. Before the battle, St Columba, who had passed away in 597, appeared to Oswald in his tent. He strengthened the Prince for the coming battle. On the day of the battle, Oswald planted a Celtic cross. He prayed to the Christian God for the deliverance of his race – implying that something close to genocidal intent was perceived in the Britonnic Christian Caedwalla.

The unlikely happened. Oswald won. Caedwalla was slain.

I will look later on at St Columba's visitation in the chapter about St Martin of Tours and his spiritual descendants. That is because there would be another significant visitation in 878, by St Cuthbert, who died 687, to King Alfred the Great: same purpose, same circumstances. I will take them both together. For now to note: Jesus Christ taught that his God is not the God of the dead but of the living because to him all were alive. Consistent with that, in the Bible's account of the life of Jesus Christ, the long-departed Elijah and Moses appeared to strengthen him shortly before the Cross. And the accounts of the visitations by Columba and Cuthbert were not made up by late-Medieval fantasists embroidering the accounts hundreds of years later. The visits were testified by Oswald at the time, and Alfred at the time. Oswald is, to some extent, a figure obscured by the mists of legend. That might make us wonder. But Alfred comes down to us in fuller documentation as a sober great.

For now, I let it stand: St Columba, a departed Scot, was active, it would seem, at this turning point in English history.

History Changing and Explicitly Christian

Oswald went on to do two history-changing and explicitly Christian things: (i) extend Christian grace to the Wessex throne that had not long before sought to assassinate the Northumbrian throne, and (ii) send to Iona for St Aidan, an all-time great of Martinian Christian spirituality.

St Aidan actually came the second time Oswald asked Iona for help. Oswald did not choose him specifically. He just asked for Christianising help, and the first person sent lacked love. He had the harshness which the self-depriving Martinian lifestyle could lead to if not matured. So any "glory" in the choice of St Aidan would not go to Oswald. It would go to the Christian God, who says he is very jealous about sharing his glory with anyone.

However, if ever there was a case of "Cometh the hour, cometh the man", it was that of St Aidan. He was active in both the revelatory and miraculous spheres of Christian Life. He was full of Christian grace and love. He walked amongst the people. In the tradition of St Columba, he could manage kings. He brought out the best in King Oswald. He gained the full confidence of the rival royal houses of Bernicia and Deira. In so doing, he enabled Northumbria to mature. He watered Christian seed that Paulinus had already planted, and he planted from scratch. In Aidan's wake came a stream of other Martinian Celtic monks. In Oswy's time, some of them, trained by Aidan, would go on to spread the Christian Identity into Mercia and London. Because these new monks were already seasoned in Christian discipleship when they came, there was no need for a two-generation-long buildout of Christian pastoral capability as there had been in 597 in Kent. And what Paulinus had been unable to build on in the North could now be made good.

So, St Aidan became the third example of the right Christian leader in the right place at the right time, all three, Birinus, Felix and Aidan being at the height of their powers as at the year 635. At this time, something truly powerful seems to have been loosed out of the Christian spiritual realm. And with it came the most transformative Christian Awakening since the Apostle Paul in Roman times. Christian Identity had its Birth in the Early English. The spirituality that was released into them then remains amongst the most transformative movements in all history.

King Oswald of Northumbria, out of all the kings who embraced and sponsored it at that time, became the protector and sponsor-in-chief.

635 – Peace with Rheged, and Rheged's Christian Life

So now, to the fateful year 635. Oswald had established himself as the King of Northumbria. Whilst he never had rest from war, he did set about making peace where he could. St Aidan, for example, would have been a great asset in easing internal Northumbrian relations between Bernicia and Deira. External peace treaties were made as well. We will come to Wessex soon, the major one. First, however, there was an almost lost one which became quite important later in the history. It pertains to the eventual defeat of King Penda of Mercia. The treaty was with a Britonnic kingdom called Rheged. No-one could have foreseen it, but it was to play a significant part in spreading Christian Identity several years after Oswald had perished. The Christian God, of course – he could have foreseen it.

The Northern Angles interacted with several different people groups of Britonnic Celts besides those from North Wales. Relationships were different with each, warlike hostility in some cases, neutrality and a will to make a treaty in others. The best relationship was with a Britonnic kingdom called Rheged. You can think of this as broadly the west side of the northern Pennines and Cumbria south of the Solway Firth. This wanted to be neutral with Bernicia.

Now, it is interesting to infer the Christian Life in Rheged. More than a hundred years before Iona was founded, St Ninian had founded a Martinian Christian centre North of the Solway Firth. Ninian had known St Martin of Tours during his life and was the link for the Martinian Christian spirituality to descend to Saints Patrick and Columba. His centre has come down to us as Candida Casa (meaning the White House: a Latin name, but the centre was set amongst proto-Welsh speakers for whom "White" had nuances of Holy). So: Holy House. It was also known as Whithorn. Interestingly, just as Queen Bertha's church in Kent had been dedicated to St Martin in 580, so too was this establishment early in the 400s when it had been the light of the age in the North.

I think we can be sure that it had been influential south of the Solway Firth, too, in Rheged. The Celtic civilisation was seaborne. The Solway Firth was a main highway. It would have been normal for a person from Rheged to cross it to the White House for the impartation of Christian spirituality. Especially since St Ninian himself had most probably originated from Rheged. And as we will see later in this work, we can infer that so, too, quite possibly did the proto-Welsh-speaking St Patrick.

Anyway, Rheged responded to Oswald's peace initiative. It stayed on good terms thereafter, Northumbria its protector. It seems likely to me that the source of the treaty was shared Martinian Christian spirituality. And the treaty bore Christian fruit which changed history. Literally. To cement the peace, Oswald's younger brother, Oswy, entered into a marriage alliance with a Britonnic Christian princess, Rhiainfellt of Rheged. The children of the union grew up to be the first boulder in the Christian landslide that was to fall across Mercia once King Penda had died, as well as the probable cause of the headlong charge of Penda into his final battle. You see, they brought Christian Identity to one of Penda's children from under him...

But in 635, that was just a twinkle in the Oswy/Rhiainfellt eye.

635 – Christian Peace with Wessex – First Step to the Christian Early English Nation

Now, to turn to the more far-reaching and better-known peace treaty: Northumbria and Wessex, 635. It was the first step on the three-hundred-year road from Anglo Saxon tribalism to unifying Early English. It was an explicitly Christian step at the time. And one of the deepest principles of Christian spirituality was embedded in it from the outset: grace to the offender. When Wessex had last engaged with the Northumbrian throne, you may recall, it had tried to assassinate it. King Edwin had subdued it. This time round, King Oswald, building on the work of Bishop Birinus, formally sponsored the Wessex throne into Christian Identity and built the treaty on that.

So, in 635, King Cynegils of Wessex was baptised into Christian Identity. Bishop Birinus had led him to that point and many others with him. At the ceremony, King Oswald of Northumbria sponsored Cynegils into Christian Identity, Oswald being his godfather. That implies a certain seniority in Oswald, both in power and in spirituality. He also married a daughter of Cynegils, thought to have been named Cyneburh.

This was a very rich seed event in which the realms of the political and of Christian spirituality were integrated. There is a tendency for the modern mind to look at any Christian treaty where there is also a political motive and dismiss any integrity on the Christian side of it. However, political motives need not disqualify Christian integrity, not even if the treaty involves tribute from one side to the other, as may have been the case here, Wessex to Northumbria. If a Christian with good standing under the Christian God makes a real world treaty, *and* has integrity before the Christian God in doing so, then they embed their Christian spirituality into the treaty. That has the effect of activating the Christian God into the affairs of the real world, long term. Which is what Oswald did here. The treaty was the first building block of a Christian nation, the Nation of the English. This was ultimately brought into being by the Wessex royal house which Oswald was now sponsoring into Christian Identity. And in that Nation, just like the origin treaty, the realms of the political and of Christian spirituality were to become symbiotically integrated.

Bearing that in mind, I can now go on to say there would have been a pressing political reason for the treaty: to present two fronts, north and south, to King Penda of Mercia. The scenario from 635 was going to be Northumbria versus Mercia for military dominion. King Penda, not least because of military alliance with Britonnic North Wales, was the strongest. What to do about him?

Well, when King Edwin had mounted the campaign that subdued Wessex after its royals had tried to assassinate him around about 626, you may also recall that the young Penda of Mercia had been an ally on the Wessex side and lost, a rare defeat for him. In the aftermath of the battle, Penda took note of the depletion of the Wessex forces. Now, you may further recall that Wessex by 634 had lost much of its northern territory to Mercia. Well, here is how: seeing Wessex forces depleted by Edwin, and taking the opportunity by about 628, Penda regathered his forces. He wrestled Wessex's northern territory away while his former ally was weak. Humanly speaking then, it was an obvious calculation for Wessex: Northumbria is offering a treaty against a common foe: we'll take it.

However, King Oswald completely embedded Christian spirituality into the political treaty. In him, there was no modern mind's dividing wall between a realm called "religion" and a realm called "reality". And the principle he embedded into the real world was a Christ-on-the-Cross one: grace to the offender, that is, Assassin Wessex. That type of Christian principle, if extended in the name of the Christian God and in genuine faith, which in Oswald's case it would have been, has the power to root down to a thousand generations. That is the teaching of the Second Commandment of the Bible of the Christian God. Therefore, in the Christian understanding, Oswald made this treaty an enduring Christian foundation for what would become the Nation of the English.

King Oswald would have had a normal, personal, human motive for the treaty as well. Again, the modern mind tends to think that would disqualify

Christian integrity, that the Christian God requires the Christian to be too heavenly minded to be of any earthly use. However, the Christian God of both the Bible and of Christian experience works deftly with personal motives if the Christian also has humility.

Having said this, Oswald's personal motive would have been this. As you will see later, there were ancient Germanic reasons for Mercia resenting Northumbria. Oswald would have known that a character like Penda would act out of them violently sooner or later. He, Oswald, would be the focal point then. Oswald would also have known that Penda's allies in Britonnic North Wales hated Northumbria, and he, Oswald, had not long slain Caedwalla their King. Oswald in person would, therefore, have been under existential threat from a regrouping of the alliance that had just wreaked havoc in the North.

Now, a Christian King could not just lie down and wait to die. His people would pay for it in blood. Even so, "Hmmm," many a modern mind might say, "wouldn't that have been the Christian thing to do? Jesus Christ did say, 'Blessed are the peacemakers.'" However, the Christian God does also say more generally that he is familiar with conditions on Planet Earth. Therefore, Jesus Christ later called the Apostle Paul to go on to say, "Make peace as far as you are able."

Which Oswald did: with Rheged and with Wessex. He also extended protection against Penda to Sigeberht's East Anglia, and that kingdom was going to make a significant contribution to the spread of Christian Identity, long before Wessex did. In fact, it was going to Save the Christian Day in Wessex, as we shall see in the next narrative chapter.

Oswald would have had no idea at the time how significant these peace initiatives would prove to be. But as we shall soon see, he would go on to become a phenomenon: Saint King, and a sort of Early English Christ figure.

Birth – Christian Identity in the Early English

- I call the Christian treaty between Northumbria and Wessex "Nation Building Step Number One" in the high-level summary with which I began this book.

- I call the simultaneous ministry of St Aidan, Bishop Birinus and Bishop Felix "Christian Turning Point Number One" in that summary.

It was in 635 that these momentous events coincided.

Taken together, I think we can safely say that in the year 635, transformative Christian Identity came to vigorous Birth amongst the Anglo Saxon people groups. And many of those Christian fusion ingredients that would make the Early English were alive at once:

- Frankish Romano

- Gaelic

- Martinian

- Latin

- Roman Catholic

Kent was still quietly building its church. In Oswald, Northumbria had a new and most dynamic Christian King. He had sent to Iona, which had sent St Aidan. Aidan came in grace and love, with the Gaelic Martinian Christian Life at its sweetest. He would restore the Christian spirituality which Paulinus had sown in the North but which seemed lost, and enrich it with his own dynamic version of it. Wessex was experiencing Christian Awakening under Bishop Birinus and the sponsorship of Oswald. East Anglia was receiving dynamic Christian Life under Bishop Felix and King Sigeberht, protected by Oswald. All the Christian strands were dominantly Martinian except in Kent, and the East Angles would soon add more of the Romano Martinian within Kent. In St Aidan's wake would come a ready-seasoned stream of Martinian Christian

Celtic monks to help him build. No need to build from scratch, as in Kent in 597.

I will look at how things went forward in the earliest formative times, 635 to the early 650s, in the next narrative chapter, the Christian Identity of the Early English in the Nursery. We will see the Nursery encounter its slaughtering King Herod figure, King Penda of Mercia. He will become a serial killer of Christian Kings.

However, we will also see King Oswald go from strength to strength in Christian terms and emerge as Saint King Oswald. So far, I have only scratched the surface of what made him Early England's most epic figure and the cherished hero of Alfred the Great's family.

Before that, however, a question for the reader:

Suppose you were the Christian God?

Before we proceed further, let's do something deeply unfashionable. Suppose you were the Christian God: how would you respond when Oswald prays to you for victory in the Battle of Heavenfield? Are you too holy to soil your hands? Your Bible says that you do not have favourites. And Caedwalla is a Christian too, isn't he? So you have to wash your hands of the whole thing, don't you?

Well, what you do is follow your principles. They are not mysterious principles, either. You have already made them known. In this particular case, the key principle has been hidden in plain sight. Thousands of years ago, you inscribed Ten Commandments on stone. In this case, consider the Third one. It says do not take the name of the Lord your God in vain because if you do, your guilt will stand.

Now, what does it mean to take the name of God in vain? In a Christian understanding of this, it means to call yourself a Christian but not be the genuine article. What does it mean, your guilt will stand? It means you will have no place of Favour with God. So if you call yourself a Christian but do not bear the fruits of it, you will have no Favour of God upon you when it comes to the crunch. It is important to understand here that the Christian God says that he does not practice discriminatory favouritism by race, gender, status, whatever. But he does say that he retains the option to extend Favour to any who are in Christ, regardless of race, gender, status, whatever, if they comply with the guidelines. It is fair enough if you think about it: the Christian God says that he also retains the option to be more severe with those who are in Christ than those who are not if the former ignore the guidelines.

Regarding the guidelines, what had Caedwalla done? Taken Christ's name. But cultivated the root of bitterness – sternly warned against for the Christian. And abrogated his God's right to revenge – expressly forbidden, and he would have known it.

What about Oswald? Well, the Christian God says that he has the power to foreknow. Therefore, he foreknows that Oswald will bear the genuine fruits of taking Christ's name. And Oswald is not after revenge. He has a rightful claim to the Northumbrian throne.

Not rocket science, is it? If you are the Christian God, you follow your revealed principles.

Well, make of it what you will. Some would say, banana oil, there is no God. Others would say there is a God, but he is not active in history. Seems odd to me, that one, though: calls himself Almighty, but is inactive? For my part, I note, mingling the political with the spiritual, as you have to do to appraise Oswald:

- After he prayed, Oswald won. It seems to have been an unlikely victory.

- The Christian God's principles would have Favoured Oswald. There is no *favouritism* in the Christian God, meaning, no discrimination by race, gender, or status, etc. However, there are spiritual principles of Favour, meaning ways you can co-operate with the Christian God for blessing. Oswald was within them.

- As for the old caricature of Anglo Saxon doing down Celt: Gaelic Celts helped the Angle-ish Oswald to do down Britonnic Celts who had been doing down Angles. And the Gaelic Celts with Oswald in the battle had a very different Christian Identity to the Britonnic Celts in the battle. The Gaelic Christians were of a Christian culture that was Martinian at the height of its vibrancy. The Britonnic Christians, as we saw earlier, were of a Christian culture that seems to have become tired; and these ones were also vengeful.

- Therefore, the Battle of Heavenfield can reasonably be seen as a complex intertwining of battle between three different ethnic warrior people groups, two of which were Celtic, with battle between two differing Celtic Christian Identities. A modern understanding might try to call the latter element a "religious war". A Christian understanding might reckon that one Christian Identity was in the right and the other in the wrong and discern in the Battle of Heavenfield, to its relief, that the right one won.

Interlude

Before I proceed to the next chapter of the narrative, the Christian Identity in the Early English in the Nursery from 635 to 650, a short interlude chapter. It is time to look Beneath the Lid at what the Christian spirituality of Oswald, and many other Christians of his time, was actually like. It should repay understanding it. After all, as it encountered and transformed the Anglo Saxon people groups, it created the English.

CHAPTER 11.

Beneath the Lid

Before resuming the narrative, I want to reflect on what was in the Christian spirituality which I call "Martinian". What was beneath the lid of the tin which the modern mind labels "Religion"? What would the Christian spirituality have been like in men such as Saint King Oswald, King Sigeberht, St Aidan and Bishops Felix and Birinus? And, although they were of a subtly different stream, what would the Christian spirituality have been like in men such as St Augustine of Canterbury and Bishop Paulinus of York?

It matters to come to terms with this because it shaped the real world history of the English. It was not locked away behind a modern dividing wall. It was at the beating heart of the culture. It was the yeast within the loaf of it, the salt curing it.

My answer? Not all that different to how it is in any Christian of today who knows the Life in the Holy Spirit of the Christian God. Not religious. Not ritualistic, either. "Sparky" would express it better. I will use that word from now on as a regular alternative to "Romano Gaelic Martinian Catholic". I will use that sort of mouthful when I want to stress the Fusion nature of the Christian spirituality which shaped the Early English. But "sparky" gives you the feel for what was in the tin.

Understanding the Sparky Christian spirituality

The best way to understand the spirituality which shaped Early English history is to consider the original seed of it, Jesus Christ. If you want to get under the skin of the history of a Christian people, then you have to come to terms with the Christ. What was in him will be in the people and their history. After all, they sought to follow his model.

Jesus Christ was… Sparky, capital S. He had very strong Life in the Holy Spirit of the Christian God. It made him a complete master of the revelatory and miraculous dimensions of Christian Life. Since the Christ set himself up as the great model for others, it follows that if Martinian Christians, or any others, the Latin ones, for example, were following the model, they, too, would have had experience in the revelatory and miraculous dimensions of Christian Life.

Which they did have. They exercised the "Charismata" of the Holy Spirit of the Christian God. And they had "Anointing" from the Christian God. These terms require explanation.

Christian "Anointing"

Pope Gregory the Great, St Augustine of Canterbury, Paulinus, Bishop Felix, Bishop Birinus, St Aidan, Saint King Oswald and many more we are yet to meet in the period from 587 to 689 all had this: Christian Anointing. It was the source of their spiritual empowerment under the Christian God.

Christian Anointing means having empowered Life in the Holy Spirit of the Christian God. I had better develop that further. What follows is not an explanation of the traditional Christian sacrament in which anointing oil is applied to a person. Although Protestant and Roman Catholic Christians literally rub people with anointing oil in various contexts, there is another and less understood dimension of Christian Anointing. You see, oil is a symbol of the Holy Spirit. The Holy Spirit is the reality signified by the oil. What is required if we are to understand Christian history in the Early English is an explanation of the reality, not the symbol. Because the Early English had the reality and encountered it in gifted Christian after gifted Christian. An explanation of the reality now follows.

Jesus Christ – The Imagery He Used

Jesus Christ came to impart Life in the Holy Spirit of the Christian God. He used two images for the Holy Spirit. One is of a wellspring of God's own spirituality from deep within the Christian. The other is of a coating or mantle of God's own power resting upon them. The original meaning of the word "Anointing" arises from the latter image, literally a liberal coating of olive oil over a person, where the oil denotes the Holy Spirit of the Christian God.

In the Old Testament of the Christian Bible, "Anointing" refers to someone having the outer spiritual coat alone, for example, King David and the prophets Elijah and Elisha.

In a New Testament Christian, "Anointing" is what arises when the two different ways of spirituality, as expressed by the two different images, are in harmony. Christian Anointing is the Life of the Holy Spirit on the inside in harmony with the power of the Holy Spirit on the outside.

The Effects of Christian Anointing

When an Anointed Christian exercises faith, the Anointing upon them can impart a certain indefinable spiritual authority. It can also have empowering effects as they exercise a specific Calling. For example, a Christian with Call and Anointing to be an Evangelist can deliver a message of invitation to receive Jesus Christ. A Christian without that Call and Anointing may deliver the same message. Many will respond to the former but few to the latter. However, that same Christian to whom few respond may be Anointed for helping Christians in a church to stay in step as a team; this is the Call of a Pastor. If the Evangelist tries the same, all trip over one another.

Put another way, Christian Anointing adds a certain je ne sais quoi of the Christian God's own powers and presence to a God-given Calling. Christians can have many forms of Anointing. In a skilful musician, it will turn a song from a dead work into an act of worship. Some Christians can even have Anointing to serve the tea. The Holy Spirit of the Christian God imparts an added measure of subtle joy to the people as they serve them. He is not too high and mighty.

Christian "Charismata"

The Biblical Apostles Peter, John and Paul all had Anointing and operated out of it in diverse ways. Paul also exercised, and urged Christians to use, the "Charismata" of the Holy Spirit of the Christian God.

The "Charismata" are gifts of the Christian God's own powers of speech, insight and faith, most often imparted within situations that need them. The word charismatic, with a small c, indicates someone with a compelling personality. With a large C, however, the word Charismata means gifts of the Christian God's own powers. A "Charismatic" Christian exercises them.

Combining Christian Anointing with the Charismata

Now, when Christians with Anointing also abound in the Charismata of their God's own powers, it can open up dimensions of the revelatory on the one hand and the miraculous on the other, at the discretion of the Holy Spirit of the Christian God. That is how it was with Jesus Christ. And, therefore, it is how you can reasonably expect things to be for his followers as well.

Hence you get, for example, St Martin of Tours. He had the Christian God's own powers of spiritual discernment. Pope Gregory the Great: he echoed the Apostle Paul's level of spiritual understanding. St Augustine of Canterbury: he had a portion of the miraculous powers of the Christ. Paulinus of York: he had the revelatory powers of the Christ and Paul just when he needed them. In the North: Saint King Oswald, St Aidan and St Cuthbert of Northumbria and John of Beverley, Bishop of York, were exceptional in Christian gifting and impact. Collectively, they had the impact that the Christ himself would have had if he had walked the North in those days. We will meet Cuthbert and John later in the book. In the next chapter, we will meet the families of King Anna of the East Angles, and of King Eorcenberht and Queen Seaxburh of Kent. Each family discernibly Anointed and familiar in different ways and degrees with the Charismata. King Anna seems to have been an important Evangelist within English history. In the next chapter, you will see him lead the relapsing Wessex throne to Christ: an English nation-shaping moment as it turned out.

Timeless Spiritual Kinship

A key point is this: Christians with Life in the Holy Spirit of the Christian God have a spiritual kinship that spans the generations. Because English history in its founding times was shaped by Christians with Life in the Holy Spirit of the Christian God, it follows that a Christian who has the same in modern times can discern it and get under the skin of the history-shapers.

Here are just a few examples of timeless Christian kinship with the history-shapers.

- Christians of today can experience deep inner certainty, knowing the Christ deep within. Those in this book would have done so.

- That certainty imparts joy in difficult circumstances, and the presence of Christ imparts love. St Aidan abounded in love, and he spread joy wherever he went. His spiritual successor, St Cuthbert, was the same.

- Some Christians with the mantle of Anointing of the Holy Spirit in modern times carry a subtle authority with them. Certain Gaelic Martinian Saints had the same Big Time: kings were in awe of them.

- Many English Christians of today love Christian song. They loved it back then, too. Some, these days, like the song to be spontaneous. Others like it liturgical. Northumbria in the times of Oswald and afterwards abounded in Christian song: some of it spontaneous, some of it liturgical.

- Some Protestant Christians of today pray for the power of God that has been on those who have gone before them to be alive and present again in their times. An example would be the departed evangelist Billy Graham. "Let what was in Billy Graham be alive in our times," they might pray to the Christian God. Alfred the Great's family, founders of the nation of the English, would have prayed in the same way about Saint King Oswald, long after he died. The modern Christian might use a book about Billy Graham to focus their praying. Alfred's family used Oswald's bones to focus the same.

Thus far, it was not much different to today. Bones revolt us, books do not. But most of us can read, whereas most of them could not. The post-Reformation caricature that has descended to us of bones and relics is one of superstition, and of faith in the bones. But it does not follow that all were superstitious and put faith in the bones. Some would have cherished the noble values which the bones represented and put faith in the Christian God for the values. That seems to have been the real world history-shaping case in the family of Alfred the Great.

Temporally, however, everything has changed. The bedrock of the Martinian way was monastic culture. It was a stricter culture. It was less individualistic. If immature, it could be harsh. Not everyone in it was in it by choice. It was within a world of Warrior culture. It was within a materially deprived culture: limited diet, little technology, no modern medicine. Enslaving was normal. Forced service was the lot of many.

I would not want to live in such times. I don't want kinship with that.

However, those things are the one-eyed side of the story. The two-eyed fulness of it is that the Christians in this book knew the Christian God within them. And they manifested his powers. Even to this day, these realms of Christian spirituality, with Anointing and Charismata, remain as an undercurrent in the culture of the modern English. They remain within some of their Christian churches. But those churches are now walled off from secular culture. In Bede's time, however, as he wrote the first history of the English, these realms of Christian spirituality were a shaping force in the whole culture, with no dividing wall between secular and church. The earliest history of the English was written by Bede out of that culture.

Furthermore, Bede's writings show a culture consistent with the Christian Bible. The revelatory, miraculous and discerning powers which Bede describes, coming from the Holy Spirit of the Christian God, are all well within the envelope of the Bible. They were the powers of Jesus Christ. He said that as it had been for him so it could be for his followers. And with these powers, according to the Christian Bible, anyway, come inner resources of the love, peace and joy of the Christian God himself. You sense those things in Bede, the person behind the writings: a good and kind person wrote the earliest English history.

Not a bad deal for the Martinian Christian to abound in such things as all these, even in a world whose externals I would not want to live in. Not every one of them would ripen into the fullness of life in the Holy Spirit. But it only needs a few ripe ones at the heart of things to transform their world, like yeast working through dough. When the Early English Christian Identity came to Birth, there were some very gifted ripe ones, and they kept on coming in the years that followed.

As for the set-apart monastic communities in the founding times of the Early English, the modern tendency is to propagandise the monastic as the privileged few. But they saw themselves as there for the benefit of the whole. When they prayed, for example, the understanding was that everyone benefits from the cleaner spiritual atmosphere created by Christian prayer, not just the monks and nuns. The Early English Christian Kings certainly saw it that way. They regarded the prayers as precious; therefore they valued them; therefore they funded them. And besides, from these communities came hospitals, care, education and much else that shapes a wider civilisation.

The Martinian Christian spirituality promoted many good things. And these good things are what would really have been under the lid of the tin that we now call "Religion" and "Ritual".

Caricature versus Reality

We tend to caricaturise the ancient Christian ways now. On TV, for example: cue shots of bare stone walls; add ritualistic background chant; add ethereal voices behind closed doors. Recite Bible quotes in a stern and thunderous actor-y voice.

The Reality, however, was transformative for the English: a slowly increasing proportion of the culture came to know the Christ deep within, with the resources of joy and love which spring from that. It made for Light in the Dark Ages. And marvellous things came to the needy as Saints Aidan and Cuthbert, for example, walked in their midst in a world of no modern medicine.

Small wonder that the Anglo Saxons embraced the Christian Identity when they encountered the true way of it in the Martinian Christians. Small wonder that they cherished it as the foundation of their unifying Early English Identity. In the spirit of saying that:

- I said earlier that the Christian English Identity was conceived in love in the times of King Ethelbert and Queen Bertha of Kent.

- I reflect now that the Christian English Identity was brought to Birth by Christian Anointing on the Sparky Martinian Christians.

Now, back to the narrative: the transformative Christian Identity of the Early English after its Birth: its time in the Nursery. The next chapter will start with much Cooing at Baby. Then it becomes Slaughter of the Innocents – Adults Only again.

CHAPTER 12.

In the Nursery – 635 To 650

635 to 640 – Fairly Quiet in the Christian Nursery

I have read that the formative years of your life, the first five, are the most impressionable. If you are loved then, you are likely to love later, as an adult. If you are rejected then, you may struggle later as an adult. And there is an old saying, "The hand that rocks the cradle rules the world." It is important who and what shapes your Nursery years.

So let's look at what came next after 635. Christian Identity in the Nursery. I date the period of that for the Early English as 635 to the early 650s. That is when the Awakening of the new Christian spirituality was at its most vibrant.

About five years passed from 635 in which there was relatively little recorded tumult. King Oswald of Northumbria probably had little rest from war and skirmishing. However, St Aidan, Bishop Birinus and Bishop Felix had shelter to build Christian foundations in Northumbria, Wessex and East Anglia. In Kent, the Christian mission jogged along.

Five quiet, formative years. Little has come down to us in the records because little happened in the way of high drama. Then again, hardly any of us have a record of our own first five years. This author was loved. There is no more than that which I can remember, and then only as a fuzzy feeling. It doesn't mean to say that nothing important happened. What could have been more important than being loved in one's formative years? In a like manner, nothing much happened in the history, except that the Early English began to be loved in the name of Christ. You might think that worth disregarding for the history, except that it was the chief historical news of the times. That and King Penda of Mercia gradually building up Mercia. And a fateful collision course developing between Penda and King Oswald.

Before we proceed to the details, we should look at two maps.

- The first is of people groups by location. It is set at about 635.

- The second is a broad-brush labelling of their spirituality by the same locations as at 635 and in play until 655.

The first map is to help you to cross-reference people and places within the narrative. The second is to help you to see how the fateful collision between Penda of Mercia and Oswald of Northumbria built up. For example, taking the first and second together, you can see how it was that King Penda's Mercia emerged. He sort of proto-federated a number of Anglo Saxon people groups, partly by force and partly by underlying spiritual affinity. You can also see the loosely allied proto-Christian Identities within other Anglo Saxon people groups. These also began to ally, not by force but by underlying spiritual affinity.

I am not saying that the Mercian federation-by-spiritual-affinity was done in full consciousness. Human spirituality works more subtly than that. The image used for spirituality by Jesus Christ was of yeast gradually permeating unseen throughout the dough.

Taken together, the two maps form the backdrop to the period of Christian Life in the Nursery. There were broadly five years of peace. Then the Nursery became a dangerous place to grow up in. The different spiritual affinities collided in the real world.

Strathclyde, Gododdin and Rheged were Britonnic Celt. First two hostile to Northern Angles; Rheged was neutral and intermarried with them. Britonnic Celts in the North of Wales were at enmity with the Northern Angles but allied with the Mercian Angles. Northern Angles (Northumbria) came to share common Christian roots with Scotic (Gaelic) and Pictish Celts.

Mercians were basically Angles, perhaps some Britonnic mixed in. Back in the Anglian origin-lands in the north of Germany the Mercian King had been the Chief Anglian King. So they resented those upstart Northern Angles (Northumbria).

Mercia, as distinct from Mercians, began as a sort of federation pulled together by King Penda. Middle Angles, Middle Saxons, and Hwicce all saw themselves belonging in it, and so did Lindsey and East Saxons. Northern Angles, East Angles, West Saxons and Kent were allied on shared Christian values.

South Saxons were isolated.

Martinian = Celtic version of the Christian spirituality of St Martin of Tours which emerged out of Gaul, mainly after 410. Strongest in the Gaels/Scots.

Britonnic = older Celtic Christian way derived out of the old Roman Empire from 177 to about 410. Some Martinian pockets, not dominant.

North Wales Britonnic Celtic Christians allied with pagan Mercian Anglo Saxons in common cause against Martinian or Romano Martinian Christian Anglo Saxons.

Mercian federation came out of the pagan people groups & semi-pagan mixture in Lindsey & Hwicce.

Mixed = Britonnic Christian stream mingled with Martinian (Rheged) or with pagan (Lindsey, Hwicce). Rheged - I infer some strength of Martinian spirituality.

Romano Martinian – except Deira, sourced from elements of the Frankish Church that had a version of the Martinian Christian Spirituality as reinforced by the Irish Pict, St Columbanus. In Deira – Paulinus's Roman planting was re-cultivated with the Gaelic Martinian spirituality.

Political alliances or hostilities up to 655 mapped on to the underlying commonalities or differences of Spirituality, and the senses of Identity built on that

Christian Kent

Kent was a relatively stable place. It had been the most settled Anglo Saxon people group for more than a century. The one with the closest ties to the Franks and the Roman Catholic church. The one that had received the mission of St Augustine of Canterbury from 597 and kept quietly building upon it.

I am satisfied that I can discern a particular characteristic in Kent's Christian ways from 597 until they lost it in 663: wisdom. Wisdom rarely makes headlines. It is one of those things of which the saying goes, you don't know what you've got till it's gone. It had been in King Ethelbert. It had been in St Augustine. He tends to be written off because he had failed to convert all the English and win over all the Britons by 604. Augustine did, however, set in motion educational processes which matured to disciple many of the Early English over the next three hundred years. The team that succeeded him had the same wisdom.

Interestingly, the Christian Bible teaches that the fear of God is the beginning of wisdom. Ethelbert's son, King Eadbald, seems to have started out foolish. But after the fear of God came upon him sometime between 616 and 619, he changed. He seems to have become wise.

So, there we have Christian Kent up to 640: slow, steady, wise. What could be more boring?

Christian Wessex – West Saxons

The progress of Christian Life in Wessex is obscure in the period 635 to 640. Wessex was not as yet the later Wessex. It lacked both lands and internal political unity. King Cynegils of Wessex had been sponsored into Christian baptism by King Oswald of Northumbria in 635. Wessex would have been paying tribute to Northumbria for several years before that since King Edwin had responded to its attempt to assassinate him by subduing it. It may still have been paying tribute to Oswald from 635 but within Christian treaty and more in the way of an ally against the common threat, King Penda of Mercia. As to how King Cynegils fared as a Christian, we do not know. However, he was initiated into Christian Identity by two of English history's great Christians, Oswald and Birinus. He would have been inspired by Oswald and well taught by Birinus.

The successor king to Cynegils, named Cenwalh, seems to have remained pagan until near the end of Birinus's life. However, given that Wessex came to cherish its Christian Identity in the long term, we can see that what Birinus planted turned out to be strong. It would survive wobbles with Cenwalh, and a stinker in 686, which I come to later in the book, and keep going forward.

From 635 to 640, however, steps in the development of Christian Identity in Wessex – obscure. Fairly quiet in this section of the Nursery. Penda was preoccupied more on his Northern and Eastern fronts. In Wessex, the highly gifted Birinus was overseeing the first baby steps in Christ.

East Anglia – East Angles

Relatively boring, on the surface, up to 640. However, there does seem to have been a vibrant Romano Martinian Christian spirituality developing. If not already like it, it would soon become "Charismatic", as defined earlier in the previous chapter, "Beneath the Lid".

The monks from Ireland were doing their bit. Bishop Felix was doing his. King Sigeberht wanted to become a monk and eventually did so.

I would say that the Christian spirituality in East Anglia in the period has been greatly underrated by history. In Christian terms, East Anglia, situated between rather staid Kent and ultra-sparky Northumbria, was plenty sparky. It was the glue in the loose alliance of the three and on terms with babe-in-Christ Wessex, too. In terms of nation-building for the Early English, well… the Christian spiritual sources in East Anglia from 635 to 640 were those that finally matured in the Early English: Romano-Martinian-Catholic with a strong flavouring of Celtic. So the East Anglian Christians were nurturing the ultimate Identity of the whole. This would suggest that the early Christian Life in the East Angles was as transformative of Identity as the more famous Christian spirituality of the times amongst the Northern Angles. However, there is less documentation of it. And there was less violence in the region to capture the attention.

Northumbria

Not quite so boring. Well, it never was, in those days – it was Early England's most dangerous neighbourhood.

The Bernician part of Northumbria was possibly at war with the northern Britons of Strathclyde and probably at war with the northern Britons of the Gododdin. Some sources have King Oswald taking what we now call Edinburgh in 638; others are not so sure. It is impossible now to tell who would have started what with whom. We noted earlier that Oswald did seal a peace treaty to the west of Bernicia with the Britons of Rheged.

I would think that Mercia and Northumbria were also sparring throughout the period.

Much the most important thing in the period, however, was the advent of St Aidan. He was of the Gaelic Martinian Christian spirituality and very sparky. King Oswald – also very sparky – had taken the throne of Northumbria in 635. In the process of securing the kingdom in military terms, he also took the step of transforming it in spiritual terms. He sent to Iona for a Christian missionary versed in the ways of the Gaelic Martinian Christian spirituality. After one false start, they sent him St Aidan.

St Aidan

Cometh the hour, cometh the man. St Aidan took the development of Christian spirituality in the proto-English to a new level. The Roman church was organised in dioceses of defined territory. The Gaelic church of Aidan was set up to reach out to tribes spread sinuously throughout wider territories. Therefore, the Gaelic church was configured, in a way that the Roman church was not, to reach out to what were then more tribal times. What is more, the Christian spirituality amongst the Gaels had been maturing for several generations. Therefore, St Aidan was soon able to import a fuller team of Christian leaders ready-matured – and sparky, too. Aidan's later team, and not just he himself, were to become of first importance for the growth of Christian Identity both within Northumbria and to the south of it as time went on.

From the outset, there was more focus on the common people than was customary in Roman Catholic ways. I am not saying that the Roman way should be sneered at for that. It had a certain robust pragmatism for the times: it is not much use to take the Christian message straight to the farmer if the local king or lord kills you. Have to win over the local leader first. Anyway, more than to the South, the Scotic/Gaelic way was for the people as well as the ruler.

Now, we should note here that the Gaelic Martinian Celtic church of St Aidan was always part of the Roman Catholic church. Its ways differed from the European mainstream, having become cut off by tumult arising from Germanic migrations, but it saw itself as part of Rome. The Britonnic Celtic church by 604 had cut itself off from Rome, but the Gaelic/Pictish one engaged if it could. As he travelled on the European mainland, for example, St Columbanus strongly encouraged the Papacy to lead well. Therefore, think of the Gaelic Celtic church, in the version that came to Northumbria, as a more innocent part of what was then a more innocent Roman church, too. Spiritually dynamic, but so, too, were some of the Romano-Martinian Frankish Christian leaders, and so, too, the Latin Christian leaders, St Augustine of Canterbury and Paulinus.

St Aidan also had a way with kings. That was the way of it with the great Gaelic Christians. St Columba of Iona had been a proto-Prime Minister and king-maker. These days, we tend to see the sphere of Prime Minister and the sphere of Saint-Monk as walled off from each other. But we can see from Bede's history that St Aidan brought out what was good in King Oswald. We can also see that not just Bernicia but also the royal house of rival Deira came to love Aidan and was loved by him. So he started to unify the kingdom of Northumbria on a shared Christian foundation.

Aidan also brought fresh nurture to the Latin Christian seed that Paulinus had planted in Deira. Paulinus had been gifted in the realm of the Christian prophetic. Now, in Aidan, Deira received an injection of the Gaelic Martinian

Christian spark as well. Between 635 and 640, there would have been developing in the Deiran part of Northumbria a spiritual fusion similar to that in East Anglia and potently transformative, too, as would be proved later. Deira would start producing bishops with strong fusion Christian spirituality within an urbane Roman Catholic outer shell. One of them, Trumhere, would become yet another Christian leader for the hour when Northumbria and Mercia were tense after King Penda's time. He built bridges upon the fusion Christian Identity which, by then, had become common to Deira and Mercia. In 679, Archbishop Theodore would capitalise on Trumhere's bridge-building to bring the two warrior-to-the-bone powers of Northumbria and Mercia to Christian peace. Transformational stuff. The foundations for each of these clerics to build on, however, were first laid by St Aidan and his winning ways.

"Winning" would be a good description of St Aidan – a most winsome man. Some of the Celtic saints were quite harsh. Some even hated the Anglo Saxons. Others were at best impatient or disdainful towards the new babes-in-Christ. There were plenty of pockets of the Martinian spirituality in Britonnic Wales, but it is hard to discern that they made a difference to the hostility of attitude. Many generations later, in the time of Alfred the Great, the Christians in what we now call Wales would make a huge contribution to blessing the English. But as at 635, it seems to have been the Scot, St Aidan, who most loved the Angles. And like infants in the nursery, they responded to the love.

Therefore, much though the modern mind might wish to focus on violence in Northumbrian history as the story from 635 to 640, it was mainly Christian love and St Aidan that were the story.

Boring? Hmmm…

641 to 642 – Definitely Not Boring

The drama of the period when Early English Christian Identity was in the Nursery began in 641. The highest drama mostly centred on Penda versus Oswald in 642, Mercia versus Northumbria. However, I will build up to that, taking things in order, from East Anglia first.

Now, sadly, there is a Nursery Story in the Christian Bible. It happened in Bethlehem within two years of the birth of Jesus Christ. King Herod, looking to snuff out the Christ, slaughtered the infants there. The proto-Early English Christian kings were about to encounter their own Herod figure: an old-fashioned Anglo Saxon, King Penda of Mercia at the height of his power.

Aided and abetted by the Britonnic Christian Celts of North Wales, and with his new proto-federation of Mercia now firm on shared pagan affinities, Penda was set to re-establish the old order of things: the ancient Germanic way, tribes in their separate places, Mercia the top dog and tribute taker. As in the old Germanic lands, top dog was defined by nearness of descent from the god Woden, i.e. Mercians.

It is important to appraise Penda's conscious motives before we proceed to the narrative. He had already killed one Christian King, Edwin of Northumbria, and was to become a serial killer of more. He was also to become boastful about it and directly provocative to the Christian God. But he was not an outright persecutor of Christians. He had little time for the Christian way. It had been witnessed to him in such a way that he had formed the basic accusation in his mind that Christians were hypocrites. However, he did not forbid the preaching of the Christian message. His conscious motive was this: the Glory of Mercia.

Now, as to Penda the accuser of Christians: it can be a perilous thing making accusations of hypocrisy at Christians. There may indeed be hypocrisy. However, the Christian God reserves the right to discipline if so. And the Bible teaches that there is a spirit which it calls the accuser of Christian souls. Unfair accusations of hypocrisy are its stock-in-trade. The Christian Bible teaches that this particular spirit is at work under the surface of accusation and when flesh and blood are doing violence to Christians.

However, the Christian Bible also teaches that the Christian God can be very patient with people like Penda, judging them by their lights. Penda was not himself a religious hypocrite, you see. Jesus Christ had made clear that it stirs the Christian God to anger if religious hypocrisy is there in his name. It was not there in Penda. With Penda, what you saw was what you got. With that sort of thing, the Christian God says he gives time and space to come round to receiving him.

So it was to be now. Penda was going to have time and space to do his… worst? … best? Depends on your perspective. The good and the bad must grow together, is what Jesus Christ taught. Only he, the Christ, on his return to the earth, has been given authority to uproot the bad once and for all. Until then, if you uproot the bad, you also uproot the good. In King Penda, that Biblical principle, and the other one that we noted earlier, that God works all things for the good of Christian Identity for those called in Christ's purposes, was about to break out in the Nursery of Early English Christian Identity.

King Sigeberht Slain

So we move to East Anglia, 641. The date is uncertain, actually, but that is what I plump for. The circumstances are also vague. The inference is that Mercia set out to subdue East Anglia because it was an ally of Northumbria. Penda came attacking.

Now, we noted earlier that King Sigeberht of the East Angles had laid aside his kingly calling for that of a monk. The people brought him out of monastic retirement to be their figurehead in battle. He went unarmed into the conflict. Penda's forces slaughtered him. I should say this: there is normally no call from the Christian God for a Christian King to go unarmed into the conflict. However, a monk may choose to do so, and it was in that calling that King Sigeberht died.

I should think that this was the event which now brought King Oswald of Northumbria into full-on collision with King Penda of Mercia. However, first of all, to note an irony.

King Anna of the East Angles

King Sigeberht's successor in the East Anglian Christian Nursery was King Anna. The ironies inherent in Penda's life now increased. So far, kill King

Edwin, who was a baby Christian, and reap King Oswald, who was a lightning rod Christian. Now, kill King Sigeberht, reap King Anna. King Anna was at least as devoted to Christian Identity as Sigeberht had been. His family can be discerned to have embraced Christian Identity vibrantly. Anna was also able to resist Penda militarily for more than ten years. And, as we shall see, he would lead the young lapsed-back-to-pagan King Cenwalh of Wessex to Christian Identity during that time. Anna's family, which seems to have partaken of that Frankish Roman Martinian Christian spirituality as reinforced by St Columbanus, would soon infiltrate that into more staid Kent, which as yet had encountered only the pre-reinforced version of the same.

Thus it was that the Christian God seems to have replied to Penda's slaying of King Sigeberht: there came to power the most underrated Christian King and Family of Early English history.

Anna probably took the East Anglian throne with Oswald's Northumbrian help, partly out of alliance against Mercia and partly as one sparky Christian helping another sparky Christian.

Collision, 642 – King Oswald Slain and Saint-King Oswald Born

And now, 642, the conflict came to a head. King Oswald's Northumbrian forces joined battle with King Penda's Mercian and Britonnic forces. The location is uncertain, most likely near the town now called Oswestry (a name thought to be derived from "Oswald's Tree"). This is now a market town in the north-west Midlands of England, close to the Welsh Border. Mercian/Britonnic North Welsh territory in those days. What was Oswald doing there? Was he an invasive aggressor? Was he a pre-emptive defender? I would favour the latter. However, no-one really knows. What I think we can say from a Christian understanding is that it was another outworking in the natural realm of a collision of different Identities in the Spiritual realm.

Oswald's reign began with one of those in 635. And now it ended with another in 642. King Penda prevailed. King Oswald was slain. As the end came upon him, he prayed to the Christian God to bless his soldiers. It seems that Oswald was prayerful all his kingly life, rising each morning to pray first and at length to the Christian God for the wellbeing of his people.

Penda had Oswald's body dismembered. The head and upper limbs were hung on stakes for all to see, much as Christ's body had once been nailed to "the tree", i. e. the Cross. Hence the old name "Oswald's tree".

This became a potent image for the people. It would have echoed Oswald as a Christ figure. There followed a sweep of yet more new-found Christian faith at its highest heat.

Therefore, the triumph backfired on Penda. Another irony. Just as Penda might have thought he had sent Oswald's name into oblivion, blow me down if the dead Oswald didn't morph into a miracle cult: Saint King Oswald was born. He had more hold on the hearts of the people in death than he had in life. Miracles and healings broke out. Even the soil he died on became the location of a miracle. So the soil was dug up and transported to be a relic along with Oswald's nation-building bones, of which more later.

Now, I am going to stick my neck out here and surmise that King Penda did two unwise things in the triumph of the dismemberment. For him, the dismembering was a sign for the people of the victory of his pagan gods over the Christian one. Here is what was unwise in his triumphing:

i. He dismembered Oswald's right arm as the sign that the arm of Penda's power had triumphed over the arm of Oswald's power. But St Aidan had earlier prayed prophetically in Christ over Oswald's right hand that what it stood for would never decay. We will come to that in a while. The point, for now, is that the Christian God would have sought to *vindicate* the prophetic prayer of St Aidan. That is the way the spiritual realm of the Christian God works. Vindication is a key principle that his Bible reveals he would follow. The entire Christian gospel could be summed up in this one phrase: God's vindication of his Christ, and, by extension, Christ's own.

So, the Christian God would find a way for the power which Oswald's arm represented to live on; at least, he would do so if that God is who he says he is with the ways that he says he has. It would be the appropriate response to Penda. And the appropriate honour to St Aidan.

And as we shall see, posthumously, the power represented by Oswald's arm did prevail.

Before we surmise the second unwise thing King Penda did, I must appear to digress. In Medieval times, in the year 1170, the then Archbishop of Canterbury, Thomas Becket, was murdered in his own cathedral. Four knights did the deed. At the climax, a priest, rejoicing in the murder, picked out Becket's brains from his broken skull on the point of a sword and scattered them on the floor. He is reputed to have said something along the lines of, "This traitor will never rise again." (Source: Michael Green, *St Thomas Becket*). Think it through: a priest complicit in murder in the sanctuary and flatly declaring no Christian resurrection. Satanic stuff, in a Christian understanding. The fashionable modern egg custard version of the Christian God would meekly bow to it, I suppose. The Biblical one, though, what do you think he did?

He did not zap the priest or the knights or King Henry II, whose ungovernable rage had set it all off. But, in regard to the dispute with King Henry II that led to the Archbishop's murder, you could say that Thomas Becket did rise from it. He won the argument posthumously and it stayed won for 350 years. Not only that, but there was an outbreak of miracles and healings that led to Thomas Becket being Sainted. He became the hero of the people, rather than the king whose knights had killed him, and a miracle cult.

Now, I am not going to go into the validity of later Medieval miracle cults. There are books about instances of corruption in them which make for sometimes angry, sometimes pitying and sometimes laugh-out-loud responses. I will say this for now. The Christian God seems to have *vindicated* the Archbishop. The Archbishop's arguments were possibly less reasonable than those of King Henry II. But after the satanic provocation in the Christian God's sanctuary, from the Christian God came *vindication*: Becket won.

These things can be no surprise if you once allow for one of the basic patterns of the Cross of Christ. The Christ had done no wrong, yet he was insulted on the Cross and triumphed over, and his God was directly challenged. In response, the Christian Bible teaches that God planned for Christian Identity to become an extended family, the Christ as its head, throughout the earth. This was to be the long-term *vindication* of his Christ. And indeed, an extended Christian family throughout the earth is exactly what has come to pass. It is quite simple, really: provoke the Christian God, especially by defiling his own, and he will vindicate his own. Quite often, after death. But not with lightning bolts of tit-for-tat death. Rather, with lightning bolts of grace, which increase the spread of the Christian extended family. Saint King Oswald was to become a lightning rod for exactly such a lightning bolt.

So now, to return to King Penda and the second point as to what was unwise:

ii.   I strongly suspect that the dismemberment was Penda's way of saying to the Christian God, as it were, "That shows you!" Which was going to leave him wide open to a reply from the Christian God. Some sort of *vindication* of Oswald in which the Christian God would be saying, to those with ears to hear it, "And *that* shows you!"

And that is what happened. Big time, as the years went by. Ironies multiplied for King Penda, and victories escalated for the Christian Identity that Oswald stood for. For example:

a)   As we have already touched on: Oswald became the Saint-King hero figure of those times and for centuries to come. The peoples rallied to the Christian Identity he had stood for. Even Penda's own people: as soon as they could escape from the older-fashioned Anglo Saxon Identity of Penda, they did so.

b) We shall come to this more fully in the chapter about the "Toddling" time for Christian Identity in the Early English. King Penda's own family became Christian. And once Penda had gone, his Mercian Kingdom took hold of Christian Identity with both hands, initially from the Gaelic Celtic Martinian saints trained by St Aidan.

So Penda won the military battle, but he lost the spiritual and Identity war. The old-fashioned, fragmented Anglo Saxon Identity gradually became the unifying Early English one: in Christian togetherness.

Note that any "glory" in this does not go to Oswald. He never meant it for a moment. He was dead. Any glory goes to the Christian God. These were just the sort of ironic things that the patterns in his Bible suggest he would do.

King Oswy of Bernicia

To round off the narrative of Northumbria as at 642, you may recall that Oswald's younger brother was called Oswy. He had been five years old in 616 when fleeing with Oswald into exile among the Gaelic Scots. Like his older brother, he had taken on Christian Identity through the mission of Iona. When Oswald had made peace with Britonnic Rheged, Oswy had married the Princess Rhiainfellt to seal the treaty. There were two children of the marriage, youngsters as at 642.

When Oswald died, Oswy took the throne. However, Northumbria had split in two, Bernicia and Deira, possibly King Penda's doing: divide and rule. Oswy had only the Bernician throne. And years ahead of him in which whoever could tear a piece off Bernicia would try to do so.

Oswy's character has come down to us as different to Oswald's. He was shrewd, even cunning. Christian Life took a more ambiguous course with him, too, as we shall see in later chapters. For now, to note, one of the first acts of Oswy's Bernician reign was to mount a daring raid into Mercian territory and reclaim the remains of King Oswald. And the primary policy was to keep the ministry of St Aidan in place and let it develop around Oswald's remains – a focal point for Christian Awakening.

We must note here, and return to it later, a further irony for King Penda. King Oswy, in spite of himself and to his own surprise, would eventually become Penda's nemesis. He was never any better a Christian than he might have been. He was not in the same Christian heroic mould as his brother. Strange, really; ironic.

Saint King Oswald – Posthumously

Now, before resuming the narrative, I want to consider some of the phenomena associated with the cult of Saint King Oswald after his death.

- One was to do with his right hand, over which St Aidan had prayed. It is said to have become incorrupt after death.

- There was an outbreak of posthumous miracles.

- There began a centuries-long reverence for his bones. Oswald's bones seem to have got involved in a proto-English-Nation-building treaty in 679 and were at the heart of King Alfred the Great's family when they founded the Nation of the English.

Now, all minds descended from the Protestant Reformation, whether Christian or atheist, struggle with things such as saints, bones, relics and posthumous miracle cults. However, some effort has to be made to come to grips with them. Otherwise, how can we understand English history? Such things were a defining cultural force, political and spiritual, for a thousand years.

The first thing to bear in mind is that there were few, if any, books or other media for drawing together common cultural memory. Bones and relics did not have to be about superstition. They could be about treasuring the values which the relic represented and retaining it in the common cultural memory. As you will see as the book develops, there was a strand of that in the long reverence for Saint King Oswald's bones. There was a very strong attachment to many Christian relics in the grandson of Alfred the Great, King Athelstan. It was he who ultimately founded the Nation of the English. In our modern times, we tend to caricature those of ancient times who treasured relics as superstitious and generally of pitiable character. But Athelstan was of noble character. What he wanted was that which was noble in the lives of those who were now his relics to be alive in his world.

As to the pitifully superstitious, the bookshelves are groaning with debunkery of Medieval bone cults. And I am not going to try to defend many of the accusations. However, I would say this about events after Saint King Oswald's death, when miracles were recorded over his relics and even on the soil he died on: consider the pattern of Christ on the Cross. The *full* pattern. Christ on the Cross had been resurrected to life afterwards. Well, so the Christian Bible says. After that, miracles abounded. There were more of those in the years after the Cross than there had been in his own life. And then his message prevailed throughout the political entity that had crucified him. The full pattern of the Christ was this: death gruesomely displayed for all to see on the Cross; then resurrected and alive; then more phenomena than before; and after that, what the Christ had stood for prevailed over the politics of the Roman Empire – long run.

Note now what happened with Saint King Oswald. There played out a similar Christ pattern. Firstly, death gruesomely displayed for all to see in an echo of the Cross. Next, in a Christian understanding, Oswald would not have been dead; rather, he would be alive with the risen Christ. Then, miracles followed through, more phenomena than before. And what Oswald stood for prevailed over the politics of the Early English people groups – long run.

A strong Christ-on-the-Cross pattern match.

Oswald would not have intended such pattern matches. However, Christians routinely live out Christ patterns without the least awareness of it until or unless someone with insight points it out to them. You see, in a Christian understanding, to live out such patterns does not depend upon the human being. It depends upon the Christian God being consistent with one of the most basic promises in his Bible: that the Holy Spirit of the Christian God will be at work to replicate Christ's patterns around the Christian.

Now, as to ancient practices of linking prayer for something such as healing or miracles to bones and relics, here is a Christian principle: if you trust in the bone, if you pray to the bone, if you pray to the saint whose bone it is, that is occult. If the bone leads you to focus on the Christian example of the saint and becomes a trigger for you to draw near to the Christ, and you pray to the Christ, that is Christian.

Post-Reformation propaganda, imbided in the mother's milk of modern English Protestant or atheist alike, assumes that the ancestors prayed to the bones. Maybe, in Medieval corruptions, most of them did. But suppose that some, especially in the founding times of Christian Awakening, did not? Suppose the bone or relic was a prompt to draw near to the Christian God, relevant in its time, as a book might be now, about, for example, the Welsh Revival of 1904? Why would not the Christian God respond with compassion, as he says he would do, to the poor and needy in a world with no medicine? Why would he not work with the grain of their culture? The modern mind might be sniffy. The Christian God might not.

The story of the right arm of King Oswald is particularly striking. It goes as follows. The King was at a banquet. An officer said that the poor had gathered for alms. Oswald not only gave them the food but also broke up the silver plates that carried the food and distributed those as well. St Aidan, witnessing this generosity to the poor, clasped King Oswald's right hand and prayed, "May this hand never decay." Apparently, it did not do so. Well, not for many centuries, anyway. I believe it is still in a reliquary in Durham Cathedral.

What to make of this? Well, the right hand in those days stood for the King's power. That was why King Penda took care to dismember Oswald's right arm. The prayer of St Aidan was in response to what King Oswald had just done. What he meant was, "May all who hold the type of power signified by a King's right hand never cease to give above and beyond to the poor, out of

Christian compassion, as Oswald has just done." I can see no reason why the Christian God would not honour such a prayer.

And indeed, it seems very clear to me that this prayer of St Aidan has prevailed in the cultural history of the English from that day to this. There has always been a cultural value, arising from a Christian root, that to go above and beyond to the poor is the right thing to do. I know that the history has been two steps forward, one step back. But stock markets, for example, never climb in a steady unbroken line. They plunge from time to time but gradually climb overall. What Saint King Oswald's right hand stood for, in terms of St Aidan's prayer, has never decayed. Perhaps the literal non-decay was a prophetic *sign* of that in its time. Embalming may have been involved as well. But that would not disqualify the sign.

I should say, in passing, that one should never underrate the power of a Christian gifted in the prophetic and revelatory realms, as St Aidan was, to speak out prayers that shape the world to a thousand generations of spiritual but not genetic descent. Of the Biblical principle behind that, more soon.

For those who want to go deeper than I have done, regarding Oswald breaking up the silver plates and distributing them as well, here is a hint. I will not develop it further in this book, but here it is: in the Christian Bible, silver can be a motif for the redemptive work of Jesus Christ. The Holy Spirit in St Aidan would have known that, even if Aidan did not.

Christ Patterns in Saint King Oswald

To sum up for now for Oswald. The Christian spirituality into which he was initiated was descended from the Christ pattern in St Patrick: grace to those who had maltreated him. Oswald's first major act as king was to extend grace from the throne of Northumbria to the assassin throne of Wessex: another Christ pattern, and a nation-seeding one. And after death, his God seems to have replicated the full pattern of Christ on the Cross around him.

Small wonder that Oswald's name descended to multiple generations of reverence and to different people groups too. *Vindicated*; most definitely vindicated.

For now, to continue the narrative of Christian Identity in the Nursery for the Early English, events after 642.

642 to early 650s

Kent

Actually, we start shortly before 642, back in boring Kent. Eorcenberht, son of Eadbald, grandson of Ethelbert, came to the throne in about 640. Three points of interest:

i.   Eorcenberht was the first King to formally forbid the worship of idols, along with penalties.

ii.   He had married Seaxburh, daughter of King Anna of the East Angles.

iii.   The eldest daughter of the marriage, named Eorcengota, was to have a "Charismatic" life marked by Christian signs and wonders.

As to forbidding the worship of idols, I address that more fully in a later chapter. To note, for now, kings *reasoned* with kings to do that. It was part of the process by which kings persuaded kings to take on Christian Identity. In those days, it meant something big. It was an Identity-Transforming step for worship of an idol to be replaced by worship of the Christ.

Anyway, Eorcenberht felt strong enough, and committed enough to the Christian God, to take the step. He would have reckoned that it was for the good of his people. In those days, they had the spiritual "seeing eye". It has been lost to us now. But back then, they could see the spiritual realm associated with the idols. They wanted their people protected from it. Eorcenberht specified penalties too. You could spin him today as an oppressor. However, in a Christian understanding, he would have been a caring liberator.

Just two generations on from the much-disrespected St Augustine of Canterbury, a King of Kent brought up to have spiritual insight and caring Christian commitment.

But there was no blood and violence. Boring, wise Kent again, overlooked in the histories: wisdom doesn't attract as violence does.

Nation-Building Event Number Two

As to King Eorcenberht marrying Queen Seaxburh, history barely remarks upon it. But I call it Nation-Building Event 2 in the high-level summary table. The royal house of Kent allying with the royal house of East Anglia: the two most civilised people groups of the time. East Anglia had within it the reinforced Romano Martinian Christian spirituality. Kent had within it the Roman Catholic order which would gradually shape much of English life for a thousand years. The marriage fused the streams. And each kingdom had a passion to develop education. If you recall, before King Anna, King Sigeberht, slain Christian king of the East Angles, had wanted Christian education for his people from 634. Bishop Felix had been gifted to help him set that up. Kent, since King Ethelbert and St Augustine in 597, had also set itself up to give Christian education. Therefore, what we have in this marriage is a union of royal families committed to common Christian Identity, each with a passion to educate. That is what I call English Nation-Building.

I think it is clear that there was a significant "Charismatic" Christian element beneath the surface of the history here as well. That had entered into the roots in Kent with St Augustine and had been in his team because it was upon Paulinus, too. This marriage now reinforced it. You see, it is clear from the life of Eorcengota, daughter of the marriage, that there was a strong "Charismatic" element in her Christian spirituality. If you have experience of that dimension, you can discern it in the family of King Anna, Seaxburh's father. So I think that Seaxburh would have inserted a sparky Martinian Christian spiritual rod into Eorcenberht's more staid Roman Catholic spine at a time when Kent may have needed the reinforcement. It descended to Eorcengota in a life of signs and wonders.

I see it like this, then: the Northumbria/Wessex Christian alliance of 635 was the first step to unified Early English nationhood, which developed on shared Christian foundations. The Kent/East Anglia Christian alliance of about 640 was a further step towards the same.

Again, all but lost to history; no blood and violence. Boring, wise Kent. Christian wisdom did more to shape England than the sword. But the fashion is to give prominence to the swordplay.

Having a Good Death in Christ

As to Eorcengota, daughter of the marriage, I want to highlight the spirituality in her as indicative of what was in the Romano Martinian Christian Franks and the family of King Anna of the East Angles. It was very high and Charismatically gifted.

We should note the account of her death. It was rather a splendid one: angels singing, and gathered up by visible heavenly light. The account is by Bede. He glories in it and recounts several others like it. That he does so speaks to a lost value of the times: having a good death in Christ. For Bede, that was a key element in English history: good deaths in Christ.

Eorcengota was in a noble tradition. St Columba had known his time had come in 597. He had made his farewells, including to his horse. It laid its head in pre-sentient farewell on his bosom. The monks saw the church in which he sat fill with light as the moment came for him to be gathered.

For Eorcengota, there was no farewell horse. But she knew the day that her God would come for her. And on the day, she saw men dressed in white enter the monastery to gather her. The monks heard choirs of angels singing and saw light come down from heaven to bear her away. The most notable of all these phenomena we will come to in the next chapter. St Aidan was seen borne up in the same manner in 651 by St Cuthbert, from which point St Cuthbert entered upon a calling to become quite possibly England's greatest Saint.

I see no reason not to take Bede's "good death" accounts seriously. Death was a fact of life in those days. Jesus Christ said that he is the resurrection and the life, so a value consistent with that would be to want a good death in Christ. And it would be consistent with the Christian God to work with the grain of the value system, rather than cut across it. Besides, it was not uncommon to witness angels singing on the roof during major summer Christian camps in England in the 1980s. That was at the height of what became known as the "Charismatic Renewal", meaning a renewed outpouring of the Holy Spirit of the Christian God. 600s and 1980s in England – similar phenomena. As to knowing your time has come, this author lodged for many years with an older couple from the "Charismatic Renewal" movement. Some years after that, the lady died suddenly. Afterwards, her husband found various notes around the house to comfort him. He also recalled a number of things she had said earlier. They seemed strange at the time. He realised they had been to prepare him. She knew.

So, as it was then, still it is now, in Christian experience. Since Bede recounts history from the perspective of Christian experience, that needs to be allowed for in appraising the history.

Wessex 645 to 648

Now, to Wessex, 645 to 648. Bishop Birinus was nearing the end of his life, and King Cynegils, the king whom Oswald had godfathered, had passed on. His son Cenwalh had opted to be pagan. I think we can infer that he wanted a war-machine version of God: one that would give him war victories, no questions asked. Well, the Christian God does give war victories. But he follows principles. We saw how complex they would have been for King Oswald in 635. This God is not a war machine, no questions asked. Maybe that is even how King Oswald perished, for all his lightning rod Christian spirituality: presuming upon war victory in 642 as he had received it in 635. Christians do make mistakes, serious ones. Only the Christ makes no mistakes. It does not mean to say that the mistakes, even to death, cannot be redeemed by the Christ. "Redeemer" is, after all, one of his great titles.

Anyway, young Cenwalh's family had been allying with Oswald to restrain Penda on the one hand but had married Cenwalh into Penda's family on the other. That was the old Anglo Saxon way: marry, but do not let a marriage alliance get in the way of the fighting. As a Prince, therefore, the young Cenwalh of Wessex had been married off to a daughter of Penda. No name has come down to us for her.

What happened next was this. By about 645, Cenwalh, now the King of Wessex, and having opted for pagan Identity, put Penda's daughter aside. Not overly wise. He must have known what had happened to King Edwin of Northumbria when he had once put aside Penda's cousin: the chop. Penda attacked. Cenwalh managed to escape into exile. The year was 645. The place of exile was the court of King Anna of the East Angles. The court with the Romano Martinian Christian dynamism.

Oops, King Penda. Another irony…

King Anna leads King Cenwalh into Christian Identity

In exile with the East Angles, Cenwalh adopted the Romano Martinian Christian Identity that he had resisted in Wessex. It is important to note that Bede, always eager to credit a cleric, did not credit any cleric for Cenwalh's conversion. He credited King Anna. If you recall, years before that, King Edwin of Northumbria had reasoned King Eorpwald of the East Angles out of idolatry and into the Christian way. Now an East Anglian king replicated the favour: he reasoned Cenwalh of Wessex out of idolatry into the Christian way.

Interesting to note in passing: King Oswald had been led to Christian Identity in exile. Ditto King Sigeberht. Now ditto King Cenwalh.

After this, by 648, King Cenwalh was able to retake his Wessex throne.

King Cenwalh of Wessex never set the world alight as a Christian. I strongly suspect that a God of war victory would have remained his partial preference. And his dealings with the church in Wessex were dubious for much of his reign. However, at the end of his life, he did do one momentously important thing, lost to history's note but history-shaping. Was it bloody? Was it a marriage alliance? Was it cunning? Er, no, he appointed a bishop who turned out to be exactly the right Christian leader in the right place at the right time. The bishop was called Leuthere. We will return to him in a later chapter.

Suffice for now to say this. In his short time, Leuthere would establish stable Christian foundations which Wessex never lost. In fact, Wessex slowly but surely built its sense of Identity upon its Christian foundations. And it was the Wessex ways of doing things which, in the end, became the ways of the kingdom of the English.

So you might say that King Cenwalh, unwise when young and pagan, ended his days as wise in Christ.

King Penda's Most Profound Irony of the Many

And we might now discern the most profound irony of the lot in the life of King Penda. If there had been no driving of Cenwalh of Wessex into exile with the Christian King Anna of the East Angles, there would have been no recapture of Christian Identity for the Wessex kings. Therefore no Christian Identity for King Alfred the Great's Wessex family to restore and embed into the English ten generations later.

That Shows You!

To develop this irony further, I must set out two little-known items from the New Testament Christian Bible.

i.   Paul teaches that one of the purposes of the Christian God is to make his wisdom apparent to beings in the heavenly realms. They can see us but we cannot see them. One way the Christian God does this is through patterns which the Holy Spirit brings out of Christian Lives as they overcome setbacks. A classic one would be the Saint King Oswald pattern: dismembered, yet the full pattern of the Cross of the Christ replicated thereafter. The *image* intended in Paul's writings would be that God turns to angelic beings, saying, "See how wise I am." As for Oswald in this, he would be present and alive and nodding agreement – well, within a Christian understanding, anyway.

ii. Even less understood than this is a teaching by Peter. After being made alive again, the Christ went to certain imprisoned spirits and *triumphed* over them. Peter does not give the triumph speech. However, these would have been spiritual kin with the type of unseen being that would have enjoyed seeing the Christ mocked on the Cross and would look with satisfaction on the likes of King Penda dismembering King Oswald. The Christ seems to have said something along the lines of, "You cheered when I died. Who's cheering now?"

I say this so you can validate the next points I make from the Christian Bible.

- When King Penda had King Oswald dismembered, it was like saying to Oswald's Christian God, "That shows you!" And malign beings, perhaps, looked on and cheered.

- However, within one generation, Penda's family and kingdom were embracing Christian Identity.

- And within ten generations, the Wessex family, which Oswald had godfathered, were founding Christian England. In a Christian understanding, that would be a fairly typical timescale of the Christian God when interacting with real world history. He plays a long game.

So, Christian God to King Penda: "And *that* shows you!"

And, to any malign beings that had watched on: "Who's cheering now?"

Christian Identity in the Nursery

To summarise so far:

There were five peaceful years from 635 to 640 for St Aidan, Bishop Felix and Bishop Birinus to cultivate Christian Identity in the founding times of the Early English. Kent continued to make steady Christian progress too.

In 641-2, there was slaughter in the Nursery. King Penda came to dominance. His ideals were in the ancient Anglo Saxon mould, his drive the Glory of Mercia. He brought death to sparkily Christian Northumbria and East Anglia. In 645 he brought exile to totteringly Christian Wessex. However, Christian Identity became stronger, not weaker, in all three.

King Oswald in death became Saint King Oswald, a person on whom many patterns of the Christ became focussed.

King Anna was, I think, a most underrated Christian King. As you will see soon, King Penda got him in the end. But not before he had done a Christian work with the Wessex King which shaped English history.

The alliance of the royals of Kent and the East Angles on Christian foundations was a little-remarked proto-England-building alliance.

And King Oswy succeeded King Oswald in Northumbria. A most complex man. We will encounter a lot more of him soon. He became the unlikely nemesis of King Penda in the end. And as to King Oswy's family: it became the first boulder in the landslide of Christian Identity into Mercia in the Toddling times soon to come. As we shall see.

However, before I continue the narrative into the times of Toddling into the Early English Christian Identity:

- I make final reflections on Saint King Oswald as a postscript to this chapter.

- Then a separate chapter will look more closely at many Christian phenomena which accompanied the time of transformative Christian Awakening in the Early English.

Postscript – More on Saint King Oswald

Christian Grace within the Peace Deal

It is possible to put an entirely cynical slant on the real-world outcome of the Northumbria/Wessex treaty of 635. As events unfolded, Penda's Mercian power was not to be contained against Northumbria. Neither would Wessex get the upper hand with Mercia for more than two hundred years. Therefore, put the event in the file marked "Heroic Failures", perhaps? For example, there was a child of Oswald's marriage of treaty, Oethelwald. As we shall see, he became something more than a heroic failure: grown up, he was to make an alliance with Penda! And if you want to look much further forward, Northumbria, three centuries later, was most uneasy about joining the maturing union of the English when Wessex finally crystallised it. And of course, Oswald himself perished at Penda's hands.

So seen cynically, maybe it was like this: good try, Oswald – failed.

However, we have to allow for the way the Christian spiritual realm works. Jesus Christ taught that a seed has to go into the ground and die for it to grow into a plant. He mainly meant himself as the seed. Most often, the principle is to be understood spiritually by a Christian, as in die to the drives of self. However, sometimes the Christian God requires it literally of a Christian. The Christ is entitled to require it: it was required of him. No Christian is asked to go where the Christ has not been. It seems to have been required of Oswald.

Over and above this, however, it is time now to consider carefully three more foundational principles of the Bible. The God of the Bible says that he applies them to peoples who take on Christian Identity. For Christians, they work as follows.

i.   A blessing once sown by Christian faith may be active for a thousand generations. That is the Christian way to understand the second part of the Second Commandment.

ii. Because the Christian God has a Holy Spirit who is for all people groups, places and times, a blessing once sown can transfer by people group and location and pop up in distant times after appearing to have gone underground for a very long while. So, for example, you can have a flesh descendant who loses the plot, e.g., Oswald's son Oethelwald. You can have a spiritual descendant who recovers the thread, e.g., King Alfred the Great.

iii. On the Cross, Jesus Christ sowed the ultimate spiritual blessing: he extended the grace of God to those who had cursed him. Then he rose from the dead blessing those who had no right to be blessed. The principle is known as grace. Slowly but surely, Christian grace has a way of blessing all that it touches. It transforms. It unites. So the Christian God says, anyway.

It follows that if a Christian extends grace in the same way, they can expect to activate from their God a spiritual inheritance of blessing, transformation and unifying that may descend to a thousand generations and in different times, places and peoples.

in 635, Oswald extended blessing in Christ from the Northumbrian throne to the Wessex throne that had tried to assassinate it. So the union activated that most profound of all Christian types of blessing: the grace principle of Christ. It activated it into the real political world in the founding times of the Early English because Oswald had real-world reasons for making the peace. In due course, in Wessex, it matured down multiple generations to more nation-unifying effect than Oswald could have imagined.

I am not saying that Oswald intended so much. No more than Penda intended to intensify the energy that was developing in the new Christian Identity by attempting to slay it. Penda became a focal point for *irony*. Oswald became a focal point for *grace*, but as the lightning rod, not the lightning.

Here are three less cynical points.

a) Northumbria and Wessex did stay at peace. In an age often characterised as one Anglo Saxon fragment warring against another, they did not make war.

b) In the following century, a combination of Wessex Christian learning with Northumbrian Christian vigour, with Kentish Christian wisdom in the mix as well, took the Christian gospel back into the old and still pagan Germanic heartlands of Europe. The transformative Christian Identity change took hold there too. It helped to civilise the Europe that descended to us.

c) Nearly three hundred years later, Northumbria had lost the high Gaelic Martinian Christian spirituality which had been in Oswald. But the Wessex royals had recovered it in modified Romano Martinian form and taken it to their hearts. However infantile the early Christian ways of Wessex kings may have been, they never ceased to cherish their godfathering into Christian Identity and union by King Oswald. We can be certain that this was so. You see, Oswald's bones were at the beating heart of their culture when they founded the Kingdom of the English. In those days, whose bones you treasured showed where your heart was.

So, in Saint King Oswald, all three Biblical principles were fulfilled in the real world history: blessing descended to multiple generations, to different people groups, and to peace-making transformation.

Saint King Oswald, then, was a potent spiritual package: another form of "mustard seed". Jesus Christ taught, if you recall, that the spiritual legacy of the Christian could become like a mustard seed: the tiniest of seeds would become the largest plant in the garden. Queen Bertha of Kent had been the first example. King Oswald was another. History shows that the Christian Identity that he sowed in 635 did become the largest plant in the garden of the English.

Saint King Oswald – White Blade

In later times, Britonnic Welsh speakers, including those in Gwynedd, whose King had been the Caedwalla whom Oswald defeated, were to give Oswald a name indicating high honour within their culture: Lamnguin, meaning White Blade – Holy Sword. In some translations, Oswald has come down as Bright Blade. However, as we saw earlier, for the people who so named him, White conveyed the implication of holiness. And I think they intended that. The Christian Bible uses the image of the Christian God's Holy Spirit as a wholesome sword of God's Word. Applying this to Oswald, and fusing it with the real-life warrior, White Blade implied "Holy Christian Warrior", a King David figure.

In their times, it would also have denoted a spiritual descendant of the Candida Casa (White/Holy House to their understanding). If you recall, this was the Martinian Christian centre which St Ninian had first dedicated to St Martin early in the 400s north of the Solway Firth. That territory in those times was Britonnic Welsh speaking, and so was St Ninian. As you will see later, Ninian actually took on the new Martinian way before he founded Candida Casa, but he would still have been of treasured memory as a great Christian of Britonnic Celt ethnicity. So the title of White Blade implies that some Britons came to understand Oswald as a descendant of the finest of Welsh-speaking Christian spirituality, as well as a Gaelic and English-speaking Christian Warrior. And they would have known back then something almost lost to us now. I will return to it more fully later. It pertains to the Gaelic Martinian Christian Life which St Columba had taken to Iona in 563 and which had descended into Oswald. Before it came to Columba's people, it had originated in Candida Casa. The implication is that the latter-day Britonnic descendants of Caedwalla could see that the Angle-ish Oswald had been of Celtic Christian spirituality at its finest.

I deduce that there must have been something very special in this Saint King for Caedwalla's people to allow him the heroic name White Blade.

There was also a political and military reason. In this case, ironically, the main enemy of the Britons of the later generations had become Mercia. Saint King Oswald – by now acquiring widespread semi-legendary status – had become a rallying example for standing against Mercia. But the epithet stuck. It would not have stuck without more general and deeper assent. And it hints at a more general perception: that the Christian God had not been on their own King's side. He had been on the side of Oswald, the spiritual descendant of Saint Ninian. Thus it was that Saint King Oswald, White Blade, came to be cherished amongst the Britons of North Wales. A lost marvel, I would say.

Victory on Saint King's Oswald Day

The family of King Alfred the Great of Wessex, the King David family of English history between 878 and 927, cherished the bones of King Oswald. And as you will see in the final narrative chapter, "Graduation", Alfred's daughter won the decisive battle against pagan Danish forces on Saint King Oswald's Day 910, his bones having come newly into her possession.

I will suggest to you later, in the "Graduation" chapter, why it would be no coincidence, under the Christian God, that the battle should have been won on Saint King Oswald's Day.

King Oswald and King Arthur

I reflect that some today hanker after King Arthur, a Britonnic Celtic figure, perhaps not seeing that the Arthur motif, the "once and future king", can be taken to be a garbled motif for Jesus Christ.

However, we do seem to have had a real Christ-like figure in Saint King Oswald. And unlike Arthur, although just like the real Christ is foretold to do, Oswald really did return to save the day.

I find it more than interesting, too, that Saint King Oswald was a product of Christian grace from Celt to Anglo. We live in times in which one hurt after another between "English" and "Celtic" has descended to us. There have been centuries of Anglo versus Celtic mutual caricature, prejudice and division. Saint King Oswald corrects them. The nearest to him in modern literature and film is the Strider/Aragorn figure, a sort of once and future king in Tolkien's "Lord of the Rings". In the film, he comes across as a rather Celtic hero. The orcs are very English. Here is the truth, though. Oswald was Angle-ish: proto-*English*. Steeped in the Scotic/Gaelic *Celtic* Martinian Christian spirituality that had first blessed him as a youth, when no blessing would have been deserved on his Angle-ish father's account. He laid the spirituality into the founding roots of the future English. And it became a uniting force in their culture.

So you see, if you allow for a Christian and spiritual appraisal, you can find a founding history more complex and ironic, but also more glorious, wholesome and unifying, arising out of the Christian Identity in the English than has descended to popular caricature.

Now, the narrative will continue into the Toddling times of Christian Identity in the Early English. There will be more to say about King Penda, and also about irony and the Christian God.

Before that, however, a further interlude chapter, "Open Heaven", to reflect on various wonders in the time of Christian Awakening in the Early English, all of them lost to or hidden from the modern English understanding of their history.

CHAPTER 13.

Precious Things

The stones of Solomon's Temple were finished in gold and studded with precious stones.

Gold for the Glory of God.

Jewels for the People of God.

For the Christian, the jewels foreshadow the People of the Christian God as Living Stones in a spiritual temple.

They also stand for Enduring Wonders of God.

You may have been taught that the times of the Anglo Saxons were mainly of Darkness and the Sword.

But the Christian Awakening of the Early English was more a time of Living Stones and Enduring Wonders.

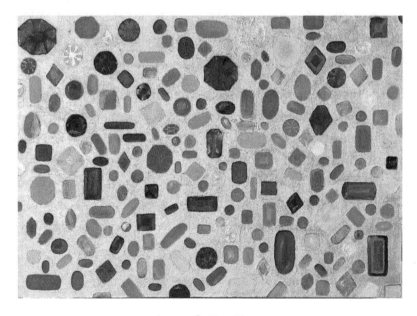

Artwork: Ben Emet

CHAPTER 14.

Open Heaven

I said in my Introduction that my focus in this work is to restore lost or hidden things. Before continuing with the narrative flow, I want to reflect on a few wonders in the Awakening time when Christian Identity was laid in the Early English. I will also highlight certain Christian phenomena in those times. As we allow these things to come back into the light, so we restore not only the vibrant spiritual atmosphere of our early history but also a deeper understanding of what made the English.

Under an Open Heaven

I have heard some Christians use the phrase "under an open heaven." It indicates a time of Blessings from the Heaven of the Christian God. This describes very well how it seems to have been in the Early English period of transformative Christian Awakening. From a balanced appraisal of history, with a willingness to see with two eyes, the natural *and* the spiritual, it was a period of phenomena and unsung wonders.

This does not mean to say that all was wonderful. All of history is a mixture of the good and the bad. All of life is. Jesus Christ taught that it would be ever thus until he returns to sort it out. Until then, it depends on how you respond, what resources are within. It was a world of land-based economy, warrior culture, lack of medicine and enslaving bands. However, the Christian God claims to offer an extra resource to those who receive him: a deposit within of his own nature. It is said to generate power to overcome difficult circumstances. A great deal of difficulty had to be overcome.

However, in the midst of much darkness, some remarkable lights shone out.

Pope Gregory the Great – his Great Heart for the Anglo Saxons

As we read earlier, Pope Gregory the Great sent St Augustine to Canterbury from Rome in 597. The first successful Christian mission to the Anglo Saxon people groups.

Much has been written about Pope Gregory, but not much of it reflects on the heart that he had for the Anglo Saxons. This man truly deserved his title of "Great". What a wonder then that his great heart was set for many years on bringing good to the Anglo Saxon peoples. Before he sent Augustine to Canterbury, and before he became Pope, Gregory had set out on his own for the shores of what had once been "Britannia" to take the Christian message to the Germanic invaders of it. The people of Rome would not let him go. But he continued to cherish the ambition.

Various motives are attributed to Gregory. For example, that he wanted to restore the old Britannia to the Roman Empire. Or that he wanted to get the Anglo Saxon people en masse to become Roman Catholic so they might then outnumber and repel the Arian heretics of Europe. I will say more about Arianism shortly. For now, it was a heresy destroying the church from the inside out.

Another motive is also presented. Gregory saw Angle-ish children in the Roman slave marketplace. By a play on words between "Angle" and "Angel", and reckoning the children looked like angels, he decided to send a Christian mission to save the angels. A bit twee, perhaps? We have the story from Bede, but he presents it as an old tradition not to be lost. There would have been something in it. Gregory would have seen such slaves. And it seems that he did pay to free and have educated some young Anglo Saxons. However, I would say that Bede uses the story more to bring colour to the history than as an explanation of motive.

Anyway, to weigh these things up. As to restoring Britannia to the Empire, Gregory would indeed have remembered the old link. But there was no Empire in the west to restore it to. There was a Church. Gregory was not an Empire

Builder; he was a Church Builder. As to Arianism, it was indeed Gregory's biggest problem. But to plan to solve it by converting Anglo Saxons en masse? Gregory was a practical man. No one would make that a master plan: unforeseeable and unpredictable.

More than any of these things, in Gregory's mind would have been this commission from Jesus Christ: "Go into all nations and make them my disciples." This is a keynote verse of the Christian Bible. It is known as "the Great Commission". Gregory's letters show that he had in-depth knowledge of the Bible. He would certainly have known the Great Commission. Every generation of Christians puts it in their top ten verses of the Bible. If you want to understand the history of a nation labelled with Christian Identity, you have to make the effort to understand Christian scriptures. They are usually a key element in the motivating forces that shaped the nation.

Therefore, the "Angels" may have given Gregory a prompt. But life and experience teach you that perilous missions, from which people will never come back even if they succeed, are not mounted because you get touched with a sentiment or harbour fond hopes. They are mounted when it is a passion in your heart which will not go away, which keeps on growing, and, for a Christian, when you can confirm it from the Bible. Confirmatory Christian scriptures are usually the clincher for the experienced Christian.

So there is a good explanation of why Gregory sent the mission. He cherished the idea for some time. It did not go away. It grew. He checked it out against what he would have seen as The Maker's Instructions. And in due time and season, the means came for action. That process is testified to time and again by experienced Christians as the way the Christian God works. They attribute to their Christian God both (i) the seeding of the idea and (ii) the maturation process to acting upon it.

To me, this speaks eloquently of an Open Heaven over the Anglo Saxon people: a Pope with a heart for them, believing himself prompted by the Christian God to go to them. What a wonder. Lost to our post-Reformation prejudices.

No Arianism – An Unsung Wonder

Arianism was a heresy which dominated the church in Europe up to and including the Christian missions to the Anglo Saxon people groups. (Note, Arianism with an i, not the Aryanism with a y of Nazism. With an i, it was an ancient Christian heresy, not a Nazi mish-mash).

Now, here is an unsung wonder. Large swathes of the European church had been corrupted by Arianism. But there was no Arian heresy in the Christian input that came to the Anglo Saxon people groups. It was not in Gregory, Augustine or Paulinus. It was not in the Gaelic Martinian Scots. It had insinuated into the Romano Martinian Franks. But St Columbanus had taken care to drive it out from the monastic foundations which he established amongst the Franks. Those Christians who came to the Anglo Saxons from the Franks were from that purified stream.

We had better diagnose the nature of the Arian infection. This is so that we can:

a) Discern the unsung wonder of the Early English *not* having been infected with it.

b) Begin to understand the far-reaching consequences for later English history and the modern world of the Early English *not* having had the infection.

I must ask you, therefore, to be patient and get into a bit of detail. There are forests of material out there, but I will try to discern the wood from the trees for you.

Arianism was within the church, especially in its high places. It was a parasitic spiritual larva which ate the living spiritual body from within. The Arian heresy went as follows:

- Jesus Christ was a created human being, therefore not divine. By way of comparison, the Christian understanding is that Jesus Christ, creator not created, is both fully human and fully God.

155

There was also this thinking along with the Arian teaching:

- Jesus Christ was a punishment substitute: the Cross visited God's wrath on him instead of on us.

The Christian understanding of the Cross is more subtle. Christ on the Cross was God paying with his own blood to redeem humankind from a hidden spiritual legal system which holds us captive. We cannot plead our own case within that. But our case has been settled: God has paid for us. Put another way, it was an expression of love more than wrath. To the extent that wrath was poured out upon the Cross, it was as much to channel our wrath upon God as his on us. The consuming nature of the suffering was to warn us how terrible it would be to be bound forever to both the place and fate of evil beings, with no-one to plead our case.

Now, there were consequences of the Arian heresy and the thinking about the Cross:

Arian Heresy	Christian Understanding
If Jesus Christ is not God, he cannot judge you.	Jesus Christ, since he is fully God, has full authority to judge you. And he can and will judge you.
Since God's wrath on you was expended on Christ, do what you like, it is paid for. The Christian God will not judge you.	Even once you have been ransomed out of the hidden courts, Jesus Christ will continue to discipline you.
For best results, let religious ritual keep you focussed on your guilt: keep utilising the blood payment.	For best results, remind yourself often of the redemption paid, letting the Christ keep activating the Holy Spirit of the Christian God within you.

You can deduce that different behaviour patterns would arise, as follows:

- The Arian heresy could lead to fatalism, religious dependency and cynicism. It had no power within it to transform the human nature. It left the believer infantile in the things of God, guilt unresolved.

- The Christian understanding leads on to accountability, Life in the Holy Spirit and integrity. It has power to impart the divine nature to the human nature, to lift accusation, to transform and to make you grown up in the things of God.

However, many times more deadly was this consequence:

- The Holy Spirit of the Christian God would not agree to work with an Arian sub-divine wooden duck version of a Christ. He would depart from an Arian church.

Now, all that is authentic in Christian Life comes from having a deposit of the Holy Spirit of the Christian God within. Jesus called that the spiritual new birth. It is the Holy Spirit who transforms; who teaches the Christian, from within, to be accountable and to have integrity; and who imparts assurance of the Christian God as adoptive Father, accusation lifted. He makes the Christian grow up, in other words. But with Arianism, there was no Holy Spirit to deposit. A Hebrew word in the Old Testament is "Ichabod". It means "The glory of God has departed." It was an Ichabod version of church, obeying all the outward rituals with none of the inner reality. A monster of Religion, in other words. It had the label of Christian but defrauded the spiritual reality of it. It had the effect of making the people infantile in Christian things.

As for secular rulers, Arianism could be very attractive for some. They could do anything they liked before the Arian version of God. Just make sure you go through the religious observances. It was also attractive to ambitious career seekers in the Church. You see, from 313 onwards, the Emperors had made the Church the place to be to get on in life. So that is where the worldly went to wrestle and intrigue for office. Any wrong they did in the process would be covered by the Arian version of God. Machiavelli, for example, would have made a fine Arian.

However, there was no Arianism in what came to the Anglo Saxons. Pope Gregory's team, the Martinian Christian Franks as reinforced by St Columbanus, and the Gaelic Martinian Celts were clean of it. St Martin himself had lived during Arianism's penetration of the Church. He had discerned it, been beaten up by it, drawn aside from the mainstream of it, and left a legacy of how to have the Life in the Holy Spirit of the Christian God.

I think that it was a major blessing of the Christian God, an Open Heaven blessing, that these Christian streams and only these were what came to the Anglo Saxon people groups. For example:

- A Christian ruler is obliged to be a lot less cynical than an Arian one, more accountable. Value system emerging: rule for the common good, even when others cannot see you, a value in English bones.

- A Christian cleric is obliged to have more integrity than an Arian one. Value system emerging: hate hypocrisy, a value in English bones.

- A Christian church would have the Spirit of the Christian God within, promoting maturity in the wider body of people. An Arian one would be Ichabod, a religious fraud. Value system emerging: let your spirituality be for real, a value in English bones.

It is necessary to make the effort to *discern* the differences. Radically different consequences emerged from them in our real history. The English gained good values from their Christian Identity. It is not helpful to lump everything about Christian Identity into a box called "Religion". It is as we discern, for example, that we can see and recover the good in the value systems of the English that descend to this day:

- Accountability in rulers.

- Integrity under a God who sees you when the law does not.

- Good things activated in you.

- Bad things disciplined in you.

What's not to like? But none of those values have descended from the Arian religious root. They descended from the Christian root.

Now, to understand the impact of the non-infection with Arianism on our real and modern world, we have to come to terms with another principle in the Christian Bible: there is nothing new under the sun. The Bible relates it to human spirituality when that lacks the transforming power of the Holy Spirit of the Christian God. Labels and outward forms change. Cultures change. But human spiritualities are shape-shifters. They do not change.

It follows that the ways of Arianism, without the label, may be on the earth at any time. For example, the Apostle Paul had a great deal to say to oppose the spirituality of Arianism, minus the label, in his letters. And throughout history, it can be discerned to have been alive and well, unlabelled, in diverse types of Christian churches and practices. Wherever we can discern superstitious or cynical Christianised understanding, we will normally find shape-shifting Arianism at the root. In the Medieval times of the English, it seems to have become a giant tendril choking the more ancient planting of the Christian Life in the Holy Spirit.

It was for this reason that the English of five hundred years ago had a Protestant Reformation. Why? To take an axe to the tendril. To say, "Goodbye, wooden duck god. Hello again, Christian God, the God in our oldest roots."

Now, this pertains to the modern Western world. The Protestant Reformation unleashed it. Protestant Christians were in the forefront, for example, of making modern political, technological and wealth creation systems. But that was not their motive: they wanted to be able to grow to maturity in their Christian God again. That was what unleashed the modern world. All those other effects are presented these days as main motives, and they tend to be attributed to secularists, as we have become, rather than to Protestant Christians, as they were. But these secular effects were the sideshows. What drove the Reformation in England was that the English, once given a sniff of a chance, wanted their Christian God back. With passionate intensity. As passionate as they had been in the founding times.

Anyway, no Arian infection in the Early English founding times. Good values, healthy ones, were planted in the roots by those who were the real deal in the Christian God. I think "Open Heaven" describes that very well.

And for what it's worth, once centuries had elapsed after the Protestant Reformation, the old Martinian Life in the Holy Spirit of the Christian God was able to cut loose once more into the wider earth. Often through Protestant English speakers. In new clothes and labels. But I run ahead…

Love, not Hate

Another wonder is that what was most authentic in the Christian Life of the Celtic peoples came into the Anglo Saxons – and that it came in at all, given that the Anglo Saxons were invaders.

You could broadly say that there were three streams of Celtic Christian attitude to the idea of the Anglo Saxons becoming Christian. One was hatred. One was impatient disdain for beginners. The third was love. The stream that hated the Anglo Saxons lost its way. The stream of impatient disdain had little impact. The stream of love prevailed. In the real and violent world. But what a wonder: there was much hatred and disdain to get past.

More subtly, we have already seen that the Britonnic Christian way had long been penetrated by a heresy called Pelagianism. It taught that a human being could perfect themselves through their own goodness. The Christian understanding, however, is that it is the work of God's Holy Spirit to perfect you. Pelagianism, therefore, downgraded the need for the Holy Spirit of the Christian God. I sum it up like this: Pelagianism = self-righteousness, or striving for righteousness of self.

In Christian terms, Pelagianism was less deadly than Arianism and more kindly. However, it would have had the effect of making Christian witness tired and the church sleepy.

The Pelagian church was one that the Anglo Saxon people groups intuitively rejected. They probably thought it was a bit wet. King Penda, for example, despised it. He noted that the practitioners could not meet the standards of righteousness by their own strength anyway; hence his accusation that Christians were hypocrites. I would surmise that Coifi, King Edwin's pagan priest, had turned from it but not found the true Christian way: that righteousness, as defined by the Christian God, is a work of God's Holy Spirit from beginning to end. When Roman Catholic Paulinus explained things to him properly in 627, the lights went on. The Holy Spirit came into him. That is when he rode off to destroy his pagan sanctuary. And set it on fire.

Anyway, this pseudo-Christian Pelagian stream in the Celts made little impact on the Anglo Saxons.

Ironically, the harshly impatient attitudes in other parts of the Celtic church were as likely to be Martinian as Britonnic. However, somewhere along the line, Christian love had not completed its work. The deprivation of lifestyle that was included within the Martinian way had stayed stuck in harshness. And here now we see two great wonders of the Christian God:

- From the Martinian Gaels, King Oswald received St Aidan, in whom Christian love *had* matured. It was Aidan who became the chief trainer of Christian missionaries to many Anglo Saxon people groups.

- Although the Pictish Celt St Columbanus had himself been a fierce and quite harsh man, what he planted amidst the Franks was mediated to the Anglo Saxons through more urbane and even mellow Franks: Bishop Felix of the East Angles, for example.

What a subtle wonder of the Christian God: love, not hate, is what came to the Anglo Saxons. And in large measure, and contrary to modern caricature, much of it sprang out of Celts. Humanly speaking, it would have been most unlikely.

Spiritual Armoury and Woden Fulfilled

A new concept of armoury came to the warlike Anglo Saxon people groups. In a Christian understanding, by God's Holy Spirit, there is a spiritual suit of armour:

- Battle belt of truth.

- Battle breastplate of righteousness.

- Battle shoes of readiness for peace.

- Battle shield of faith.

- Battle helmet of salvation.

- Battle sword of the word of the Christian God.

The call would be to wear that spiritual armour. A most wholesome message: truth, righteousness, peace, faith, salvation and hearing what the Christian God says. Presented in a resonant way for warrior times. But much more peaceful. Small wonder that the Anglo Saxons, as they progressed to becoming the Early English uniting on shared Christian foundations, did that by peace more than the sword. Not the fashionable view of history, I know, but a more accurate and, in the end, more glorious one. A time of Open Heaven indeed, to seed peaceful armour into a warrior world.

There was another resonant message, much overlooked, more mysterious, but also a wonder in its way: most of the Anglo Saxons were bound in with a god called Woden. Those who were classed as royal had found a way of tracing and validating (perhaps by force) descent from him. One thing you rarely hear is that Woden was temporary. One day all things in Woden would be wrapped up into a greater and unknown God.

Now, compare the Christian message. Jesus Christ is the one greater than Woden into whom all things in Woden will be subsumed. As to the effect of receiving the Christ: it makes you royal in the sight of the Christian God – anyone, commoner as well as aristocrat – and you do not have to validate your royal standing with force. You validate it with love.

A most culturally transforming and relevant message. And I really do think that coming to terms with the detail of the Christian message does much to restore and add colour to the real world history.

Not One but Two Apostles to the English

Some call St Aidan the Apostle to the English. Others give the title to St Augustine of Canterbury. I would say that each warranted the title in part and taken together were one complete Apostle. And I reflect upon a wonder and also a Christ pattern:

- What a wonder, for not one but two quite different but complementary Christian greats to be active amongst the Anglo Saxons in the one epoch.

- Jesus Christ sent out his followers in twos. So in Aidan and Augustine, we have another Christ pattern. And they were gifts from an Open Heaven, the pair of them, as a Christian understanding might see it.

St Aidan and St Cuthbert – Elijah and Elisha Pattern Replicated

We will encounter more of St Cuthbert later. Ministering after St Aidan had died in 651, he became, in many ways, the most purely great of all the English Saints. We will look here at the event that crystallised his calling. You might call it literally an Open Heaven event.

On the night in 651 that St Aidan died, Cuthbert was a young soldier or shepherd on night watch duty in the Scottish borders. He saw a light descend to earth and return carrying, it seemed to him, a human spirit to heaven. He gave up soldiering after that and went into monastic training, emerging as St Cuthbert: more gifted in some ways, certainly in the miraculous, than even the great St Aidan had been, and sweeter in nature, too, if that were possible. What Cuthbert had seen in 651 was St Aidan gathered up.

Now, within the Bible which Christians use there is a vivid original of this pattern. Two of the great prophets were Elijah and Elisha. Elijah came first; Elisha succeeded him. Elisha was more at home with miracles, and possibly the sweeter character. There was a condition for Elisha to inherit Elijah's mantle of spiritual power. He had to witness the moment when Elijah's time on earth would end in his being carried up to heaven. Elisha witnessed precisely that. Whereupon he inherited Elijah's mantle of power and more.

The pattern was replicated in Aidan and Cuthbert. Cuthbert saw the moment that Aidan was carried up to heaven. He went on to be more gifted in the miraculous and the sweeter character. So, from a Christian way of confirming things, the Bible pattern validates the account of Cuthbert's calling.

The point I would make is this: it was a significant highlight phenomenon within the times. But it was also relatively typical of the times: Open Heaven. In this case, literally, and within the framework of the Bible.

Bishop Birinus

There are some things that have come down to us which I think were *not* wonders. Bishop Birinus of Wessex, for example, is alleged to have walked on the sea. He forgot a special cloth used in celebrating the Eucharist. But his cross-channel ship was already under way. Rather than make a fuss, he walked back to retrieve it.

Birinus did gradually become another miracle cult after death. It was never as popular in Wessex as the cult of St Swithun. My mother told me that St Swithun is the saint who might make it rain for forty days if it rains on St Swithun's Day. I don't believe everything my mother told me these days.

Now, Birinus must have been striking in life. What was consistent and credible was that he was a fine teacher and preacher looked up to by the Wessex leaders. In terms of fulfilling the Great Commission of Jesus Christ – go and make disciples – he was front rank.

Regarding St Augustine of Canterbury's miraculous powers, the Bible teaches explicitly that some can have them, and Pope Gregory the Great confirmed them in writing. Regarding the revelatory powers of Bishop Paulinus of York, they were those of the Apostle Paul, well within the Bible envelope.

However, as to Birinus walking on the water, well, the Bible tells us that the Apostle Peter *did* manage it for a short moment. And he would have been a hero for Birinus. But Peter's faith wavered in no time. And we have to exercise discernment. The tale derives from the twelfth century, by which time it had become custom and practice to embellish accounts.

That is most often the clue – when was the account from? If from Bede, early 700s, you can reckon it likely to be valid. If from Medieval times, you can more often smell a kipper.

It tends to be the stock-in-trade of the modern English approach to its early Christian history to recount a kipper-y Medieval tale and then smile indulgently, patting the ancients on their wide-eyed little heads. However, I do not need to use Medieval standards to find remarkable wonders of the Open Heaven period whose lost history I am recovering. The next three that follow, for example, are authenticable crackers.

And yes, they did open eyes wide at the time.

The Monk Fursa

You may recall that when King Sigeberht of the East Angles retrieved his throne, he sent for and received Christian help. Contemporary with Bishop Felix, he received some monks out of what we now call Ireland. Amongst them was Fursa, the Scotch bonnet chilli pepper in the East Anglian spiritual stew. Now here is an insight into the times, how they were spiritually vivid.

Monks might engage in the most intense spiritual battles. Fursa – who also made an assiduous contribution in the real world – was taken by an angelic escort along a narrow way with flames either side of it. Devils and people were within the flames. This was *not* a vision of hell. It was a vision of the effects of reneging on baptismal vows, covetousness, sowing discord and practising injustice. This was the actual *interpretation* given to Fursa.

In the Christian Bible, the Apostle Paul wrote of a visit that he was given into heaven. He could not tell whether he was in the body or out of it. It was similar for Fursa. As he walked between the walls of flame, a man on fire was hurled at him from out of the flames. In the encounter, Fursa was scorched on shoulder and jaw on one side. Afterwards, the scorch marks were physically visible on his body. According to his angelic escort, Fursa had had a link to the man's sin that had not been renounced.

This was the sort of spiritual life in some Celtic Christians of the Martinian stream. This same Fursa was also a most reasonable man who persuaded people to take on Christian Identity by teaching and by example of virtue, faith and love. These days we would say, you can keep Fursa and the flames; just give us the example of love. But with Fursa, the spiritual visionary was integral with the man of reason and love. And his was the type of spirituality impacting East Anglian Christian Identity in those times. If you recall, the East Anglian Christian Identity was a formative forerunner of the ultimate Early English one.

Now, you can read that Fursa's story became the starting point for later and more lurid Medieval "Visions of Hell" literature. Some of those may have been manipulative. It is necessary to exercise discernment about them. However, Bede, being of a culture which understood such things, indicates that Fursa did *not* have a vision of hell. He was taken in spirit through the consequences of four types of sin, within a vivid experience. Within the experience, he was given an *interpretation* of it. That is usually the key, down to this day, when you hear a story of a heaven or hell experience. They are much more common than you might think. The key to them is often, what was the interpretation given?

The experience may have been wild. But the interpretation was not. To remind ourselves, it was a warning to be passed on about the effects of reneging on baptismal vows, covetousness, sowing discord and practising injustice. Later Medieval Visions of Hell literature might have been manipulative, but in Fursa's time, and any other time, what could be more helpful than a vivid warning against practising injustice?

Anyway, I took an interest in the story of Fursa because in my own lifetime I can remember hearing a related Christian TV testimony at the beginning of the twenty-first century. An occultist had just died. Prayed for by Christians, he was sent back to this world. He had been in flames. As he returned to this present world, others in the flames cried out, "You brought us here – don't leave us." He looked back at them. With that, the fire scorched one side of his face. The marks remained on it when he returned. This is said to have happened in a part of the world receiving the Christian message for the first time and within systems of idolatry. Within a time such as Fursa's, in other words.

Now, some might call that Christian TV claptrap, probably followed by an appeal for money to the gullible.

But there are many strange things, past and present, arising from Christian power-spirituality when encountering other spirituality. You couldn't make them up. Here now comes another cracker. I said we would look more closely at how the Fear of the Christian God came upon King Eadbald of Kent, Ethelbert and Bertha's son, between 616 and 619.

This will test you. Thinking caps on.

The Conversion of King Eadbald of Kent

King Eadbald of Kent was the son of King Ethelbert and Queen Bertha and the brother of Queen Ethelburgha who married King Edwin of Northumbria. Eadbald had taken the throne of Kent by 616. He seems to have lacked his father's Christian sincerity. He reverted to paganism. He took his father's wife (not Bertha, who had died, but a second one).

The then Archbishop of Canterbury, Laurence, from Augustine's old team, was very discouraged. King Ethelbert had tried a Christian mission to London, but that had failed. The East Saxons, who held London, were not to be dislodged from their pagan preferences. They had expelled his old colleague, Bishop Mellitus, who left the country. Laurence was minded to do the same. After much prayer, and tears, he lay down to sleep. In the night – and this begins to sound like a Medieval tall tale – St Peter appeared to him. St Peter told him to stand fast for the sake of his flock and then *scourged* him. The marks were visible. In the morning he showed them to King Eadbald.

The king was amazed, wondering who would inflict such injuries on an Archbishop. Laurence explained that it was for the sake of Eadbald's salvation. Eadbald became very afraid. He banned idolatrous worship, gave up Ethelbert's wife, embraced Christian Identity and was baptised. Thereafter, he promoted the interests of the church.

How about that under an Open Heaven: St Peter scourging the Archbishop of Canterbury, no less? And the Fear of God – which the Christian Bible declares to be the beginning of wisdom – making a direct hit on the top political leader? Thus shaping the real world history – what to make of it?

What you tend to read in history books is this: King Eadbald reverted to paganism. The circumstances were nudge, nudge, wink, wink. Then he became a Christian. No further info, but there's maybe an implication of a controlling church. No-one gets to grips with what is said to have happened. Airbrushed from our history. But really, could you make it up? Did Laurence fake it? Was Eadbald a simpleton? Was it a tall tale by Bede?

Well, Bede used some very difficult material by the understanding of our own times. But he was careful not to tell tall tales. In his time, such accounts as this were a highlight but not too abnormal. There is an old dictum, attributed I think to Sir Arthur Conan Doyle's Sherlock Holmes: when you eliminate the impossible, what is left, however improbable, is the truth.

So, let's look into it. First: was Laurence a faker? I should think it unlikely. He was from a team that had integrity. Brought up to believe that liars go to hell. And it was an adult king he was dealing with – and probably afraid of, as we shall see – not a junior to be manipulated.

Next: was Eadbald a simpleton? His general life story indicates shrewdness. Was the church controlling him? He had more authority over it than it had over him. He was not converted through fear of the church. It feared him more than he feared it.

Well then, let's authenticate the story both from context and by drawing upon the teaching of Pope Gregory the Great, no less, to validate it from the Bible.

It was not uncommon in pagan culture for a son to take his father's wife after the father had died. When he was alive, St Augustine had sought written advice from Pope Gregory on this matter. Gregory had written a stern reply with an injunction against it. The point he made was that to do so was something forbidden in the Old Testament. It was a form of "uncovering your father's nakedness". Ethelbert had been one flesh with his second wife. Uncovering her nakedness, Eadbald also uncovered Ethelbert's and dishonoured him.

Now, Christian Life is not based on Old Testament Law. However, Christians sometimes understand that many details of Old Testament Law give insight into a hidden spiritual realm. Out of it can come either that which will bless you or that which will curse you, depending on your conduct. Uncovering your father's nakedness is a major fail; it comes with a promised curse: you will not live long in the land given by God. That is the curse which comes with breaking the Fifth Commandment, which is to honour your father and mother. So, to complete the Gregorian type of logic chain: if you have uncovered Ethelbert's nakedness, you have dishonoured your father and will not live long in the land that God gives. Therefore, do not do it.

We have to try to see things as if we were the Christian God now. How his revealed character would see it here. Eadbald may have activated the Fifth Commandment and its curse into play in his life. However, Ethelbert, his father, had been a most genuine Christian. The Christian God would want to extend grace – i.e. relief from curse – to Eadbald for Ethelbert's sake and, in the process, rescue Ethelbert's honour.

As to Archbishop Laurence, how would the Christian God see it? Maybe this God would want Eadbald to see that he had dishonoured his father. But why then scourge Laurence rather than Eadbald in order to bring Eadbald to account? This God is supposed to be fair, isn't he?

Well, the Christian God says that he is gracious as well as fair. And he would have been extending grace to Laurence as follows. I think it was like this: Laurence may have been holding back. He must have been afraid to bring up Gregory's old warning with the king. I would reckon that Laurence had the letter containing it. But rather than use it to remind Eadbald, he held back. He likely feared expulsion or even for his life. However, the Christian God would have expected the Archbishop to risk rebuking the king whatever the consequence. Not doing so would be a disciplinary matter for Laurence.

In grace *and* in fairness, therefore, the Christian God killed two birds with one stone. He gave Laurence a supernatural scourging as much less damaging than maybe incurring the wrath of Eadbald. And put the fear of God into Eadbald in the process.

This may not correspond to some modern images of the Christian God as a jellyfish, having no spine, Baby Jesus Meek and Mild. But it maps straight onto the Bible of the Christian God. In this, a letter to the Hebrews teaches that the Christian God reserves the right to visit painful discipline on his children out of grace. Now, you would not normally experience that as flagellation. You would normally be taken through a salutary experience which brings you down-ity when you have been getting uppity. However, it would seem that in Laurence's case, the Christian God took himself literally. It was within the Bible envelope, though.

As to whether it was literally St Peter doing the scourging, well, why not? There is no Saint a Roman Archbishop would have respected more. In a Christian understanding, Peter would have been alive with Christ. Why not delegate him? The God of Jesus Christ delegated the departed Elijah and Moses to visit the Christ.

As to Eadbald, it is clear from Bede's account that he already respected Laurence. He would have been clearly instructed in the rights and wrongs of idolatry – one would think by his father. And also instructed not to take his father's wife: the letter from Gregory would have been part of his upbringing. Dad would have seen to it. I think we can be certain of that: Augustine may have sought the guidance, but it would have been Ethelbert who prompted it. It was guidance for an Anglo Saxon culture: Ethelbert's, not Augustine's.

So if you think about it from the point of view of the Christian God and what he says he is like, it would have been gracious, not controlling, of that God to put the fear of God into Eadbald. It would call him back out from under an activated curse. He had known from his youth that what he had done was unacceptable. Which would also explain why he came under conviction there and then: he already knew he was in the wrong.

So, underneath the apparent tall tale, the scourging, the apparent controlling and the instilling of fear, we have grace. To King and Archbishop alike. The hidden hallmark of the Christian God. In most unlikely circumstances for the modern mind. But within the Christian envelope.

Thus it seems to have come to pass that King Eadbald of Kent, wilful in the flesh, morphed into the underrated King Eadbald, shrewd by the Spirit of the Christian God.

Open Heaven, but within a very different world to this one. A world to be appraised on its own Christian terms, perhaps, if you want to come to grips with it.

St Augustine the Demon Scorcher

We're back with St Augustine of Canterbury. And with scorch marks again.

St Augustine is a much-disrespected man. We've already covered some of the reasons. There is another. When his team set out from Rome for Kent in 596, they got part way but were overcome with fear of the dangers ahead. Augustine returned to Rome. Pope Gregory gave him a ticking off and sent the team back on their way. You can see this in children's books in Augustine's old cathedral of Canterbury: St Augustine-the-scaredy-cat, as it were.

I wonder. Perhaps Augustine and his team were right to be scared. A couple of points:

- Pope Gregory had failed to equip them with the paperwork, the first time round, for calling on Frankish help en route. Second time round, they had it, and they were going to need it.

- As I understand it, they took a different route the second time round. Perhaps they had been right: I have read informed speculation that the original route had killer brigands in its path. More to the point, however, as I understand it, each route, first and second, took Augustine via the island monastery of Lerins. This monastery is where, as you will see later, the Anointing on St Martin of Tours had gone and where St Patrick had been spiritually empowered, too, as you will also see later. When Augustine arrived at Canterbury, he seems to have had a portion of the old powers of St Martin. I speculate that the first time round, Augustine's eyes were opened to the Martinian Anointing at Lerins. The second time round, he received it.

So I do wonder: perhaps the Christian God fulfilled his principle of working things out for good for those called in Christ? Maybe put that in the books for children?

Anyway, to press on, one more strange story, with St Augustine of Canterbury at the heart of it. Again, it restores the vivid spirituality of the times.

It also shows the allegedly staid Latin monk Augustine making with sparky powers similar to those of the more romantic St Patrick.

It was often the custom of the Roman church to set up its places of worship on older pagan idol sites. This was not in order to mingle with paganism. It was in order to declare the victory of Christ over the forces behind the idols. That is why you see some demonic gargoyle heads on some cathedrals. The intention was not to invite the people to worship the demons on display. The demon's head was on display as if it were a literal severed head hung from the walls of a castle after a battle, as might have been done in those days. It represents the spiritual war spoils of Jesus Christ resurrected. The message of the cathedral gargoyle is, "Come inside and worship the one who has defeated me."

Now, before you could begin to worship in a newly dedicated Christian sanctuary established over an idol site, the bishop had to perform a rite of exorcism. He had to expel, in the name of Jesus Christ, the demons associated with the previous idols. It was custom and practice. The thing is, though, in those times it wasn't always just words. It could become more than a rite. You might witness shenanigans as the demons went… get insight into their character… see that Christ's name was stronger.

A most vivid example came with St Augustine of Canterbury. King Ethelbert would have witnessed it and perhaps Eadbald as a child, wide-eyed. It may explain some of Eadbald's speed to come under the Fear of God in later years, as already recounted. It would have been a headline event and recounted in Queen Ethelburgha's formative years. Ethelbert may even have testified about it to other kings. Lost to history, though… airbrushed out…

Here's the story. In Canterbury, within the site of what is now known as St Augustine's Abbey, Augustine dedicated a small chapel to an early Christian, St Pancras. He performed the exorcism rite. It turned out a bit like Gandalf versus the Balrog in *Lord of the Rings*. Maybe the author of that work was drawing on this almost-lost account or others like it. The building of St Pancras was shaken as if by an earthquake. And the departing demon of the idol, so I have read, left a scorch mark on the wall.

St Augustine the scaredy-cat? Or St Augustine the demon scorcher? I don't see why it would not have happened. It was a St Martin-anointing type of thing. It was of the times. It was of the ilk of St Patrick, spiritual descendant of St Martin. It was an out-of-the-ordinary highlight, but not an unknown one. And it was during an epoch that Christians might call "Open Heaven". Jesus Christ himself declared that he saw Satan fall *like lightning* from heaven, so flames and scorch marks *would* be within the Biblical envelope of a Christian exorcism.

I suppose these days we might say, "You can keep St Augustine the demon scorcher, thanks. We like our archbishops genteel, and the only stuff broken by them the communion wafer." Or, "We prefer Saint King Oswald the grace extender." But the two different ways that Christian Identity worked out, demon expelling and grace extending, were symbiotic within the ways that the Christian God seems to have tackled things. You couldn't take out the one without taking out the other.

It is difficult for a modern mind to come to terms with many of these types of phenomena. But they were highlights that actually shaped the real world history. If we want to restore the history, we have to restore the phenomena too. For that reason, I include them but with modern Christian reasoning and explanation of how they fit within principles of the Bible and the revealed character of the Christian God.

King Reasoning with King

Another notable thing – to me, the most "Open Heaven" wonder of them all – is that kings reasoned with kings to give up idolatry. Probably Ethelbert with Raedwald. And more successfully, Edwin with Eorpwald; Anna with Cenwalh; and as we shall see soon, Oswy, once he had become the King of Northumbria, with the King of London, another and different Sigeberht.

Firstly, note the word *reasoned*. When there is reference in some modern commentary to turning from idolatry when persuaded by a Christian king, there can also be an implication of oppressive force used on the pagan king. Now, a Christian *is* allowed to be forceful: the Christ commended it. If you actually read his life, rather than settling for caricature spin on it, Baby Jesus burst out of the straps that kept him in his cradle. He grew up to be Jesus Christ the Forceful. However, he always reasoned. And the model he set was that he never oppressed. Neither, I should say, did Christian king oppress newly Christian king in this period. I should say that if anyone oppressed, it was pagan King Penda of Mercia, not the Christian kings. In a later chapter, I will deal with an exception in Wessex, a rogue king, another and different Caedwalla. He became a curse on Christian Wessex for four generations following the way he dealt with what we now call the Isle of Wight. We will come to that.

For now, and to note, king *reasoned* with king. Apparently, the Christian kings preferred that to the sword. Boring. Poor TV. That is the history, though.

Secondly, we need to dispense with another standard modern assumption: that rulers would have taken on a nominal label of Christian purely for political reasons. That might have happened in later centuries. But not the earlier ones. That standard assumption allows us to disregard the many transformative implications of Christian Identity, lob them into the box marked "Religion" and move smartly on.

However, to get more balance than that, to open our Second Eye to the history, we would do well, instead, to enquire into Anglo Saxon idolatry or, more to the point, what a king would understand to be at stake in turning from it. In the world that then was, to give up idols would be a major step to change of Identity.

Now, let's join up some dots. The leaders in suppressing idolatry were Northumbria, Kent and East Anglia. The chief civilising kingdoms of the epoch were... Northumbria, Kent and East Anglia. I would suggest it is not a coincidence. It is related. As they abandoned their idols, it was a transformation of spiritual Identity. And this particular change, a Christian one, had this effect: it civilised. It gradually turned the Anglo Saxons into the Early English.

But how? Why? Well, that which is genuine in Christian Life has always promoted civilisation. However, the Anglo Saxon version of idolatry seems to have been integrated with cultural values which held the people back. Long history has intuitively ascribed the title "Dark Ages" to the Anglo Saxon times of idolatry. I know the title has the technical meaning of "little documented". But it also has a commonly accepted shiver of recognition of darkness in it, too. If we once allow ourselves to enter the spiritual understanding of those times, we can come to terms with the shiver. So let's do that. Here now, in modern language, is the Christian insight of the ancient kings. The English had this understanding for more than a thousand years up to the Great War, 1914-18. Here is why kings and clerics sought to ban idolatry.

Idols can have a spiritual force behind them arising from the demonic realm. When you worship an idol, you unintentionally invoke a dangerous feature of a hidden spiritual legal system. The demonic is well versed in it. The human being is ignorant of it. But ignorance, as in ignorance of any law, is no defence. And these beings have no concept of mercy. The danger is as follows. If you worship idols, you risk activating a mysterious entitlement within the system: the spiritual beings associated with the idols gain the right to cross over from their realm to yours. And some of them might mess with you.

Now, I mentioned this hidden legal system earlier in the chapter. The first work of Christ on the Cross was to redeem us out of the jurisdiction of its court. However, if a person does not take advantage of that redemptive work by receiving Jesus as the Christ, the Christian understanding is that the person remains subject to it. And to whatever the demon of the idol wants to infiltrate into their life.

It might not be a modern understanding. But it was the time-honoured one of many generations.

The Christian Bible is extremely forceful against occultism and idolatry. The Christian God reckons these beings are real. He reckons that they also intend harm. And he perceives them to have entitlement in court. Therefore, for our good, and not because he is a crotchety old repressor, this Christian God does not want us conceding rights to spiritual beings to mess with us. So determined has he been in real world history to put a stop to the powers of this court that this Christian God says that he actually paid with his own blood to redeem us out of its entitlements.

Well, strange to the modern mind. But that was the understanding of Christian rulers in those times. Idols have demons, and if you worship the idols, the demons have rights. That was the understanding of every stream of Christian Life which came to the Anglo Saxons. It would have become the understanding of kings when they converted to Christian Identity and submitted to Christian discipleship: idols hurt your people.

It matters to recover this lost understanding of idols and what was at stake. Until we do, we tend to judge the ancients by modern standards and find them wanting. But within their own standards, there may be things for us to learn. Take, for example, King Eorcenberht of Kent, Eadbald's son, Ethelbert and Bertha's grandson. He was the King of Kent from about 640, into whose Roman Catholic Christian spine the East Anglian Queen Seaxburh inserted a Martinian Christian rod. He banned idols and imposed penalties. How will we see him today? "Religious, misguided; we are superior beings now"? "Crotchety old repressor – throw off the restraints"?

Well, the Christian Bible does say that without powers of Christian revelation, the peoples do throw off restraint. And in the process become subject to beings that mess with them. So here is an alternative view, one with some Christian revelation: Eorcenberht would have been a Christian enlightened by the Holy Spirit of the Christian God. With spiritual insight and with the Christian God's own understanding. And out of that, he acted as a carer for the well-being of his people.

We could see Eorcenberht like that. But there is a real risk that the modern mind would see him as follows: "Huh, deprived his people of their human rights. And didn't fight with anyone – boring. Omit from the history books." But Eorcenberht and kings like him shaped the founding history of the English. We have to recover and come to terms with his Christian understanding if we are to see our history whole. Because Eorcenberht's Christian spirituality with regard to idols is what passed into the Early English. It remained in the English until the Great War, 1914-18.

This implication of Christian Identity – deliverance from the oppression of demonic powers – really mattered to the Early English kings. As they *reasoned* together about idols, they had in view the spiritual liberation of their peoples. As their peoples turned to Christian Identity and gave up idols, they civilised. That is why I take king reasoning with king over the implications of idolatry to be a chief wonder of its times. It is kings, not clerics, who make the decrees that shape national history. It is not controlling churches that do that: it is rulers. Few decrees have shaped English Identity more than those which stopped idol worship. Because the ultimate effect was not just to change the religious label of a people group; it re-shaped their civilisation and brought light into it. I would see that as a stand-out wonder in times of "Open Heaven".

Now, I know that some people still practised idolatry, lurking in the forests. But so what? Spiritual things take many generations to mature. Slowly, idolatry faded out. A brand new course was set in the transformative Christian Awakening of the Early English: civilisation.

History was more than we imagine

I return to Birinus walking on the sea. The account was given long after. However, I think we should not toe the line with an approach to English history that makes no allowance for phenomena within it that have arisen in times of Christian Awakening. When we cut Christian understanding out of the history of a nation which had Christian Identity for more than a thousand years, we diminish our capacity to understand the history of that nation. There have always been phenomena in times of Christian Awakening, integral with events that turn out to be history-shaping. We should weigh them up on their own merits within the envelope of the Christian worldview, not dismiss them out of a purely secular one. That way, we can see history with two eyes, not one.

I would see it like this: the veneer of Anglo Saxon history was who did what to whom and when and for what gain. But the substance of Early English history was uniting around Christian Identity towards civilisation. If you want to restore the substance of English history to the modern English, you have to apply a discerning Christian understanding within it. Dismissing it all as "Religion" would be the worst form of what I believe is called these days, in other contexts, cultural appropriation. Put another way, secular writing that omits the vibrant Christian dimension of Early English history, or calls it "Religion", making no effort to discern within it, deserves to be seen as another form of what I believe is called "blacking up".

In a Christian understanding, English history was much more than we conventionally assume. So just think of that Christian dimension: much of what is now the United Kingdom was under what Christians would call an Open Heaven, notwithstanding a land-based economy, a warrior culture, a lack of medicine and enslaving bands, when the Christian rootstock was being planted and the English Identity took its first baby steps into the world.

The many Christian phenomena were not the regrettable tall tales of ancients who were dimmer than wot we are. They were part of the world of ancients who encountered a different spiritual realm from wot we do. They fitted with the Christian Bible, too.

We can move back to the narrative now. Christian Identity emerging from the Nursery, the Early English learning to Toddle with it.

CHAPTER 15.

Toddling – 650s to 663

This chapter is mainly focussed on Mercia and King Penda. You can think of Mercia as broadly the Midlands of what later became England.

There will be a couple of other highlights regarding (i) Christian Identity coming to the East Saxons (i.e. London) and (ii) a much-overlooked appointment to Canterbury, Archbishop Deusdedit. These two highlights occurred in the year 655.

It was also in 655 that the decisive battle took place in the conflict between Mercian pagan King Penda and Northumbrian Christian King Oswy. Mercia adopted Christian Identity after that. Once it did so, the gates were opened wide for all the Anglo Saxon people groups to be transformed into Christian Identity.

So, London, Canterbury, Northumbria, Mercia: the year 655 brought significant moments in the history of each. It was a watershed year in the more general history of the Early English.

Kent, East Anglia, Wessex, Northumbria

Before we turn to Mercia, and how it adopted Christian Identity in dramatic circumstances, how were the existing Christian kingdoms getting on with Christian Identity? You could say that they were Toddling in it, each in their different ways.

- Kent was, well, Kent. Boring, wise, stable. Its Christian educational capabilities were developing. King Eorcenberht and Queen Seaxburh had strong Christian Life. The Christian Identity was slowly permeating the people. You could see Kent like this as a Toddler: an easily instructed type of Christian child. Steady on its feet, as well.

- <u>East Anglia</u> had much harassment from King Penda of Mercia. King Anna had taken the throne with Northumbrian help. As part of the more general Mercia versus Northumbria conflict, King Anna was a target. Guerrilla warfare and much hiding was his lot. One of his brothers, pagan, was plotting to ally with King Penda as well. The Christian clerics and monks, however, were embedded and making steady progress with spreading and educating a Christian Identity. You could see East Anglia like this as a Toddler: a gifted type of Christian child, but from a threatened home. Swift on its feet.

- <u>Wessex</u> was ever so slow on the uptake. Who would have dreamt it would become the chief of the kingdoms and the most devotedly Christian? King Cenwalh was not getting on at all with the person he had appointed as Bishop, named Agilbert. Scholarship progress was being made amongst clerics and monks, but the kingdom itself was internally unstable. You could see Wessex like this as a Toddler: a slow learner type of Christian child. Not always listening. Prone to fall over.

- <u>Northumbria</u> was much harassed by King Penda of Mercia. King Oswy was serious about Christian Life but in need of restoration to good standing in it following the murder of King Oswine of Deira in 651. I will deal with that in the next chapter, "Loss of Innocence". Oswy's children were serious about Christian Life, too. And his marriage and kingdom were serious about Christian Life. But all of them, children, marriage and kingdom, were divided in its expression. We will also cover that in the next chapter.

A young man named Wilfrid was on the rise, a most gifted man. He would become Bishop Wilfrid of York: brilliant and partisan for Roman church ways versus Gaelic ones. Of him, more in later chapters. However, the inner Gaelic Martinian Christian Life of Northumbria remained dynamic. St Aidan passed away in 651, but he had trained a team of sparky Christians. His spiritual successor, St Cuthbert, was in monastery training in the early 650s.

In later years, Cuthbert and Wilfrid would exist side by side. Wilfrid would become a Colossus of Northern churchmanship. Cuthbert would step aside, give him the field. But Cuthbert would become the Colossus of not just Northern Christian Spirituality but also Early English Christian spirituality. These patterns were on the rise by 655.

So, Northumbria was more than Toddling with its Christian Identity; it was running and jumping. However, Northumbria, the gifted Christian child, you might say, had also stumbled badly. And it was becoming a house divided on the inside and threatened from the outside.

Summary – Mercia Adopts Christian Identity

The story of how Mercia came to Christian Identity is complex. I will set out a summary before going into detail.

- Mercia was set on a course of military dominion. The resolutely pagan King Penda of Mercia harassed Christian King Oswy of Northumbria.

- If you recall, in King Oswald's time, he had sealed a peace treaty with Britonnic Rheged (Cumbria) by marrying brother Oswy to Rhiainfellt of Rheged. There were two children, Princess Alhflaed and Prince Alhfrith. On maturity, they married children of King Penda. Alhfrith married Princess Cyneburh. Alhflaed married Prince Peada.

- Early in the 650s, Prince Peada, Penda's son, wanted Oswy's daughter, Princess Alhflaed, in marriage. King Oswy would only let Peada marry his daughter if he submitted to Christian baptism.

- Peada agreed to be baptised as a Christian. He would have been prepared for it by St Aidan's Martinian Christian team – nothing nominal about the Christian in them. Such was their impact that Peada said that he would adopt Christian Identity even if Alhflaed were to be denied to him.

- King Penda may have seen all this as Oswy subverting his son. He forced a decisive battle with King Oswy in 655. A most unlikely result occurred. Oswy won. Penda was slain. Oswy probably couldn't believe it. Only a short time before, he may have offered the biggest wealth tribute in Anglo Saxon history to keep Penda at bay.

- When Penda died, his son Peada already had sub-king status in Mercia. Oswy re-affirmed and increased it but took the overlordship of Mercia.

- Oswy sent the Martinian Christian saints marching into Mercia. Mercia received them happily. It never sought to throw them out despite later political ructions in which Peada was murdered and Oswy's rule overthrown. Christian Identity was taken hold of with both hands, and they took care to integrate it into the Mercian sense of Identity.

With Penda gone, the road to Christian Identity became safer for the Early English as a whole. However, Mercia's initiation into Christian Identity was highly politicised from the outset. And Mercia, more than any of the other kingdoms, gradually turned the politicisation of Christian Identity into an art form. It is not so much that it lost innocence as that it was never innocent from the start. You could say that as from 655, Mercia adapted very quickly to Christian Identity; it was an intelligent child, but it tried to run with the Identity before it could walk in it. It was given to domineering and somehow never quite listened to Nanny's Christian Message about that.

Now, to more detail.

Formation of Mercia

We had better understand a difference in the early 600s between Mercians and Mercia. Mercians were one of many invading people groups which made their way to what we now call the Midlands of England. Penda was a Mercian. Although his name possibly implies unrecorded family intermarriage with Celtic North Wales, he seems to have identified as an Anglo Saxon. People groups contiguous with the Mercians included those called Lindsey, in what is now Lincolnshire; they seem to have been a co-existing mixture of Briton and Germanic Invader. There were also the Middle Saxons, in broadly the counties adjacent to the north of London. The Hwicce were along the Severn Valley, and there were a number of other smaller people groups too. Mercians were central to them all and adjacent to Britonnic peoples in what we now call North Wales. They had also had, in the ancient continental homeland, the most prestigious ancestry of any of the Anglo Saxon tribes.

During Penda's lifetime, by force of his might and prestige of his ancestry and through deeper spiritual affinities, the various Germanic ancestry groups – Mercians, Lindsey, Hwicce, Middle Saxons and a few others – merged into the one federation or loose Kingdom of Mercia. The affinities that brought the groups together have been lost to formal history. However, a map of the various territories by spirituality shows you the obvious affinity. With the exception of Lindsey and Hwicce, which seem to have been semi-pagan semi-Christian (Britonnic root), Mercia became a federation of those that retained the old Germanic paganism. It seems to have unwittingly formed its Identity in opposition to those that had embraced the Martinian version of Christian Life, namely, Northumbria, East Anglia, Wessex and Kent.

Here I partially repeat the maps used in the chapter "Christian Identity in the Nursery".

Mercians began as an invading People Group in the late 500's.

Mercia was the federation or loose Kingdom which King Penda formed in the 600's out of adjacent People Groups including Lindsey, Middle Angles, Middle Saxons, Hwicce and a few other smaller ones

People Group Relations & Nuances of Mercia vs Northumbria

Mercians were basically Angles, perhaps some Britonnic mixed in. Back in the Anglian origin-lands in the north of Germany the Mercian King had been the Chief Anglian King. So they resented those upstart Northern Angles of Northumbria.

Martinian = Gaelic version of the Christian spirituality of St Martin of Tours which emerged out of Gaul, mainly after 410.

Britonnic = older Celtic Christian way derived out of the old Roman Empire from 177 to about 410.

North Wales Britonnic Celtic Christians allied with pagan Mercian Anglo Saxons in common cause against Martinian or Romano Martinian Christian Anglo Saxons.

Mercian federation came out of the pagan people groups & semi pagan semi Christian (Britonnic root) Lindsey and Hwicce

Spiritual Influences In People Groups to 655

Mixed = Britonnic Christian stream mingled with Martinian (Rheged) or pagan (Lindsey, Hwicce)

Romano Martinian – except Deira, was sourced from elements of the Frankish Church that had a version of the Martinian Christian Spirituality as reinforced by the Irish Pict, St Columbanus. In Deira – Augustine & Paulinus's Roman missions became reinforced with Gaelic Martinian spirituality.

Political alliances or hostilities up to 655 mapped on to the underlying commonalities or differences of Spirituality, and the senses of Identity built on that

1
4

King Penda of Mercia relentlessly harassed Northumbria in the early 650s. I think there is a clue as to why, in addition to the difference in spirituality. It harks back to the Germanic lands before the migrations. You may recall that families were defined as royal by tracing a lineage back to the god Woden. Some were more royal than others. In the homelands, Mercians were the most royal; were the most looked up to; received the most tribute; held the highest honour; and honour was in war. So Mercians had a rooted sense of entitlement, which they fed by war.

In what we now call England, however, the Mercians had been latecomers. The East Angles had settled before them. And their new Christian spirituality would have led them to turn away from the old world of Woden and, therefore, away from acknowledging Mercian entitlement. As to the Northern Angles, i.e. Northumbrians, insufferable: not acknowledging Mercian entitlement *and* throwing their weight about. For example, always trying to spread their big feet into neighbouring Lindsey. Take them down...

For Lindsey, it was most likely a choice of who to dislike less out Mercia or Northumbria. It seems to have hated Northumbria more. It is notable that it had an element of Christian Life which Paulinus had been seeking to regenerate by 632, before the death of King Edwin of Northumbria. Some element of that may have mingled with older Britonnic Christian roots. But Lindsey's aristocracy leaned towards Mercia, resenting the domination which Northumbria kept imposing on it.

I should say here that just because the Northumbrians had become Christian, it did not follow that they drew back into their own territory to lie down like doormats and await the next conquering power to come along. They were of the ancient understanding of a land-based economy: if you are supine within that, your own people will perish. So the Christian Northumbrians did throw their weight around. It was the system. The options were all worse. However, for King Penda, no way were they going to get away with it.

It is important to note that quite a lot of Penda's power was founded on military alliance with neighbouring Britonnic Christian Celts in what we now call North Wales. He may have had an element of blood descent from them. He died on the day they left him without their support in battle. I mention this because it flatly contradicts the traditional notion that evil Anglo Saxons steamrollered innocent Celts. The pagan Anglo Saxon Penda, in league with Britonnic Christian Celts, steamrollered Martinian Christian Anglo Saxons.

Leading up to the Battle of Winwaed 655

The Battle of Winwaed, 655, was a defining military climax: the Big Two, Mercia versus Northumbria, Penda versus Oswy. Mercia had become much the stronger in military might. Northumbria had become much the stronger in Christian spirituality.

By 655, King Penda was the military Colossus of the Anglo Saxon people groups. He had also become a serial killer of Christian Kings: Edwin of Northumbria, Sigeberht of East Anglia, Oswald of Northumbria, Anna of East Anglia. His chief motive was The Glory of Mercia. However, he had become boastful about the slayings too. His dismemberment of Oswald's body was the triumph of his gods and a direct challenge to the Christian one.

By 655, Penda wanted Christian Oswy's notch on his belt as well. He had been harassing him for years. He may have taken a huge bribe of tribute money in a subduing campaign in the north not long before. We can infer that he had also been engaging in intrigues:

- The successor to King Anna was a pagan brother, Aethelhere. He took the throne of East Anglia when Penda finally cornered and slew the Christian King Anna in 654. Aethelhere then joined forces with Penda in 655 against Oswy. One would infer some plotting and for some time.

- The son of King Oswald through his marriage to Cyneburh of Wessex was named Oethelwald. He allied with Penda to overthrow Oswy in 655. One would infer more plotting, perhaps the promise of puppet kingship on the Northumbrian throne. Good job Oswald's legacies were spiritual...

However, Penda's own family were reading a different playbook. Prince Peada, sub-king of the Middle Angles, wanted to take Oswy's daughter by

Rhiainfellt of Rheged, Alhflaed, in marriage. It seems that Oswy's son by Rhiainfellt, Alhfrith, had also married a daughter of Penda, another and different Cyneburh. Now, concerning marriage between the children although the fathers are at war, the old-fashioned Anglo Saxon way was fine with it. You just didn't let it get in the way of the fighting.

But Peada was prepared to go further than the old-fashioned way. He was willing to take on Alhflaed's Christian God as well. Bede credits the brother-in-law, Prince Alhfrith, with persuading him. Family relationships are always complex, but one would imagine Alhflaed herself had a word. Anyway, King Oswy insisted that Peada must adopt Christian Identity before he would consent to the marriage. That was a firmer condition than the old Bertha/Ethelburgha arrangement, i.e. that the Queen must be allowed to maintain her Christian faith.

Various motives are attributed to Oswy, but no-one really knows. You can be purely cynical: Oswy's cunning streak – steal Peada from under his father Penda's nose from one Identity into another. Or you can even be unfashionably trusting: Oswy really cared about promoting Christian Identity and to double-safeguard it in his daughter. Given Oswy's general life, the truth would most likely be in the middle. Oswy had a crafty streak. And he was sincere about Christian Identity in his daughter.

Bede does take care to say that the Christian message was explained carefully to Peada. His response was that he would become a Christian even if he were denied the hand of Alhflaed. I see no reason to doubt that. Prince Alhfrith may have been a decisive influence, but we have to remember who would have given this Christian baptismal teaching to Peada: the Gaelic Martinian Christians trained by St Aidan. Peada's teachers would have been the Anointed brigade. There was no nominalism of Christian Identity with them. The Christian Life in them would have been sparky, very sparky. I see no reason why Peada would not have genuinely wanted what was in them.

So, Peada was baptised. And not in a nominal way. The question would be how would his father, King Penda, react to that? The right arm of his Mercian power had already dismembered Oswald's right arm of Northumbrian power: in battle, man to man, the approved way. Now this, behind his back? Bede tells us that Penda would tolerate the Christian message in his kingdom, but he had no time for it personally. As we saw previously, he may have had a garbled witness to it. As to his children... they had their own lives. One imagines the old warrior rolling his eyes. But as for crafty Oswy infiltrating his many times already defeated and rather wet God into them... that was going too far.

That is my surmise. No-one knows. But it explains a lot because, not long after a triumphant campaign which had already intimidated Oswy, Penda went hastily on campaign again. This time, not to subdue. This time, to kill. Something made it personal. I would infer it was Oswy's infiltration of his Christian God into his family. Penda decided to settle things with Oswy once and for all.

The Battle Of Winwaed 655 – Nation Building Event Number Three

Penda forced a battle. The location of Winwaed was somewhere near the city now called Leeds. He had his own troops and three other forces as allies. One was from Britonnic Celtic North Wales. This alliance had long been a secret of Penda's success. Another was from East Anglia, led by Aethelhere, that pagan brother of the slain Christian King Anna. A third was led by Oethelwald, son of Oswy's brother, the late Saint King Oswald, allying now with his own father's dismemberer. He had become sub-king of Deira in 651, but it seems that this was not enough. One can infer that he wanted Penda's help to take the whole Northumbrian throne occupied by Oswy's sons. Or maybe he just hated crafty Oswy, of whose complex court more in the next chapter, or was in some way under the protection of King Penda. Perhaps it was some of all of those. Bede accords Oethelwald respect as a sincere Christian. But it is difficult for a Christian understanding to discern any guiding hand of the Christian God.

Anyway, Oswy was desperate, having no choice but to fight. He was expected to lose. His older brother, Saint King Oswald, had prayed the most noble prayers before the Battle at Heavenfield in 635. Now Oswy, in a semi-pagan way, offered various eve-of-battle bribes to the Christian God in 655. We can expect the revealed character of the Christian God to have turned a deaf ear. However, Oswy did at least pray his heart out. And we will see in the next chapter, when I spend a lot of time on Oswy, how the Christian God really would have responded in the light of the character and powers that he reveals himself to have.

For now, to keep it simple, it went like this: Oswy won the Battle of Winwaed 655.

Penda's allies from Britonnic North Wales withdrew after Oswy prayed. Either they already had all the tribute they needed from the recent campaign in the north, or they were tired of fighting. On the day, Oethelwald, son of Oswald, also stood aside. His forces did not join in. One can only imagine the conflict in the young man. Aethelhere of East Anglia was slain. His kingdom reverted to a Christian brother of Anna.

Penda himself was rash. The combination of personal enmity to Oswy and ingrained habit of warrior fury caused him to fall on Oswy's forces in a storm that could not be sustained. He lost, for the first time since King Edwin of Northumbria had won the field when Penda had been allied with Wessex in 626.

It was a watershed moment in the whole of Early English history. After 655, nothing could stop the Anglo Saxon people groups, two steps forward one step back, the pattern recurring, from becoming the unified Christian Early English. For this reason, like many, I call this Battle a Nation-Building Event. For me, number 3 of those in the period.

Of Oethelwald son of Oswald, sub-king of Deira, I have found as yet no record of what befell him. Alhfrith, son of Oswy by Rhiainfellt, was often a great annoyer of his father. However, he stood by Oswy in the battle. He was given the Deiran sub-crown instead.

Oswy also honoured the promises he'd made to the Christian God before the battle. These included giving over an infant daughter named Aelflaed to monastic life. She later oversaw the famous establishment at Whitby. Today it is a much-visited and evocative ruin. In those times, it was also in a group of monasteries which harboured a young man named Caedmon. He became the first great Anointed "singer-in-the-Spirit" of the Christian proto-English. He has successors all over the modern world today. The English language developed as he rang out praises to the Christian God. That is the culture which Aelflaed was given to share during her life. We can stress her deprivation. Or we can stress her privilege. Or both. You choose.

As to King Penda of Mercia, the decapitator was decapitated. Who lives by the sword will die by the sword, Jesus Christ once said. And the measure you give to others comes back to you; the Christ taught that as well. In a Christian understanding, the Christian God is very slow and patient in allowing those principles to prevail. Note that they are not active judgements: they are *principles* of judgement baked into things. They are principles that grind exceeding slow but also grind exceeding fine. Sometimes they only come into play after death when, within a Christian understanding, the one who may be dead to us remains alive to the Christian God – and to the justice due to them.

In Penda's case, the principles would seem to have prevailed in life. Mind you, he had a whole generation to stride the stage. Time after time in that period, the Christian God extended grace, replying to provocation by increasing the Christian Life in the peoples whose kings Penda put to the sword and, from 655, in Penda's own people.

We will appraise King Penda more fully later in this chapter. For now, to continue the narrative.

Christian Identity Comes to Mercia

King Oswy made himself over-king of Mercia in 655. He affirmed Peada as sub-king of the southern parts of Mercia and directly ruled the northern parts himself.

There now fell to Oswy a decision: what revenge to take on the Mercia that had harassed him, despoiled his people and their property, and possibly taken from him record-breaking tribute.

It was his finest hour. Oswy sent the Martinian saints marching in, secure under his authority. How very non-Anglo Saxon. The sparky Christian Life of Gaelic Martinian Christian Iona *had* been real in him, then. Something of St Patrick's grace-extending Christian spirituality found expression in him. The example of his epically heroic brother, Saint King Oswald, extender of Christian grace to Assassin Wessex, *had* been noted and acted upon. How very Early English.

There would have been a political motive for Oswy: Christianise the enemy. But that does not disqualify Christian integrity. If anything, we can discern Christian Wisdom: what's not to like about infiltrating peace?

Now, a conventional commentary might appraise the Battle of Winwaed as that alone which removed the chief obstacle in the way of the Anglo Saxons uniting into the Christian English. However, we might think more carefully. There is something else to add in. Indeed, the Battle closed down an older Germanic way of life. But it was the *Christian decision* of Oswy afterwards to send in the saints which paved the way forward to the new English Identity, not just the battle. Because it was around the Christian Identity that the peoples united to become the English. So you could say that by extending Christian grace instead of revenge, King Oswy shaped real world history from 655 and for centuries to come. Because you see, from 655, proud Mercia – the most militarily dominant of the powers and the centre piece of the jigsaw that interlocked many people groups – now took hold of the new Christian Identity with both hands. And they became very serious children with regard to embedding it and spreading it.

Mercia's way forward

We should note in passing here that, yet again, in Alhfrith and Peada, one royal prince had persuaded another royal prince to adopt Christian Identity. It was something the leaders wanted. It was not just a churchy thing, or a nominal label type of thing. It was a commonly held shaping thing for their proto-states, taught by dynamic monks who had sacrificed all normal comforts for their Christian God.

Anyway, from 655, Mercia took hold of Christian Identity with both hands. It was a fusion in Christian terms. The outward ways of the Roman church were favoured by both Prince Peada and his Northumbrian influencer, Prince Alhfrith. The missionaries given to Mercia, however, although mainly ethnic Angle-ish, were steeped in the sparky spirituality that came from the Martinian Christian Life as mediated by the Gaelic Scots. And the bishops that followed through later were to be of the strong and sparky fusion Christian Identity of Deiran Northumbria – legacies from Paulinus, St Aidan and his team, and James the Deacon: strong Christian gifting within the urbane Roman Catholic shell.

As time went by, Mercia would eventually lose much of the spark. Before that, however, it would become even more eclectic in its Christian contents. It would absorb the sparkily Romano Martinian Christian territory of East Anglia. That never recovered its military strength after the slaying of King Anna. Mercia would also integrate Kent's longer-established Romano Martinian Catholic Christian fusion and, with that, the top clerical appointment of them all at Canterbury. From both kingdoms, it also absorbed significant educational prowess.

So Mercia took in and spread the Fusion which became the Christian Identity of the Early English: Romano Martinian Gaelic Catholic. But it would never cease to politicise Christian ways for the Glory of Mercia as well.

For example, there was a subtle but deep difference between the Mercian Christian way and the Christian way that would develop in the family of Alfred the Great of Wessex. We can compare and contrast Mercia's later and greatest king, King Offa, 757-796. Offa seems to have been favourable to Christian Identity as a badge of civilisation and a political tool, but it took second place to the Glory of Mercia. Alfred's family felt called to protect and develop the polity of Wessex and the growing English sense of Identity, but that took second place to Christian sincerity. It was Wessex that ultimately prevailed. In the real world. Interesting.

However, we should note that Mercian Christian Identity originated in the times after the transformative Christian Awakening had been at the height of its spirituality. It developed in consolidatory and less innocent times. Wessex was birthed into Christian Identity with Saint King Oswald, lightning rod of the Christian God, replicator of Christ patterns. Wessex never ceased to cherish that root. Alfred the Great's family elevated it to the highest place in their culture. Mercia, however, was birthed into Christian Identity with crafty King Oswy. A more ambivalent man. A Christian and a Politician, capital P.

Roots shape the plant. Well, the Christian ones do, anyway. So it would seem.

Peada Murdered, Oswy overthrown, forward with King Wulfhere

As at 655, Oswy had the Mercian over-throne, with Peada his main sub-king. That meant that Peada would be seen by the Mercian court as a Northumbrian stooge. They murdered Peada within a year, in 656. In 658, they overthrew Oswy's rule as well. On the throne they set Wulfhere, Peada's brother, one of their own.

It was a very tense time. However, the Mercians did not overthrow the chain of Christian leaders which had been introduced into Mercia by Oswy. And out of that chain, in 658, emerged another bishop who just so happened to be exactly the right person in the right place at the right time. His name was Trumhere. He had the confidence of King Wulfhere and of King Oswy. He was a Fusion Christian. He was from Deira, the Yorkshire part of Northumbria, and a relative of Queen Eanflaed, once a refugee in Kent. Trumhere was of the Roman Catholic outward forms that were favoured in Deira and in Mercia. However, the contents of the container included the Celtic Martinian Christian spirituality which was beloved of King Oswy and winning friends and influencing people in Mercia. An urbane outward Roman shell – much respected – and a sparky interior – much wanted.

Anyway, Bishop Trumhere built bridges of shared Christian spirituality to keep the powers uneasily at peace. So did other successors. And as we shall see later, in 679 the great Archbishop Theodore would walk on these bridges of common Christian Identity to seal the deal.

As to Oswy in 658, he had the sense to know that he could not hang on to over-kingship of Mercia. He backed down. Perhaps that came out of the wisdom of his Christian God. Oswy turned out to have held power just long enough to ensure that Mercia would embed the new Christian seed and let it grow.

As to King Wulfhere, the little-remarked thing was his marriage. Militarily, he was Mercia through and through, his father Penda's son. One of a long line of formidable warriors building the Mercian prestige. That sort of thing is much noted in the histories. But we should also look at his marriage. Little noted. But another Kentish Christian corker.

Wulfhere had married Eormenhild of Kent, a daughter of the strongly Christian King and Queen of Kent, Eorcenberht and Seaxburh. Little is known of Eormenhild. But in the previous chapter, we already inferred sparky Christian Life in her parents and her sister, Eorcengota. We can assume that Eormenhild carried on the tradition of great-grandmother Bertha, great aunt Ethelburgha, older cousin Eanflaed and mother Seaxburh and inserted a strong Christian rod in the royal spine. Wulfhere did behave like it. He was a warrior like his father Penda and devoted to the Glory of Mercia. But he took great care to make and receive good bishop appointments and Anointed Christian mission into Mercia.

Anyway, this was the peaceful way that the Kentish Christian wisdom infiltrated the Mercian powerhouse. In the next generation, after the Kentish royals had lost their Christian wisdom, things became less happy between Mercia and Kent. But in the times when Mercia Toddled into Christian

Identity, there was the Kentish Christian wisdom in the ruling family to help hold it steady.

After Bishop Trumhere passed away in 662, he was succeeded by Bishop Jaruman. In those days, Mercia was absorbing Essex/London. When London began to fall away from Christian Identity in 664, King Wulfhere sent Jaruman in to fix it. That is how seriously the Mercian kings began to take the promotion of Christian Identity as the foundation of their emerging state as it grew. Quite a change: in 654, pagan London was in the orbit of Penda's pagan Mercia, but in 664, post-Penda Christian Mercia was making sure London retained the Christian Identity.

Appraising King Penda of Mercia

King Penda was Old School. I think he could meaningfully be titled "The Last of the Anglo Saxons". I know that is contrary to all conventional labelling, but I think it is fair. I think we should rethink all our labelling rather than dismiss it. I do not mean it literally. I mean it in the sense that his demise was a watershed moment: after it, the demise of the old Anglo Saxon Identity became irreversible.

By his lights, Penda was not the pantomime villain of the age. He was not an empire builder in terms of territory. If he subdued a territory, it was for tribute and the honour of Anglo Saxon Mercia. But as long as they gave first place to Mercians, he let the other Anglo Saxon people groups keep their own Anglo Saxon place. It was proto-colonial. And it was proud. But it was according to his lights. However, it is hard to see Penda as a hero of civilising progress.

Penda did not forbid the Christian message. He had rejected it himself, but I doubt that the Martinian Christian understanding was ever received by him. Within that, all Christians are works in progress to be perfected in their resurrection. But Penda did not know that. He seems to have thrown out the Martinian Christian baby with the wet Britonnic Pelagian bathwater. Penda rejected the Christian message on account of those who fell short and were hypocrites.

By his lights, Penda was not a hypocrite. What you saw was what you got. There can be little doubt that he got high on victory and on taking tribute. But I don't think he was driven by greed for tribute, nor by a set desire to slay Christian kings. I think he wanted a reset to the older Germanic culture which the Christian one threatened: the people groups in their places, with Mercia the top dog as it had been in the old Germanic lands and in high standing with Woden. Material things were a byproduct; honour was key, and honour was in war. This fostered a certain pride. He would look down on those who, like Oswy, would not readily man up for war with him.

However, as we have seen already, in the process of asserting the Glory of Mercia, Penda became a serial slayer of Christian kings: Edwin of Northumbria; Sigeberht of East Anglia; Oswald of Northumbria; Anna of East Anglia. And he did boast about it. In the case of Oswald, we should note again what Penda did. He had Oswald's remains dismembered and shown off as a triumph. The intent would have been a type of witness: (i) my gods are stronger than your God; and (ii) behold Oswald's dismembered right arm: my right arm is stronger.

He could, maybe, have got away with it if history was a system closed to the Christian God – or there is no Christian God. But if the system is not closed, and there is that God, and he is who he says he is with the powers he says he has… And if the prayer of a Christian gifted in the prophetic, such as St Aidan, has any real power in it, praying as he did that what Oswald's right arm represented would not decay… well… Penda would have activated the hidden spiritual realm and its courts.

And the Christian God had also been issued a challenge. Penda to the Christian God, as it were: "My gods are stronger!"

The fashionable modern Christian God might acquiesce. The Biblical one, however – he might reply. In Penda's case, as you will now see, seven times over.

The Seven-Fold Reply of the Christian God

For a being who says he is all-powerful, as the Christian God does, but who also says that he has compassion on us, knowing that we are dust, there are complex principles to take into account when provoked. The Apostle Paul teaches in the New Testament of the Christian Bible that there are circumstances in which the Christian God takes account of the integrity of the likes of Penda within their lights. And besides, the Christian God's revealed character is not one that replies with a kneejerk.

Therefore, we can see that throughout Penda's life, the Christian God, ever patient, seems to have forborne much. He did not reply to Oswald's dismemberment by wiping Penda out. He replied through an unfolding sequence of unstoppable grace. Now, what follows is a hallmark of all hallmarks of the hand of the Christian God in real world history. This is how he really would work when being consistent with his revealed principles:

i.   The successor King to Christian Edwin of Northumbria was Oswald, greater in Christian Life.

ii.   The successor to Christian Sigeberht of the East Angles was King Anna, as strong in Christian Life but militarily the stronger.

iii. Cenwalh of Wessex, driven into exile with King Anna by Penda, was led to Christian Identity by King Anna.

iv.   After King Oswald was killed, Saint King Oswald emerged. Christian Life became stronger, not weaker, in Northumbria. As we saw, the full resurrection pattern of Christ on the cross replicated around Oswald. And what King Oswald's right hand had stood for, his Christian kingship, did not decay... St Aidan's prayer fulfilled.

v.   In the end, Penda's children started to convert from under him.

vi.   Oswald was followed by Oswy, perhaps the more astute one; certainly Penda's nemesis.

vii.   When Oswy finally overpowered Mercia, he did not take vengeance. Instead, he sent the Martinian Christian saints marching in. Mercia took hold of Christian Identity with both hands and spread it.

I make that seven replies. Seven is the Christian Biblical number for perfect, complete. The Christian God to Penda, or so it would seem: "Whose God did you say was the stronger?" It is not exactly a subtly hidden hallmark this time, either. It is a trumpet reply to a trumpet challenge.

An unstoppable wave.

The Christian God to King Penda of Mercia,

And to any unseen powers watching on:

What Penda had stood for – swamped.

Artwork: Ben Emet

Given all of this, it is interesting to see how King Penda is more conventionally appraised these days. The majority view is that he was the great figure of early Anglo Saxon history. Using my definitions, i.e. that "Anglo Saxon" describes the old people groups, but "Early English" describes those people groups uniting around a transformative Christian Identity, it would be fair enough. However, the sense in which it is typically intended is that Penda was *the* great figure of the times. Hmmm… he did lose, actually. What he stood for faded out. That is why I would call him "the Last of the Anglo Saxons." Not literally, but his death was the watershed moment in the process.

However, King Penda was indeed great as the military Colossus of the time and the knitter together of Mercia. And the formation of Mercia was to become a major building block in forming the nation of the English because once it had adopted the fusion Christian Identity that Penda had resisted, it did a good deal to consolidate, systematise and spread it.

Irony

For me, however, by far the most significant thing to address in the life of King Penda of Mercia is *irony*. Few careers can have been more ironic. His sword unintentionally did as much to trigger Christian Identity in the Early English as Saint Aidan, Bishop Birinus and Bishop Felix put together: seven times over, as I have just shown you above.

To understand the ironies, it is time to look at principles of the Christian God again. Three of them. Penda seems to have activated them in the real world history.

1. In all things, God works for the good of those called in Christ's purposes. As we noted earlier, for those called *in Christ's purposes*, and "good" means for the development of Christian Identity as a whole. An individual Christian may perish.

If you leave out the Christian understanding that the perished one would not have actually perished, there is a certain ruthlessness, you may think. The next two are also quite ruthless. The third is even disturbing.

2. The good and the bad must grow together. Jesus Christ taught that only he can sort out the tangle of them and only when he returns. Until then, if you uproot the bad, you will also uproot the good.

How frustrating is that? If God quashes King Penda, he loses all the replies. Well, it was the Christ who taught the principle. In order to reinforce the point, the Apostle Paul added to the teaching. What follows is very uncomfortable. But the Christian understanding would be that it was the Holy Spirit of the Christian God who helped Paul to express it as follows:

3. The Christian God has bound the whole creation over to frustration. It will be so until all Christians have received their resurrection. Until then, all is in bondage to frustration.

Taken together, these three principles can make for great ironies. The Christian God, it would seem, is the hidden author of irony. However, to note carefully: the ironies tend to be activated when human beings seek to bend all things to their own control and self-will.

Here are the typical ironies that arise from 2 and 3. The seeds of fall will be present at the height of your power. The seeds of recovery will be there in your fall. Sometimes, the good you intend will lead to bad; the bad you intend will lead to good. In a Christian understanding, the Christian God will search out and one day judge *the intent*. But until that day, nothing will stop the ironies manifesting.

As a reminder, here are some of the ironies that worked out in the real world history:

(i) No aggression from Penda of Mercia, no Christian conversion for Cenwalh of Wessex. Therefore, no Christian tradition for Alfred the Great of Wessex to restore. Therefore, no England as we know it because Alfred's family did not set out to build England as such; they set out to secure their Christian Identity. England emerged as the after-product.

(ii)   No dismemberment of Saint King Oswald to challenge the Christian God, no increase of grace upon grace from that God to the peoples of Northumbria and Mercia.

Very frustrating for Penda's intentions. Human beings, according to these principles of the Christian God, do not have what they would most crave: control. As to what to do about it, in a Christianised system, the choices are stark. Either commit life to him or shake the fist at him. Maybe try punching him with the fist. But in a Christian understanding, Baby Jesus has grown up to be granite: we will hurt our fist. The Christian Bible is explicit about Jesus Christ: he set his face *like flint* to all accusation and to the cross that would most completely accuse him. Any fist blow that could be landed on the Christian God fell on him then. Resurrected now, he is invulnerable and, in what he declares to be a loving way, ruthless: he will not change these principles of irony and frustration until the time comes for his return. Whatever the cost meanwhile.

Anyway, the point, for now, is this. There can have been few greater examples in human history of bondage to frustration leading to irony upon irony than King Penda of Mercia. Bringing down Christian kings was real life and bloody whack-a-mole for him. He started to boast about it. But every time he whacked a mole, the Christian Life in the mole came back stronger.

Very frustrating. King Penda would appear to have activated these profound and disturbing Biblical principles in real life and ultimately nation-shaping history. Because the Mercia he built with blood, sweat and toil, once harnessed to the Christian Identity he had no time for, did much to spread that Christian Identity through the whole. It had the Martinian Christian spirituality within a Roman Catholic container. That is the spirituality which the family of Alfred the Great would later rescue when all seemed lost. Mercia did a lot to embed it. But it was all very New School. Penda was Old School.

So, the Battle of Winwaed 655: a significant and nation-shaping event during the times when the Early English were Toddling with their Christian Identity, and the climax of one of the most ironic periods in all of human history. But we must remember to add King Oswy's non-vengeful Christian decision after the battle in order to see the history with two eyes. That is what shaped a nation. The battle merely made it possible.

East Saxons – Essex and London from 655

Now, to turn to the territory of the East Saxons, Essex as it became. It sat between the Christian territories of Kent and East Anglia. However, until 655, its loose affiliation was to pagan Mercia. It is noteworthy in that it included what we now call London.

As at 597, when St Augustine arrived at Canterbury, Pope Gregory the Great, thinking of how things had been in the old Britannia, had intended London to be one of two great Archbishoprics, the other being York. However, Augustine had his success at Canterbury, not London. London had received one of his team as a bishop, Mellitus. That would have been under the influence of King Ethelbert of Kent. The King of the East Saxons was a sort of sub-king to the King of Kent. However, reading between the lines, London doesn't seem to have been all that keen. As soon as it could, it reverted to an older god.

Gregory seems to have accepted the reality that Augustine should settle where he was really wanted, which was Canterbury. Augustine, for his part, was acting within the spirit if not the letter of Gregory's original intention. After all, Jesus Christ taught that one should build on spiritual rock, not spiritual sand. As conditions were at 597, Canterbury was rock in Christian terms, London was sand.

The East Saxons seem to have been different in their spiritual heritage to the Anglo Saxon mainstream. Most Anglo Saxons were attached to Woden. As we saw earlier, there was a resonating Christian message for those who were in Woden. Woden was temporary. The Christian God was the permanent God into whom all things in Woden would be subsumed. The Anglo Saxons were generally quick to receive the Christian God when offered the opportunity by sparky messengers.

However, there was no such resonating message in London. The East Saxons seem to have been attached to a more obscure god called Seaxneot or Saxnot. And they proved very sticky about accepting the Christian God instead. However, as at 655, King Oswy of Northumbria was suddenly and unexpectedly ruling the roost. The East Saxons became open to diplomatic overtures from him. And here once again, king *reasoned* with king. Oswy persuaded the King of Essex and London, another and different Sigeberht, to give up idols and adopt Christian Identity. And then, as he did with Mercia, Oswy sent the Celtic saints marching in. Not as an army with metal swords to subjugate; rather an army with spiritual swords, meaning words of the Christian God, to liberate. Well, liberation is how the Christian understanding would have seen it, anyway.

The name of one of the Celtic greats, St Chad, later to be Bishop of York and then of Lichfield in Mercia, is still embedded in Essex place names. Another one, St Cedd, is highlighted in Bede's history. Many were baptised in Essex locations. Bede records that both king and people had joy. He also records the following highlight which brings out the atmosphere of the times.

As I said earlier, the saints of the Gaelic Martinian Christian heritage had a way with kings: king-making, king-encouraging and king-disciplining. They were also tough. And intolerant of sin. Cedd was of the mould. A particular nobleman had been excommunicated by him for unlawful marriage. Cedd had also ordered that no-one should eat with him in his house. King Sigeberht, however, did eat with the man in his house. I would infer, given later events, that it was in the hope of appeasing a violent man. Whatever the case, as he left the house, he encountered Bishop Cedd. The king leapt from his horse and *prostrated himself* before the Saint.

It might be fashionable today to label this as "controlling church". But look at the stature of St Cedd. He had no sword. The king had that. There must have been some spiritual power and authority upon Cedd: Anointing, the Christian would call it. Besides, as we saw earlier in the conversion of King Eadbald of

Kent, that arose through the Fear of the Christian God, not controlling church. The Fear of God was abroad in those days. The Christian God declares the Fear of him to be the Beginning of Wisdom.

Sigeberht would have been wise to have listened earlier, however. Cedd touched the king with his staff and foretold that he would meet his death at the hands of the man he had just left. Sadly, this came true. Sigeberht was later murdered at the man's hands, in about 662. The reason given was that Sigeberht was too forgiving of enemies.

You could accuse Cedd of imposing a controlling curse. Or you could reckon that Cedd could discern what was in people: he knew a murderer when he saw one. Keep away, had been his firm counsel. Sigeberht would have done well to listen. Whichever way you see it, I think we can see that there was nothing nominal in Sigeberht's Christian Life: too forgiving and high respect for the Bishop. Essex and London probably had little choice but to adopt Christian Identity in 655. Everywhere else around them or affiliated to them was going that way. But for a while at least, until Sigeberht perished, it enjoyed the change.

There were to be no ironic rebounds of Christian Life getting stronger in this case. There was no King Penda to reply to. And by the early 660s, the pristine fires of Christian Awakening were dying down. Consolidation and systematisation time had come. London would soon wrap into Mercia. Mercia after Penda became determined to build its proto-state upon Christian Identity. Growing in power, it did much to consolidate Christian Identity far and wide and to systematise the way of it. And thus it went for London: Christian Identity survived Sigeberht's death, as well as further wobbles following a plague in 664. But after Sigeberht's time, it was rarely as sparky again.

However, in 655, London's people group did join all those others that were Toddling into Christian Identity. It was an important piece in the jigsaw.

Deusdedit – Archbishop of Canterbury 655 – Nation Building Event 4

Finally, we come to what I call Nation Building Event number 4. It is much overlooked in the history books, to my knowledge. It was the appointment of an undistinguished scholar to become the Archbishop of Canterbury. His name was Deusdedit. Written off because he accomplished little. However, it is not what he accomplished that matters. It is what he represented.

Firstly, he was the first indigenous Early English Archbishop. However, the indigenous Archbishop was not quite up to the task himself. There would be a further gifted "import", Theodore, from 668.

Secondly, more significantly, Deusdedit was a Wessex scholar, not a Kent one. Because Wessex was unstable politically, and its kings immature in Christian understanding, it tends to be assumed that Christian Identity was making little progress in Wessex. On the contrary, beneath the radar, it seems that Wessex was taking its Christian Identity seriously enough to produce the first indigenous Archbishop.

The Nation Building aspect of Deusdedit, however, was the Wessex/Kent linkage of churchmanship. Beneath the radar of warrior banging chest with warrior, the churches of Wessex and Kent would develop the ultimately-stronger-than-that-sort-of-thing Christian educational contents of a civilisation. Kent would soon become very troubled by Mercia. So, too, would Wessex. But Wessex would always have Christian Identity at its heart and emerge in the end to ascendancy. One thing it would ascend with would be King Alfred the Great's passion to restore education. The educational system that he wanted to restore originated, in large measure, as a product of Kent and Wessex Christian linkage.

Now, let's take stock of the Nation Building Foundations so far:

- 635 – Northumbria and Wessex make Christian and political union, nation-founding.

- 640s – Kent and East Anglia make Christian and political union, civilisation-building.

- 655 – Northumbria secures much Christianisation into Mercia, nation-building.

- 655 – Kent and Wessex make Christian linkage, civilisation-building.

The significance of all this goes further still. In the 700s, Northumbria's high Gaelic Martinian-derived Christian spirituality would get into the mix with Kent and Wessex Christian learning. The effect would be a successful Christian mission into the old Germanic lands, one of the last and strongest pagan redoubts of mainland Europe. The effect would be a transformation into Christian Identity there. That changed Identity descended to multiple generations. It helped to shape the world of today. Deusdedit's appointment can be seen as the mustard seed of that overall outcome – the mustard seed being, if you recall, the illustration by Jesus Christ of the tiny seed that becomes the largest plant in the garden.

Christian Kent and especially its Christian Women

I turn to another piece of stocktaking now. Have you noticed what a difference Christian Kent made to everything? Yet it rarely, if ever, lifted the sword between 597 and 655. Not the stuff of TV. Not the history that sells. But look:

- Queen Bertha and her team – the original mustard seed of Christian Identity for the nation of the English. The overlooked Christian influence on King Ethelbert of Kent.

- St Augustine of Canterbury and team – wise, underrated builders of indigenous pastoral structure and learning.

- Bertha's daughter, Queen Ethelburgha of Northumbria, "Tate", the lively one. The overlooked Christian influence on King Edwin of Northumbria.

- Queen Seaxburh of Kent, out of the "Charismatic" Christian East Anglian family of King Anna. Reinforcer of King Eorcenberht of Kent, forbidder of idols. Influence overlooked by history. Also the mother of Eormenhild.

- Queen Eormenhild of Mercia, holder of the Mercian Christian Toddler's hand, out of Eorcenberht and Seaxburh's dedicatedly Christian Kentish family. Influence overlooked by history.

Concerning all the female rulers, none of them went about killing and they do not seem to have had affairs. Therefore, they get airbrushed out of the history. They seem to have shaped it, even so. Or, to be more accurate, with the Christian Life within them, they seem to have shaped it.

Still to come in addition to all these, though referenced already, Queen Eanflaed of Northumbria, the Kent-educated daughter of Ethelburgha. She would contribute to Nation Building Event number 5, next chapter.

It is interesting to see so much Christian shaping coming through the women of Kent. The Christian Bible does teach that with regard to the powers of the Holy Spirit of the Christian God, there is no difference between male and female. Circumstances, practicalities of life, and nuances of character may differ. The Christian God works with the grain of those. But Christian spirituality does not differ. The Holy Spirit of the Christian God will work with any who follow the guidelines in Christ.

I find it interesting, too, to compare the Infant Christian character of Kent to the character that has come down to us of the original seed of it, Queen Bertha. Kent was the most compliant Christian Toddler. Bertha has also come down to us as compliant. Roots shaping the plant again, in Christian terms. However, quiet or not, Kent's Early Christian Wisdom Spirituality got into nearly every element in the foundational shaping of the nation of the English.

The ways of the world might overlook a quiet one like Bertha. However, the Christian spirituality of the quiet one would appear to have shaped the real world history. That would be another subtle hallmark of the Christian God. The

Apostle Paul taught that the Christian God specialises in using those overlooked by this world to transform it. The principle works whether they know it or not and for multiple generations after their faithfulness has set the ball rolling.

Adding yet another figure to the almost lost Christian female side of things, the "Graduation" chapter of this book will highlight Osburh of Wessex. The Christian mother of King Alfred the Great. Nothing evil known of her. Airbrushed out of history. However, she did do one thing that shaped history: she shaped the Christian worldview of her son, Alfred the Great. The Christian hand that rocked the cradle really did shape the world. We'll come to Osburh later.

Summary: Toddling

So, a momentous year, 655: the gates were flung open to build the nation of the Early English upon Christian Identity. They were very much Toddlers in that as at 655. And as we shall see in the next chapter, already losing innocence in it. But then again, toddlers do. Meanwhile, to reflect: what a transformation of Identity, 635 to 655. I think it was breathtaking.

And what a reply of the Christian God to King Penda of Mercia, or at least, so it would seem: victorious, complete and gracious, yet overwhelming and fearsome in its way as well. Interesting: those are the ways of the Christian God as his Holy Spirit has inspired the portrayal of him in his Bible. They seem to have been set loose in the real world of the Early English.

CHAPTER 16.

Innocence Lost – 650s to 668

The Christian God declares of himself that he is perfect. He declares of human beings that they are not perfect. However, he says that he is patient with them. As to Christians and the church more specifically, I once came across an apocryphal tale. Jesus Christ, having ascended to heaven after being resurrected from the dead, met up with the angels. "Well done, Lord," they said. "And now, what is Plan A?" Jesus looked down to earth and pointed to his disciples at contention with one another. "Them," he said. "They are Plan A." The angels looked and asked, "What is Plan B?" Jesus replied, "There is no Plan B."

Well, Plan A sprang a leak in Early England as the 650s went on. Out of what a modern Christian understanding would call "contentious spirit", the Christians – let's call them "Church" – lost their innocence. And so too, in murderous circumstances, did Christian King Oswy of Northumbria – let's call him "State". Each together, Infant Church and Infant State, lost their Christian innocence.

As this chapter goes forward, I will focus mainly on King Oswy of Northumbria and Christian Identity as it developed in Northumbria during Oswy's time. Events there were to shape Early English history and Identity beyond Northumbrian borders as well as within them.

Refresher and Preparation

Before we go ahead, a refresher as to terminology that I use, and also a few points to prepare the way.

I take care to distinguish between differing streams of Christian Life that were encountered by the Anglo Saxons. All were contained within the Roman

Catholic whole, but it is essential to discern by each type within that. I use terms as follows:

- Roman Catholic – representing the mainstream practice of the Church of Rome at the time.

- Gaelic Martinian – The Christian way practised amongst the Celtic Scots (a.k.a. Gaels). It was descended from St Martin of Tours, hence "Martinian".

- Romano Martinian – Mainly the Christian way that came to the Anglo Saxons via the Germanic Franks of Gaul. It too was descended from St Martin. However, the Franks were more in the Roman cultural mainstream than the Gaels.

I also call both types of Martinian "sparky". In the times I am writing about, there seems to have been plentiful life in the Christian realms of the revelatory and miraculous, and coming out of all three of the streams.

However, by King Oswy's time, certain cultural differences were developing that had the potential to impart different senses of Identity:

- In terms of those types of cultural expression which tend to impart a distinct sense of Identity, the Roman way had more focus on order and outward display, e.g., grand buildings.

- The Gaelic way was focussed more on the interior spiritual life. It was orderly in its way. But in terms of those cultural forms which tend to impart a distinct sense of Identity, it was happy to express itself in humbler ways.

- The two had different ways of setting the dates for Easter. The results did not coincide. This is important because Easter is the main Christian festival. By the 650s, the Gaelic and Roman churches were in more regular contact than they had been. Easter dating was a live issue between them, and tensions were developing.

- Latent differences in sense of Identity arising from the different cultural expressions were starting to add heat to the Easter debate. This was starting to give rise to what Christians call contentious "Party spirit" – "I am of the *Gaelic* Easter Party." "I am of the *Roman* Easter Party."

Now, people can sometimes exaggerate the division between the Gaelic and the Roman. The Gaelic church was part of the Roman one and eager to engage with it. It had developed different cultural expression because of being cut off from the mainstream of Rome by varying groups of Germanic invaders. However, in this chapter, you will see that this particular growing divergence within inner Christian circles did make a significant impact on the entire forward history of the British Isles.

Northumbria the Volatile

What we call "Northumbria" comprised two Angle kingdoms, Bernicia and Deira. Bernicia stretched broadly from the River Tees to the Firth of Forth; Deira incorporated what we now call Yorkshire and north of that to the River Tees. The two had been joined with contention from the outset.

I said of Saint Aidan that his Christian spirituality did a good deal to calm down rivalries between the two and help Northumbria to mature into one. However, in a Christian understanding, "the flesh" is always at war with "the Spirit". So it was with Northumbria. Any time the leaders in Bernicia and Deira, whether leaders clerical or leaders aristocratic, stepped into "the flesh", contention between the two, Bernicia and Deira, could flare up, even with St Aidan there.

In the times I am writing about, when much of the Christian spirituality in Northumbria was as sparky as it gets, there were certain differences in the senses of Christian Identity in Bernicia and Deira. The differences will be seen coming into play in this chapter in a heated way. They had nation-shaping consequences.

Bernicia identified firmly with the Gaelic Martinian Christian way. Deira was more complex. It was Romano Martinian Christian but from an origin different to the other small kingdoms. Its Christian life had been seeded not by the Franks but by the Latin Roman Catholic, Paulinus. Deira identified firmly with the Roman Catholic way. It was also keeping up to date with that. However, in the days of Saint King Oswald, Deira also happily received the Gaelic Martinian St Aidan and team. So Deira was a fusion. You could reasonably call it Romano Gaelic Martinian Catholic Christian. That most nearly describes it. It may sound long-winded. But if you descend from the English, that is the Identity you most nearly descend from, whether Protestant Christian, atheist, whatever. May as well come to grips with it.

So, in the mid 600s, Bernicia was Christian-sparky. And so was Deira. But with different understandings of their spirituality, different roots for it and different cultures to encase it. Cultures which were also long-standing political rivals.

So… let's look at the times when the Early English lost their Christian Innocence.

Murder of King Oswine of Deira

King Oswy of Northumbria had taken power during the turmoil that ensued when Saint King Oswald, his older brother, was slain by King Penda of Mercia in 642. However, Oswy did not at first take all of Northumbria. The kingdom broke into its older constituent parts, Deira and Bernicia.

Oswy became King of Bernicia. Like Oswald before him, he had taken on Christian Identity in the exile days at Iona. However, he has come down to us as a more ambivalent and crafty Christian than his Saint King brother.

As we saw previously, one of Oswy's first acts was to launch a daring mission into Mercian territory to reclaim Saint King Oswald's remains. His ongoing domestic policy was to continue to promote Christian Identity in

Bernicia, Saint Aidan and team staying in place. In regard to all else, the first years were about securing Bernicia from existential threat on many sides.

Slowly but surely, Oswy secured the half-kingdom. Then he set out to become the over-king for the whole of a restored Northumbria. However, Deira did not play along. It preferred its fusion Christian spirituality as enriched by St Aidan. And it had its own royalty. They were content with the broken-apart political status quo. And besides, Oswy was not always, shall we say, a Nice Guy. I am not sure I would have wanted crafty Oswy ruling me if I had been in their shoes.

Anyway, to achieve control, Oswy tried marriage first. In the later 640s, either Rhiainfellt of Rheged died or he put her aside into monastic life. He sent for Princess Eanflaed from Kent to be his new wife. Eanflaed had been that daughter born on the night when the Wessex royals tried to assassinate her father, King Edwin of Northumbria. She was the first-baptised in Northumbria, following promises made by Edwin before his campaign to subdue Wessex. After King Edwin perished in battle with King Caedwalla of Gwynedd and King Penda of Mercia in 632, Eanflaed was taken as a refugee to Kent by Paulinus and her Kentish mother, Ethelburgha. She was brought up in Christian Kent, then the most Roman Catholic of the kingdoms in its outward ways. Eanflaed brought north with her the Kentish Roman Prestige and the Roman Catholic outer forms more favoured by Deira. She was also a blood royal of Deira by King Edwin. Oswy may have hoped that marriage to her would help Deira to accept him as over-King. However, the Deiran court seems not to have co-operated.

Now, the Deiran King, Oswine, was of sincere Christian character. It is possible that he actually was a Nice Guy. St Aidan seems to have had at least as much time for him as for Oswy. However, reading between the lines, Oswine seems to have had a malleable character that made him unable to resist being used as a focus for intrigues by his Deiran court in response to the intrigues of Bernician Oswy. In 651, Bernicia and Deira came to battle. Oswine of Deira withdrew when it came to the crunch, rather than become a focal point for bloodshed. Afterwards, however, Oswy had him murdered.

After this, Oswald's son by Cyneburh of Wessex, Oethelwald, became King in Deira. It is not clear whether Oswy enforced this, as sub-King subordinate to himself, or whether Deira did it when Oswy was looking the other way. Whichever, this was the Oethelwald who would later conspire with Penda against Oswy in 655.

Anyway, murder: In 635 the Anointed Christian King Oswald had prevailed in battle over the bitter Christian King Caedwalla. But in 651, the rather crafty Christian King Oswy accomplished the sincere Christian King Oswine's murder. There would have been a significant difference under the principles of the Christian God. Bede's history makes no bones about the wrongdoing. The Northumbrian kings were greatly looked up to in Bede's writings, but he didn't look up to Oswy over that.

Queen Eanflaed brought about the reconciliation of the two royal families through pragmatic Christian peacemaking, rather than through kinship vengeance. She used monastic establishments and the institution of regular compensating prayer within them. However, it is one thing to satisfy human blood honour by devices of monastic prayer. It is another to satisfy the hidden courts of the spiritual realm. And yet another to satisfy the Christian God. The whole episode would have cast a dark spiritual shadow.

Innocence Lost.

St Aidan seems to have known it was coming. He had previously lamented that Oswine did not have the ruthless streak of a king and it would cost him his life. The implications are (i) that Aidan knew things were brewing up for a Bernicia versus Deira royal showdown and (ii) that Oswy, whom Aidan knew well, did have a ruthless streak.

Satisfying the Christian God

So now we come to another of those moments when we pose the question, if *you* were the Christian God, how would you deal with Oswy over this murder? Oswy calls himself a Christian. He has therefore taken your name in vain. What would satisfy you? A caricature version of this God might hit Oswy with his biggest stick. A mind which seeks to cry "Foul!" in the Christian God might criticise him for not doing so. These days, Oswy would do jail time. A long stretch. As for the caricature God, he might also reward Deira at the expense of Bernicia. Indeed, if the Christian God is a *vindicator*, as I have said in an earlier chapter, perhaps he really *ought* to make a way for Deira to prevail?

Well, as you will see later, in a lost and hidden way, *Christian* Deira *did* prevail over *Christian* Bernicia. But at the personal and political level, Oswy seems to have got away with it.

It is time to understand more of the deeper principles of the Christian God now, and how they might come into play with a real and imperfect Christian ruler. King Oswy, we must note, was not given over to bitterness and alliance with the pagan, as the Britonnic Christian Caedwalla had been. Oswy had fallen. But his heart was not beyond restoration. He wanted his proto-state to continue as Christian. He provided the lands for Eanflaed's Christian peacemaking. He wanted Christian ways going forward as he could understand them by his lights. He was a mixture. If *you* were the Christian God, how would you handle the mixture?

Well, you could sum up the revealed character of the Christian God, and in a way the entire Christian Bible, in one short phrase: The God of the Second Chance. Further to that, the Christian God says that he works with grace with what he has got, rather than throwing out all the toys on account of what he has not got. Therefore, Oswy, murderer in 651, was going to get a Second Chance.

Let's look again at that Battle of Winwaed, 655. To his own amazement, Oswy had defeated King Penda of Mercia. On the eve of the battle, the fallen Oswy offered desperate prayers to the Christian God, semi-Christian bribes.

"I'll build you monasteries. I'll sign over my baby daughter to monastic life. Only save me!" I have paraphrased. But what do you think? If the Christian God is as perfect as he says he is, would that prevail with him?

Well, Oswy did win an unlikely victory. Penda's allies deserted after the prayers. And the Christian God seems to have done what he could for the life of baby Aelflaed: she grew up in Christian circles that had dynamic Life in the Holy Spirit of the Christian God. Jesus Christ had promised life in all its fulness to those with the Life in the Holy Spirit. Aelflaed's later career indicates that she would have shared in it.

But here is what I think. The Christian God can be defined as the God of the Second Chance. And he knows the future, he says. Therefore, he can look ahead to the future to discern whether a Second Chance might arise, rather than responding with a big stick in the immediate present. For Oswy, the Second Chance would come like this. He was going to have to pass a test. The test would be this: Oswy is going to win the Battle of Winwaed; what will he do with the victory?

The Temptation of King Oswy

Here now is the test before Oswy: he had won the Battle of Winwaed, 655. The temptation to make a hideous example of defeated Mercia must have been enormous. It had tormented Northumbria for years. It could be seen as grimly fitting that King Penda, the decapitator, had been decapitated. Live by the sword, die by the sword. The measure he had given to Oswald came back to him. Those were principles spelt out by Jesus Christ. So as to King Penda, that's one thing. But as to Mercia, the urge would have been this: "Violate the violator. Loot the looter. It's what we have always done. Look what Penda did to Oswald's body: dismember the kingdom of the dismemberer. Break the kingdom of the one who broke Northumbria in two."

Well, Oswy did break Mercia in two, installing himself as King in the north and over-King of the whole, with newly Christian son-in-law Peada as King in the south. But he refrained from vengeance. Instead, he used his new power to secure Christian mission into Mercia. Oswy, to his everlasting credit, took a leaf out of Saint King Oswald's playbook when he extended peace to Assassin Wessex, and out of St Patrick's playbook when he went back with the message of Christian Life to those who had enslaved him. He even acted out a Christ-resurrected pattern, no less. As follows: The response of the resurrected Christ to his crucifier, Old Rome, had been to send his disciples into it, with the Anointing of the Holy Spirit of the Christian God, to transform its ways. Oswy now sent the Christian saints marching into Mercia, the Gaelic Martinian Christian Anointed brigade trained by St Aidan.

That is what would satisfy you as the Christian God. Second Chance test passed. Oswy restored under the Christian God. Set up all the monasteries you want, institute all the regular prayer you like, that does not restore you. Extend grace in Christ in place of vengeance, that does.

Anyway, this is the sort of thing that happens when the Christian God is patient with the likes of an Oswy rather than responding with knee-jerk and a big stick. Oswy had his finest hour.

It was Oswy's Christian decision, not the Battle of Winwaed itself, that was a turning point for the development of a Christian Identity within the slowly uniting Early English people group. The Christian decision was the transformative thing. Oswy was to be overthrown by 658. But Mercia never looked back after adopting the Christian Identity. It stayed with that and did a large part to embed it into the slowly building nation of the Early English.

One might infer that the Christian God would find satisfaction in that as well.

Nation Building Event 5 – Synod of Whitby 663-4

Now, the Mercia into which King Oswy sent the saints was never innocent in its Christian Life. As I said in the previous chapter, it was always a domination-seeking entity. There was always an element of using Christian Identity as a political tool. However, the Mercian ways did gradually come to have a more civilising light mixed in with them. Its kings wanted to build Christian proto-states that were enlightened by older standards.

So too did King Oswy. And in late 663, securely established as over-King of all Northumbria, he made a major attempt to cement the union of the two components, Bernicia and Deira, at an event known as the Synod of Whitby. A Synod is a gathering of Christian leaders. In those days, they included secular leaders as well. So they combined the Lords Spiritual and the Lord Temporal. The UK House of Lords down to modern times descends from the concept.

This particular Synod was called and presided over by King Oswy. It is quite difficult to appraise it. However, we must do so, because I call it Nation Building Event Five. What Oswy intended at Whitby was the shaping of Christian Life for a Christian proto-state of Northumbria in isolation. What emerged unintentionally was a further-reaching convergence of unified Christian Identity for the Early English more generally.

The Synod of Whitby had its good points and its bad points. The bad ones amount to a significant moment of Lost Innocence within the inner Christian circles. However, Jesus Christ taught, remember, that until his return, if you try to uproot the bad, you will also uproot the good. And there was Christian good as well as Christian bad in the Synod.

So, let's have a patient look at this event, the Synod of Whitby 663/4. Whitby is a town on the northeast coast of what is now called England. Great fish and chips. Evocative ruined Abbey. In those times, Whitby's monastic life harboured some of the most vibrant Christian Life on the planet. There is a modern movement in the Christian world called "Hillsong". I think it came out of Australia in recent times. I would see one of its earliest precursors as the Caedmon I mentioned in the previous chapter. He came out of a little group of related monasteries in the Whitby area. He developed the Old English language for inspired praises to the Christian God. Different culture, different media, different world, but his "Holy Spirit-filled-song" tradition carries on.

Oswy's pre-occupations, however, were more pragmatic, less innocent, than Christian song. He had a problem that the Synod was called to solve: the dating of Easter. He and Bernicia used one system. Queen Eanflaed and Deira used another. The results were different dates for Easter every year. If you are trying to build a proto-state on Christian foundations, it matters for the component parts to use just the one method for dating Easter because other dates in the calendar derive from it. Different dates for that, different dates for other things too. Bernicia and Deira were tense together within the Northumbrian whole. Multiple different significant dates didn't exactly help to unite them.

There was a difficulty within Oswy's family, too. Bede highlights it. Queen Eanflaed, product of Deira and Kent, used the Deiran dating for Easter. King Oswy, product of Bernicia and Iona, used the Bernician dating for Easter. Now, before Easter, it was customary to practise a long period of reflection and self-denial, called Lent, before ending it in an Easter feast. There was one year in which King Oswy set about his Easter Feast while Queen Eanflaed, working to dates that were later by a whole week, was still in her Lenten Fast. Eanflaed has not come down to us as a shrinking violet.

So, Oswy wanted a unitary way forward over Easter dating.

Now, as it happened, Eanflaed's Deiran Easter date was also the Roman Catholic method. Oswy's Bernician Easter was of the Gaelic method. Therefore, Oswy would have to choose one or the other. The two ways had similar underlying Christian spirituality: Romano Martinian and Gaelic Martinian, each one having Life in the Holy Spirit of the Christian God. But one and only one of the outward ways of encasing the spirituality was to be chosen at the Synod of Whitby for all future state-building purposes. King Oswy would lead the Synod, hear the arguments and make the decision. It was going to be a momentous one: which way forward? Roman Catholic? Or Gaelic?

And remember: the inner Christian circles of the differing ways were not at peace beforehand about the outcome. Tensions had been building. Different senses of outward Identity were at stake.

Before we come to Oswy's decision, we should develop some of the characters who converged at Whitby in late 663.

James the Deacon

The character most overlooked is also, for me, the most interesting. We referenced him as a young man in the chapter "Labour Pains", surviving Caedwalla's ravaging as at 633. Thirty years on now to 663 and he was an old man, from Deira, the Yorkshire part of Northumbria: James of York, the Deacon, he who had shared with Paulinus in ministry up to 632 when King Edwin perished. James, if you recall, was a Christian singer. But of a more orderly method than the later and more inspirational Caedmon. Orderly, in the Roman Catholic way. But James had also been through not one but two waves of Christian power Anointing in Deira. First with the prophetically gifted Latin Paulinus. Then within the vibrant spirituality which broke out from the Martinian Christian Gaels in King Oswald's day. He was of the complex fusion Christian Identity that shaped the English, in other words. During all those years from 633 to 663, he had kept his head down, quietly building pastoral capabilities to sustain Christian Identity. He had survived through political times of chaos, bloodshed and divisive intrigue. He came to Whitby on the Roman Catholic Easter team.

Bishop Agilbert

There was another cleric there, too, for the Roman Catholic Easter team. Bishop Agilbert, recently sacked from Wessex. He represented the continental European Roman Catholic Easter practice. He is thought to have been the prestige Roman Catholic figure at Whitby. Only one problem, he had no language skills. That was why he had been sacked from Wessex: it seems that he struggled to make himself understood in the Anglo Saxon language.

The Young Wilfrid

Not a lot of use to have prestige if you can't make yourself understood. For that reason, the Roman Catholic team came with a new and budding star. We referenced him in the last chapter. His name was Wilfrid.

Wilfrid was of the Northumbrian aristocracy. Although he had been educated at the Gaelic Martinian monastery of Lindisfarne in Bernicia, his life shows that he had no sympathy for its ways. Lindisfarne had been too insular for his taste. Wilfrid identified in a partisan way with the Deiran fusion Christian spirituality. And he had larger horizons. He travelled extensively on the European mainland and several times to Rome. He would become one of the great Christian clerical figures of all Europe. He became devoted to all things Roman Catholic, including order, display and grand building. However, a post-Reformation Protestant understanding of "Roman Catholic" would fail to capture his essence. I discern from some accounts that he had within his Christian Life some of the same Christian "Charismatic" giftings that were alive in Deira in those times. These would have descended spiritually from Paulinus, Bishop of York, after 627 and were still in Deira a generation after Wilfrid under a Bishop of York named John of Beverley. I will look at this John in a Postscript following the later chapter about Archbishop Theodore and his times.

Anyway, this made Wilfrid a complex Christian package at Whitby, having some of the Bernician Gaelic spiritual heritage from Lindisfarne but a partisan representative of the fusion Christian spirituality of Deira and its prestigious Roman Catholic outer forms.

To add to all that, Wilfrid had charisma in the general sense: he was a captivating and brilliant person. He also, as I shall show you soon, had a domineering streak. And as the Synod of Whitby was to prove, he was ultra self-confident when young. He was to be much humbled later in life and learn from it. But as at 663, the young Wilfrid was a bulldozing combination: (i) forcefully charismatic in personality, (ii) "Charismatic" in the more technical Christian sense of gifted by the Holy Spirit of the Christian God, and (iii) partisan for Deiran Christian spirituality and Roman Catholic outward ways. A highly complex mixture. Wilfrid went on to have a highly complex life; for me, he was possibly the most difficult to appraise of any Christian within the history of the English.

Now, as at Whitby by 663, the young Wilfrid had become a favourite of Queen Eanflaed. It is not clear whether King Oswy had any time for him. But Oswy's son Alhfrith favoured Wilfrid too. This Alhfrith, if you recall, was Oswy's son by Rhiainfellt of Rheged. He has come down to us as an annoyer of Oswy but also as committed, like Wilfrid, to Roman Catholic outward ways rather than Gaelic ones. He seems to have been accepted in Deira from 655 when Oswy had made him the sub-King there in place of Oethelwald after the Battle of Winwaed.

This might seem like a lot of detail, but it matters because Wilfrid carried the day at Whitby. We should try to understand what was in him and his sponsoring sub-King because Wilfrid and Alhfrith became influential not just in Northumbria, especially Deira. They also became influential in the way that the Christian Identity developed in Mercia, and Mercia would embed its newfound Christian ways far and wide.

One thing about the Christian Life in Wilfrid: it was not innocent. For example, sometime between 655 and 663, Wilfrid and Alhfrith between them managed to engineer one of Christian history's more notable negative achievements. In the process of Romanising the then-Gaelic monastery at Ripon, now part of Yorkshire, the pair of them managed to expel the young St Cuthbert. So there was a domineering side to Young Wilfrid.

Bishop Colman of Lindisfarne

Bishop Colman of Lindisfarne, of the Iona tradition, was the leader of the Gaelic Martinian Christian party that came to Whitby. His tradition had enjoyed the favour in Northumbria of Saint King Oswald and then after him King Oswy. St Aidan had died in 651, succeeded by Bishop Finan. Finan had been influential in the original Northumbrian Christian mission into Mercia from 655. Colman had succeeded him. Colman was of an honourable and dynamic Christian line from St Martin of Tours via the all-time Celtic greats: St Ninian, St Patrick, St Columba and St Aidan. In the next chapter, I will take time out to explore that line further.

It was Colman's task to argue for the Gaelic method of calculating the dates of Easter.

Outcome of the Synod

Oswy heard arguments for the different Easter dating methods from Colman for the Bernician way and Wilfrid for the Deiran one. He chose the Deiran way, Wilfrid's, the Roman Catholic one. That could be seen as quite big, a Bernician favouring the Deiran.

Oswy's decision would appear to have hinged on a Christian worldview of yesteryear. The Bernician Easter method was said to have descended from the great Apostle John. St John was the Spiritual Confidant companion of Jesus. He wrote the gospel of John in the Christian Bible. The Deiran Easter method was the way of the Roman church that was said to have descended from the great Apostle Peter. St Peter was the Action Man companion of Jesus. I think that the Biblical gospel written by Mark derives from him. Now, Jesus Christ said that he gave to St Peter the keys to the kingdom of heaven. In Oswy's mind, or so it would seem, if you wanted a permit to enter the Pearly Gates after death, best to be on good terms with St Peter. So King Oswy chose St Peter's way.

Well, it would not be my way of understanding the keys to the kingdom of heaven. And the Apostle Paul had warned in his letters about choosing one Apostle over another. Reconcile the lot of them in Christ had been Paul's advice. Don't even show favouritism to me, Paul. Whatever the case, Wilfrid won. He was of the Roman Catholic church devoted to St Peter.

However, I can't say I find fault with Oswy. I prefer to forgo the modern fashion for patting the ancients on their naïve little heads. I have a subtle and complex mind, but the details of Easter dating methodology make me go cross-eyed. Union in the Holy Spirit of the Christian God is what would win my vote.

It would have been what Oswy was after, too. He had to decide something out of what he could understand. Or more likely, I should think, explain his decision in a way that would not have involved communicating very arcane detail that would be absorbing to the ecclesiastics, the Lords Spiritual, but bamboozling to his court, the Lords Temporal.

Anyway, Oswy did and did not get union in the Holy Spirit of the Christian God out of his decision. He also sowed consequences far beyond what he could have expected. Good ones. And bad ones. We should look at the consequences.

Consequences of the Synod of Whitby

Here is what was Nation Building at Whitby for the Early English. King Oswy decided to build Northumbria as a Christian state on Romano Martinian Catholic church foundations rather than the previous Gaelic Martinian monastic foundations. The effect was that Northumbria came on board with the Romano Martinian Catholic Christian Identity developing in all the other kingdoms. Northumbria was then the kingdom in the ascendancy militarily and the most sparky spiritually. It pressed the accelerator towards the new fusion Identity, Romano Martinian Catholic Christian with plentiful Gaelic spark. The Early English sense of nationhood gradually coalesced around that.

As you will see in a later chapter, Mercia and Northumbria were going to fight again. But after Whitby, they developed this same fusion Christian spirituality, so they finally came to Christian peace; and the peace endured. King Penda's era of endless Mercia versus Northumbria fighting would soon be over, bar one more episode, after Whitby.

Therefore, the Synod of Whitby was a significant step forward to ultimate nationhood of the English. I would call that good, not bad, in the grand scheme of things. Unless, in our own times, you want England to devolve back into fractious sub-kingdoms, I would think that is fair.

It *could* have been a purely good outcome in Christian terms, too, in that the whole of Northumbria after Whitby remained strongly Martinian in its

Christian spirituality, and in that the other kingdoms also had inward Martinian Christian spirituality acquired via Frankish or Gaelic Christian sources. The Synod unified the inward Christian spirituality of many kingdoms on the sparky Martinian Christian rootstock of Life in the Holy Spirit of the Christian God.

However, we're not perfect, are we? And that includes the ecclesiastics. There were consequences you might call bad and would, by any objective standard, call sad.

There had been tensions in the inner Christian circles, remember? Young Wilfrid the bulldozer cracked a water main. As follows:

I can only suggest that you get hold of Bede's Ecclesiastical History and read Wilfrid's speech at the Synod. (i) I am an older man. If a young man spoke about me to a King in front of me in the way in which Wilfrid spoke to Oswy to diss the older Colman, it would have got right up my nose. I mean, read the speech – bumptious or what? (ii) If I had also, like Colman, long enjoyed the favour of that King, who then turned to the young man's way without having first sounded me out – the whole thing looking like a bit of a fix, crafty Oswy and all that flimsy reasoning – it would have done more than get up my nose. I would have had a sense of being betrayed. (iii) I might even have seen it like this. That conceited young product of Angle-ish aristocracy. And that crafty Angle-ish King. They have closed ranks against my Scotic race.

Talk about the Law of Unintended Consequences...

In what I would hold to be the saddest moment in the history of the British Isles, Colman and team packed their bags. In 664, the Martinian Christian Scots departed from Lindisfarne and ultimately made their way to Ireland. The generations have paid for it ever since. That is a negative example of the power of Christian Identity to shape real world history. Out of a division in outward forms of Roman and Gaelic Christian expression, where in truth there was shared Martinian Christian spirituality, came a lasting sense of fracture of more general cultural Identity of Angle and Scot. And something truly precious was lost to the Early English. They had their most vibrant Christian stream of any out of the Gaelic Scots.

The most redolent example, for me, in modern popular fiction would be Tolkien's elves sadly departing Middle Earth for the West.

This did not all come out of the blue from a decision by King Oswy or even out of Wilfrid the bulldozer. Tensions had been developing for a while between Roman and Gaelic Christian camps over the Easter issue. One method may have been objectively right and the other objectively wrong, but six of one and half a dozen of the other in terms of contentious attitudes building up.

However, I can find no fault with Bishop Colman. I would be sitting in judgement on what I might have done myself. I do feel sorrow about it, though.

As to Wilfrid, you will see in the next chapter but one that his Christian God would appear to have disciplined him as life went on. In the end, he was greatly humbled, and after that, his God seems to have given him a gracious old age. It is not for me to cut across the grain of that. Wilfrid was what he was in 663.

Meanwhile, what are we left with after the Synod of Whitby?

Innocence Lost in the Christian inner circles, I should say. And a couple of mixed spiritual legacies:

i.   In terms of the ongoing development of Christian Identity in the Early English, the Northern Celtic way had been fitter for purpose in more tribal times. But the Roman way, with territorial dioceses, had more legs for nation-building. It had more education in it. And it had more continuity of order in it. A local clergyman might be only a few rungs up from the devil, but the materials he would use were only a few rungs down from the Apostle Paul. So the Roman way of doing things was proof against much clerical incompetence generation by generation. However, it could also devolve quite easily into Religion, outward form without the inward Reality.

ii.   On the other hand, the Gaelic Martinian spirituality was not much bothered about outward forms. Therefore, it would always be likelier to express Christian Identity as Life in the Holy Spirit: inward reality; sparky. However, the Christian spirituality in the likes of a Saint Cuthbert, an Angle but of the high Gaelic Martinian spirituality, is more difficult to maintain. It can go off the boil or devolve into sectarianism. The spirituality of a Cuthbert – I will come to his fuller story soon – would never be lost, but it might be expressed only from time to time down the generations. His ways endured a couple of generations down to Bede but after that tended to run more like an underground river than an overground one.

Both the patterns have been active throughout all of English history. The result in Christian terms for the English became a robustly enduringly fusion Christian Identity. But sometimes it would devolve into Religion, and from time to time Awaken back into the Reality. The example of (i) and (ii) combined par excellence would be the Protestant Reformation. That restored the reality but became sectarian. Once it had spent 400 years getting past that, it can be seen as having eventually freed the underground river of the Martinian Life in the Holy Spirit of the Christian God, which had been in the likes of St Cuthbert, to surface overground again in the wider earth.

Anyway, what would appear to have come true in real history after the Synod of Whitby is the frustrating principle expressed by the Christ: the good and the bad must grow together until his return. Until then, if you uproot the bad, you will also uproot the good. Jesus Christ taught that this frustrating mixture is a fact of life in a world in which, according to the Christian God, Innocence was Lost from the very Beginning. Only he, Jesus Christ, can sort it out, and only when the time comes.

The Hidden Victor at Whitby

One point I must pick up before moving forward. I said in an earlier chapter that the Christian God has declared a purpose to vindicate his Christ, and by extension Christ's own, in real world history. Early in this chapter, I said that a vindicating Christian God might make a lost and hidden way for *Christian* Deira to prevail following the murder of King Oswine of Deira, the sincere Deiran Christian King who was murdered by the calculating Bernician Christian King. I return to that most underrated of all figures, James of York, the Deacon.

Now, can you see how *vindication* worked out? Is it coming to light for you? James was of Deira. Of the Roman Catholic orderly way. Of the Latin Christian Awakening in Paulinus's time. Of the Gaelic Christian Awakening in King Oswald's time. He was the original of the spirituality that came to Whitby in young Wilfrid. But he wasn't bumptious. And he had been through the fire: chaos, bloodshed and intrigues all around. Still standing. Quietly building. It wasn't young Wilfrid who won at Whitby. Within that mysterious spiritual realm of the Christian God, by the hidden hand, it would seem, of the Holy Spirit, it was James who won. What he had stood for throughout a lifetime prevailed.

James seems to have been another mustard seed – his type of Christian Identity spread out after Whitby to become foundational in the Christian Identity of the Early English. Romano Gaelic Martinian Catholic, but also tried and tested. James's seed has been buried deeper from view even than Queen Bertha's. However, this was common to each of them: quiet, life-long Christian faithfulness. James the Deacon seems to have been the spiritual victor at Whitby – without saying a recorded word. He seems to have been an innocent Christian at Whitby in times of lost innocence. Yet his lifetime of hidden spiritual victory would appear to have shaped the real world.

Well, I might be stretching it. But long Christian experience would tell you that this sort of thing is what you would expect in the real world as a hidden hallmark of the Christian God as revealed in his Bible. It accords with the Christ principle, you see: vindication of faithfulness. And with another teaching, this one by the Apostle Paul: that the long-run victors are those in Christ whom this world overlooks. It seems to have worked out in James of York, as well as in

Queen Bertha of Kent. *Christian* Deira did prevail. But in more mixed circumstances in 663 than in 597.

Christian Identity Leaderless and Hanging in the Balance

After the Synod of Whitby, we have this as at 664:

Northumbria, Mercia, Wessex, East Anglia, Kent and London moving forward within a Fusion Christian spirituality. The pristine fires of Christian Awakening were dying down. But they all wanted to consolidate their proto-states on Christian foundations. Christian Identity was looking as unstoppable as the wave which overwhelmed King Penda.

But by as soon as 668, they were all close to losing it.

There has to be Anointed Christian leadership, you see, for Christian Identity to make headway. By 668, there was a vacuum in it.

Wilfrid Frustrated, Trouble Brewing

After Whitby, Young Wilfrid was wanted by Alhfrith, sub-king of Deira, to become the Bishop of York. However, Wilfrid did not take up the post immediately. There was no-one in the British Isles whose orders he would respect to consecrate him. He journeyed into Europe for consecration. And he tarried there for reasons unknown. Meanwhile, Alhfrith vanished from the history records, possibly a victim of plague in 664, or lost from sight after turning on King Oswy.

Over-King Oswy, meanwhile, growing impatient in Wilfrid's absence, appointed one of the Bernician Saints team, St Chad, to Deiran York. There was a certain amount of tension beneath the surface of the appointment. Chad seems to have been a humble person in an invidious circumstance, forced upon the Deirans.

Wilfrid eventually returned and wanted his entitlement to York, but he did not get his way. He settled for a while at his Abbey at Ripon in Deira and had regular and influential contacts with Mercia and Kent. But this most gifted and influential of clerics had little formal power anywhere in the years just after the Synod of Whitby.

I should think that Wilfrid was also a focal point for ongoing contentious spirit in the North. I doubt King Oswy had much time for Wilfrid, whatever his decision may have been at Whitby. Wilfrid's ally, Alhfrith, sub-king of Deira, had departed the scene. King Oswy was also ageing, and his favoured heir, Prince Ecgfrith, was to become a King of implacable and warlike character. He would be just the type to renew conflict with Mercia. Ecgfrith would love St Cuthbert. But he would loathe Wilfrid.

A certain loss of Christian stability was looming. As at 667/8, all was not well in the Northumbrian Christian Identity. Trouble brewing.

Kent Loses its Wisdom

King Eorcenberht of Kent died on the day that Archbishop Deusdedit died, says Bede. It was in 664. The vacancy went unfilled for nearly five years. The Early English were leaderless in their top Christian appointment.

Christian King Eorcenberht's successor was King Egbert. There was an internal family dispute over his claim. The rivals were murdered. Egbert was not involved at first hand. And who knows what option he may have had. Egbert sought both legal and religious means of expiation. Unlike King Oswy, however, there does not seem to have been a truly restorative moment in Christian terms. In another of those sad turns of history, Kent's polity was never the same again. Its Christian Life had made a special contribution of Christian Wisdom in the founding times of the Early English. But out of complex family inter-relationships, what Egbert had done seems to have caused offence within Mercia. Kent paid for it later. Wulfhere's successor, King Aethelred of Mercia, sacked Kent, for a variety of reasons including Egbert's murders. Mercia went on to absorb Kent.

Yep… Christian Wisdom: as the saying goes, you don't know what you've got till it's gone.

East Anglia and London Absorbed into Mercia

The vibrant Christian Life of the East Anglian royals had been wounded when King Penda had slain King Anna in 654. East Anglian military strength had also ebbed away after its new pagan King had taken Penda's side at the Battle of Winwaed 655 and been defeated there. Once Mercia had taken a course towards Christian Identity after that battle, weakened East Anglia bowed to absorption into it. It meant that Mercia took in, beneath the surface of things, an injection of the Romano Martinian spirituality that had come in from the Franks. But the vibrancy of that began to go underground.

Mercia was also in the process of absorbing the East Saxons and London. The bishopric in London came into the Mercian gift. Before that, the Christian King of Essex and London, Sigeberht, whom we saw in the previous chapter, "Toddling", had been murdered for being too forgiving. London seems to have become spiritually schizophrenic after that, part reverting to pagan, part hanging on to the sparkily Christian. The reverting element did so under pressure of the plague of 664 which followed the Synod of Whitby. The Christian God, it seemed to them, could not be real if you can get the plague. Anyway, the Mercian King, Wulfhere, sent his new Bishop, Jaruman, to call them back to Christian ways. It seems that he was successful. However, the two great St Aidan-trained Saints who had brought Christian Awakening to London were no longer there. St Chad had been appointed to York. And the dynamic St Cedd died in the same plague of 664. He took it as the ticket home to his Christ.

One wonders to what extent Mercia might have forced compliance to Christian Identity on London after Sigeberht was murdered. I have read that Sigeberht's murderer received baptism in East Anglia some time afterwards. But if he had meant it, I think the baptism would have been in or near London. One has the impression of a hidden hand of Mercian enforcement. (East Anglia was folding into Mercia by now.) Mercia was a serious child about embedding

Christian Identity. Not killing for it, note. No more guilty, in promoting a Christian Identity it saw as Light and suppressing idolatry it saw as Dark, than a modern government could be held to be for enforcing rules to promote vaccination and stop the spread of disease.

However, one senses a loss of Christian spark in London. As you will see shortly, it did manage to have a bishop as the 660s went by, but in what we might see as dubious circumstances. It all gives the impression of loss of Christian Innocence in Essex and London by 668.

Mercia – Christian Identity Precarious

Mercia itself was becoming quite an eclectic mix of Christian influences in the 660s. It favoured the Latin-Deiran Romano Martinian Catholic outer forms. However, it had been helped into Christian Identity by the Gaelic Martinian spirituality. It was also absorbing the Frankish Romano Martinian Catholic spirituality of East Anglia. And it was setting course to absorb the Roman Catholic Prestige of Kent. All these streams fused into the Early English as Mercia gradually worked its way to dominance. King Wulfhere, and many others to follow, became very serious about basing their expanding proto-state on Christian foundations.

From 658, Mercia had as its Bishop, at Lichfield, the gifted Trumhere. After Trumhere died in 662, it received Jaruman. Both were of the favoured mixture, Northern Romano Martinian Catholic, with the underlying Celtic spark fused in.

However, Jaruman also passed away in 667. At that point, you could say that Mercia, a Toddler-in-Christ with the arms of a heavyweight boxer, was without formal Christian leadership to help it towards maturity.

Mercia also remained tense with Northumbria. As we saw in the previous chapter, "Toddling", it had overthrown Northumbrian King Oswy's over-kingship by 658. Mercia had defined itself for a generation before that as the chief military opponent of Northumbria. Bishop Trumhere, as we also saw in that previous chapter, had taken a good deal of steam out of the conflict. And King Oswy had had the sense to draw back as well. But things were delicately poised. Mercia could have slipped back to older ways.

There was a particular risk of that in 668. Bishop Trumhere had passed away by 662 and his able successor, Jaruman, by 667. These both had some of the Christian way in them that promoted humility in kings. Proud Mercia had lost that subtle influence for Christian humility. And it had lost formal Christian leadership whose spirituality, being Northumbrian-derived, had been a force for reconciliation of the two powers.

Not good, when King Oswy was ageing in Northumbria, warlike Prince Ecgfrith was waiting in the wings and equally warlike King Wulfhere of Mercia had arms to flex.

Wessex – Struggling for Direction

As to Wessex, its King Cenwalh, converted by 648 in the court of King Anna in East Anglia, was struggling to find a way forward with Christian Identity. After Bishop Birinus had died in 650, Bishop Agilbert had been appointed, he who struggled to make himself understood in the Anglo Saxon language. Cenwalh sacked him. After that, a man named Wine had been appointed. However, Cenwalh fell out with him. Wine made his way to the Mercian royal court and bought the bishopric of London.

As at 668, Wessex was lacking formally ordained Christian leadership and influence. Its King had been a waverer between the Christian and the pagan too. There was a serious risk of losing its way, in Christian terms.

Canterbury and Most Everywhere – Vacant

In Canterbury, Archbishop Deusdedit had passed away. The appointment of a replacement fell into a power vacuum. The post remained vacant from 664. The monastic foundations were still building quietly there. But from the most directive Christian post of all, there was no direction.

As at 668, only two bishoprics were filled: Wine in London, having purchased it, and Saint Chad, uneasily, at York. Chad's orders were also technically suspect.

The Northumbrian set-apart Christians remained vibrant. The Celtic way was reliant more upon the monastery than the church and its bishops, and the monasteries continued strongly spiritual in the tradition of the Scots. At Lindisfarne, Saint Cuthbert was coming into the maturity of his high Christian powers. He was also rebuilding the life there since Colman's departure. But Cuthbert had little interest in appointments, titles and humanised authority structures. Wilfrid was influential in Mercia and Kent, but without formal powers, and a divisive figure in his home kingdom of Northumbria. King Oswy was ageing, sub-King Alhfrith of Deira was no more, and Oswy's likely successor, Prince Ecgfrith, was to be of implacable and warlike character, likely to spoil for a fight with Mercia once Oswy had passed on.

Mercia was very young in Christian Identity, very tense with Northumbria. The two had a newfound commonality of Christian Identity. But Mercia could easily have resumed more adversarial military ways. Sparky East Anglia was declining in its Christian spark. Wessex was not at ease within its new Christian self.

Altogether, as the year 667 rolled on to the year 668, Christian Identity was struggling for direction in the proto-English. I would say that the Christian Identity that had been born in them had entered a period of Innocence Lost. And seen purely from the perspective of Jesus Christ's Great Commission – go and make disciples – lack of leadership risked snatching defeat from the jaws of victory. Another widespread relapse, as had happened with Paulinus in 632/3, was all too possible, and this time even more catastrophic.

To the Rescue

It would need a Christian Leader of stature to pull things round. From the most unlikely of sources, in 668/9, one came. To Canterbury, as Archbishop. His name was Theodore. A Greek. Not an Ancient one, but improbably aged, even so.

Theodore understood two types of "Architecture" – Architecture Spiritual and Architecture Temporal. How to build a unified spiritual body; how to build a unified administrative body; and how to build the two as one in disparate territories in days when communication and travel were difficult. And he more than commanded the respect of Kings: they watched his ways of governing the church as a proto-national entity within their separate kingdoms and learned more unifying ways from them.

Such was Archbishop Theodore. Figures with gifts such as these are rare throughout all of history. But in 668, coming as the choice no one wanted, the proto-English got one.

He achieved greatness in his old age. He was not of royal Kent, but he was all that had been wise in Christian Kent and more. His legacy was to be a symbiotic integration of Church and State for the proto-English. It bequeathed a culturally uniting sense of Christian Identity which endured for more than a thousand years.

Before we look at Theodore, however, the next chapter will address a thread that has been running throughout every chapter of this book: "Martinian". The time has come to take note of St Martin of Tours and his spiritual descendants in more detail. Theirs was the Christian spiritual legacy which Theodore secured in the English.

CHAPTER 17.

Cosmic Seed

St Martin of Tours never married or had children.

But St Martin was a rich spiritual seed.

He had a host of highly gifted Christian descendants.

The spirituality in those descendants transformed the pagan Anglo Saxon peoples into the Christian Early English.

Artwork: Ben Emet

CHAPTER 18.

Saint Martin of Tours (316-397) and His Spiritual Descendants

In order to come to grips with what shaped the founding identity of the English, it is necessary to meet the life and Christian spirituality of St Martin of Tours.

His spirituality was as follows:

- Humble
- Powerful
- Truthful
- Deep
- Prophetic
- Discerning
- Cleansing
- Wise

This spirituality was released into the rootstock of the Early English in their founding times by spiritual descendants of St Martin, in a pincer movement that swept in from Celtic Christians in what we now call Scotland and from Germanic Frankish Christians in what we now call France.

Martin's Dates

Martin (316-397) was a citizen of the Western Roman Empire. He was born in a territory called Pannonia, in a location that is now part of modern Hungary. His father had been a Roman soldier with firm pagan views. Martin, as a young man, showed a deep affinity for Christian Life. His father, to "cure" him of it, arranged for Martin to be pressed into the Roman Army, against his will, at the age of just 15. He emerged from it at the age of 40, having given a mandatory 25 years' service. During that time, Martin's Christian Life became profound.

The Church in his young days

In Martin's young days, the church as a great institution had scarcely begun to exist. The famous Roman Emperor, Constantine the Great, had decreed official tolerance of Christianity in the year 313. He had also made it clear that the Christian way was henceforth to be the way he preferred for the Empire. Until then, the Christian church had been persecuted on and off for 250 years. As at 313, what was left of it was just emerging from the most systematic persecution ever, under the Emperor Diocletian.

The culture of Christian Life that impressed the young Martin was the one before the effects of Constantine's edict had percolated through the church. He was of the church ways that Diocletian had sought to exterminate. Martin's was the church of martyrs: of little structure; you were in it for life or death, quite possibly death. It taught commitment of discipleship. It existed by its spirituality. It had a name for looking after its own in a way that no other movement did. But it could do few works of public good – it was not supposed to exist. Such good as it could give to the wider world was of its spiritual influence. That was a top priority back then. The days were already numbered for that understanding of church when Martin was young. But it was still the understanding that shaped his earliest days in Christ. Because what started to happen in Rome after 313, the church becoming a place for career preferment, had not reached provincial Pannonia in his youth.

From Commitment to Commitment

Martin's approach to Christian Life was shaped by his years in the Roman Army. The 25 years' service required complete commitment. Every day, the Roman soldier was drawn into the most disciplined life on the planet. His life was free and yet not his own. What we call the monastic movement developed in large measure in the west from former Christian soldiers of the Roman army.

They carried over what they had known within the military institution into monastic institutions: set-apart; disciplined; totally committed. Their life was still not their own; only now it belonged not to the Emperor, by contract, but to the Christian God, freely surrendered.

The Roman soldier might also learn a trade for later life. Martin became an army medic. That also shaped the way his Christian Life worked out later. His spiritual life coalesced with medical experience to make him gifted in bringing wholeness to the poor, the sick and the mentally disturbed. And it imparted a missionary passion to lead the people out of an idolatrous way of life that held them back into a Christian one that could take them forward.

Martin also emerged from 25 years of danger in the Army with a calm and quiet disposition. He was going to need it.

A Changed World

The Christian world into which Martin emerged from the Army in 356 bore little resemblance to the one of Martin's youth. Constantine the Great, his mother Helen, and his son and successor Constantius, had taken a great interest in the Christian church. It enjoyed the state favour; some might say for better, some for worse.

Anyway, as at 356, there were a couple of problems in the church which would have been a big deal for the Christian God. The first one was this: after 313, you could get career benefits if you had a good position in it. By 356, very gifted people were in church leadership but not exactly gifted in the realm of spiritual influence: gifted in worldliness. That is not fatal before the Christian God if such leaders will, at least, submit their shrewdness to God, defer to one another and work humbly with civil authority rather than trying to dominate it. But it would be a problem.

The second problem was much deadlier. Much of the church in the west had succumbed to a heresy favoured especially by Constantius. It was called Arianism. I've already analysed it in the chapter about "Open Heaven" where I pointed out the wonder that no trace of this heresy was in those gifted Christians who first came to the Early English. That was because their Christian spirituality descended in great measure from St Martin. And St Martin had left a spiritual legacy which inoculated against it.

As a reminder, sorting out the wood from the trees about Arianism, there was no spiritual new birth in it. All things that matter to the Christian God spring from the spiritual new birth in Christ. The Arian church was a dead work: fake. The Roman church, whatever its faults, maintained doctrines that would still enable the new birth if a person really sought the Christ. The Arian church, by contrast, was a devil. The only problem was when Martin came out of the Army in 356, the devil was winning. The Arian church had become dominant in the Empire.

Martin seeks advice

Martin was one of the few who had not succumbed to Arianism. It is clear from his subsequent life that he had much exposure to its progress within the church during his Army days. And that he came to a decisive opinion about it. We can infer what it was from this: twice he was beaten up by Arian church gangs. We can also infer it from this: emerging from the Army, he made his way to Poitiers in Gaul, or France as we now call it. There he came to the dwelling of Bishop Hilary. Hilary had his bags packed. He had been sentenced to exile by Constantius for a strong open letter opposing the Emperor's Arianism. He awaited the imperial contingent who would shortly come to take him away. Martin wanted advice from Hilary: where to go to and whom to study with to be trained further in Christian Life.

One can only wonder at how it would have seemed to Bishop Hilary. Soon to go into exile; all seemed lost. Now here was this Martin, and it would have been obvious to him – it seems to have influenced everyone, some loving it, some hating it – that this Martin had in him a depth of spiritual greatness and he had a true understanding of the Christian gospel: that it depends upon the

Holy Spirit of the Christian God from beginning to end. There was hope, after all.

The Christian Journey begins

There was time for Hilary to equip Martin with sound doctrinal teaching and to appoint him to be an exorcist. And when Martin expressed the desire to walk over the Alps from Poitiers in Gaul (France) to his parents in Pannonia (Hungary), Hilary equipped him with letters of commendation for hospitality en route. Martin's objective was to lead his parents to Christian commitment.

Crossing the Alps, Martin fell into the hands of robbers. One raised an axe to kill him, but another stopped the blow. This latter, leading Martin off bound, asked Martin who he was and whether he was afraid. Martin replied that he was a Christian and that he grieved not for himself but the robber. The robber released Martin, asked him to pray for him and afterwards sought to lead a Christian lifestyle. Arriving in Pannonia, Martin's father proved obdurately pagan. His mother, with friends and neighbours, received the Christ.

Moving on from there, Martin came to Milan, in what we now call northern Italy. This was then, as it still is today, one of Europe's great cities. He got there just as a best-seller hit the stands. It might not sell today, but it certainly sold back then. It was a biography of the life and example of a hermit monk in Egypt called St Antony. These days, the keenest young Christians of the English-speaking world will go to conferences and events with highly gifted speakers and inspired music to develop their Christian Life. Sometimes they come back on fire. Those days, you had to settle for a book about a hermit. But it set the keenest Christians of the western Roman Empire on fire. It set St Martin on fire. Martin felt a draw towards the monastic life. Now, here was a newly published how-to-do-it manual derived from its earliest great practitioner.

It is interesting to note that the author of the book was called Athanasius. He was the leading figure of them all in opposing the Arian spiritual death and upholding the types of small c catholic doctrine which modern Protestant Christians would easily agree with. Indeed, you could say that the English fought the Protestant Reformation to recover it. It seems that Athanasius had the sort of evangelising gifts and understanding that would likely give him the platform at many a Protestant evangelising rally of modern times. The gifting seems to have been present in the book.

Martin set up a community in Milan with a few friends, intending to imitate what they read. However, he came to the attention of the Arian, i.e. heretical, Bishop of Milan. The bishop's retainers beat him up. Martin and his little band made their way to a small island off what we would now call the Italian Riviera. There they almost starved themselves to death in the cause of developing intimate spiritual communion with the Christian God; such was their zeal to reduce "the flesh" and promote "the Spirit".

Bishop – against his will

Five years had elapsed since Martin had left the Roman Army. He reined in the starvation side of things a bit and, in 361, made his way to the Loire Valley of Gaul, the political conditions having become more favourable on the mainland. He set up a small Christian community in a village named Ligugé. There he spent the ten happiest years of his life. In 371, however, the people of nearby Tours wanted a new bishop. By now it was known that the strange monk at Ligugé had something very special in him. So they carried off Martin against his will and put him forward for candidature. The various other regional bishops, whose will would normally have prevailed, did not want him. Not their type. The people shouted them down and carried the day. Martin submitted to it. Make of that process what you will: it shows that the Christian whose spirituality was going to descend with history-shaping impact into the world had popular acclaim.

Martin did fulfil his bishop's duties, but he did not exactly conform. He set up headquarters outside the city at Marmoutier, building a monastic establishment in the caves there. The local people had to come out to him. The keen Christian young of Europe flocked to the caves to be mentored by him. He became a seed of living Christian spirituality into them. To the scandal of his peers, he insisted on wearing rough garments. To the scandal of all, instead of a throne, he sat on a three-legged milking stool: a sign of humility but also a symbol of Father, Son and Holy Spirit, the Three-in-One Christian God.

A Gifted Ministry

From time to time the sick were healed. At the time of writing this, a painting in Canterbury Cathedral shows Martin praying to raise a dead baby back to life. On at least one occasion, he resuscitated a dead person, following the pattern documented in the Bible in the account of the prophet Elijah. When Martin did go into church in Tours, he would spend time amongst the mentally ill who would come freely into it. Some were delivered, and he cared about all of them. He would lie down amongst them without fear and let them wander round him as he prayed. In community with the young enthusiasts at the cave monastery, the basic idea was to learn to hear from God and speak it out and to discern the Holy Spirit from other spirits.

On missionary adventures amongst the country people in Gaul, Martin was a destroyer of idols and pagan sanctuaries. These days, we might take the libertarian high horse with him about that. How dare he infringe their human rights? Martin's understanding was that demons were associated with the idols and they meant the people harm. So he had the people's well-being in mind. He did not just destroy: he ministered the replacement life of Christ. And he usually proceeded with permission. The most famous incident was over a sacred tree. He wanted the villagers to chop it down. They said they would follow his Christian God if he would lie on the spot where they knew, from their experience of tree felling, that the tree was certain to fall if they felled it. Martin agreed. They tethered him to the spot. As the tree fell towards him, Martin stretched out his hand in the sign of the Cross and the tree fell the other way. The villagers adopted Christian Identity. These days we might see Martin as a sort of Jedi Master. In those days, the Gallic region being Celtic by culture, they would have seen him as a sort of Super Druid. Martin was not a Druid. The druidical tended towards the elevation of nature, whereas Martin worshipped the Christian God. However, he was also a set-apart holy man, and the idea of the set-apart holy man was also at the heart of the druidical culture. And Martin had powers over normal nature. So there would have been a missionary resonance in Martin's way that impacted the people strongly.

Forebodings (i) – Tours

Towards the end of his life, there were a few things that would have filled Martin with foreboding. The first will seem very strange to the modern mind. Martin could see that his likely successor was going to be a more worldly person who would diminish his spiritual legacy locally to Tours. Why not just force him out while you still have the position to do so? But Martin did not. He could only have perceived it to be part of God's mysterious plan.

Forebodings (ii) – An Evil Seed in the Church

I need to introduce a distinction before we proceed. I find it helpful to discern a difference between Large C Catholic and small c catholic. The Roman Church of today calls itself Large C Catholic. Most Protestant Christians of today remain 80-90% small c catholic. I will explain as we go on.

The second foreboding for St Martin was that in 380, seventeen years before his death, the Roman capital C Catholic Church, where the capital C denotes a sense of Identity set upon domination, came into being. What gave it this new Identity was imperial insistence that the direct descendants of St Peter, represented by the Papacy, had formalised supreme authority over the church, along with secular powers of coercion, and anyone in the Empire who did not line up could be coerced.

Until 380, I find it helpful to think of the Roman church, whatever its formal title, large C or not, as catholic with a small c. Its Papacy had premier prestige and influence but had not formalised sweeping domination with added rights of coercion. Interestingly, the Early English, structuring though they did their world around the Christian church, never conceded formal dominion to the Pope. Instead, they accorded the Papacy premier prestige and influence and co-authority over the highest clerical appointments. That remained so with the

Norman conquerors. It was the Plantagenet King John who first conceded dominion powers, which the Protestant Reformation later cast off.

The word catholic with a small c has a range of meanings, such as universal, wide-ranging or inclusive. More technically, it can be taken to mean "of commonly understood, tested and approved Christian doctrine, as descended through those who validated it under the Holy Spirit of the Christian God and within corporate review processes". As such, it describes the Christian church right back to when it was born without any title in year 33 when Jesus Christ ascended to heaven and the Holy Spirit of the Christian God came upon it. So if a Protestant thinks they belong to that, they would be small c catholic as well.

A significant validation process for Christian doctrine took place during the earlier years of Martin's life without his direct involvement, although he had clearly been aware of it. In response to the deadly Arian false doctrine – which was the spiritual killer of all spiritual killers – the Roman church slowly but surely began to write out the true doctrines that would provide a foundation for the spiritual new birth. It therefore documented and developed various Creeds. To this day, the Protestant Anglican Church will happily stand by the greater part of them, and most UK Christians, whatever their title, will recite 80-90% similar versions without misgiving. That is because most UK Protestants are 80-90% catholic with a small c. That applies in many nations outside the UK, too, however spectacularly gifted the church may be in latter-day spiritual streams of Christian Life. It applies even if the church gives itself the words Reformed, Baptist, Methodist, Presbyterian, Pentecostal, Kingdom, Redeemed, Strict, Particular, Fire, River, Community, Full Gospel or many other things besides in its titles. Most Protestant Christians sing the heart of the catholic doctrine with a small c every Christmas, without blinking, in the famous old carol "O come all ye faithful": "God of God, light of light, Lo! He abhors not the virgin's womb. Very (i.e. truly) God, begotten not created."

Anyway, St Martin subscribed, like most Protestants, to small c catholic understanding as it developed in written Creeds during his earlier years. But St Martin, like any Protestant, did not buy into the Roman Catholic Church with a large coercive C from 380. The people who had decreed it that way had meant well, by their lights. It was to be, for example, a solution to eliminate the Arian spiritual death if all else failed. However, they had not bargained for ungodly clerics abusing their newfound powers. No sooner did these have them than Martin was obliged to become involved in a plea for clemency after a worldly bishop had engineered the trial of a sect of over-zealous Christians in Spain. They were in error, not heresy, and the error was not that far off how Martin had been from 356 to 361, over-starving himself off the Italian coast.

Within the plea process, Martin found himself obliged to share holy communion with the other bishop as a condition of the release of the captives. He did share in it – and felt drained of spiritual force for long afterwards. The deal was reneged on, anyway. The other bishop backed out, but the imperial powers still put the offenders to death.

Martin was a spiritually sighted man. That sort of thing, as the Roman Catholic Church with a large C was born, would have filled him with foreboding. If Martin was the seed form of great goodness, he had just encountered the seed form of great evil – and inside the church, not outside it.

Now, it will be no surprise to a non-Christian reader to see that evil came into the Christian church. Maybe a Christian reader might baulk. However, a Christian reader might be inclined to confirm whether this is possible within the church from the Christian Bible. In that, you can discover an evil seed in the leadership within the very earliest and as yet untitled church. You find it in the tiny letter called 3 John. You find there, in the character called Diotrephes, the seed that was to grow into the Dark Side of the Medieval church. The seed was in this: Diotrephes loved to be first – wanted to dominate, in other words. But Jesus Christ had taught that who coveted coming first would come last, whereas who would submit to coming last would come first. St Martin, fully compliant with Jesus, would always let himself come last under God. But the Roman church in his lifetime had begun a long journey to covet coming first: domination.

Now, I must stress that I am not saying that the Roman church is like that now. But it seems difficult to argue that it did not become like that for a time. The large C Catholic title remains. And the authority of the Papacy, although overthrown in the Protestant church, remains in the Roman church. But it seems to have been pruned severely of the old Coercive powers. And it cherishes its ancient Saints. Protestants can learn from that. Some of those Saints were the origin seed of modern-day Protestant Christian spirituality. The Protestant Reformation secured the spiritual heritage of those Saints when it was in danger of being lost. However, it also put it into new clothing and developed new labels. And accompanying those new labels was an indiscriminate loathing of the past. So the heritage *seems* lost. But Christian spirituality does not change. Labels change. Shapes shift. But in Christian spirituality, although degrees of revelation vary by generation and location, Jesus Christ is the same yesterday, today and forever.

Now, returning to the little letter of 3 John: in contrast to Diotrephes, who was *not* commended, there was someone who *was* commended. His name was Demetrius. He was the genuine article Christian. But… no more is said of him in the letter, meaning that he would have to make his way in the church under God, whatever the likes of Diotrephes might get up to.

Saint Martin was a Demetrius figure. Filled with foreboding: Diotrephes was rising.

Forebodings (iii) – Tumult of Empire

The third thing that would have filled Martin with foreboding was that he would have seen in his lifetime the secular western Empire heading to its tumultuous downfall. Martin himself was no stranger to emperors. The day before his release from the Army, he had stood up to one when put in a situation that would have compromised his sense of Christian integrity. What a temptation. One day to go after 25 years' service: go for the easy way. But no, Martin would not. The outcome was that Martin found himself, on his very last day of 25 years' service, in a position unarmed on the battlefront where he was certain to be killed. The opposing force stood down on the day. Martin walked free. That is how narrow a squeak it was for the Christian spirituality which would one day transform the Anglo Saxons into the Christian Early English and ultimately descend to many peoples. The point for now, though, is that Martin would have known of general decline going on, and with it came much violence.

It has been written of Martin, in a book by a former minister of the tiny church of St Martin's in Canterbury, Christopher Donaldson, that he and his band would not have much cared whether civilisation sank or swam. Very likely. But it made for a turbulent backdrop to his life. And he would have seen what was coming. In the century after his death, the old western Roman Empire descended into chaos as various Germanic tribes overran it.

Martin's Spirituality Prevails

I should give one more example of St Martin's spirituality. Before I give it, I should say that one of the most important "Charismata" that the Christian can have by gifting of the Holy Spirit of God is called "Discerning of spirits". It is the gift that keeps the Christian flock grounded in truth. Jesus Christ was the great example. St Martin specialised in it. For example, he was perturbed by a local miracle cult. He had a bad feeling about it. He enquired of the Christian God. Instead of a dead saint, it transpired that the focus of the cult had been a highway robber. St Martin was shown the man's shade. He sent it to its place. I can't help thinking that many Christian leaders in the world today would say to Martin, if they met him, "Come along and show us how it's done."

Well, St Martin died in harness as Bishop of Tours in 397. His spirituality did not die with him. Locally, Tours was going to hold his relics and a cult of them. But his spirituality was going to prevail far and wide. You could put that down to one of those things. Or you could note that it is a familiar pattern of the Christian God, which is that his own may prevail posthumously. Like, er, Jesus Christ. For St Martin, there were two mechanisms involved:

A. One of the invading Germanic tribes, the Franks, came to treasure what Martin stood for.

B. He had a chain of great Celtic Christian Saints for spiritual descendants.

Both these streams of Christian spiritual legacy matured down to the Anglo Saxons and transformed them.

A. The Franks

Politically appraised, the Franks, or at least their rulers, were a violent people, given to bloody civil war in later generations, and a gift to any historian who wants to portray history as Hallowe'en Horror for the children. However, there was more to them than that. To see our history in a balanced way, we also have to consider the Christian spiritual dimension of them.

Spiritual Principle – Healthy Eye, Healthy Body

To appraise the Franks spiritually, we first have to come to grips with certain cryptic teachings by Jesus Christ. He said that the eye is the lamp of the body. If your eyes are healthy, your body will be full of light. But if your eyes are unhealthy, your body will be full of darkness. Before that, he had also said that a light or lamp must be put on its stand and not hidden.

What he meant, drawing upon a few other things he said too, was this. The healthy eye is the spiritually empowered group of Christians bearing the Christian message. The body is the earthly context in which they live – language group, tribe, nation or empire. The lampstand is the language group, tribe, nation or empire that will let the spiritual Christian group with the message of the Christ shine like a light on the stand rather than hide it. As long as there is truth and goodness in the spiritual Christian group, the surrounding language group, tribe, nation or empire will benefit. Even if they have a dark heritage and a mixing in of dark ways, there is hope for them, and the Christian God will promote light in them. If the Christian spirituality becomes blind, then the language group, tribe, nation or empire that was once a stand for the light will also become blind. The Christian God might ultimately take his hand off it, and such ditch as it might fall into will then be fallen into. As for the Christian witness that has lost its way, Jesus added a further cryptic teaching: the point will come when, all God's patience having been exhausted, he will remove the lamp from its stand.

Applied in the Real World

Now, the real world point is this. One of the so-called Barbarian tribes put Martin's Christian lamp on its stand. All the others put an Arian fake lamp on their stands. Their names are the stuff of shuddering memory, such as Vandal and Goth. The Martinian tribe was the Germanic Franks. In the end, much of France became their land and the whole of it was named from them.

The Franks were no angels. They were as brutal as the rest. There was no special appeal in them compared to the others; nothing of their own goodness to commend them. But then again, with the Christian God, he makes it clear that humankind's own goodness is a lesser concern to him. What is of greater concern is what light is on the lampstand.

In the history of the Franks, it went like this. The Germanic Franks had swept into Gaul. More than a hundred years after Martin had passed away, in 507, the brutal King Clovis of the Franks faced a battle with the King of the Arian Goths, Alaric II. The location was Poitiers, where Martin in 356 had met Bishop Hilary and near where, at Ligugé, Martin had spent the happiest years of his life. Winner took Gaul.

Now, Clovis had a Christian wife named Clothilde. She was the grandmother of the future Queen Bertha of Kent and a most remarkable Christian. Influenced by her, Clovis had already called on the name of Jesus Christ during a battle he was losing and won it, whereupon he had been baptised.

Now, there may or may not have been Christian integrity within the baptism. However, now that he faced the Goths, Clovis, out of superstition perhaps, or out of at least an atom of Christian faith, insisted that his troops do no harm to the neighbourhood in order not to offend the late St Martin. When one trooper stole, he killed the man himself. Then he sent messengers to nearby Tours, to the basilica containing Martin's body, to seek an oracle as to the outcome of the coming battle. As the messengers entered the basilica, the monks were reading words of King David in the Bible: "You gave me strength for the battle... humbled my enemies ...that I might destroy them." Encouraged by this report, Clovis joined battle and defeated and slew Alaric. Later he went in person to the basilica of Tours in triumph and there, wearing a purple tunic like a Roman potentate, had himself crowned. He established his seat of government in Paris.

Clovis, a pagan willing to honour St Martin, had just defeated an Arian. Neither he nor his descendants, in all their dissolute violence, would ever say a word against St Martin thereafter. The Frankish people adopted the Roman Catholic church doctrines; they were the only major tribal group of the times not to go Arian. Pilgrimage to Martin's sites became part of their culture. He became their hero saint. Given the goodness that had been in Martin, compared to the brutality in the Franks, what's not to like about that?

What to make of Clovis?

There are a number of ways to reflect on this. Clovis certainly would not have won by magic. He was made of pungent stuff as a warrior and a general. So you could say it was by his own might that he prevailed. It was a coincidence that he had involved St Martin: there is no God, or if there is, he is not active in human affairs.

Hmmm... God, who is Almighty by his own estimation, is not active in human affairs? Really? It is a consistent position if you are an atheist, but a difficult one if you are a God-believer.

Well then, you could say, Clovis was into superstition: do not offend a dead saint. Would God favour him over that – are you kidding?

Time to ask the question again: if *you* were the Christian God, how would you weigh up Clovis?

I would see it like this: dead saints and superstition may not have been the chief concern of the Christian God at the time. He plays a long game. He works with what there is, not with what there is not. The future of the Christian message of salvation through Jesus Christ might have been at stake in Clovis, in the Christian God's reasoning. That would have been a big deal to him; a very big deal. It is why, in the Bible, God favoured King David. The future of the messianic line to Jesus Christ was at stake in David's battles. David did not fully know at the time. It was not for his own goodness that God gave him Favour. It was for the Christ to come. Perhaps it was similar with Clovis.

Because here is the point I would make: the basilica at Tours, for all its worldly harbouring of relics, still held to good doctrine as descended from St Martin. This means that there was a healthy eye in the local body. Its relics were a focal point, relevant to the culture of the times, for the unlearned to draw near, maybe in superstition for some, but maybe in faith for others, to seek the word of the Christian God. And the Tours basilica doctrine was not Arian and fake. It was Christian. By then, of the Roman Catholic church with a large C but still harbouring the old catholic with a small c understanding that was in Martin and capable of imparting the spiritual new birth.

Anyway, under Clovis, the Franks adopted Christian Identity and took the Martinian way of it to the heart of their churchmanship. Few others in mainland Europe did. Therefore, although some Frankish leaders may have been dark, they lampstanded, in their church, an eye with light in it, and it brought light to the body of their people. The spiritual health in it descended to the Early English in the real world.

So, if you want to understand our history, you have to permit yourself to discern the Martinian Christian light on the lampstand in the Franks. You can't recount only their secular brutality, holding your nose at them, holier-than-thou; history as frightening the children into a pleasant sense of easy superiority to the past.

These days, as descendants of the Protestant Reformation, even historians who do acknowledge the Frankish church tend mainly to highlight corruptions in some of its bishops. However, the fuller truth is that the Franks had some great Christians in their earlier church generations. And the way they dealt with the Anglo Saxons, with whom they had common Germanic heritage and good ties, was not to make war on them to subjugate them. Instead, they sent their best Christians to promote Christian Life, all of those that came to the Early English being spiritual descendants of St Martin.

Queen Bertha of Kent was one of them. Bishop Liudhard, her chaplain, would have been another. Bishop Felix of East Anglia, a key figure, was another. Although there is no absolute certainty, I am not the only one to infer that Bishop Birinus of Wessex was of the Frankish Martinian spiritual heritage as well. Birinus was at work in Wessex when, with the Gaelic Martinian Saint King Oswald of Northumbria as godfather, the first foundation of the English Identity was laid within Christian treaty: the two Martinian streams, Frankish and Gaelic, fused in the foundation time.

The East Anglian court of Kings Sigeberht and Anna was on intimate terms with the Martinian "Charismatic" stream of Christian Life in the Franks. Coming out of East Anglia, Queen Seaxburh added extra Martinian spark to the Kentish Christian ways of King Eorcenberht. And East Anglia, sitting between Northumbria and Kent both geographically and spiritually, helped the three kingdoms to go forward into Early English Christian unity by way of peace, not sword. It was the Romano Martinian Catholic Christian King Anna of the East Angles who led the lapsed-into-paganism refugee King Cenwalh of Wessex into Christian Identity too.

These were Christian English Nation Building things, mediated via Frankish or Frankish-connected Martinian Christians.

So, through the Frankish church, the Martinian Christian Life came to the Early English like the southern claw of a great pincer.

B. Great Celtic Saints

We turn now to the more famous Christian spiritual descendants of St Martin: in a golden Celtic chain, St Ninian, St Patrick, St Columba, St Columbanus, St Aidan, St Cuthbert. These were the Northern claw of the pincer movement of Christian Life to the Early English. We generally call them the great Celtic Saints.

In the days of Ninian and Patrick (early 400s, broadly), the term "Celt" spanned different people groups with different senses of Identity in the territories of what we now call the United Kingdom. The Britonnic Celts had a proto-Welsh language and an old stream of Christianity descended from the old Roman Empire from 177. That stream seems to have become a Christian lamp taken off its stand. The Picts had a similar language to the Britons. The Scots had the quite different Gaelic language. Picts and Scots were largely heathen. However, in the 400s, they each gradually took on the newer Martinian Christian way. That became like a replacement lamp on the stand.

In the secular world of the early 400s, the various groups used to fight and sometimes enslaved one another. The Britons, for example, were much troubled by the still-largely-heathen Picts and Scot/Gaels.

Martin's Spirituality Migrates

St Martin passed away in 397. In 410, the Western Roman Empire fell into chaos. There followed a century of Germanic invasions which overran mainland Europe.

The remains and cult of Saint Martin stayed at Tours. They were to play a part with King Clovis in 507, as we saw. However, long before that, the Martinian *spirituality* migrated.

- It went offshore of what is now the French Riviera to a monastery known as Lerins on an island now named after St Honoratus, who founded it.

- It went across the sea to monastic pockets in what we now call Ireland.

- It journeyed into monastic pockets of what we now call Wales.

- It pressed on, monastically, into what we now call Scotland – in two phases.

I have heard it said that these small monastic pockets could be credited with saving Western Civilisation, no less. The detail omitted tends to be that they were pockets of migrated Martinian Christian spirituality. It is customary to omit that detail. To my mind, if you omit it, then you do not actually teach what really shaped the history. Nor can a person from the Western Protestant world, including the atheist, discern their descent.

Now, before we go any further, yet another reminder not to see the Celtic church as somehow not a part of the Roman Catholic church. As you will soon see, it was the Pope or his envoys who sent out the great Celtic Saints to the North in the first place. As to St Martin himself, he sought to live at peace as far as he was able within the overall envelope of the Roman Catholic church.

St Ninian

Shortly before 397, the starter Northern Celtic saint, St Ninian, was sent out by the Roman Pope Siricius. Ninian was a Britonnic Celt, commissioned out of Rome. He was from what we now call Cumbria in England, the south side of the Solway Firth. We have encountered it already in this book under its Britonnic name, Rheged.

It is important to note that after the Pope commissioned him, Ninian took a detour. He may have been Britonnic ethnic, but the detour made him Martinian spiritual. He went to learn from St Martin. Ninian was contemporary with Martin in the closing days of Martin's life. He was also a friend of one of St Martin's inner circle, a man named Paulinus of Nola (in Campania, southern Italy). Of this Paulinus of Nola, more when we come to St Patrick.

Not long before 397, when Martin died, Ninian and Paulinus of Nola became immersed in the Christian spirituality of Marmoutier, Martin's cave monastery near Tours. It was *after* Ninian had taken on that mantle that he went back to his homeland with the Papal commission to evangelise. He crossed the Solway Firth and went into what is now Scotland. He went to the pre-Martinian Christian Britons of the North and also to the heathen Picts, a far Northern Celtic people whose language was not dissimilar to the Britonnic. The Picts began to adopt Christian Identity. Ninian founded a noted and long-enduring centre of Christian learning on the north side of the Solway Firth known as Whithorn or Candida Casa (the White House, where White has implications of Holy). Just like Queen Bertha's tiny starter seed church at Canterbury nearly two hundred years later in 580, Candida Casa was dedicated to St Martin. It became a major centre for the development of Celtic Christian discipleship. The building of it was under way when St Martin died. This was the first phase of the migration of Martinian spirituality into what we now call Scotland.

Ninian went on to establish a chain of monastic centres and a safe route for Christian missionaries into the Pictish interior of what we now call Scotland. The vibrant power of the Christian God is said to have been on Candida Casa, and the monks he seeded into the small establishments became a byword for peaceful light amidst the people.

His mission complete there, the Britonnic Ninian crossed to the Picts of what is now Ireland. The Martinian spirituality took root there, far west of Germanic invasion and tumult. This territory of Ireland was then also full of Scots. The languages were quite different: Scots held to what we now call Gaelic, Picts to something like Britonnic (forerunner of what we now call Welsh). The Martinian Christian Life that Ninian founded in Ireland would later spread to the Scots. When the Scots began their migration out of Ireland into the west of what we now call Scotland, they took it with them. This was the second phase of the journey of the Martinian Christian spirituality into Scotland. And this second phase of it was going to become transformatively important for the Angles later. Kings Oswald and Oswy of Northumbria were going to partake of it in their exile amongst the Scots. [To note in passing: Kings Oswald and Oswy of Northumbria, called Irish speakers in some history books, would actually have been masters of Gaelic (as well as the Old English of their childhoods) because of their exile among the Gaelic-speaking Scots.]

St Patrick

Turning to the sequence again, in about 405, a young Britonnic Celt was captured and enslaved by Scotic (Gaelic) Celts, being carried off to what we now call Antrim, Northern Ireland. He was a proto-Welsh speaker. He may have been from North Wales. It is also possible – I think likely – that he was from territory in what we now call England: Cumbria/Rheged, like St Ninian. His name has come down to us as Patrick. Later, St Patrick to you and me, green beer and all that.

Before we look at St Patrick's career, we must return to what became of St Martin's spirituality at Tours. Martin's temporal successor, Bishop Brice, took his relics to the basilica at Tours and began the process of turning them into a cult. In the time of Clovis, they were a trigger for events already described. But what of Martin's many spiritual successors, other than St Ninian and Paulinus of Nola, who had trained under him at Marmoutier? As it happened, through coincidence you may say, or by the design of the Christian God you might alternatively reckon, Martin was given, as his time drew to a close, a biographer who trained with him. His name was Sulpicius Severus.

It is important here to note the word "biographer". Many lives of Saints have come down to us from what we call "hagiographers". These were writers, often of the Medieval period that we associate with corruption and the fantastical, who produced exaggerated or whimsical lives of saints. The ones that sold big in their days, and kept the pilgrims coming, but to which we now respond, "Yeah, and I'm Elvis." The Protestant Reformation had a visceral loathing of them. It has descended into modern atheism. However, *biographers* write reasonably and with feet on the ground. Such was Sulpicius Severus: a rare commodity down the ages until after the Protestant Reformation. To him it was given to write the Life of St Martin.

When published, in about 395, it had, in its time, the same impact as the Life of St Antony had on Martin in Milan in 357. It set the keen Christian young of Europe on fire and kept alive much that Martin had stood for. One of those in whom it was alive was to become known as St Honoratus. He took the old Martinian route to an island off the Riviera, the French side of it this time, founding in 410 a monastic community known as Lerins on the island now called St Honorat. This held the light of Martinian spirituality while the mainland was troubled for a century by the Germanic tribes. It was even to prove a staging point for St Augustine's little team as it made its way to Canterbury in 596/7, quite likely imparting the Martinian "Anointing" en route. It was also the place where Bede's mentor, Benedict Biscop, stopped off to "get the Anointing", to use a modern phrase from some Protestant circles which promote the Life in the Holy Spirit of the Christian God. Pause here: the earliest historian of the English, Bede, was mentored by someone who had detoured to Lerins for the Martinian Anointing. No wonder Bede's history is full of the phenomenal. The Martinian Christian times *were* phenomenal.

Anyway, we must remember this Lerins as we return to the Britonnic-ethnic Patrick. He spent many years as a slave amongst the Scots in Ireland and was not badly treated. But he did want his freedom. The day came that he escaped by ship. It seems that he had a dream that instructed him to set off to seek the ship. The port was two hundred miles away. It must have been quite a journey. This was the first of two life-changing dreams. Guidance through dreams is well within the normal envelope of the Christian prophetic. But the dots to join up to explain the whole episode are lost to us now.

To continue, Patrick was like Ninian in this way: Britonnic ethnicity, Martinian spirituality. After his escape ship docked in ravaged Gaul, it seems to have been a priority in Patrick's mind to use his freedom to develop his Christian Life. And the sources he sought were all Martinian. It is clear that Patrick was of the Martinian chain. He was baptised in Ireland during his slavery by Saint Caranoc. Caranoc was a living link to St Ninian. Some think St Caranoc did all the "sowing, watering and reaping" into Christ of St Patrick. I think it more likely that Caranoc "reaped" St Patrick out of an earlier exposure than that to the Martinian way: either in North Wales or, as I would think more likely still, out of Candida Casa. What could be more normal for a young Christian of the Celtic seaborne culture than to cross the Solway Firth, from his home turf of Rheged, for impartation of the vibrant Christian spirituality planted there by his Rheged hero, Saint Ninian?

Anyway, once Patrick had escaped, he visited what he had hoped would be the central source of Martinian Christian spirituality, the basilica of St Martin at Tours. However, his time had not yet come; the region was in a period of Germanic invasions, and there he also realised just how little Christian understanding he had. Patrick returned eventually to his Britonnic home and family. However, later in life, he was to journey again to seek the Martinian Anointing in different locations. He was hungry for it. He searched far. He became highly motivated for a fresh impartation.

Here is why. Once back in his homeland, a second life-changing dream came to Patrick. In the dream, the Gaels who had enslaved him asked him to return to them and walk among them. Patrick took this as a call from the Christian God to take the Christian gospel to his enslavers. We have no date for the dream.

Now, people get quite embarrassed to recount that a dream was involved. We don't believe in that sort of thing. However, there is no problem with a dream inviting you to take the Christian message to a specific territory. It is well within the envelope of the Christian Bible: the Apostle Paul was guided in exactly that way on one occasion. The people of a particular territory asked him in a dream to come to them.

In response to the dream, Paul went immediately. Patrick, however, delayed. In that way, he behaved exactly as Paul had taught in another respect: he took time to come to the end of his own strength and acquire sufficient empowerment from the Holy Spirit of the Christian God. You see, after the dream, Patrick spent numberless years in preparation to answer it. To paraphrase his words, written at the end of his life, he went to Ireland when he had come to the end of his own strength. In Patrick's case, one of the things he would have come to the end of his own strength about was any lingering desire for vengeance on his enslavers.

But what did Patrick do in the numberless years before he answered the Call? He hunted down the Martinian Anointing. As follows:

He returned to Gaul to seek out studies. At some point in the proceedings, and what a wonder is this, Patrick made his way to southern Italy, to Paulinus of Nola, then a very old man, for advice on how to develop his Christian Life. Paulinus of Nola was the oldest remaining one who had known St Martin in life. Paulinus advised Patrick to follow a course which included staying at the Lerins monastery of St Honoratus. There Patrick drank in the Romano Martinian Catholic Christian spirituality. He "took the tonsure", meaning a haircut which denotes a life set apart for Christ. He got a good sight more than a tonsure. Judging by his later life, he also "got the Anointing" – Big Time. Jesus Christ, if you recall, had used an image of the Holy Spirit of the Christian God as a mantle or overcoat of power. There can be little doubt that Patrick got the mantle. Then he was ready. By then it was about 431/2.

Let's take stock here: St Patrick became immersed in the Martinian Christian spirituality in the same place that St Augustine of Canterbury visited en route to the English, as well as Bede's mentor, Benedict Biscop. And note: this great Celtic Saint was empowered out of the *Romano* Martinian stream, *not* the Gaelic one; the Gaelic Martinian Christian spirituality that descended to the English was not even born yet.

St Patrick's Commission

So, in the year 432, St Patrick responded to the dream imparted by his Christian God. He went back to the Scots in Ireland who had enslaved him and took the Christian gospel to them. He had a wondrously successful ministry. Sadly, it was written up later in a legendary way. However, we should step aside from the modern predilection to reject all that was phenomenal because we hate Medieval embroidering. By the time Patrick was done, Ireland was the leading Christian light of Europe. You don't achieve that without there having been abundant spiritual power at work. Many long-enduring centres of Christian discipleship were established. And that, if you recall, was the Great Commission set by Jesus Christ.

Now, it is necessary to drill deep as to why Patrick was successful. There would have been more to it than simply the power of the Holy Spirit of the Christian God. We have already seen why, when we recounted the great principle of Christ that became embodied in the life of the future King Oswald of Northumbria: grace in Christ extended to the assassin. We traced the spiritual lineage of that back to St Patrick. It was like this when Patrick went back to Ireland in 432: blessing was extended to curse: freedom in Christ was extended to slavers. *Christian grace* was Patrick's ultimate response to a great evil. He had spent numberless years preparing to extend it. I think we can reasonably say, from a Christian understanding, that his God would have made Patrick successful in the extreme because he had extended grace in the extreme.

St Patrick's life was not, as you might get the impression these days, like this: "A mythical goodie-goodie had a mythical dream and went off to fulfil it immediately, and tall tales ensued. Now, let's drink to that in green beer." Instead, it was like this: "A real-life former slave had a dream of Christian guidance exactly like the Apostle Paul in the Bible. He studied numberless years away from home in response to it. He journeyed to southern Italy and sailed to a French Island to encounter the real people with the real spiritual power he would need for the task. He came, like the Apostle Paul, to the end of his own strength. Finally ready, he went in obedience to the call. Christ-like, he extended the most profound of all forms of grace: blessing to slavers. Whereupon, exactly as Jesus Christ had taught would happen if you followed that pattern, signs and wonders abounded in his Christian ministry." There has never been a finer example in all history of the principles of the Christian Bible being made flesh in a Christian. What a pity that Medieval embroidering has focussed the modern mind on debunking tall tales rather than the complete pattern of the Christ in St Patrick.

Anyway, the result was that what we now call Ireland became the leading Christian light of Europe. In the monasteries there, a strong contribution was made to saving what we call European civilisation. What you might read in the history books is that the contribution was made by a few "Religious" monks in Ireland copying Bibles. What it was really saved by was the Martinian Spirit-filled Christian Anointing borne in a human vessel who followed exactly the patterns of Jesus Christ and the Apostle Paul. The monks developed vibrant Christian Life and copied Bibles as an outworking of that.

Saint Patrick to Saint Columba – Profound Grace

St Patrick's spiritual legacy was to have a further profound mark of the grace of the Christian God in it. The key link in the spiritual chain that led from Patrick to the conversion of the Northumbrian Angles was to be St Columba, more than a century later. Now, here is a wonder of Christian grace: *St Columba was a direct descendant of the Scotic family that had kidnapped and enslaved the young St Patrick.*

We should make the effort to discern basic Christian principles here. In a Christian understanding, the Christian God has worked certain basic principles into the creation which he has subjected, for the time being, to frustration. There are principles of judgement. They work exceeding slow and grind exceeding fine. And there are principles of blessing. They work like a seed, or an exponential S-curve over time, or a snowball being rolled through snow. Starting small, they end up abounding.

Now, here is what came of the initial seed of grace sown by St Patrick. Remember, here, that spiritual things are not bound by time and to genetic succession. The grace descended to St Columba, descendant of slavers, once St Patrick had broken a cycle of evil by returning blessing in Christ to the enslaving family. The grace was extended in turn, by those Columba went on to train on Iona, to Oswald and Oswy, children of the violent Angle-ish invader.

Out of that emerged Saint King Oswald, extender of peace to Assassin Wessex. Out of that peace was laid the first foundation stone of an entire nation with Christian Identity: the English. Such, in a Christian understanding, is the profound grace and mystery of the Christian God, such his power to transform the worst of evils down the generations. Small start, abundant finish.

Interesting to think that the English owe much of their originating Christian Identity to a seed of Christian grace sown by St Patrick. Much more glorious than a conventional understanding, too. Centuries of later hurt and grief have hidden it from view. How much happier it would be to recover it.

Now, like St Ninian, St Patrick was sent out with Papal authority. The community of Lerins was of the Roman Catholic church. Patrick was confirmed in his mission, and later made a bishop, by St Germanus, a senior envoy of the Pope. Later in his life, unjustly done down by fellow bishops, Patrick appealed to the Pope for restoration, and the Pope granted his appeal. Patrick's Christian Life, like St Ninian's, was not of a Celtic church that somehow or other was not Roman Catholic.

By the time Ninian and Patrick had done, the territory we now call Ireland had become a leading light of spiritual Christian Life in Europe. Pict and Scot, otherwise warlike in nature, were side by side in the monasteries. And those monasteries became civilisation-savers. The Escape Pod of real-world history in Western Civilisation was a Christian Pod through and through and Martinian Anointed in the underlying detail.

St Columbanus and St Columba

You can liken what descended from St Martin via St Ninian and St Patrick to a golden chain. After them, the Christian spirituality that was to descend to the Early English bifurcated into two lines: St Columba and the similarly named, but very different, St Columbanus.

a. St Columba was of the Northern pincer movement of the Martinian Christian spirituality to the Early English. His spirituality descended to them directly via St Aidan and on to St Cuthbert. St Columba was a Scot/Gael. He became exiled from what we now call Ireland, having sparked off bloodshed by his high temper, it is thought. He founded a notable monastery at Iona off the west coast of what is now Scotland. It is probably where Saint King Oswald of Northumbria was converted. Earlier in life, St Columba had been trained by St Finnian. Finnian, in turn, had been trained by the Patron Saint of what we now call Wales, St David. David himself had finished his education at the Candida Casa established by St Ninian. So, we might note in passing, St David of Wales was in the golden Martinian chain.

I have read that St David may have made his way through what we now think of as Anglo Saxon territories in the 540s. However, it would have been to take a Christian message to residual Britonnic peoples there. Most of the Anglo Saxons at that time had been forced back to the European mainland by "King Arthur". In the end, as we saw earlier, the various pockets of Martinian spirituality in Wales seem to have made little impact on the Anglo Saxons. The Davidian disciplinary regime was also thought of as harshly self-denying, even by Celtic standards. However, via St Columba, you could say that, in a sense, the Welsh Saint did infiltrate the Anglo Saxons.

You can also see that this St Columba had not one but two great "Patron Saint" seeds in him: spiritual lineage from St Patrick of Ireland (notably the North of Ireland) and St David of Wales. And we might therefore note in passing that, via Iona of the *Scotic* Columba, there came into the founding roots of the English Christian Identity the Martinian Christian spirituality of *Northern Ireland* and parts of *Wales*...

For what it is worth, St Columba had also been to the trouble of buying a Bible from the basilica at Tours: one that had lain on the remains of St Martin...

b. St Columbanus, a Pict in the territory of Ireland, was the lost-from-sight reinforcer of the southern pincer movement of the Martinian

Christian spirituality to the Early English. He went out of Ireland to minister in mainland Europe, starting with the Franks. He brought spiritual reinforcement to the Frankish church at a crucial moment. He came on the scene as the Frankish church was sliding into corruption and being infiltrated by Arianism. He shored it up and founded Martinian monasteries which guarded the Christian doctrines of the life in the Holy Spirit. Bishop Felix of East Anglia emerged from one of these. Kings Sigeberht and Anna of East Anglia had their Christian understanding out of them. And I would think it very likely that Bishop Birinus of Wessex was also a product.

Now, let's take the two, Columba and Columbanus, side by side:

St Columba - Scot from Ireland	St Columbanus - Pict from Ireland
A royally descended man of high temper, charismatically persuasive, gifted with creatures as well as people. Bold, courageous and a diplomatic king-maker. Descendant of the kidnappers of St Patrick. Founder of monastic settlements which reached out to Scotic tribes in Ireland and Scotland.	A man of biting tongue and high temper, gifted with creatures, charismatically forceful with people, fierce with royalty. Came out of a monastic settlement in Ireland to found more of these in Frankish Gaul and parts of what later became Switzerland and North Italy.
I have read that Columba anointed to kingship the dynasty which descended to be the Scottish line of the royal family of the United Kingdom.	Columbanus prophesied destruction to the royal Merovingian house of the Franks – the prophecies came all too terribly true.

St Columba appeared after death to King Oswald on the night before Oswald's battle with Caedwalla 634/5. He strengthened him for the unlikely victory which gave Oswald the Angle-ish Northumbrian throne.	
Died in 597 as St Augustine of Canterbury was starting up in Kent.	Criss-crossed paths with St Augustine of Canterbury but never met him.
Sparked off bloodshed as a young man in his high temper. Founded the monastery at Iona as an exile penance. Iona became great amongst the monasteries he founded. It became a refuge from 616 for Angle-ish Oswald and Oswy of Northumbria.	The Frankish church had fallen into some confusion and discouragement. Arianism had resurged in Europe and insinuated itself amongst the Franks. Columbanus collided head-on with Arianism and with failed churchmanship. Founded monasteries after the old Martinian model in Frankish territories as an antidote. Forcefully wrote to urge the Pope to be worthy of his station.
St Aidan and St Cuthbert descended from this Ionan stream. Both highly gifted under the Christian God. St Aidan a.k.a. the Apostle to the English, not only brought transformation into Northumbria.	Bishop Felix of East Anglia descended spiritually from the monastic foundation that Columbanus set up to reinforce the Frankish Christian Life. Most likely so, too, did Bishop Birinus of Wessex. Via the family of King

He also opened a way for many gifted Celtic saints of similar spiritual background. After his death, in King Oswy's day, these went into the areas of Anglo Saxon territory that had most opposed the Christian Life, i.e. Mercia and Essex (incl. London).	Anna of the East Angles, this same stream of Christian Life influenced Kent and Wessex, as well as East Anglia. Columbanus would quite likely have dealt with the Anglo Saxons with fierce disdain. Those from the Life stream he brought to the Franks, however, dealt with the Anglo Saxons kindly.
The North of England, the Midlands and London were helped into Christian Identity via this stream of Gaelic Martinian Christian Life.	The Kentish, East Anglian and Wessex parts of England were given added impetus towards Christian Identity via this different stream of Romano Martinian Christian Life.
St Cuthbert appeared two centuries after death to King Alfred the Great. He strengthened him for the unlikely victory that led to his royal house not only reasserting Christian Identity but also founding the nation of the English. So you could say that this Northern Celtic Christian stream, spiritually, got into the founding of the whole of England.	

And so it came to pass that what had been in St Martin of Tours descended to find its most complete expression in the founding times of the Early English, through Germanic Frankish Christians and great Celtic Christians.

St Martin of Tours – Common Root

Do you see now how so many roads lead back to St Martin of Tours? His was the Christian spirituality that was laid into the foundations of what was ultimately to become English-speaking civilisation. That grew up around its church. The first church at Canterbury was the starting point to the South: dedicated to St Martin. The first foundation by St Ninian in Scotland, starting point to the north: dedicated to St Martin. And to the east, there is a place called Dunwich on the Suffolk coast. It was Bishop Felix's seat amongst the East Angles. Most of it is now under the sea, and with it, many churches. The churches furthest out under the sea are those which were the oldest established. One of the churches furthest out to sea was… dedicated to St Martin.

The founders in the earliest times all seem to have thought St Martin was their common root. If we accept that he was, then let's recap the nature of his Christian spirituality. It was a foundation for much that has brought light into the earth in the midst of much that has been dark. His spirituality was:

- Humble
- Powerful
- Truthful
- Deep
- Prophetic
- Discerning
- Cleansing
- Wise

Quite a wholesome root, one might think. Worth recovering and celebrating, perhaps?

Visitations of St Columba to King Oswald and St Cuthbert to King Alfred

I included a couple of visitations of departed saints in the table previous. St Columba appeared to encourage King Oswald on behalf of the Christian God.

St Cuthbert appeared to King Alfred the Great with similar encouragement. I tend to see the Christian Life in Alfred as the further-developed plant which first emerged from Oswald's spiritual seed. In a like manner, Cuthbert was a plant that developed out of Columba's spiritual seed.

On each occasion, the visitation was to strengthen them shortly before turning-point battles. On each occasion, long-run Christian Identity was at stake. In 635, Oswald overthrew the bitter Caedwalla, took the throne of Northumbria and invited St Aidan in. Later, in 878, Alfred defeated the Dane, Guthrum, when all seemed lost to the invading Danish paganism. Within two more generations, his family so thoroughly rolled back the pagan tide that explicitly Christian England was founded. This battle with Guthrum was the tidal turning point.

However, it is very much the fashion not to include such things as visitations by departed saints in the histories these days. Gloss over them. Don't excite the children – unless you can find some atrocity to highlight instead. We don't believe in visions, anyway. Even if we have a Christian belief ourselves, keep quiet: we might get made fun of. The Reformation got rid of that sort of thing, didn't it?

However, the visitations seem to have played a part in our real history. They would also indicate that our real history was not lived out in a closed and humanist system. The Christian God has interacted with it. These days, many would deny that at all costs. But we have to evaluate them, surely? It is less than justice not to. The witnesses who told of these visitations to those who wrote them up were Oswald and Alfred themselves. They thought the visions mattered.

Ah well, you don't believe in any of that old malarkey, do you? If you are an atheist, it is consistent not to. You are calling the testifiers liars or deluded ancients who, testifying to them at the time, didn't know as well as we do now, more than a thousand years removed. It is consistent with our present-day culture to patronise them like that. We know better. Note, however, that it is Oswald and Alfred that you are calling either liars or perhaps over-imaginative.

Formidable kings in the real world. And Alfred, for example, comes down in all reasonable estimation as a true and thoughtful Great. So that is a big call.

However, if you are any form of God-believer, why not believe it? In particular, if you are a Christian using the Bible to validate the visions, why not? Something similar happened with Jesus Christ. In his time of preparation for his own defining battle, the Cross, Elijah and Moses, both long departed, appeared to him on the mountain top to encourage him. Jesus said that as things had been for him, so they could be for his followers.

You could water things down by saying it may not really have been Saints Columba and Cuthbert; it was something understandable in their times that was given from God to Oswald and Alfred. Pat them on the heads, the poor old souls: they weren't enlightened like wot we are. But there is another option here: honour the ancients; we aren't enlightened like wot they were. Take Elijah and Moses. No-one ever says they were not Elijah and Moses. They either say, consistent with their beliefs: banana oil; never happened. Or they say, consistent with their beliefs: it really was Elijah and Moses.

Well then, why not Columba and Cuthbert for real as well? God is not the God of the dead but of the living because to him all are alive, is what Jesus Christ said. So they would still be alive in the Christian God. And it is not as if Columba or Cuthbert sought worship. Like Elijah and Moses, they are said to have come from God with the purpose of strengthening Christian Life before a decisive ordeal. That is within the Biblical Christ pattern.

What you are left with, if you do decide to accept the testimony of Kings Oswald and Alfred, are visitations by two departed Gaelic Martinian Christians entrusted with messages from the Christian God. And they were manifest at decisive points in the real-world history of the English.

CHAPTER 19.

Charts of Martinian Christian Spiritual Descent

Notes

The charts that follow are lines of *spiritual* descent.

- A full line indicates a short lapse time and/or obvious impact.

- A dotted line indicates a long lapse time and/or subtle impact.

A few detailed points:

- On the chart of descent to Northumbria, Mercia and London, the birth mother of Prince Alhfrith was Rhiainfellt of Rheged, not Queen Eanflaed. However, Alhfrith was of Eanflaed's Roman Catholic preferences via Bishop Wilfrid, who was favoured by Eanflaed. That is what the chart shows.

- King Oswy of Northumbria had three sons. Alhfrith is on the chart because he played a role in the onward transmission of Christian Identity into Mercia. Two other sons of Oswy are omitted: (i) Ecgfrith, son of Eanflaed. He became King after Oswy. (ii) Aldfrith (with a d, not Alhfrith with an h), son of Oswy's earliest relationship, which was with Princess Fina amongst the Gaels. Aldfrith became King after Ecgfrith. A Postscript after the next chapter will say more about these two sons of Oswy. For now, to note, it was in Aldfrith's time that Northumbria entered its famous Christian Golden Age. You can think of him on the chart as being in the spiritual lineage of Iona.

- The phrase "Viking *Incursion*" indicates partial Danish settlement. For Northumbria, I use the phrase "Viking *Invasion*". This indicates more complete Danish settlement, most notably in old Deira.

- I have supplied the chart about descent to Scotland, Wales and Northern Ireland as a courtesy for others who may wish to develop it further. I have omitted a lot of detail. I offer it because it is impossible to explain the history of the Christian Early English without touching on the history of the Martinian Christians who originated from the old Celtic parts of what is now the United Kingdom. Especially since some of them, via Saint King Oswald of Northumbria, sowed spiritual seed which descended into the present royal family of the United Kingdom.

A lot of research has gone into these charts, and I have tried to be accurate. However, they are unorthodox, and my intentions with them are not academic. My intention is to recover the ancient roots of transformative Early English Christian spirituality.

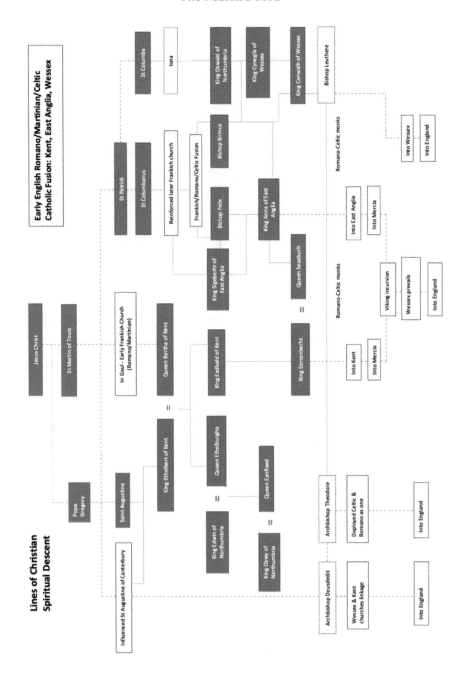

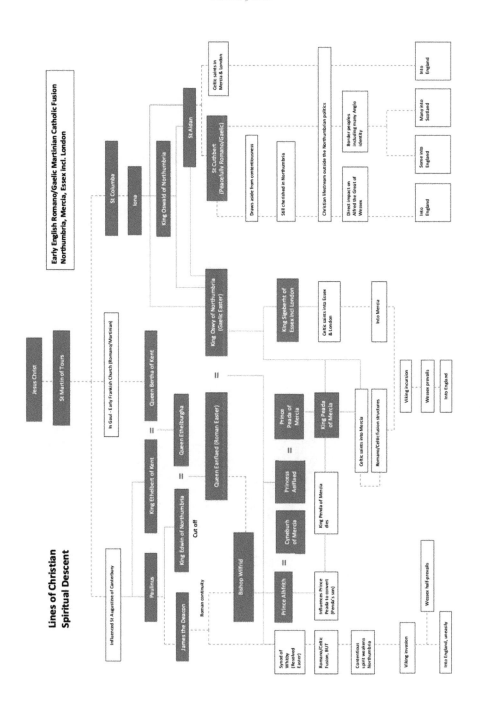

Lines of Christian Spiritual Descent

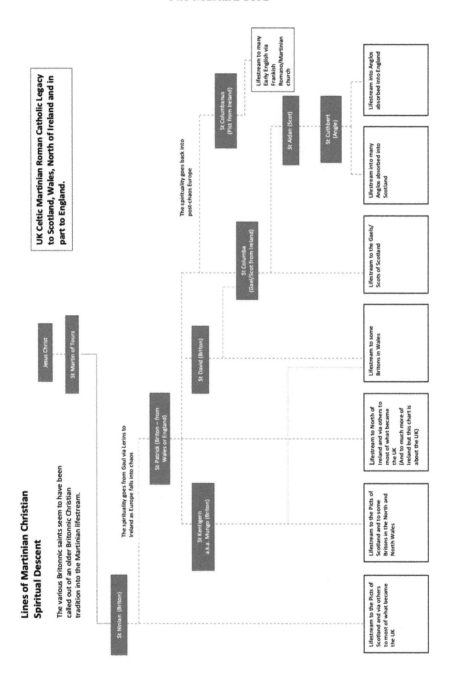

Lines of Martinian Christian Spiritual Descent

The various Britonnic saints seem to have been called out of an older Britonnic Christian tradition into the Martinian lifestream.

UK Celtic Martinian Roman Catholic Legacy to Scotland, Wales, North of Ireland and in part to England.

Jesus Christ

St Martin of Tours

The spirituality goes from Gaul via Lerins to Ireland as Europe falls into chaos

St Patrick (Briton – from Wales or England)

St David (Briton)

St Kentigern a.k.a. Mungo (Briton)

St Ninian (Briton)

St Columba (Gael/Scot from Ireland)

St Columbanus (Pict from Ireland)

The spirituality goes back into post-chaos Europe

St Aidan (Scot)

St Cuthbert (Angle)

Lifestream to many Early English via Frankish Romano/Martinian church

Lifestream to the Gaels/ Scots of Scotland

Lifestream to some Britons in Wales

Lifestream to North of Ireland and via others to most of what became the UK (And to much more of Ireland but this chart is about the UK)

Lifestream to the Picts of Scotland and to some Britons in the North and North Wales

Lifestream to the Picts of Scotland and via others to most of what became the UK

Lifestream into many Anglos absorbed into Scotland

Lifestream into Anglos absorbed into England

276

CHAPTER 20.

Off to School – Archbishop Theodore – 668 to 669

Three great figures dominate this chapter, Archbishop Theodore of Canterbury, Bishop Wilfrid of York and Saint Cuthbert of Northumbria. They were at the height of their powers together within Theodore's primacy, which was from 668 to 689.

These were real people. However, there is a sense in which each one of them was to become Typical, capital T. They left different but complementary legacies which were foundational and enduring.

668 – In the Balance

Wessex and Kent

Deusdedit, Wessex scholar and Archbishop of Canterbury, had died by 664. The relationship that he signified between Kent and Wessex churches would turn out to be a civilisation-building foundation. However, from the death of Deusdedit, the Canterbury vacancy was unfilled for five years. And by 666, Bishop Wine of Wessex had fallen out with King Cenwalh of Wessex and decamped to London. There was no replacement. Therefore, as at 668, there was no-one in senior Christian Leadership in either kingdom to build on the civilising foundation.

Northumbria

In Northumbria, King Oswy had unintentionally laid a foundation for the building of the nation of the English. He had done that by deciding to join the Romano Martinian Catholic Christian mainstream at the Synod of Whitby in

663. But the Christian Leadership in the North was struggling. Alhfrith, sub-king of Deira, had wanted Young Wilfrid to become Bishop of York. Well, Wilfrid would indeed become a dominant leader in Northumbria. But in the years after 663, he went off to Europe and remained there too long. King Oswy installed the Gaelic-trained Bishop Chad in his place. There were technical flaws with St Chad's ordination. And he would have had a lot to do just to secure his position at Deiran York: not Deira's choice.

Wilfrid, on his late return, did not over-press to take York from Chad. He based himself at the monastery at Ripon in Deira. He seems to have been active in Mercia and Kent, but otherwise he awaited developments. Bishop Colman and many others of the old Gaelic Martinian Christian team had left Bernician Lindisfarne. St Cuthbert was still there and was coming into his high spiritual powers. Towards the end of his life in the 680s, he would come into a formal bishop's role. But as at 668, he was not much interested in titles. Northumbria maintained sparky Christian spirituality in both Bernicia and Deira. But it was rather leaderless.

Mercia and Others

In Mercia, Bishop Trumhere had been the man for the hour when Mercia overthrew King Oswy's over-kingship in 658. He commanded the respect of both King Oswy and new King Wulfhere of Mercia at a time of high tension. Trumhere would have been a lost and hidden reason why Mercia and Northumbria did not slide back entirely into the old endless fighting: bridge-building on newly shared common Christian Identity. However, the situation remained unstable and tense. In 662 Trumhere died. Trumhere, if you recall, had that Fusion Christian Identity which Mercia derived from Northumbria. He had an able successor, Jaruman. But he, too, died in 667. King Wulfhere remained serious about building a Mercian state on Christian foundations. His Kentish Christian Queen, Eormenhild, may have been a lost and hidden influence. It seems that Mercia was also consulting from time to time with Wilfrid at Ripon. But as at 668, Mercia was formally leaderless in Christian terms.

East Anglia, meanwhile, the unsung shaper of the Fusion Christian Identity of the Early English in the earliest years, had lost its force and was merging into Mercia.

Kent's royal house had compromised its Christian integrity and, with that, its wisdom after 663, in the days of King Egbert.

As for London, that had Bishop Wine but in rather unedifying circumstances, buying the Bishopric in 666 from Mercia, under whose control London had come.

Would it end well?

There you have it in formal Christian Leadership terms. Just two bishops as at 668, one having bought the office, the other in an uneasy position and of doubtful technical qualification. The Christian set-apart monastic communities throughout the land were sparky in their Christian spirituality from mainly Martinian sources. The kings of the Big Two, Northumbria and Mercia, wanted to build states upon Christian Identity. But in terms of engagement of trained Christian Leaders with rulers, there was little.

Where was the Christian Leadership going to come from? Would the people groups go forward together from the Toddling Christian Identity which had Lost its Innocence? Or would they slide back discouraged into the older pagan Anglo Saxon? There was that possibility.

In 668, it was all in the balance.

An epic beginning had been made to the Christian adventure of the Early English. But as I said earlier in this work, in the chapter called "Gestation", the task set by Jesus Christ was not to make a good beginning, with raw converts; it was to make a good end, with seasoned disciples. Would the call be answered?

Yes.

Archbishop Theodore

In 668, Archbishop Theodore was appointed to Canterbury, arriving to take up the post in 669. I call this Nation Building Event Six and Christian Turning Point Two.

As to Theodore, a principle to keep in mind is that the Christian God claims to have a speciality of using the least likely if he can. Theodore was a most unlikely success.

Those were uncouth times. Theodore was couth. They were also warrior times. Theodore was an intellectual. They were short age-span times. Theodore was already old when he came to Canterbury. His appointment would have needed the royal favour. Theodore was not the royal choice. And they were times when the Archbishop appointment should have Papal sanction. Theodore was not the preferred Papal choice.

However, the uncouth came to respect him. Rulers learned to govern their kingdoms by his example. Warriors set aside their warfare for him. He lived an abnormal lifespan. And the Pope, perhaps, came to enjoy congratulations on the wise choice made.

Theodore was of the ancient and learned Christian civilisation of the Greek East. He came from the city which the Apostle Paul had called home, Tarsus. He was educated in the city of Antioch, centre of the early great prophets of the Christian church. That was the centre which had set apart Paul for the mission of turning the Roman world upside down. What a Christian Spaceship to land amongst the Barbarians. Theodore commanded Greek, Syriac and Latin languages; was a scholar of Bible exposition; had experience of Persian culture as well as Byzantine (Eastern leg of the Old Roman Empire) and had grown up amidst wars and tumults. He was a refugee of sorts. It had not been a sheltered life, whatever those achievements.

Seriously, what a package to send to the Toddling-into-Christian-Identity Early English.

Yet this package was not the expected one.

As it happened, the same day that Deusdedit died, so too did the Christian King of Kent, Eorcenberht. There was a hiatus in arranging a replacement for the Archbishop. The Kent royals had an internecine episode in which actors for King Eorcenberht's son, King Egbert, killed two rivals.

By 667, however, Egbert had engaged in dialogue with King Oswy of Northumbria about filling the Archbishopric. They selected a cleric named Wigheard to go off to Rome for Papal affirmation. This candidate no sooner got to Rome than he died before he could be consecrated. However, this meant that the Pope was now on the case, and Pope Vitalian searched for a replacement.

Vitalian wished to appoint a scholar named Hadrian. He was based in southern Italy and of North African origin, fluent in both Latin and Greek. Hadrian declined. He felt that to be an Archbishop would be a level of responsibility beyond him. He suggested an alternative, but he too declined. Therefore, Hadrian was asked by the Pope to reconsider. Instead, he looked around again and alighted on Theodore, then already 66 years old. He recommended Theodore, but the Pope was not keen. Theodore was more embedded in Greek customs than Hadrian. Pope Vitalian also worried that Theodore might have taken on Eastern ideas that were rejected in the Western church. However, Vitalian came to an arrangement. If Hadrian would travel to Kent and be the number two, his role being to keep Theodore on the Western straight and narrow, then he would release Hadrian from the call to be an Archbishop and indeed appoint Theodore, who was willing.

Thus it was that they came to Kent together. The Early English got two for the price of one. Theodore was installed as Archbishop of Canterbury and Hadrian as Abbot of St Augustine's old Abbey there. Theodore was freed by Hadrian's scholarly presence to spend his energies on government. And Hadrian was freed by Theodore's governing presence to spend his energies on scholarship and education. They were one of the great double acts of all history, and they shaped the real world of the Early English. The effects of the two of them in tandem were as follows:

i.   Gradual governmental integration. Theodore became the first Archbishop to whom every small kingdom church of the proto-English would defer. It was a consistent and unifying Christian Identity that was deferred to. Kings participated in Theodore's church councils, watched how he did things, liked what they saw and began to incorporate into their diverse local ways of governing the practices which they observed in the nationally unifying church way of governing.

ii.   A significant progression of Christian scholarship within the educational realms, hence Civilisation Building. Hadrian made a strong contribution.

I think we can safely say that in Theodore's time, the Infant Christian Identity of the Early English went Off to School. It began a centuries-long journey to symbiotic integration of Christian Identity with National Identity.

Before we go further, we should note again the multi-ethnic infusion of Christian Life to the Anglo Saxons. These diverse Christian sources passed into the founding rootstock as the people groups morphed into the Early English:

- Latin (St Augustine & team, Paulinus)
- Frankish (Felix, Birinus, and still to come, Leuthere)
- Pictish via the Franks (St Columbanus)
- Gaelic Scot (St Aidan and a multiplicity)
- Greek (Theodore)
- North African (Hadrian)
- Out of Ireland (Fursa & Co in East Anglia, and a new monastic establishment soon to come into Wessex which would become important in the following century).

- Welsh Christian scholars were used by King Alfred the Great in the days of the restoration of Christian Identity in the Early English from 878.

By the standards of the time, this was very diverse. To this day, what we now call the United Kingdom is amongst the most international of nations. Seeds contain the plant.

These inputs all came within the framework of a Roman Catholic church which was the civilising and integrating force of the times. It knew no borders as we know them now. It worked with chaos all around and somehow or other transcended it. It may have had its faults. None are perfect, said the Christ, except God. There was worldliness. It was gnawed at from the inside by the deadly heresy of Arianism. Yet it somehow managed to send only its purest Christians to the proto-English. Coincidence? Or the hidden hallmark of a Christian God who works with a frustrated and mixed-up real world?

Now, we should note a few highlights of Theodore's ministry:

In the North, Theodore removed St Chad from office as Bishop of York. He made good Chad's questionable ordination and then appointed him as Bishop to Mercia. Chad was wanted there and back in his depth again.

In place of Chad, Theodore appointed Wilfrid as Bishop of York. Northumbria got a Colossus. One it would later jail and strip of lands.

You can see that, in reusing Chad, Theodore made no room for division and discrimination between the "Roman" and the "Celtic". He harnessed those in whom he could sense Christian "Calling" whatever its source. In that respect, Theodore was an Architect Spiritual of unifying spirituality. He sent a Romano Gaelic Martinian Catholic Fusion Christian Identity out into all of what would become England. Long-winded, but that does specify the founding English spiritual root. The church of every kingdom was becoming of the one coherent Roman Catholic outward form, with common infusion of the inward Martinian sparky spirituality from multiple sources, and containing those small c catholic doctrines which the Protestant Reformation would recover a thousand years later.

Wilfrid's approach, meanwhile, was firmly Roman, Roman, Roman…

Theodore went on to appoint many competent new bishops and develop various administrative church territories for them (called "dioceses") throughout most of what became England. Although there were later additions, the structures he built, except in the North, endured to modern times. Theodore instituted all-kingdom councils for governance of the church. The church of every kingdom co-operated in them. The secular rulers were present on the councils and applied what they learned from them. In that respect, Theodore was an Architect Temporal of unifying government.

However, Wilfrid would attend the councils by proxy, not in person.

As the various rulers participated in the new-fangled way of talking things through, rather than saying it with spear points, there began the model for proto-Parliament. Now, I know there were always diverse assemblies, but Theodore's time saw a step change from tribal to proto-national; things were done in a conscious and unifying sense of accountability to the Christian God, by Lords Spiritual and Lords Temporal together.

The royal house of Wessex, Alfred the Great's family, tends to be credited as the inventor of proto-Parliament. However, Alfred saw his mission as recovery and restoration. Two hundred and fifty years later, the royal house of Wessex would recover and restore the Christian foundations and then build the kingdom of the English on them. You can think of those Wessex royals as Builders Temporal and Builders Spiritual on Theodore's Architectural foundations.

Bishop Leuthere of Wessex

Bishop Leuthere was not one of the Big Three of this chapter, but I must highlight his appointment into Wessex early in Theodore's time.

You may recall that King Cenwalh of Wessex struggled with his bishops after Birinus passed away in 650. He sacked Agilbert and then Wine and left the vacancy unfilled. However, there seems to have been a wrinkle about early Christian Wessex and where it would seek its Christian leaders from. It seems that until Leuthere came, in 670, Wessex saw its church as parented from the Frankish mainland, not Canterbury*. That is important for two reasons. (i) In the political world, it was an obstacle to coherent unity. (ii) In the world of Christian spirituality, it was an obstacle to completing the recipe of the wise old Pope Gregory: all bishops to be united under just two Archbishops on what would become English territory.

> * This is a reason why I speculated in the chapter "Birth" that Wessex may have put out feelers for their own "Wessex Brand" Christian input rather than a Kentish hand-me-down.

Leuthere came from the Frankish church but was consecrated by Theodore and taken into Canterbury's parenting structures. That turned out to be important in two ways.

i.   The first was in what this change represented. In coming under Canterbury, the Wessex church moved into line with the old plans of Pope Gregory and came more fully into the orbit of Theodore, Architect Spiritual and Architect Temporal of the proto-English. With that, the Kent/Wessex Church linkage began to fulfil the promise in the original Deusdedit appointment of 655. The linkage thenceforward became a strong Nation Building foundation.

ii. Secondly, Leuthere was personally gifted at being a Bishop. Wessex rulers would soon spend several generations in the wilderness, as we shall see in the next chapter, "Graduation". However, the Wessex Christian Identity would not lose its light. Wessex Christian understanding would re-emerge and prevail in the rulers and shape the nation of the English. The Wessex Christian Identity that kept going through dark times did so from two chief sources:

a. One of them was that in the year Leuthere died, 676, a mission came out of Ireland which established gifted monastic life at Malmesbury.

b. The other was that Leuthere was gifted enough to lay enduring church foundations.

It was not the Wessex *rulers* that carried the small kingdom as a coherent whole through several generations in the wilderness until its royal family could emerge to build the nation of the English. It was the Wessex *Christian scene*. Leuthere did a lot to set that up.

Leuthere himself seems to have been yet another gifted Christian Frank. I am not sure of his spiritual heritage. However, he was one in a chain of Christian bishops who just so happened to be right person, right place, right time. Coincidence...? Maybe. But you can be sure that every one of them would have given control of their lives to the Christian God.

Bishop Wilfrid

We come now to Bishop Wilfrid of York. There is a lot to say about him because there are so many things he Typified and embedded in Early English roots. I called him a Colossus. He was. He could also be styled as a Saint, as was one of his titles. But I think Bishop Wilfrid styles him better.

Theodore appointed Wilfrid as Bishop of York in about 670. We've already seen Young Wilfrid in the previous chapter, carrying the day at the Synod of Whitby. There can have been few more forceful Christians in all history. And as I said in a previous chapter, for me there has been no Christian harder to appraise in all history.

First, to note, it had always been part of Pope Gregory's plan that York should become an Archbishopric. It became so in 735. Gregory had also intended that York, like Canterbury, should oversee multiple subsidiaries. In Theodore's time, the South and Midlands participated in the multiplication. The North, led by Wilfrid, did not. Wilfrid kept York as one great monolith. He opposed splitting it up with every ounce of his strength. He co-operated with Theodore's councils, but by proxy rather than in person. Ironic: Wilfrid drank in the borderless grandeur of Rome yet insisted on a separate Northern fastness. He was most forceful in imposing his rights there. Many of them were, indeed, his rights. However, he even went so far as to claim primacy, from York, over Ireland. After all the hurt of Whitby in 663/4.

Roman Order

Wilfrid stood for Roman Catholic Order. He forcefully imposed it. That is most unfashionable today. However, we should make the effort to enter his times. I should think that what Wilfrid stood for would have been preferred by many to the chaos from which his world had emerged.

Wilfrid made the most tremendous Christian impact on the North. We must remember the world he came from: violent, chaotic. Wilfrid forcefully carried the day for the primacy of a more peaceable and orderly Christian Identity in his society of the time. He asserted it in times when assertion would have been needed. Even if, today, you incline to looking down on the Christian Identity he asserted, in its time it was peace, light, proto-social security, proto-health service, and civilising by comparison to what had gone before. In a Christian understanding, it was more than all that, too: it embedded the possibility of eternal salvation into systems of church that could be developed for the many.

He was forceful, too, with the set-apart Christians in northern monastic life. Some loved him, and some could not stand him. However, what he actually sought to impose was the Order of St Benedict. Ironic, really, in one so dominating: the main focus of Benedict's Order was deference of one to another within Christian community.

Anyway, in the process of imposing this Order, Wilfrid expelled the young St Cuthbert from monastic life at Ripon in Deira. However, the Order itself was a kindly force in an unkind world. As English Christian spirituality developed, Benedictine set-apart communities did a lot to shape it. There was a disciplinary side to the Order, but you can blow that out of proportion. It was mostly a kindly shaping that they imparted. I have read the modern Church of England describe itself as basically a kindly organisation. That seems broadly fair to me. It was the likes of Wilfrid who forcefully embedded the monastic spirituality which fostered kindness. It descends to this day on a taken-for-granted basis. But they embedded it within a world that was far less kind than our modern one.

Wilfrid's favoured version of Christian Life was very Roman Catholic orderly. These days, English Protestant Christians with Life in the Holy Spirit might prefer something with more than a hint of the spontaneous. However, what Wilfrid set up was a style of church that could endure. You see, it could give high-grade set-service-of-worship materials to local leaders who might be indifferent at best. The high-grade set worship materials became a thing to unify the peoples around and a higher form of civilisation than they had known before.

Besides all this, when reading his life, it can be discerned that Wilfrid was personally familiar with the "Charismatic" gifts of the Holy Spirit of the Christian God. This might come as a surprise to a modern English Protestant Christian understanding which might not expect that in one so militantly Roman Catholic. However, he was. And so, too, were other Bishops of York, beginning with Paulinus from 627 and including John of Beverley, Bishop of York from 709. Wilfrid had sparky Christian spiritual heritage from the Latin Paulinus in Deira and the Gaelic Martinian Lindisfarne. He incorporated Frankish and Benedictine influences too. There was a lot of spark in all of these influences in their origin times. Wilfrid would have been a potent personal spiritual mixture. There would have been more to him than the modern caricature of a "Romaniser", as he tends to be known.

Wilfrid Brought Low

As time went by in the North and Wilfrid came to dominate, he lost the goodwill of the Northumbrian royals. After King Oswy died in 670, the successor king was his youngest son, by Queen Eanflaed, King Ecgfrith. Ecgfrith seems to have inherited some of the implacable and warlike character of his pagan grandfather, Aethelfrith, he who Raedwald and Edwin had overthrown in 616. Ecgfrith was a bad king to cross. However, Wilfrid did cross him, for various reasons. So began his long journey to being thoroughly humbled.

For example, Wilfrid sided with Ecgfrith's first Queen over her wishing to remain a virgin for Christ rather than concede conjugal rights. That marked his card. And possibly Ecgfrith never ceased to resent Wilfrid for having prevailed at Whitby for the Roman way over the Gaelic. In due course, Ecgfrith's second Queen humiliated Wilfrid. He was badly treated at that time. And then, Archbishop Theodore and King Ecgfrith between the two of them began to rein him in. Theodore was tired of Wilfrid's failing to co-operate with the division of his enormous diocese into more manageable subsidiaries. Ecgfrith and Theodore enforced a split of York into four. Interestingly, Theodore appointed as new bishops those who were of the Gaelic spiritual lineage where possible. The modern caricature of the church history of the times tends to paint it as Roman Church versus Celtic Church. However, in the days when the Early English went Off to School with their Christian Identity, Archbishop Theodore harnessed Roman and Celtic as one to teach it. He was the Architect Spiritual of a Fusion Christian Identity.

In the reorganisation, Wilfrid was given the reduced remnant of York. However, King Ecgfrith went on to expel him. Wilfrid then journeyed to Rome to appeal to the Pope; in other words, he went over Theodore's head. He returned with papers to uphold his earlier rights. In response, King Ecgfrith jailed him.

After his release, Wilfrid journeyed via Mercia to the South Saxons, what we now call Sussex and Hampshire. There, by invitation of the local king, he established Christian structure in the 680s. That was the penultimate Anglo Saxon domino to fall to Christian Identity. From there, in dubious circumstances, he went on to do the same on the Isle of Wight, the very last domino to fall. I would not like to say that either location went into full-on

Christian Awakening as in the King Oswald days. They went into full-on Church, capital C; similar maybe, but not quite the same.

Wilfrid found time, too, in all of this to blaze the trail for the Christian message into the old pagan Germanic heartlands of Europe. He made little headway but was ahead of his time in trying it. Next century, a fuller team of Wessex, Kent and Northumbrian Christians would take to the trail and succeed.

Towards the end of Theodore's life, he and Wilfrid were reconciled. In 687, Wilfrid was restored to a northern Bishopric at Hexham. That was after King Ecgfrith had perished in 685. Ecgfrith's successor was the oldest son of King Oswy, whom we have not yet encountered. We will look at him further in a Postscript. His name was Aldfrith. (Not Alhfrith; we have met him, sub-king of Deira, Wilfrid's friend). In Aldfrith's time, Northumbria entered a golden period of Christian civilisation, which was to make it a chief light in Europe by Bede's day.

However, in 691, Wilfrid managed to fall out with Aldfrith and get expelled again. Wilfrid, it seems, agitated for Aldfrith to overturn Theodore's old decision and restore the former massive York diocese to him as one. Aldfrith refused. There may have been undercurrents. Aldfrith grew up with the Scotic Gaels. One would imagine, therefore, that Wilfrid also got into some lost but heated Roman versus Gaelic argument with him.

Anyway, this new expulsion was a considerable negative achievement on Wilfrid's part, given that Aldfrith seems to have inherited what was best in both Oswald and Iona. Not quite as negative an achievement as Young Wilfrid expelling the Young St Cuthbert out of Ripon. But notable, even so. What goes around comes around, to paraphrase Jesus Christ; the measure you give is the measure you receive: expel... get expelled.

Eventually, Theodore's successor, Archbishop Berhtwald, called a council of all the Northern church leaders to consider Wilfrid's case. They upheld the expulsion and confiscated much of Wilfrid's northern lands. This might suggest that his peer group had become, by now, rather frustrated with him, shall we say.

I note in passing that this was after Wilfrid had accepted lands in dubious circumstances on the Isle of Wight in 688. More of that in the "Graduation" chapter.

Wilfrid journeyed to Rome again to appeal to the Pope. Meanwhile, Archbishop Berhtwald convened another council to restore Wilfrid to communion and to some of his northern lands. Concurrently, Wilfrid's appeal to the Pope was upheld. On his return with yet more papers of entitlement, however, Wilfrid fell ill. It was by now 705. It seems that the Christian God spoke to Wilfrid at this point and took him in hand. Through the Archangel Michael, no less, he told the sleeping Wilfrid that he would have four more years of life. He was to retire to what was left of his lands, be peaceful and quiet, and prepare to meet his Maker. Make of that what you will. Wilfrid was no false prophet. Four years he did have. He passed away in 709, those last four being the most peaceful years of his life.

Since that is how Wilfrid's God is said to have dealt with him in the end, that is also how I choose to appraise him. Rest in peace.

Bishop Wilfrid – Unintended Consequences

There were certain Unintended Consequences to Wilfrid's career. Now, as I said in the chapter appraising King Penda of Mercia, the Christian God says that he judges intentions. However, life is also full of ironies. The Christian God takes partial responsibility for those. They arise, after all, from this God's having bound the creation over to frustration, but only if human beings precipitate them by fixated insistence on having their own way. Out of Wilfrid, two seed ironies did arise. They sprout to this day.

i. As we've already seen, the Synod of Whitby had fractured the Christian union of Angle and Gaelic Celt. Wilfrid's combative attitude contributed to that in the first place, I think. Sadly, he did not exactly help to repair the fracture. Claiming a bishop's jurisdiction over all Ireland out of York, after the upset he had caused at Whitby in 663... not exactly fence-mending. More likely to give traction to further ethnic resentment and, out of that, opposing senses of Identity.

ii.   The other irony was more subtle. It was hardly down to Wilfrid in isolation, but I think he became a seed of this: within the slowly uniting proto-English, a seed of North/South cultural divide was being sown. Wilfrid, highly gifted and brilliant, jealously guarded his Northern dominion. He would brook no interference with it. However, Theodore, who wanted to interfere, did have authority to do that. And Pope Gregory, the greatest representative of the Papacy that Wilfrid kept appealing to, had originally stipulated multiple bishoprics in the North.

I suppose Wilfrid had a case not to comply. York was not an Archbishopric at that time. Gregory had prescribed any subdivision out of an assumption that there would be authority for York over all the subdivisions. But at all costs, Wilfrid would not let his seat at York be divided up. And he was absent in person when all the other peers were setting the patterns for multi-kingdom united government. Instead, he was present by proxy. He went along with things. But that is not the same as the personal presence of one so great amongst his peers. Rather than be in council with them, he built his Northern dominion. And wherever he did appear in person, he seems to have been highly combative until his old age.

It is ironic in the extreme: this most travelled of the early clerics, who had found Lindisfarne horizons too small, who was coveted on mainland Europe, was always, somehow, jealous to be separate in a Northumbria which part of him had no time for at all, given how much attachment there was in it to Gaelic Christian ways.

There were to be several other and later factors which would amplify the sense of North/South divide. Viking Invasion from 793. Identification with the Danelaw up to the Norman Conquest. William the Conqueror brutally harrying the North in 1069/70. Tudor monarchs failing to win it over for the Protestant Reformation. However, in Wilfrid, somehow, I sense an early planting.

Contentious spirit, I sense. Spiritual things have a way of spreading like yeast through a loaf. That was the image used by the Christ. A contentious spirit got loose in Northumbria long before the Vikings came. Wilfrid's life story bears the hallmarks of its seeding. Of course, Bernicia and Deira were always rivals, contentious from the origin point. But Christian grace can overcome contention. The likes of St Patrick and Saint King Oswald, somehow, in Christian grace, overcame deep things. And yet, for all the phenomenal spiritual brilliance of the North, I discern that it could not get free of contention.

Bishop Wilfrid made a dynamic Christian impact upon the North, irresistibly bringing order where there had been chaos. He intended that. He spread a great deal of consistent Roman Catholic order proto-nationally. He intended that, too. And he helped to unite the monastic Christian spirit proto-nationally, again intending it. Wilfrid had strong personal spirituality, but he seems also to have sown contention between the sense of Identity in various people groups. I doubt he intended that. And whereas Archbishop Theodore harnessed Roman and Gaelic Christian spirituality as one, and Wilfrid had some of that Gaelic spirituality in him, for Wilfrid, it was the Roman way and only the Roman way. He must have been convinced he was right. However, he was brought low, not once but twice. After which his life came to a good end under the Christian God.

What a complex journey. The good and the bad, said Jesus Christ, grow together. Until the time comes, if you uproot the bad, you will also uproot the good. Few Christian leaders, to my mind, ever demonstrated that more fully than Bishop Wilfrid.

Anyway, it was Theodore who put Wilfrid into York. Theodore who later reined him in. And Theodore who eventually became reconciled to him. Quite an Off-to-School experience for the great Archbishop himself in his old age, one would think.

Northumbria and Mercia – Peace – And Saint King Oswald's Bones

We must return to Archbishop Theodore and a defining triumph: in 679, brokering peace which endured between Northumbria and Mercia. Also, we must take note of Saint King Oswald's bones: they got involved too… Yet again, we can't address only the political triumph, as the modern mind would like to do. We must also come to grips with an accompanying Christian phenomenon. Sigh.

Fighting over Lindsey

King Oswy had made himself the over-king of Mercia in 655 when King Penda of Mercia perished at the Battle of Winwaed. By 658 the Mercians had overthrown his power. Oswy came to terms with it. Bishop Trumhere of Mercia, brought up in the Deiran church and of the same Christian expression and inheritance as both kingdoms, built bridges of shared Christian values between Oswy and the Mercian king, Wulfhere. There was an uneasy peace.

Oswy passed away in 670 and was succeeded by the implacable and warlike King Ecgfrith of Northumbria. Meanwhile, the formidable King Aethelred had succeeded to Mercia.

The territory known as Lindsey, now Lincolnshire, came back into focus. You may recall that it had long been a bone of contention between Northumbria and Mercia. Northumbria would not let it rest in Mercian hands. In 674, Ecgfrith took it, but further battle was joined when, in 679, Mercia wrested it back. Two forceful kings with plenty of the Old School in them.

Theodore brought them to peace in the Christian New School.

Two things came to pass out of this, but before we spell them out, we should take note of something rarely drawn out in the history books. These tend to focus on the warlike and the battles. However, during the uneasy period of 658 to 679, and even while kings were coming to war again, the Christian communities of Northumbria and Mercia were at one, in peace, and developing into a common Christian Identity. Trumhere, Wilfrid, Jaruman, St Chad and many others: Romano Martinian Catholic with plenty of Gaelic influence and all of it spiritually sparky. They were in both kingdoms and inter-communicating.

For example, King Oswy had sent Gaelic-spirituality Christians into a Mercia which favoured Roman outward forms. Archbishop Theodore later followed the example by appointing St Chad as Bishop of Mercia. When, after that, Wilfrid was trying to eliminate Gaelic-descended Christian ways from Northumbria, in favour of entirely Deiran Roman Catholic outer forms, Theodore broke Wilfrid's power and reintroduced Gaelic Christian leadership into the new Northumbrian dioceses. The Big Two powers were becoming a fusion in Christian Identity terms: Romano and Gaelic. Which lent a uniting impetus, not a warring one.

When, in 679, Theodore brokered the peace between the Big Two, Northumbria and Mercia, it was on that shared fusion Christian Identity, which he had already helped to shape, that it was founded. And bar one hiccup in the 740s, the peace endured. It was a nation-enabling peace. A Christian peace. And another way that Theodore, Architect Spiritual of the English, was also an Architect Temporal.

Now, two notable things came to pass after Theodore brought the warring kings of Northumbria and Mercia to peace:

1. Northumbrian military ambitions were deflected away from the South for good. King Ecgfrith turned his warlike nature to the North and West, to the Picts and to Ireland. Therefore, a stumbling block in the way towards union of the Early English was removed. However, a further stumbling block between English and Celtic senses of Identity was to become embedded instead. More about that in the Postscript about Oswy and his sons. History books conventionally say that the peace endured between Northumbria and Mercia because Northumbrian power was broken. However, peace endured because Mercia was too strong for Ecgfrith *and* the Christian Identities of the

two were fusing into one. That is our history when seen with two eyes and not just the one.

2. The late Saint King Oswald became involved via a phenomenal sign to seal the deal. Through his bones. We had better come to terms with the account. Seeing with the Second Eye, and all that. Here is the story.

King Aethelred of Mercia had married a daughter of King Oswy, Osthryth. Hope you can pronounce that without showering your neighbours. Osthryth wished to place her late Uncle Oswald's bones in the monastery at Bardney, in Lindsey. She sent them there on a cart. Bede tells what happened next. The monks wanted nothing to do with Oswald's Northumbrian bones. Mercian Identity was their preferred Identity. Differences with the old Northumbria ran deep. Oswald's bones sat beneath a tent on the cart outside the monastery, rejected. All that night, a column of light stretched from the cart to the heavens, visible through all Lindsey. The monks were persuaded that the Christian God had spoken. They took in Oswald's bones. Various miracles ensued.

What to make of it? More of Bede's old tingle tangle, he will insist on interweaving it with the history, if only he would stick to the facts?

Well, where did the light show? Lindsey. What had the fighting been about? Lindsey. What was the context of the phenomenon? A peace deal after a dispute about Lindsey. Why was Osthryth wanting the bones there in Lindsey? In her Christian understanding, to seal the peace deal between her father's kingdom and her husband's kingdom on earth as in heaven.

And what had defined Saint King Oswald? Peacemaker as far as he was able, and original seed-founder of the uniting Christian English when he made peace with Wessex. What did his bones represent then, in that culture? Peacemaker as far as possible, within a uniting Christian culture.

What was the sign to be interpreted then, given from the Christian God by way of the miraculous light? (i) God's approval: peace on earth as it is in heaven. Just what Osthryth wanted. And what she also got. And (ii) God's gracious rebuke to the monks of Bardney: how faithful were they being, in their prejudice, to their Christian Identity? Not at all faithful. Therefore, what might the Christian God want to say to them, assuming he would have something to say? "My Christian people are already becoming one in Mercia and Northumbria. Get with it. Since when did Mercian Identity trump Christian Identity? Wakey, wakey – see the light."

And in token of that, their God gave them a light.

Well, why not? After all, what exactly had brought King Oswald to his death in 642? Northumbria versus Mercia conflict. How fitting that a heavenly light over his bones should signify a lasting end to that. After all, the Christian understanding would be that Saint King Oswald would still be alive with the Christian God. Therefore, and thinking out of the box here, what might the still-living Oswald want more than anything else in conversation with the Christian God? Northumbria versus Mercia conflict resolution. What could be a more exquisite reward for him from the Christian God than that – and involving his bones to seal the deal?

Now, Oswald's bones were bones. They were not Oswald. Oswald, to use a Biblical understanding, was hidden with Christ in God. But the bones were culturally relevant for focussing faith on the Christian God. They had become a widespread focus for that. And light from heaven to the bones can be seen as a confirmatory sign, to that culture, that what Oswald stood for had come to pass.

Not modern thinking, I know. Out of the box. Bewildering to a modern Protestant Christian mind and ridiculous to the atheist mind that descends from that. But perfectly reasonable in a Christian God for whom time and death are no constraint and who might have been less sniffy about saints and bones than modern fashion would think.

Phew.

For the Protestant Christian mind, can we map this onto the Bible? Yes: signs follow those who are faithful. Posthumously? Why not? It worked out that way with the Christ himself.

And remember Queen Osthryth: wanting peace on earth as in heaven. Why would a Protestant Christian object to a wondrous sign that says to her, "Your prayer has been heard"? If the sign were not dressed up in old-fashioned Roman Catholic clothing of a bygone culture, many a modern Protestant church would cede the pulpit for the testimony: "I prayed for such and such a thing as best I knew how, and God gave me this wonderful sign to reassure me." That sort of testimony is normal in a modern Protestant church with Life in the Holy Spirit of the Christian God. Why should it not have been Osthryth's?

So, perhaps a message to the modern Protestant Christian, as to the monks at Bardney: Wakey, wakey. Look beneath the surface. Open Second Eye.

And to note, as well, it was a sign of what Christian life could be like in those times. For Bede writing it up, it was a notable sign, but not an impossible one. Theodore harnessed as bishops, in the founding times of the Early English, those who had been lifelong immersed in this kind of spirituality. I should think Theodore found his time amongst the Early English… sparky.

St Cuthbert

St Cuthbert was contemporary with Archbishop Theodore and Bishop Wilfrid. He became the defining hero Saint of the Early English and of the Anglo-Danish who later overtook his Northern manor. He was also the hero Saint, along with Saint King Oswald, of the royal family of Wessex when it established the Nation of the English.

Between 651 and 687, as far as I can see, he never set foot outside Northumbria. He spent a fair bit of that time self-marooned on a tiny island too. Yet… he shaped his times – in the real world as well as the spiritual.

He was perhaps the ultimate fulfilment of what had been seeded in St Martin of Tours: gifted in the realms of the revelatory and the miraculous, yet humble, discerning and wise.

Saint King Oswald would have loved him. Saint Aidan would have rested in peace on account of him.

As briefly as I can, I will review what St Cuthbert came to Typify, capital T.

St Cuthbert – Career and Priorities

I am not going to go at length into St Cuthbert's detailed powers of revelation and the miraculous. Bede devoted a short book to them. To the modern mind, it looks hagiographic. However, if you have experience of Christian spirituality, you will discern a number of authenticating hallmarks of the Christian God. Maybe one day I will write them up, but not now. Suffice to say that St Cuthbert was Christ-like in his ways and of a power spirituality that has rarely been replicated before or since. Wherever he trod, he took a fragrance of heaven with him.

The young Cuthbert entered the monastic life at Melrose in 651, after seeing St Aidan gathered up to heaven. We covered that in the chapter "Open Heaven". Melrose is in the Scottish Border country and in what we now call Scotland. In those days, it was in the Bernician part of Northumbria that stretched as far as what is now Edinburgh.

At some point, Cuthbert entered monastic life at Ripon in Deiran Northumbria until he was expelled from there by Bishop Wilfrid in the late 650s. King Oswy's son, Alhfrith, the sub-king of Deira, had invited Cuthbert there originally but later enforced the expulsion as he came under Wilfrid's influence.

Cuthbert returned to Melrose. In those days, he walked in the Scottish Border country spreading Christian goodness, peace and healing. He was already much loved. Following the upset of the Synod of Whitby in 663/4, which we covered in the chapter "Loss of Innocence", many of the Gaelic monks had moved to Ireland, led by Bishop Colman. Cuthbert was asked to move to Lindisfarne in Bernician Northumbria and became the replacement Abbot (i.e. head) of the monastery. From this time on, St Cuthbert adopted a non-contentious Fusion Christian Identity. He was a Germanic Angle, yet as high an expression as you will ever get of all that had been in St Patrick and St Columba within the Gaelic Martinian Catholic spiritual heritage. However,

Cuthbert set himself to abide by all Roman Catholic forms as decreed after the Synod of Whitby and to encourage all others in his charge to do the same.

For a while, he walked amongst the people. He also became much loved by the Northumbrian royals. In the end, however, even the small Lindisfarne was too great a place for him. He moved to a tiny island and took up the life of a hermit. His life became entirely devoted to prayer.

St Cuthbert – Value System

St Cuthbert had powers of prophecy, revelation and miraculous healing, but they all came second to intensive relationship prayer with the Christian God. (Christian prayer is not asking for things; that is a sub-set of it. Christian prayer is relating with God with a view to prevailing.) Anyway, here is the point: this priority order was also that of St Martin of Tours.

If you recall, the Christian understanding with which St Martin grew up was that the church was not in the world to do good deeds. That was impossible in the church until after 313. It was not supposed to exist. The church in its origin seed form was in the world for its spiritual influence and to call the people out of idolatry into the Christ. Even a remarkable miracle would be seen by the likes of St Martin, who mediated many, as a by-product, to be allowed to manifest as the Holy Spirit of the Christian God would decide. The first objective was to have spiritual influence and authority within the hidden realms. Out of that, the understanding was that an influence for much good might be sown into the unseen. The good would descend to the generations and surface from time to time in the world that is seen. But not in a way that any human being or outward form of church organisation would ever be able to control.

That was the understanding of St Cuthbert in his hermit years. All over the world today, in nations where English speakers once took the Christian message, there are prophetic, revelatory and wholeness Christian communities which see themselves as having similar priorities. They do things differently.

They are not in hermitage. But they have a similar understanding: spiritual influence comes first.

Social Benefit

In the secular world of England today, by contrast, a church normally wants to have status as a charitable institution. To have that, by order of government, a church therefore compiles a statement of objectives. Those must be expressed as various types of impact and be measurable in the one-eyed human way of seeing things. Annually, a church reports how it got on with them. It is a sort of social benefit test.

However, in the two-eyed Christian world of the Early English times, it was different. In every kingdom, kings and lords would fund set-apart monastic communities for a different social benefit function: to pray; to command the unseen spiritual realm; to be an influence for cleansing in it. In the process, the communities also became proto-health service and proto-social security. But those were the by-products. Rulers wanted the benevolent spiritual influence first. They wanted it for their people. And they wanted credit with the Christian God for bankrolling it.

Because of this last point, this has all come to down us in Post-Reformation caricature as if the kings were superstitiously trying to buy or manipulate favour with the Christian God. And indeed, by late Medieval times, all manner of manipulation was in the church; hence the Protestant Reformation's mission to put an end to it. But it is best not to apply the caricature to the much earlier times when the Early English Christian rootstock was being laid.

You see, kings and rulers back then would have seen it like this: Christian prayer had *value*. They had the Seeing Eye of a world emerging from idolatry, so they could see the value of Christian spiritual influence as it developed out of prayerful communion by monks and such like with the Christian God. The Gaelic Martinian Christian monks, for example, were not the gluttonous caricature of later Medieval times. They had given up every comfort in a quest to imitate the Christ's spiritual power and authority.

Jesus Christ was the great example. In his ministry, there were occasions when he was sent for to help persons afflicted by malign spiritual beings, but sometimes the demonic had a way of departing before he even arrived. That was because the Christ had profound prayerful communion with the Christian God. It was integral to his nature. Out of that, he carried spiritual authority around with him as an innate attribute. Because of it, some of these beings could see him coming from miles away, and they scarpered, quick.

The Martinian Christians wanted to let the same develop in them to the extent that they could. I say this so that you can now authenticate a particular miracle within Bede's account of St Cuthbert. An afflicted Christian lady, whose husband had sent for Cuthbert to deliver her, found that a tormenting spirit departed before the Saint even got there.

That sort of thing does not come out of the blue or by magic. It comes because the Christian concerned has become so immersed in a life of relationship prayer with the Christian God that the power required flows as a by-product out of their authority within the hidden realm. Jesus Christ was the model. St Cuthbert was the copy.

Kings, rulers, people all saw this sort of thing and much more like it. It would have been the talk of all Northumbria. I mean, what else was there to talk about in those days?

So, for the rulers in the Early English founding times, the beneficial effects of set-apart Christian prayer were seen to be of social benefit to their people. There was value in it. Since there was value, kings and rulers would pay handsomely for it by establishing foundations to nurture it.

As to the modern caricature of a so-much-more-ignorant-than-we-are-now king doing this to buy eternal favours: well, there would be an element of that. But who made us pure enough to judge him? The Christian God declares himself to be all pure; yet the character he reveals is that if he were to find not much more than an atom of innocence in the king, he would take note of what was good in the king's intention.

Well, why not? You will favour an innocent child who is looking for a treat. You will even favour a half-manipulative child. For goodness' sake, a dog will be looking at you with those big brown eyes to manipulate a treat. A cat will wrap you round its paw for a treat. You smile and give the treat. In a like manner, the Christian God might favour a king bankrolling a monastery. He would be no more sneery than you would be with the dog. Well, so they would have understood it then, anyway. No holier-than-thou post-Puritan modern mindset, you see.

Shaping Earth as in Heaven

Artwork: Denise Critchell

Saint Cuthbert shapes things on earth as in heaven.

From his tiny hermit island.

St Cuthbert's career included much time isolated on a tiny island. From there, he shaped things on earth as in heaven through something invisible and unmeasurable: Christian prevailing prayer. He became Colossal in it. And it came to pass that the rulers and the people loved St Cuthbert then as much as when he had walked in their midst, and maybe more. The Northumbrian royals, expelling Wilfrid, became devoted to the oracle of Cuthbert, seeking it when they could.

In the end, King Ecgfrith arranged with Archbishop Theodore to call Cuthbert back into public life as the Bishop of Lindisfarne. Cuthbert was appointed in 684 and consecrated by Theodore at York in 685. Ecgfrith perished that same year, so Cuthbert became active in that formal leadership role in the first year of King Aldfrith, which was also to become the first year of the Christian golden age of Northumbria. He had two final years as a legend in his own lifetime, walking as a bishop throughout Bernician Northumbria before passing away in 687. Archbishop Theodore followed on in 689.

I am struck by what a meeting it must have been in 685 when Theodore consecrated Cuthbert at York. Theodore would soon be reconciled with the other Colossus too, Wilfrid, in 687.

Archbishop Theodore, founding Architect of the Early English, ordained each of them as bishops, Wilfrid a Colossus of the Christian Church and Cuthbert a Colossus of the Holy Spirit of the Christian God.

Now, Theodore may not have actually met Cuthbert until 685. But here's a thought. Why do you think that Roman Catholic Theodore gave so much of Wilfrid's old giant diocese of York to other bishops of the Gaelic Martinian Christian way when he split it up in the 670s? Political manoeuvring within the church and to please King Ecgfrith? That would be a normal modern one-eye explanation. True in part. But it is time to Open Second Eye again: the Gaelic Martinian spirituality was of such high repute that Theodore wanted to embed as much as he could of it in the emerging Early English church.

St Cuthbert – No Contention in him

St Cuthbert makes an interesting contrast picture. Compare first Bishop Wilfrid, the Church Colossus of the North. St Cuthbert let him have the field. He retreated to a tiny island for many years. He communed with the Christian God, seeking, like St Martin of old, to shape things on earth through the spiritual influence of heaven. And indeed, as the years went by, the Northumbrian royals would expel Wilfrid but implore Cuthbert to help shape their earth.

Then compare him to Archbishop Theodore. Theodore, from the ancient civilisation of the East and the world of the Apostle Paul, had a Calling to Architect Spiritual and, albeit not by his own design, Architect Temporal of the Nation of the English. Whereas Cuthbert… prayed, within closed monastic life, and, as far as we know, never set foot outside Northumbria.

The three legacies were complementary. Theodore: enduring Christian State; Wilfrid: enduring Christianised Culture; Cuthbert: enduring Christian Spirituality. All three factors, not the sword, are what made the Early English out of the Anglo Saxons.

Towards the end of his life, Cuthbert submitted to being made the Bishop of Lindisfarne. He wandered Northumbria one last time, imparting life and peace wherever he went. For those who like to highlight those years as being a time of conflict between the Roman and the Gaelic Christian ways, on account of the likes of a Wilfrid, Cuthbert gives the lie to it. He was of the highest order of the Gaelic Martinian Christian spirituality. However, as Bishop of Lindisfarne, he ended his days strongly opposed to faction: he wished to express his spirituality entirely within the Roman Catholic church and wanted everyone else to rest in peace and do the same. He seems to have come to that decision at Lindisfarne directly after the Synod at Whitby in 663 and despite the indignation of many of his fellows there.

The thing about Cuthbert that made him special in the North was that *he had no contention in him*. That would be why he later retreated to the small island. Contention disrupts Christian spirituality. Cuthbert would not let it.

So, did those feet in ancient times (meaning, Jesus's own) walk upon England's mountains green? I should have some reservations. However, in Cuthbert's shoes, they do seem to have walked in Northumbria.

St Cuthbert – A Different Type of Colossus

All forms of Christian expression derive from an original seed: the Christ and the original church. All are united beneath the surface of otherwise huge diversity by this: the one Holy Spirit of the Christian God. In these ways, Christians are of one common spiritual family and descent.

However, the Apostle Paul taught that there are families *plural* which "take their name" from God in heaven *and* on earth. By "take their name" he meant "are authorised by God". By "families" he did not mean nuclear families. He did not mean genetic families. He meant spiritual families. The families exist in *heaven* as well as on earth. They descend through time, in other words; there can be spiritual progenitors and, later in time, spiritual descendants. The new families derive from and remain part of the one common and original spiritual family in Christ. But they also diversify and enrich it down the generations.

When I first came across St Martin of Tours, I realised that I was looking at a spiritual progenitor. What had been in Martin came to the Anglo Saxon people groups via the Gaels and the Franks. For the Gaelic Saints, he was their starter seed. For the Franks, he became their hero Saint.

St Cuthbert was both a descendant and a progenitor. He became one of the highest expressions of the original Gaelic Martinian Christian spirituality and a hero Saint whose example sowed a common cultural seed for the Early English.

I think of the spiritual legacy of the likes of a Martin or a Cuthbert – discerning, revelatory, miraculous – as an underground river. The likes of

Bishop Wilfrid bequeathed an overground order of service which could descend robustly generation by generation whatever the quality of the priests. However, inspirational powers require inspirational communities of a similar standing to recur. You cannot guarantee those generation by generation. They have a way of surfacing in future times and in different places to the origin point. Modified in expression and outward forms, yet somehow the same underneath: Jesus Christ the same yesterday, today and forever.

In modern times, the revelatory powers that were in St Cuthbert, and the miraculous too, have surfaced again. All over the world wherever English-speaking Protestants have taken the Christian message. That is because the Protestant Reformation, once it had spent four hundred years outgrowing sectarianism, made a way for the old underground river to surface again.

Therefore, although St Cuthbert is long departed, his spirituality is not. Out of the three great figures, his legacy needed no specific type of church building or organisation to express it. Therefore, to this day, what was in him can express as and when and where and in whom the Holy Spirit of the Christian God would choose. The only provisos would be a life surrendered freely to the Christian God and a value system in which "the Kingdom of God", expressed as Life in the Holy Spirit of the Christian God, comes first.

St Cuthbert's Body – Not Decaying

St Cuthbert's body did not decay for more than a thousand years until after the Protestant Reformation. What to make of that? There are two different modern approaches:

i.   Wide-eyed ancient simpletons.

ii. Clever embalming technique.

There will be truth in the reply about embalming. But one eye of truth. What would Second Eye make of it?

Saint King Oswald's dismembered right arm did not decay for a very long time, either. We already covered that. Saint Aidan had prayed that what the arm stood for would not decay. It was, if you recall, Christian good from ruler to people above and beyond the call of duty. The value system which covets that has never decayed. It remains in English bones. The non-decay was the *sign* of that.

So, let's find the *sign* in Cuthbert's body. In fact, there were two, one in the non-decay and the second in the post-Reformation timing of the decay.

As follows:

(i) Many generations of Medieval decline of English Christian integrity would wrap around the ancient Martinian Life in the Holy Spirit of the Christian God like a giant tendril. However, the potential for the spirituality to break out once more would no more be lost than Cuthbert's body would decay. In due time, the Protestant Reformation would take an axe to the tendril. The non-decay was the *sign* of that.

(ii) Four hundred more years would elapse before the Protestants would become grown up enough to handle what was in the likes of Cuthbert once more. However, it has broken out again, and is being handled, all over the earth. Different clothing, different degrees of revelation, for the most part in different nations and often in different ethnicities. But much of it seeded from English-speaking Christians of many nations. They share this with St Cuthbert: Life in the one Holy Spirit of the Christian God, modelled on Jesus Christ the same yesterday, today and forever. In that Cuthbert's body decayed *after* the Reformation, the prophetic *sign* was this: what the Reformation had done would lead to his old spirituality being released once more. You see, once the crop has started to sprout again, you no longer need the old seed.

Summary – Off to School

The Christian God reveals himself to have an overarching purpose for those who take the label of "Christian": to bring them to maturity in that Identity. The purpose is not fulfilled by magic. It is fulfilled by a combination of experience and how we respond to experience and through help from people who have a Call from that God to impart maturity.

In their different ways, both St Cuthbert and Archbishop Theodore had such Callings.

St Cuthbert passed away in 687 and Archbishop Theodore in 689. By then, each one of them, in their different ways, had taken the infant Christian Identity of the Early English Off to School. Rulers learned from each of them; in Cuthbert's case, so too did the people.

Each was obliged to deal with much contention. Cuthbert drew aside from it. Theodore had to make the best of it. He brought Kings to Christian Peace, defused Wilfrid, and later became reconciled to Wilfrid.

In Theodore's time, the Christian Identity of the Early English, that which became the founding rootstock of a nation, became Romano Gaelic Martinian Catholic. And sparky, with Life in the Holy Spirit of the Christian God. The underground river of Christian Spirituality within the English to this day remains of that fusion. The main difference is that large C Catholic has become 80-90% small c catholic. Many new spiritual families came into being with the Protestant Reformation. With different names and labels. But that underlying Christian fusion ancestry remains the more ancient foundation.

The underlying sparky spirituality of the more ancient times, call it "Charismatic", "Anointed", "Prophetic", "Revelatory", whatever, is in the wider earth today wherever latter-day English-speaking Christians took the Christian message after the Protestant Reformation. And in England itself today, if you look under the lid of the label "Church", you find that this ancient spiritual stream is recovering. It is not exactly an irresistible tide as it was when overwhelming what King Penda of Mercia stood for. But it continues to flow. Many churches die off. But not the ones with this in it.

Archbishop Theodore's legacy, the intertwining of Church with Government and of Christian Identity with National Identity, endured pretty much intact until the Great War, 1914-18.

St Cuthbert's legacy, being more of heaven than of earth, sustained less damage at that time.

Bishop Wilfrid's legacy of orderly church and orderly monastery under Roman rule endured for better and for worse down the generations too. There would always be the tendency in it to run to Religion, outward form without the inward reality. English history is in some ways a story of that trend punctuated by the restoration of what was in the likes of a Saint Cuthbert. I personally dwell more on the life of John of Beverley, contemporary with Wilfrid and a successor at York, as a better indicator than Wilfrid of what passed from York into the founding Christian spiritual rootstock of the Early English. Wilfrid made a profound impact on church history and had strong personal spirituality. But Theodore reined him in, and the Protestant Reformation broke what he stood for in the English. It was the likes of John of Beverley who added to the underground spiritual river which still flows in the English. He features in the Postscript that follows, which is about King Oswy and his sons.

After the Postscript, I will end the narrative with a chapter that looks ahead from "Off to School" to "Graduation", 878 to 927. We will encounter Saint King Oswald's bones again in 909/10 and Saint Cuthbert too. He may have passed away in 687, but he made an impact in 878. Both of them impacted the family of King Alfred the Great as it brought to fulfilment much that had been good in the Christian seed that had been Conceived, Born and taken Off to School between 597 and 689 in the Anglo Saxon people groups.

CHAPTER 21.

Postscript – King Oswy of Northumbria and His Sons

The lives of two of the sons of King Oswy of Northumbria overlapped with Archbishop Theodore. Here is a short look at those sons, followed by a final reflection on the life of King Oswy himself.

There is also a short reflection on John of Beverley. He was contemporary with Bishop Wilfrid and at different times held two of Wilfrid's old posts, Bishop of Hexham and Bishop of York. I will compare them.

Kings Ecgfrith and Aldfrith

King Oswy died within a year of Theodore's arrival in Kent. Two of his sons, Ecgfrith and Aldfrith, related with Theodore and, in their different ways, also embedded certain things in the Early English roots.

King Oswy of Northumbria had sons by three relationships:

1. Before he returned from the Scots with his older brother, Saint King Oswald, and during his exile from 616 to 634, the young Oswy fathered a child, thought to be out of wedlock, by a Celtic Princess, I think called Fina. I would assume she was a Gaelic Celt. This child was Oswy's oldest son, Aldfrith. He and Theodore met when each of them was elderly.

2. Out of the marital union with the Britonnic Celt Rhiainfellt of Rheged, which arose from Oswald's peace initiative with Rheged in about 635, came Princess Alhflaed. She became the wife of Prince Peada of Mercia. The other child was a son, Prince Alhfrith. This was the son who persuaded Peada into Christian Identity and then stood by Oswy at the

Battle of Winwaed 655. He became the sub-king of Deira then. He was also the close companion of the Young Wilfrid. We don't know what happened to Alhfrith after 664. Maybe he died of the plague or fell out irreparably with Oswy. He never met Theodore.

3. Out of the marital union with the Kentish Queen Eanflaed came King Ecgfrith. This was the son who seems to have been of implacable and warlike nature. He was the one who took the throne of Northumbria in 670 when Oswy died. He encountered Theodore as peacemaker between Northumbria and Mercia and as consecrator of St Cuthbert to Bishop of Lindisfarne.

There were a couple of other complications in Oswy's court:

i. Oswy's older brother Oswald had a son by Cyneburh of Wessex after sealing the peace deal with Wessex by marrying her in 635. This boy, Oethelwald, when still a teenager, was made sub-king of Deira by Uncle Oswy in 651, after the murder of King Oswine of Deira. Oethelwald is the one who then allied with King Penda of Mercia at Winwaed in 655. He stood aside from the battle but was never heard of again after that. Looks like he did not get on with Uncle Oswy.

ii. There was also a brother older than Oswald, Eanfrith. This was one of the two royals who perished in 634 at the hands of the Britonnic King Caedwalla; one of the two that Bede called "Apostate". The complication was that Eanfrith had been exiled from 616 with the Picts, not the Scots. And he, like Oswy, had a son during exile, brought up as a Pictish royal. His name was Talorgen or Talorcan. Oswy seems to have intrigued with the Picts in this nephew's interests as time went by. Oswy's son Ecgfrith would escalate to full-on war with them.

A Box of Frogs

Arising from all this, if the life of King Penda of Mercia can be summed up as irony upon irony, the life of King Oswy of Northumbria can perhaps be summed up as a box of frogs. There were Bernicia versus Deira intrigues. Political relationships with many of the Northern Celts were warlike or filled with intrigue. His Kentish Queen had different Roman Catholic customs to his own. And there were no set succession rules in those days. I can imagine intra-family intriguing over that: Oethelwald allying with Penda, and who knows what else. It must have been quite some achievement for King Oswy to become the only seventh-century King of Northumbria to die in his bed, what with King Penda of Mercia after his head as well.

King Ecgfrith of Northumbria, 670 to 685

Anyway, I want to look briefly at Oswy's sons. Alhfrith I've already covered in other chapters. He did a great deal to promote Christian Identity in both Deira and Mercia. Ecgfrith I also touched on in relation to Bishop Wilfrid. However, there were a couple of other points with Ecgfrith, who was Oswy's chosen heir:

a. Ecgfrith sent a campaign into what we now call Ireland. Sorry to relate, it dealt far too violently there. In some understandings, it was a raid for wealth and slaves. An alternative understanding I have read is that Celts based in Ireland had raided the Northumbrian Celtic protectorate of Rheged (Cumbria), perhaps for slaves. Perhaps it was a re-run of what happened to the young St Patrick. In this understanding, Ecgfrith stood by the Britons of Rheged. He sent a campaign into Ireland to quash the raiders.

Even Ecgfrith's own court thought his forces went too far, and those were hard times. And there you see it: bad blood between Christian proto-English and a Celtic territory which had been a source of much Christian grace to the proto-English. It was a dark seed sown.

b. Through complex family intrigues or assertion of entitlements or whatever, things seem to have got out of hand with the Picts. It was a complex and warlike region to the North at that time. Most of the kings involved bore the name of the Christ, although it is hard to discern much of the fruits of that name in Ecgfrith's time. However, I can't go through every violent twist and turn. Here is the point. Ecgfrith reigned from 670, but he perished in 685 when he went on an ill-advised campaign against the Picts. And there you see some more of it: bad blood again between Christian proto-English and Celtic territories. None of the rulers in the people groups, Angle, Scot or Pict, comes out of those times as an angel, even though they still had the high Martinian Christian spirituality in common in the monasteries.

Anyway, notwithstanding that King Ecgfrith later took steps to bring St Cuthbert into the heart of Northumbrian culture, those were grim legacies to leave in times when Angle and Celt were still capable of union in Martinian Christian spirituality.

On the occasion when Jesus Christ taught that the good and the bad must grow together until his return, he had begun the teaching with a parable. A man had sown good wheat seed in his field. In the night "an enemy" had planted other seed alongside it. For what it is worth, the word "Satan" means "Enemy". The seeds in the parable were what are called "tares". These are weeds which look like wheat but are poisonous. On discovery of the mischief, the instruction of the man who had sown the good seed was to let the two seeds grow together until the harvest. Sort them out then. One senses that the parable came into play in the real world of the time in the North, even while Angle and Celt had the one-in-Christ Martinian spirituality.

King Aldfrith

After Ecgfrith, there was to be a fresh harvest of good seed from the Northumbrian Christian field. He was succeeded by Oswy's oldest son, Aldfrith, son of Princess Fina. We're back with the one least likely again, as with Theodore. Aldfrith was already quite old by the standards of the time when coming into kingship, like Theodore. Was couth in uncouth times, like Theodore. Had twenty years in authority, like Theodore. And had dedicated his life to the Christian God. Like Theodore again. They overlapped by four years, Aldfrith reigning from 685, Theodore dying in 689.

Aldfrith grew up mainly away from King Oswy's court, remote from Northumbria and from contention. He devoted himself to Christian learning at Iona. It is not clear whether he had his father Oswy's favour or not. He was not Oswy's chosen heir. I like to think that he had the favour of his mother, the almost-lost-to-history Princess Fina. I like to think she prayed for him. Whatever the case, I think we can be certain of this: Aldfrith had a vibrant Christian Life. The Christian spiritual legacy of his uncle, Saint King Oswald, seems to have borne fruit in him. And the Gaelic Martinian Christian mantle which had been in Iona seems to have rested upon him, too.

Amazingly, in times of much contention, after Ecgfrith died, the Northumbrians appear to have agreed, peacefully and at one, to invite the already aged Aldfrith, scholar more than warrior, Scot more than Angle, to be their uniting Christian King. And then... a Christian Golden Age ensued. After all that bad blood – stunning.

There is a prosaic explanation for Aldfrith's peaceful accession. Northumbria had exhausted its military strength, defeated by Mercia in 679, then by the Picts in 685. What else was there to do now but turn inwards and go Back to School regarding that Christian God who had turned out not to be a simple Military Favour Slot Dispenser? More than that, the Scots and Picts had the upper hand militarily after 685. They would also have had a fair bit to do with installing the peaceful and Scotic-sympathising Aldfrith. Sigh of relief after Ecgfrith. Those are fair enough explanations, as far as they go.

However, there is also a Christian explanation. An old Christian hymn captures it: "The arm of flesh will fail you, you dare not trust your own." St Patrick went to Ireland when he had come to the end of his own strength. Christian Northumbrian royalty, descended from him spiritually, had come to the end of its own strength too. It was ready and open to seeking its Christian strength back. And Aldfrith did represent all that had been best of that in Northumbria; more than that, he was of the Anointing that had produced it.

There was a hidden force at work as well. A force that was heartily fed up with a contentious spirit and warlike ways. A force that had, however, let the warlike and the contentious have the field and their hour in the sun. A force that had spent much of its time on a tiny Farne island even smaller than Lindisfarne. A force that brought peace wherever it trod. A force that knew how to shape the unseen by prayer in the tradition of St Martin of Tours. A force called… St Cuthbert. Aldfrith came to power as Cuthbert's life, like Theodore's, drew to its close. Cuthbert would have been greatly fulfilled in the accession. In fact, he is said to have recommended Aldfrith. And everyone listened to Cuthbert, any ethnicity, any rival kingdom. Saints such as Cuthbert, who shape the real world largely unseen, also shape it in the realm that we do see when the moment comes.

Anyway, from 685 there ensued under King Aldfrith the flowering of a Northumbrian Christian civilisation which became, as I previously noted, a chief light in the Europe of its time. It gave us Bede, the first English historian. It led on to a great Bishop of York, John of Beverley, famously gifted, highly "Charismatic".

Aldfrith also, I believe, secured the repatriation of those whom Ecgfrith had taken slave on his violent campaign into Ireland.

John of Beverley

We should look forward briefly to the career of this John. Our modern times focus one-eyed on the bad seeds in our history. John of Beverley gives our second eye a clue to the good seed alongside it. Before John was appointed to Bishop of York at the end of Aldfrith's reign in 704/5, he was appointed as Bishop of Hexham from 687, late in Theodore's time, early in Aldfrith's reign. John was a product of Theodore's number two, the North African Abbot Hadrian, and of the dynamic Christian community at Whitby: a rich new variant of Fusion Christian Identity.

We might compare John to Bishop Wilfrid. In 687, contemporary with appointing John to Hexham, Theodore and Aldfrith restored Wilfrid's Colossal spirit to Bishop of York. By 691, further contentions had led to Wilfrid's being deposed, expelled and rejected by his Northern peers. Again. This storm blew up after Wilfrid had gone perilously close to the Dark Side on the Isle of Wight in 688, as you will see in the next chapter.

Meanwhile, however, Bishop John grew in grace. James the Deacon's quiet Christian heritage was on him. He became another of the Christian greats of the Early English, his biography somehow typifying the legacies of King Aldfrith, Theodore and Hadrian. I see no reason to doubt the many miracles recorded in his life. They were Christ-like in a Bishop who sought the Christ-like mantle. They were "Charismatic" in a Deiran culture which understood those powers, descended as a fusion from the Latin Paulinus and the Gaelic Scots. And they were normal enough in their time: normal in the times of Bede, in other words, the first historian of the Early English.

John, you might say, poured pure water into the underground spiritual river of the Christian English.

Light in the Darkness

During Aldfrith's reign, Bernicia and Deira seem to have rested from strife a while. Anglo and Celt seem to have been at one at that time too. What an unlikely flowering it all was. The epic Christian spirituality in Saint King Oswald had been... dismembered. The mixed Christian spirituality of King Oswy had brought a mixture of darkness and light. The implacable warrior Ecgfrith seems to have brought darkness more than light. Then along comes this most unlikely King Aldfrith: and he seems to have been a flowering of the seed that had been in King Oswald. I can only tell you that this has all the hallmarks of the Christian God as he reveals himself in his Bible. Darkness tries to put out the light, but the light shines through. That is a founding principle of Christian scripture. It was made manifest in the real world of the Northumbrian Early English in the founding times.

As to Aldfrith's end, early in the eighth century, he emulated his father Oswy in that most unlikely of achievements for a Northumbrian King of the period. He died in his bed.

King Oswy – The End Seen from the Beginning – Postscript to the Murder of King Oswine

I must now make one more point about King Oswy. It is completely out of the box for the modern mind. But from underneath Oswy's wriggly life story, we can bring to the surface a little-rated perspective that the Christian God would apply to real world history when rulers take on Christian Identity.

The Christian God says that he sees the End from the Beginning. Well, why not? He says he made all things, and that would include time. This is not to say that the Christian God does not submit himself, for now, to work with the linear progression of human beings within time. But ultimately, this God sees all the generations as one.

Anyway, this power to see the End from the Beginning would have an impact, would it not, if *you* were the Christian God and you were weighing up King Oswy of Northumbria after the murder of King Oswine of Deira.

You see, Saint King Oswald, King Oswy, King Aldfrith – the line of succession is not linear in your eyes. They all live before you at once, whether dead like Oswald, or when still a twinkle in Oswy's eye, like Aldfrith. This God is not the God of the dead, said Jesus Christ, but of the living because to him, all are alive. And we were each one of us foreknown to this God, taught the Apostle Paul, before the world was founded.

So, if you are the Christian God, Oswald, Oswy and Aldfrith all live before you, regardless of their succession in time, each one with their rewards or otherwise. Therefore, work it out, how might you deal with King Oswy, murderer? Wielding your biggest stick might seem appropriate; it might even seem immoral of you not to wield it.

I've already looked at the Christian God as the God of the Second Chance in dealing with King Oswy. Here, now, is another aspect of the Christian God: seeing the End from the Beginning. It would affect things as follows:

- Saint King Oswald: are you going to overthrow Oswald's Christian legacy by destroying his successor brother, Oswy, because Oswy has gone astray?

- Future King Aldfrith: are you going to sentence King Oswy to destruction and in the process nobble the Christian Golden Age that you foresee Aldfrith will usher in?

It's a good job you're not God. These are difficult powers to use fairly. However, if you really are God, then once again, you apply your stated principles. In this case, the principle we can discern to have been applied is the one called grace. Grace can be defined as "undeserved favour". It seems to have been applied to King Oswy. But not just for Oswy's own faith; more likely, on account of King Oswald in the past and King Aldfrith to come.

You see, those who go before you in Christ – such as an Oswald – leave a Christian legacy of a seed of grace that descends to you when you yourself deserve no blessing. Its right to descend is stated in the Second Commandment. Those who will come after you in Christ – such as an Aldfrith – will bring a Christian blessing into their times that brings mercy to your own. Therefore, extending grace to the likes of an Oswy would be a reward to the likes of Oswald and Aldfrith.

Those are perspectives of the Christian God, and they come into play in the history of nations with Christian rulers. They came into play in the mixed real world of King Oswy.

Very unfashionable thinking. I think that, in old hymns, some English Protestant Christians of yesteryear intuited it. But it is anathema to the modern mind because it would mean that human history is not a closed system. Instead, for peoples with Christian Identity, history would be open to the Christian God. However, it is perfectly reasonable in a God who says that he sees the End from the Beginning.

And a God with the revealed character of the Christian God is not going to let holier-than-thou condemnation of King Oswy take precedence over grace to Kings Oswald and Aldfrith in the way he exercises this power. Even if we might conclude that we are holier-than-him over it. Instead, he will extend grace to Oswy to preserve the legacy of Oswald and open the way for Aldfrith. But Oswy will still have to pass his Second Chance test, refraining from vengeance at Winwaed in 655.

Very out of the box. Very Christian God. And very much, it would seem, what happened in the mixed real-world founding times of the Early English in their Christian Identity.

CHAPTER 22.

Graduation – The Nation of the English – 878 to 927

It remains to look ahead from the days of Archbishop Theodore, who died in 689, to the times of King Alfred the Great of Wessex and family, in three generations from the year 878.

Alfred's family reaped what Saint King Oswald of Northumbria and Archbishop Theodore of Canterbury had first sown. In the process, they founded the Kingdom of the English. Oswald was their great, great, many times great godfather in Christ. Theodore was the Architect on whose foundations they built a nation in which Christian Identity was symbiotically integrated with all other realms of life.

However, this family did not set out to build the Kingdom of the English. Although they developed the idea of "the Kin of the English", setting up a Nation of the English emerged as an afterproduct. They set out to rescue and restore a people group that had developed around a shared Christian Identity. It had an Anglo Saxon ethnic origin. They had a drive to rescue that. But the creative drive in Alfred's family was to restore the shared Christian Identity. That was what made them Early English.

This seems clear from the records. There was an all-conquering invasive force abroad in the land: Danish Vikings. They were defined in Early English eyes by one peril that could not be surrendered to at any cost. They were pagan, "Heathen".

There was an existential threat and, with it, a motive to survive. But it was the Christian Identity that supplied the spark for Alfred and family to create and build. They rallied the in-peril people group, with the utmost vigour, to unite around that as well as their ethnicity. And in the process, they put Christian devotion at the heart of all that they did.

When once Alfred's family had prevailed, in forty-nine years from 878 to 927, consensus formally called the rescued people group, in whom Christian Identity was foundational, "The English". Later than that came the definition of their territory as "England".

So, let's look ahead and see how Alfred the Great and family bequeathed a Christian Nation of the English and how it became "England".

Summary of the History

In this final chapter of the narrative, I delve into lost or hidden elements that emerge from Christian insight into the history. The central character in this chapter, Alfred the Great of Wessex, the only English king who ever had the word "Great" to describe him, was profoundly Christian. That was a key element within his Greatness. There is a general tendency to downplay the key role which Christian spirituality played in him. For that reason, in this chapter, I will go to some lengths to bring that side of him and his family back into the light. Christian principles will be coming at you thick and fast so that you can see how they came into play within the real world history.

However, so that we can keep a grounding, here is a summary of the history first:

1. In 686 the ruler of Wessex committed an atrocity and commended it to the Christ.

2. Between 688 and 802, Wessex came largely under Mercia's domination.

3. The Christian Identity that had been so sparky throughout all the kingdoms between 597 and 689 was slowly cooling down in the latter part of the eighth century. Christian Identity was taken very seriously and embedded into everything. However, those Church practices that would lead to the late Medieval period becoming a byword for Religiosity slowly began to be

asserted. Meanwhile, King Offa of Mercia, defining figure of the period from 688 to 802, seems to have perfected the politicisation of Christian Identity, without the sparky integrity of it, to an art form.

4.   The family of Alfred the Great came to power in Wessex from 802, in the person of King Egbert, a tough warrior. He had been sponsored by Charlemagne the Great in a manoeuvre to score political points at the expense of King Offa of Mercia.

5.   In 825 King Egbert fought a defining battle with Mercia which overthrew its dominion. Wessex did not get dominion either. From 830 the two powers existed as equals with improving mutual relationships. A hidden force towards the improvement was a period of growing maturity of genuine Christian ways on each side.

6.   In 839, the son of Egbert and father of Alfred the Great, Aethelwulf, came to power in Wessex. He and his wife, Osburh, had sincere Christian spirituality. Western Mercia had the same more generally. It seems to have recovered Christian integrity after a dubious patch.

7.   During the 800s, raids and incursions from the East by Danish Vikings became more and more serious and developed into a full-on invasion attempt. Eastern Mercia was greatly troubled, but Western Mercia less so. Wessex had Eastern Mercia as a buffer for a while too. So both Western Mercia and Wessex, regenerating in Christian integrity, were not under existential threat from the Danes until the 860s onwards.

8.   The Danes had a pagan or "Heathen" Identity. The Early English – not yet named that, and still thinking of themselves as Wessex, Mercia, Northumbria – had a Christian Identity.

9.   Northumbria was overrun. Its sense of ethnicity became part Angle, part Dane. Its old Christian Identity slowly began to infiltrate the whole, but semi-paganised.

10. Things took a more polarised course to the South. The ethnicities barely mixed; nor did the spiritualities. The Danish pagan Identity gradually swept all before it and progressed steadily westwards.

11. King Aethelwulf of Wessex had five sons. One died before Aethelwulf. The next three all reigned and died in short order after Aethelwulf died in 858, spanning the period from then to 871. King Alfred of Wessex, the youngest son, succeeded to the Wessex throne in 871 and reigned until 899.

12. Alfred had strong Christian spirituality. He was also a true "Great".

13. As at 871, the Danish invasions were becoming an all-consuming crisis. Northumbria had been overrun. Mercian power had collapsed in the East and was in trouble in the West.

14. As at 877, the Wessex royal family was at the point of extinction. Alfred had retreated into marshlands in Somerset.

15. In 878, Alfred was able to rally forces for one final battle, prevailed, and caused the Danish leader, Guthrum, to accept Christian baptism. Shortly before the battle, St Cuthbert, who had died in 687, appeared to Alfred to strengthen him. That was Alfred's own testimony, and all his writings have gravitas.

16. In 878, when Guthrum accepted Christian baptism, a treaty was made which conceded the eastern side of what is now England to become "the Danelaw" and the western side to Wessex.

17. What was left of Mercian leadership began to integrate, mainly peacefully, with the Wessex leadership, but the polities remained distinct. Wessex became the main power of the two.

18. There were twin forces towards the increasing integration. Political and military dire necessity. And growing Christian maturity, cultivated increasingly from 830 onwards and before the dire necessities arose. Histories conventionally present to you the first force only.

19. Between 878 and 899, Alfred organised his peoples, still identifying as Wessex and Mercia, for a further military confrontation with the Danelaw which he sensed must come. What motivated him in those years was to restore his peoples to Christian education and civilisation. The military and organisational build-out was to safeguard that.

20. Alfred took law-making to the next level. He built it on Germanic and Christian codes interwoven. He enforced knowledge of the law in the courts. More generally, historians see proto-Parliamentary ways in his approach. You could say that he took to the next level Archbishop Theodore's old legacy of bringing together the Lords Temporal and the Lords Spiritual.

21. Alfred gave much prominence to the concept of the "Angelcynn", meaning "English-Kind" or "Kin of the English". He came to be styled as "King of the Angelcynn". However, that could be taken to be an over-claim at the time. He was effectively an over-King of the separate polities of Wessex and Mercia, and not a ruler of those Angelcynn who were under Danish rule. Mind you, Alfred may have had a vision for more than that, hence the styling.

22. In 899, Alfred was succeeded in Wessex by a son, Edward the Elder. Edward defined his Identity as a Christian Warrior, albeit not with all his father's spirituality. However, he was formidable in war. At the onset of his reign, his right to rule was challenged from within Wessex. Danish forces came in against him with the challenger. From then on, it became no holds barred. Edward defeated the Wessex challenger and his Danish allies and from then on gradually reconquered the Danelaw.

23. The Danelaw south of the Humber was by now making baby step progress towards Christian Identity. However, for Edward the Elder and his people, they would have seen the reconquest as an existential necessity. There had been a long track record of Danish forces betraying treaties.

24. King Alfred had a genius daughter, Aethelflaed. She had both the Christian spirituality of her father and the military generalship of her brother. In the 880s, she was married into the by-now-weakened Mercian royal family, to King Aethelred of Mercia. When this king died in 911, the Mercian court, without demur, made Aethelflaed, native of Wessex and female, their ruler. Given the old tradition of Mercia versus Wessex rivalry, and male versus female roles in the ancient warrior times, that can stand as a measure of Aethelflaed's greatness. From 911 onwards, she comes down to us as "the Lady of the Mercians".

25. Before 911, Aethelflaed had been the driving force, in league with her brother, King Edward the Elder of Wessex, for the ever-increasing rollback of the Danelaw. In 910, their forces won the defining battle of the period, at Tettenhall in the Western Midlands of what is now England. Danish forces were decisively broken. Hindsight shows Tettenhall to have been another nation-building milestone.

26. The Battle of Tettenhall took place on Saint King Oswald's Day. Aethelflaed had not long laid his bones in her new church at Gloucester. Those same bones had sealed the nation-building peace between Northumbria and Mercia in 679. Her brother, Edward the Elder, had deliberately retrieved them out of Danelaw territory through an expedition in 909.

27. Edward the Elder of Wessex had three wives. He had sons by each and preferred the sons of the latter two. The eldest son, by the first wife, was named Athelstan. When Edward took his second wife, Athelstan was packed off to Mercia to be brought up. Effectively demoted. He was brought up by Aethelflaed, Lady of the Mercians.

28. Aethelflaed passed her genius, which was also Alfred's genius, of being both a devoted Christian and a gifted warrior, on to Athelstan. Rejected he may have been, but it would be he who would found the Nation or Kingdom of the English.

29. King Alfred the Great had singled out the young Athelstan, his grandson, for special honour. He had done this when Athelstan was just five, in an echo of Alfred's own singling out, also at age five, in Rome, by the Pope.

30. Edward the Elder died in 924. He had by now completely retaken Mercia, including all its Eastern parts, and East Anglia. Mercia and Wessex remained distinct entities under his strong over-ruling. Edward's preferred successor son passed away sixteen days after Edward. The others were all quite young. Mercia unilaterally declared Athelstan king of Mercia and Wessex combined. There was opposition in Wessex, but Athelstan was in the end crowned in Kingston-upon-Thames, on the Mercia/Wessex border, as their joint king.

31. By 925, the following title was used in a formal way to designate Athelstan: he became the King of the English. However, as at 925, that was still only Wessex and Mercia, now as one.

32. In 927, King Athelstan took Danish York, and with it Northumbria, without a fight. It came under his direct rule. At that time, he became King over all the Christian peoples of Germanic origin and also those of more mixed Anglo-Danish culture. He went on to style himself as King of the English and Ruler of Britain, the latter meaning what we now call Wales and Scotland.

33. It would be an exaggeration to say that Athelstan won over Northumbrian hearts and minds, but in 927, "King of the English" was no longer an over-claim. The Nation of the English now existed much as we came to know it. Ruler of Britain was an over-claim. He had the co-operation of the Welsh but the resentment of the Scots. However, between 927 and 937, King Athelstan sought to affirm that title as his power.

34. Athelstan ended his reign by overreaching in terms of "Ruler of Britain" but with the English as a cohering nation in which shared Christian Identity was foundational. Athelstan went on to embed that and also Alfred's models of law and government. He set up English government practices in

forms recognisable to this day. Athelstan was profoundly Christian in his sense of Identity. To embed Christian Identity under his rule was his passion.

35. The word "Engla-lond" – England – had come into existence by Athelstan's time. It was to designate the polity of the Christian English, but the territory was fluid and the term little used.

36. King Athelstan was a Christian Warrior through and through, always a difficult Identity to manage with integrity. But like Alfred and Aethelflaed, he was no hypocrite as a Christian.

37. So: Aethelwulf & Osburh, Alfred, Aethelflaed and Athelstan. Five strong Christians in four strong generations, defining themselves without hypocrisy by Christian Identity. By the time they had done, there existed the Nation of the English. Conceived 597. Born 635. Off to School 669. Graduated 927. Every stage a profoundly Christian one.

38. Many Anglo-Danish settlements remained, and Christian Identity developed in them. Meanwhile, English Christian standards declined. Then a new wave of Danish invaders came. Around about 1016, a Danish King, Canute, newly converted into Christian Identity, took the English throne. This came as the culmination of reprisals for a treacherous massacre of Anglo Danes in 1002. The first Danish baptism amongst the English was in 878. The first Danish Christian King of the English: 1016. What an outcome for Alfred's approach of sealing treaty by baptism in 878.

39. Canute's court embedded the name of "Engla-Lond" into full official existence to denote the territory of England as distinct from his Danish lands. The borders by then were similar to today. So, Alfred's family established the Christian English. To all intents and purposes, it was the Christian Danes that named England.

40. Until the Great War, 1914-18, the English never ceased to be passionate about their Christian Identity. It defined them, whoever ruled them.

Now, to look ahead from 597 to 689 to the story of Alfred the Great of Wessex and family, 878 to 927, recovering things that have become lost or hidden from sight.

A Rogue King of Wessex

We begin with a dreadful episode for Christian Wessex.

In 686, the ruler of Wessex committed an atrocity and dragged the name of Christ into it. A rogue king, a sort of usurper, another and different Caedwalla, had taken the throne in violent circumstances in 685 and had four short and violent years of reign.

This Caedwalla committed near-genocide on the Isle of Wight. That is a large island off the south coast of what we now call England. It harboured at that time Jutish peoples who were the last of the invader Germanic people groups to remain in favour of pagan identity.

Now, the people of the Isle of Wight, with a violent King of Wessex on their doorstep, may have engaged in political intrigues in league with Mercia against Wessex. That may be why Caedwalla put them to the sword. However, he seems also to have vowed that, if he won, he would give a quarter of the lands to that new Christian God he had heard about. It is important to understand, as Bede tells us, that Caedwalla was not Christian at this time.

Now, Caedwalla may have known no better. Church leaders, on the other hand... The response to Caedwalla's massacre was dubious. Bishop Wilfrid, who had been at work in nearby Hampshire at that time, accepted a quarter of the Isle of Wight from Caedwalla as land for him to build a capital C Church on.

Wilfrid seems to have had contacts beforehand with Caedwalla, but I am not going to imply connivance in the slaughter, as some do. Wilfrid did have a streak of The Church Militant in his theology. But there is no evidence. And from a Christian perspective, his God seems to have dealt with him too graciously at the end of his life for him to have connived. A rogue ruler is a rogue ruler is a rogue ruler. Church leaders of the time would work with the grain of it as best they could. However, to have accepted the gift has a dubious ring about it. In similar circumstances, the original spiritual example figure for the Christian in the Bible, Abraham, refused to accept. I find it interesting that Wilfrid, soon afterwards, managed to get himself expelled and stripped of lands for a second time in the North in 691, a difficult negative achievement at the time. Accept dubious new lands, lose much more of your old lands... it has the feel of the hidden hand of discipline from the Christian God on one of his errant own. It would have much been worse if Wilfrid had actually connived.

Later, Caedwalla, injured in all his fighting and sensing that he would not recover, journeyed to Rome to die there. Perhaps Wilfrid had been mellowing the brigand king. Or perhaps it was that Rome was – allegedly – closer to heaven than Wessex. Or perhaps both. Anyway, the churchmen of Rome gave Caedwalla an epitaph saying that he had laid aside barbarous rage for new birth. They also baptised him into a new name, Peter. You could spin that as flattery or spin it as signalling a king wishing to mend his ways. And there, in 689, baptised on his death bed – a practice which might hint at superstition or immature Christian understanding – Caedwalla passed away.

Grunt. A certain amount of sweeping under the carpet, perhaps?

Where was the Christian God? What would he do about dragging his name into genocide? He seems to have restored the murderer, King Oswy. How would he handle this one, then?

The Christian God seems to have applied the Second Commandment. So far, I have only brought to light the reward side of the Commandment, which is that blessings sown in faith can descend to a thousand generations. There is also a penalty side. The curses of that which is not of faith will descend for four generations. You will note that the blessing is much greater than the curse. But curse there can be.

And curse the Christian God would appear to have imposed because the ruling house of Wessex went into the wilderness for four generations. It did not cease to exist. It formulated laws. Neither did its subsequent kings replicate Caedwalla's proto-Crusading Reward-Points-with-God seeking behaviour. Wessex churchmanship grew in learning and power. The Wessex Christian scene mounted a civilisation-transforming expedition into the old Germanic heartlands. But the baton of Christian leadership and rulership in general amongst the Early English to the south of Northumbria passed, for four generations, to Mercia. By and large, Wessex was under the Mercian boot for that time. There was the occasional fightback. But rival Mercia had what is known as Supremacy. And it rubbed Wessex noses in it.

Fair enough, I should say, to Wessex. Generous even, of the Christian God, to confine the discipline to four generations. Not half hard enough for the modern post-Puritan mind. However, this God says in his Bible that he does not punish forever those who bear his name. And a couple of other points too:

- The Christian God would foreknow the family of King Alfred of Wessex. That family would restore Christian Integrity. The time would come to make a way for them, in a Christian understanding.

- At the end of the four generations, Christianised Mercia had used its Supremacy to perfect Christianised hypocrisy to an art form. For the Christian God, it would have become fair to reckon, "Time for the baton to pass on."

So it came to pass that in 802, the family of King Alfred of Wessex took the Wessex throne and set out down the path to Greatness. Irritated with the blatant manoeuvrings of King Offa of Mercia, the Emperor Charlemagne of the Franks sponsored Alfred's grandfather, King Egbert, to the throne of Wessex as a way of sticking his tongue out at Mercia. A human cause. But perhaps a hidden hand. As for King Offa, it was maybe a case of the biter bit.

Sword Point or Free Choice?

Of what happened after 802, more shortly. However, we should return to this slaughter on the Isle of Wight. I have seen at least two headlines in recent years that the Early English were forced into Christian Identity more generally at the point of a sword.

This event seems to be cited as evidence for that claim. However, it is hard to find it as general within the history. What you mainly find there is king reasoning with king; prince persuading prince; queen freely retaining Christian Identity and prevailing with it.

You find the pagan priest Coifi, given free choice, voluntarily destroying his old sanctuary in the first flush of living Christian faith. Ten thousand volunteering for Christian baptism in St Augustine of Canterbury's first year; Paulinus with crowds flocking to him for baptism in the North.

There *was* a sword point wielded in earnest during the period from 597 to the times of Archbishop Theodore: King Penda of Mercia, a pagan, became a serial killer of the Christian kings. However, the Christian Identity of those kings kept resurging stronger than before, and peacefully as far as possible. King Penda's own people took hold of the Christian Identity with both hands from the moment they were free to do so. At that time, you find Christian King Oswy of Northumbria, with all of Mercia at the discretion of his sword, sheathing it, and sending the Christian Saints marching in instead.

You find St Aidan bringing love. You find St Cuthbert spreading a fragrance of goodness wherever he walked, even implored by an implacable warrior king to walk freely amongst a people who loved him. You find Archbishop Theodore teaching Christian government and reason, and every people group and ruler copying how he did things.

You find the bulldozing Bishop Wilfrid brought low more than once under the discipline of his Christian God – the second time being after accepting the dubious gift on the Isle of Wight – and restored in old age.

You find John of Beverley, product of Abbot Hadrian's teaching, getting into the stride of his great and Anointed life as a bishop even as Wilfrid accepted Caedwalla's dubious gift. John was much loved.

One does have to wonder about a headline which presents Early English history as being one of Christian Identity enforced at sword point.

The general rule was free choice, as you would expect of a Christian God who says that it is for freedom that the Christ sets us free.

Like many a rule, however, there was one exception to prove the rule: Isle of Wight, 686, under a king, Caedwalla, who was pre-Christian, barbaric and confused. In response to having had his name linked with evil, the Christian God would appear to have passed judgement, precisely following the principles he claims to have written in stone more than two thousand years before.

Now, to press on to Alfred the Great and family. And to the Vikings who unintentionally made a way for them.

Viking Incursion

Between 787 and 878, incursion by pagan Danish Vikings became steadily more invasive and overwhelming to the Anglo-Saxon-ancestry inhabitants of what we now call England.

From a modern perspective, it was yet another migration for all the normal material causes. Pick a fight and win: glory. Take spoil: get drunk. Take land: settle down.

From the perspective of the times, as recorded in the Anglo-Saxon Chronicle and arising from their Christian worldview, it was a judgement from the Christian God for lapsed and hypocritical Christian practice. That was also how Alfred the Great came to see it later.

A Christian perspective with hindsight of more than a thousand years might also see it like this. Christian standards *had* declined. There *was* hypocrisy. Once a people group takes on the name of the Christian God but turns to hypocrisy, there can be sharp teeth in the contractual fine print. It is possible to go through a period when the Christian God lifts off his protective hand and you suffer. At the end of the period, however, the same God's Biblical pattern is that he will raise up a Deliverer. That seems to have been the pattern followed between 787 and 878 in Christian terms: in this case, the Deliverer in 878 was Alfred of Wessex. This is a regular Biblical pattern. It can be discerned to have played out in the real world history of the Early English.

The Vikings certainly had an impact. Even so, it is strange to see how we are taught about them these days. They are subtly glamorised to our children. They are implied to have been a major shaping force in English history. In truth, they left little impact in the long run within English Identity. As to that, once they settled down, the Viking Danish invaders adopted the Christian Identity that they found in the English. And they gradually Anglicised upon it.

Therefore, a Christian might be inclined to say that, in judgement, the Christian God remembered mercy. Another Biblical pattern working out in the real world.

So, a Christian perspective on the Danish Vikings is a subtle and difficult one to establish. They did Christianise in the end. Before that, however, Early English Christians of those times suffered much, and they thought the Danish Vikings to be a human agent of the judgement of God. Maybe they were not being superstitious ancients... Maybe they were right... But the Biblical pattern they lived through was not a simplistic one.

A serious point now, out of all this. The great Martinian Christians who came before the Vikings are not even mentioned to our children. The Vikings are the anti-heroes peddled to them instead. But it was the Martinian Christians who shaped the Identity which descended into English history. The Danish Vikings went with the flow of it. In the end, they rallied, for example, around the late St Cuthbert, just as the Germanic English did. Therefore, the Christian spirituality which had been in the Martinian Saints also shaped, in a hand-me-down sort of way, what the Danish Viking invaders became. That one salient big-picture fact is the one salient big-picture fact which is routinely airbrushed from the histories.

Three Nutshells

Before the Vikings settled, however, there were many terrible events. The extremity of the times is summarised in this one incident, the murder of St Alphege, Archbishop of Canterbury. This was as late as 1011/2. Taken captive by Danish invaders, he was beaten to the point of death with ox bones when no ransom was paid for him. He was put out of his misery by a death blow, compassionate, from a Dane who had just the day before been Confirmed into Christian Identity by the Archbishop in his captivity. That one nutshell sums up the trauma of more than two centuries; and the Danish Identity transition; and its backdrop. Here are two more:

i. By the year that the Viking Invaders first came, 787, King Offa of the Mercian Supremacy, a lifelong politiciser of Christian Identity, had set the highest reaches of the Christian church of the Early English against one another within his drive for the Glory of Mercia. That old chestnut. Nothing new under the sun again, eh? It may not have helped that the Archbishop of Canterbury at the time seems to have been pushed back into the role of a sort of Kentish Nationalist from within the office of Theodore, founding Architect of the Nation of the English. Christian Integrity seems to have been devolving in both church and state. There had been an epic Christian mission into Europe a generation before that. And there remained much Christian sincerity in many of the set-apart Christian communities. But it is hard not to discern Christian standards slipping.

ii. In 793, the Vikings sacked the Lindisfarne of Saints Aidan and Cuthbert, of all places. It was an enormous shock. If there was one place that the world of the Early English would have thought to be under the protection of the Christian God, that was it. To this day, an atheist will point out the event with the implication of, so much for the Christian God then. I will say just one thing about it. Jesus Christ taught, when a building had collapsed and those within it had perished, that those who had perished were not worse than anywhere else. Instead, it was a warning to all: change course or likewise perish. I would note in passing a noticeable lack of handwringing in this teaching, coming as it does from the Christ who is said to personify the Christian God.

Northumbria was to be comprehensively invaded by the Danish Vikings and settled by them. Christianising began, but in a rather paganised way; a bit of a throwback to King Raedwald of the East Angles, 616, of whom we read in the chapter "Gestation". The southern part of Northumbria, old Deira, became Danish with subject Angle mixed in, slowly Christianising. The northern part, old Bernicia, remained a cut-off Angle-ish territory with a Christian heritage less sparky than it had been in its glory days.

To the south of the Humber, the territories were subjected to ever-increasing Viking Incursion from the East and partial settlement. The Christian Identity was in crisis. And within a process which was traumatic, the power of Mercia was broken.

However, a Christian Deliverer arose. Alfred the Great of Wessex. He and his family had integrity in their Christian spirituality. And they would prevail militarily when all seemed lost.

Alfred's Roots; and Two Notable Christian Resources

In the year 802, the warrior King Egbert came to the throne of Wessex. Alfred's grandfather, he was sponsored there by Charlemagne the Great with a view to frustrating King Offa of Mercia. After many years of consolidating power within Wessex, Egbert prevailed in battle in 825 to end the dominion of Mercia over Wessex. However, he took no dominion himself. And from 830, the two powers co-existed with equal respect. A common enemy was harassing them, the Viking invaders. And Christian standards were being recovered in each kingdom. Each factor was a force for unity where once there had been ingrained rivalry.

When the time came, Alfred would draw greatly upon Christian scholarship from Western Mercia to restore the Christian Identity in Wessex as well as Mercia. Hearteningly, and to note, Alfred would also draw upon Welsh Christian scholars. Pagan Wessex had once fought with the Christian Welsh in the old Britonnic Christian days. In these later times, the Christian Identity had become common, derived from the times I have already recounted at length.

Alfred's Parents

King Egbert passed away in 839 and was succeeded by his son, King Aethelwulf. His wife was Osburh. I would like to call her Queen Osburh. However, in those days, Wessex tradition was to accord no such title. Osburh had no title.

These were the parents of Alfred the Great. It will be instructive to recover their much-overlooked role in the history. It was predominantly a Christian role.

The Christian God did not *vindicate* the event in 686 on the Isle of Wight. But when the time came, he did *redeem* it. An aristocratic young Christian woman named Osburh came out of the Isle of Wight and married into the Wessex royal family. Little is known of her except two things:

- She had strong Christian faith.

- She was the mother of Alfred the Great, committed to educating him.

Osburh is another one airbrushed out of history. However, as I noted much earlier, they do say that the hand that rocks the cradle rules the world. I have no idea whether Osburh did the actual rocking or if she delegated it to a nanny. However, she seems to have contributed a Christian worldview to her infant son, Alfred. Out of it, he became a Deliverer.

Alfred's father, Aethelwulf, was not of wolfish character, as his very tough father, Egbert, may have hoped when naming him, but Aethelwulf had this in common with Alfred. (i) He was profoundly Christian. And (ii), he knew how to fight battles. He had some success at holding the Danish Vikings in check.

So: Alfred's parents were both Christians of devotion and integrity.

It is instructive to see how some historians have appraised Aethelwulf. "Religious nutter" about sums it up. However, it would be fairer to say that he was conscientiously faithful to the Christian God. Not the same thing as "Religious". And not the same thing as a nutter. Thankfully, in recent times, his reputation is being restored.

Now, Aethelwulf did have a late-life crisis, getting his head turned by a teenager after his wife had died. Nudge, nudge, wink, wink. However, here is the greatly overlooked thing which he did before he had his late-life crisis. He gave away a tenth of all that he had. There is much debate over the details of how it was disposed of. But the details do not matter as much as the one salient point: it was out of honour to the Christian God that he gave.

I find that highly significant. Who honours me, I will honour, says the Bible of the Christian God. And here is another Biblical principle: if you express that honour as giving a tenth to honour the Christian God, that God will bless you. The modern English tend to scoff. However, according to the Bible, it is so. You might have a manipulative heart over it: if I give, I will get. Or a legalistic heart: I will tithe as a Box Ticking Exercise to Please the Unpleasable God. Or you might have a genuine heart over it: I love the Christian God, and he has put love in my heart; love speaks in actions not words, so I will give a tenth of all I have in honour to the Christian God. We live in cynical times, but many a Christian in the world today gives a tenth out of a genuine heart. I do not know of many a cynic who gives even approaching a tenth.

Anyway, I can see no reason why King Aethelwulf should not be accorded the motive of a genuine heart. It would be consistent with his life and character. There were plenty of ways in his culture to attempt to manipulate the Christian God other than giving a tenth, far less demanding: basically, follow various pseudo-Christian rituals which were set on their long course to devolving into later Medieval Religiosity.

So that was the example set to the young Alfred: integrity of Christian expression. And one which came with an explicit promise in the Christian Bible, from Jesus Christ himself: give to God and it will be given to you, full measure, cup running over. And we must remember the more general Biblical principle already seen in this book: Christian faith will bless the generations which come after you. Cup running over for them, therefore, to link up the Biblical logic. Aethelwulf's tithe, or Decimation as it tends to be known, if made from a genuine heart, would have released a principle of overflowing blessing into his family. And… the history shows… it really did.

Now, there was a political dimension to Aethelwulf's gift. The modern English mind, seeing politics as one side of a wall and "Religion" as the other side of it, tends to see the political aspect of the gift as invalidating the Christian dimension of it. But the Christian God recognises no such walls. In 635, Saint King Oswald had sown Christian blessing into the future course of political life in what would become England when, with political motives mixed in, he extended Christian grace to King Cynegils of Assassin Wessex. Multiple generations later, King Aethelwulf of Wessex, with a heart of Christian grace, expressed the Christian principle of tithing into his political realm. The effect was as it had been with Oswald. Blessings of the Christian God were released into the political realm. King Alfred inherited them in full measure, cup running over.

Mind you, as well as that, Aethelwulf incurred consequences of his late-life crisis. Trouble ensued. Osburh had died by 855. Aethelwulf went on pilgrimage to Rome. He took his time returning, diverting en route home to the Court of the Western Franks and marrying a teenage princess, Judith. During his absence, his eldest son stole the throne of Wessex. I can't go into all the human undercurrents. I would observe that the son, Aethelbald, later married Judith after his father had died. Another case of uncovering your father's nakedness, and there was a well-known Christian injunction against that in those times. It infers a throwback pagan disposition in this son.

Aethelwulf defused the situation with Christian humility, conceding half of his kingdom to the son. It set a Christian example to his family: avoid strife, accommodate one another, remember the common threat, the paganism of the Danes. Wise, I should say, from a root of Christian wisdom.

The example came to matter, Big Time. By 865, there were only the two youngest sons of Aethelwulf surviving, Aethelred and Alfred. Aethelred was to become a king of short reign but of Christian integrity. Before that, the throne-stealer, Aethelbald, had inherited the whole kingdom in a proper way when Aethelwulf died in 858. But Aethelbald died young. Aethelred had a claim to the throne at that time. However, he deferred to another brother, Aethelbert. He, too, died young. Whereupon Aethelred got the throne anyway, without strife, from 865. The pressure of Danish invasion became so great in Aethelred's time, 865 to 871, that he made a pact with Alfred, youngest of the brothers. If Aethelred died, there would be no internecine succession strife. His own young children would not take the throne. It would pass to Alfred as a mature adult able to carry the battle.

It turned out to be a pact born out of Christian wisdom. It descended from their father's wise example of Christian humility.

Aethelred died of wounds fighting the Danish Invaders in 871. Alfred came to the throne of Wessex in that year. He inherited or benefitted from:

1. His father's Christian humility.

2. His mother's Christian worldview.

3. The mystery of redemptive Christian grace that one senses in her coming out from the Isle of Wight.

4. His father's Christian example to the family to cohere under pressure to disintegrate.

5. Both his parents' general Christian integrity.

6. The seed of Christian blessing sown in his father's tithe.

King Alfred the Great had these attributes, too:

7. He could fight.

8. And rally.

9. And build a kingdom.

10. And was passionate about educating on restored Christian foundations.

Conventional analysis, seeing with one eye, gives him four out of four, the last four above, and the last of those truncated at the word "educating". Balanced analysis, seeing with two eyes, gives him ten out of ten. And no truncation of the Christian element. King Alfred comes down to us, a mixture of all of these, as a true Great.

I will give a brief account of the narrative flow of events shortly. Before that, there was something else that Alfred inherited, something most mysterious: Papal Blessing. He was singled out by the Pope to be the future king. As a young child, and the youngest of his brothers.

We had better look at this first.

King Alfred – Singled out by the Pope

My translation of the Anglo-Saxon Chronicle says that Alfred's father Aethelwulf sent Alfred to Rome. There, Pope Leo IV consecrated him as king and took him as his son at confirmation. Alfred would have been maybe five years old.

It adds a certain mystique to Alfred: set apart so young for a special destiny.

Some writers of earlier times, more willing than the modern mind to admit the Christian God into the real history of a people with Christian Identity, saw in it the prophetic hand of the Christian God. There is a certain consistency in their approach. The modern mind, by contrast, seems to avoid any such conclusion. Its approach is consistent with believing that we all came from blind process and that all things arise out of impersonal forces, which seems to be the underlying modern belief system of the English.

I can't help thinking that the earlier writers had more sense, though. If you call yourself Christian, as Alfred's people did; and the Christian God has a prophetic dimension, as he insists in his Bible and showed in his Christ that he does have; and the prophetic dimension is available to people who call themselves Christian, as the Christian Bible says it is, then why might there not be a Christian prophetic element at work in the life of young Alfred?

It is not as if, in modern times, we have had no similar example. Sir Winston Churchill knew from age 16, and said so, that he had a destiny to be a Deliverer. It was out of a Christian spirituality which had first been imparted to him as a young child by his nanny, Elizabeth Everest, that the teenager matured into this prophetic sense of destiny. And Sir Winston Churchill turned out to be no false prophet.

That being so, I can see no reason why Pope Leo IV would turn out to be a false prophet either. To my mind, who better to indicate a special future for Alfred under the Christian God than a Pope?

Alfred was singled out and set apart, ahead of his time, and ahead of older brothers. That might worry you if you take no account of Biblical example. But there is no problem with it in the Bible. The exact same happened with King David, whose life King Alfred the Great was to echo. You can dig around to find political motivation in the Pope, appraising the event as having arisen out of that alone. Or accept the obvious: that the hand of the Christian God was upon the young Alfred. English history was not a system closed to the Christian God.

Now, to note the word used in conjunction with the event in the Chronicle, the Pope took Alfred in "confirmation". A cleric "confirms" those whom they are sure have received the Christ by the indwelling of the Holy Spirit of the Christian God, i.e. have received the Christ for real rather than gone through the motions. Would a child aged just five be able to receive the Christ that way? Well, I have heard of it in modern times in some types of English church. And I knew a Christian minister whose young son, aged six, said one night at bedtime, having recently been exposed to good Christian teaching, "I want to receive Jesus, Daddy." And on his bed, as his father led him in prayer, the child received the indwelling Christ by the Holy Spirit as easily as breathing. He bore all the fruits of it as he grew up. Alfred's life bore all the fruits of that, too.

I see no problem at all, therefore, with accepting that the young Alfred, aged five, already influenced by his mother, Osburh, received the Christ in Rome and knew it. In a like manner, as a modern example, I would infer that the young Winston Churchill received the Christ in his nannied years. His subsequent life completely failed to conform to Christian stereotype. But it was always Christian. If you cut him some slack, as the Christian God says that he inclines to do in all from the least to the greatest, Sir Winston Churchill's life bore the hallmarks of having received the Christ via his nanny but having remained un-churched.

Interesting pattern here, in passing; I can't resist a wry smile. King Alfred the Great, Deliverer, hero of Sir Winston Churchill, Deliverer, received the Christ through aristocratic parents and a Pope. Sir Winston Churchill, aristocrat personified but neglected by aristocratic parents, received the Christ through his nanny, Elizabeth Everest. From Chatham. Working class personified. And female. Known to have had a sense of mission to impart the Christ and a Christian worldview into any child given into her care. Having this in common with the aristocratic Osburh, however: untitled and airbrushed from the history. But this in common, too: a world-shaper. The Christian hand that rocked the cradle…

I invite you to meditate on that pattern. The ironies within it could not be more typical of the Christian God.

This is for certain: King Alfred the Great was singled out and set apart within an explicitly Christian framework and his life bore all the hallmarks of that: in the real world.

And again, think of another pattern here. Where were the Anglo Saxons first conceived into Christian Identity? In the mind of a Pope, Gregory the Great. What a completely satisfying pattern, then, for the rescuer and rebuilder of that Christian Identity, Alfred, to be confirmed into that destiny by another Pope. If you believe you came from blind process, there is no pattern to see. And yet… the Christian pattern does seem to be there, hidden in plain sight. And how much more satisfying to see it.

Alfred the Great – Career

Alfred succeeded to the throne of Wessex in 871. At that time, the Danish forces had been making significant gains, increasing in number and beginning to settle. Mercia, once Supreme, was downtrodden. Wessex faced existential threat. The two spiritualities, pagan and Christian, were not mingling in the way that they were doing north of the Humber. Neither were the ethnicities.

By 877/8 Alfred, in an echo of the Biblical King David hiding in a cave before coming into his kingdom (which in itself was a Christ pattern, where the cave equates to the tomb and the kingdom to the resurrection), had been driven into hiding in the marshlands of what we now call Somerset. The future was bleak for King and people. It seems that Alfred was asked to keep an eye on some cakes being cooked, but they burned: his mind was elsewhere.

Maybe it happened. It used to be taught to all the children. The actual thing that Alfred said did happen seems to have been less taught to the children: St Cuthbert, who had passed away in 687, appeared to him. Early in 878, Alfred was sending out messengers to rally forces for a breakout and one final attempt to roll back the pagan tide. St Cuthbert appeared to strengthen him for the battle. I will look at this quite closely later.

Alfred won the Battle of Edington, 878. In the aftermath, he came to a treaty with the Danish leader, Guthrum. The Danish forces could have the Eastern side of what we now call England. Its name became "the Danelaw". The people of Anglo-Saxon origin in those territories had to come under Danish rule. The Anglo-Saxon-ancestry forces of Wessex and Western Mercia would have the Western side of what we now call England. A condition of the treaty was that Guthrum must undergo Christian baptism. And that the Anglo-Saxon-ancestry Christians in the East must have toleration of their Christian practices. Guthrum agreed to the conditions.

There are some notable things just below the surface.

- Danes had a long track record for striking treaties and betraying them as soon as possible. In this case, they were eventually going to break the military aspects of the treaty but not the Christian side of it.

- I find myself thinking, how unlikely an outcome, humanly speaking, that Alfred won. Guthrum's forces were the more hardened. Maybe they had over-reached. But how unlikely that, losing just one battle, the Danish forces settled for ending a war of three preceding generations. Maybe the offer to settle for half the country was acceptable to Guthrum. He could always betray it later. But (i) the military peace was to hold for long enough for Alfred's forces to grow in strength. And (ii) the Christian peace was to hold until the English betrayed it more than a century later. Unlikely, both points.

A most remarkable irony would emerge in the end as well. The Apostle Paul taught that the Christian God may do above and beyond what the Christian who sows in faith can imagine. Well, here is something that Alfred can neither have imagined nor intended. It was seeded, however, out of his Christian peacemaking and the baptism of Guthrum. It would fall to a Christian Danish King, Canute, to systematise the use of the name England to designate England. I will explore more fully later.

First, however, to complete the narrative. Alfred spent the rest of his reign, until 899, building and restoring the peoples of Wessex and Western Mercia. Western Mercia retained its distinct polity, but the overall leadership gravitated into the Wessex royal family. The Danelaw developed its own ways, tolerating Christians of Anglo-Saxon ancestry, adopting some of their ways. However, there was simmering tension between East and West.

Alfred could foresee a recurrence of existential conflict in the future with the Danish forces. It was the track record. Alfred made peace as far as he was able, but he was not an idealist. The Christian God indicates in his Bible that he, too, is not an idealist. Instead, he is a realist. So, Alfred was consistent with his God. And he turned out to be no false seer as to conflict to come. The wonder is that he had so long to prepare for it. There were battles, but an uneasy peace held, by and large.

With great energy, Alfred overhauled procedures for military call-up. He built out a string of new fortifications. As to the Christian side of things, Alfred promoted the restoration of much that had almost collapsed. He promoted education, on Christian foundations. He pioneered the use of Old English in place of Latin for that. Alfred also shaped the legal framework for the English which has descended, in part, to this day. He paid much attention to government, combining Christian spirituality with political nous. He saw himself as responsible for every aspect of the wellbeing of his subjects, spiritual as well as secular. There was no division in his outlook over that, no dividing wall. The policy for Christian spirituality was to place gifted Christians into high authority. He drew on West Mercian and Welsh establishments to recruit them. His biographer was Christian Welsh. One may infer a steady tendency towards reconciliation between Christian English and Christian Welsh since earlier times. Christian Welsh had made a growing contribution of goodness to the Early English by Alfred's time.

Alfred brought to the fore the concept of the "Angelcynn" – Kin of the English. I go into this further, and how it developed, later in the chapter. The concept was interwoven inextricably in his mind, in his family, and in his people, with Christian Identity. It became more and more a rallying concept.

It now remains to see how the English and England came to be after Alfred had passed away.

King Edward the Elder of Wessex

Edward, a son of Alfred, reigned over Wessex from 899 to 924. His accession to the throne was disputed by a cousin, a son of one of Alfred's older brothers. There were no succession laws as we know them now. Edward had to fight for it.

Within the process, Danish forces came in on the side of the rival claimant, Aethelwold. Edward had prevailed by 901, and Aethelwold had perished in battle.

From then on, it was no holds barred with the Danish forces south of the Humber. Edward spent the rest of his reign rolling back the Danelaw and consolidating Wessex royal power. By the time he had done, Eastern Mercia and East Anglia were under the Wessex rule, but Danish remnants within them were tolerated and Christianising.

Edward continued his father's Christian policies but without quite the same spiritual spark. He increased the number of bishoprics but at the same time made the role of bishop a lot more military. Very Medieval; not quite the modern mind. However, you can see that it was Christian Identity he was fighting for. You could spin him as a dominating aggressor. Or simply as realistic within his times. If he did not win, his people's Christian Identity would fall. Within the framework of the Christian Bible, to let his people down over that would be to fail in his kingly calling under the Christian God. Alien thinking to a modern mind, including many a Christianised one. But not outside the Christian Biblical envelope. The Apostle Paul taught that the state could use force for the peace of its subjects. Within the context of this teaching was an unstated assumption by Paul that the purpose was to safeguard the freedom to live a Christian Life. The Roman church and all kings influenced by them understood the role of forceful protector of Christian Identity to be a foundational role for rulers. And it is not as if Edward was enforcing conversions at the point of a sword.

Edward also played a key role in 909 in liberating Saint King Oswald's bones out from the Danelaw territory. We will come to that. To modern appraisal, it might indicate cultism. In Edward's, it would have meant participating in the sense of destiny, under the Christian God, which had been awakened in his father, Alfred. I will develop this theme later in the chapter.

Edward built an ever-more-centralised state, proto-England in the making. When his sister Aethelflaed, Lady of the Mercians, passed away in 918, he took the over-rule of Mercia in a dominating way that Alfred had never attempted. To do so, he imprisoned Aethelflaed's daughter. At that time, much of what we now call England came under Wessex domination. However, Wessex and Mercia were not yet one and Edward was not yet in full possession of the Danelaw. Edward also sought titles and submissions with Welsh and Scots, although with how much effect is not clear.

All in all, something of a conqueror, Edward the Elder. Most ambiguous to appraise for the modern mind. A more engaging character, perhaps, would be his sister Aethelflaed, Alfred's Genius Daughter.

Aethelflaed of Wessex, Lady of the Mercians

Aethelflaed was married out from the Wessex royal family in the 880s to King Aethelred of Western Mercia. Her father, Alfred, was the over-king. In later life, Aethelred became ill. After he died in 911, Aethelflaed ruled alone. She was accepted and loved by the West Mercians. She must have been a most remarkable figure. The Lady of the Mercians as she then became known: a Wessex royal loved as a ruler in Mercia. A female loved as a ruler of warriors.

Aethelflaed was full of Christian devotion. And she was a military general. She joined forces with her warrior brother, Edward the Elder, in campaigns to roll back the Danelaw. She was, in many ways, the lead figure in reclaiming Eastern Mercia. And two most significant things came her way.

- In 910, her forces destroyed the strength of the Northumbrian Danes at Tettenhall in the West Midlands. Hindsight makes that the decisive battle in the years after King Alfred. The Danelaw south of the Humber lay open, with no Northern reinforcements to protect it.

- In 918, the Northumbrian Danes at York sounded out for a voluntary treaty to submit to Aethelflaed's rule. At the time, they were under threat from Norwegian Viking forces, more violent and more pagan than the Danes had by then become. The Northumbrian Danes were by now getting into a Christian stride of sorts, attracted, for example, to the late St Cuthbert. Interesting to note here: Cuthbert was a hero saint in Wessex as well as Northumbria: his Christian spirituality was beginning to make a bridge. It would seem, airbrushed from any historical appraisal that I have read, that Christian Aethelflaed was seen as the better option than the ethnically more related pagan Viking. So much for those Vikings being the influential and shaping force in the Early English history, eh? The ethnicity-reconciling Christian Identity seems to have been the stronger, just as the Bible teaches it would be; a conclusion hiding in plain sight.

Now, Aethelflaed passed away before she could fulfil the peace invitation. However, the opportunity was not lost, as you will soon see. But there were a couple more things we should note about her now. The first is the apparent role in her career of the late Saint King Oswald. The second is that she brought up King Athelstan. It would be he who would fulfil the peace feelers from York.

Aethelflaed and Saint King Oswald

We left Saint King Oswald's bones at Bardney, in what is now Lincolnshire, in 679. This was in the chapter about Archbishop Theodore. You may recall that a pillar of light from heaven to earth upon Oswald's bones accompanied a significant peace deal.

Have there ever been more phenomena clustered around a Christian than around this Northumbrian King?

- In life, an Anointed Christian.

- In death, a Christ figure.

- A more-like-King-Arthur-than-King-Arthur figure.

- He embodied reconciliation, in Christ, of Scot and Angle.

- His later title of "White Blade" indicates a measure of reconciling, in Christ, between Britonnic Welsh and Northern Angle.

- He inherited the civilisation-saving Christian spirituality that had been in St Martin, St Ninian, St Patrick, and St Columba and set it loose through St Aidan.

- In Christian peace, Oswald became the great, great, many-times-great godfather of Christian Wessex. Nation Building in the end: Christian Wessex emerged as Christian England.

- His bones were at the heart of the phenomenon in 679 which accompanied the Northumbria/Mercia peace – Nation Building once more.

And now for another phenomenon.

In the year 909, one year before the Battle of Tettenhall, King Edward the Elder led a raid into Eastern Mercia, to Bardney, to recover King Oswald's bones. For some reason, he gave them to Aethelflaed rather than keeping them for himself. One ponders an unremarked Christian integrity in the tough warrior brother in conceding them to an exceptionally Anointed sister.

Aethelflaed, along with husband King Aethelred of Western Mercia, placed the bones in a newly built church at Gloucester. There, with the full agreement of brother Edward the Elder, fervent prayers would have been offered to the Christian God to fulfil all that had once been in the late Saint King Oswald. The prayers would not solely have been to a war god for war victory. Of course, they would have prayed for war victory. However, they would also have prayed to the Christian God to fulfil what had been started in Oswald. That is a many times more rewarding way of seeing things. And as it happened, they did fulfil what Oswald had started.

Anyway, here's the point: Aethelflaed's history-turning-point victory at Tettenhall was to be on August 5th in 910. August 5th is Saint King Oswald's Day. What to make of that, then? Well, it needs careful teasing out, and to do so here would interrupt the narrative flow too much. I will return to it later in the chapter

Bringing up Young Athelstan

The second thing of note was that Aethelflaed brought up the Wessex youth who became King Athelstan, first King of the English.

There was a certain irony about Athelstan's accession. His father, Edward the Elder, had effectively overlooked him, favouring children of a later marriage than the one which produced Athelstan. The boy was packed off to Mercia, perhaps to become sub-King there one day. And there the Genius Aethelflaed, Lady of the Mercians, moulded this somewhat lost and rather great figure of Early English history. It was he who took York peacefully. We come to him now.

King Athelstan – King of the English

When King Edward the Elder of Wessex died in 924, his nominated successor died within 16 days of him. The other children were young.

Athelstan, brought up in Mercia, was a battle-experienced Christian Warrior, noble, fit to rule and, for Mercians, one-of-our-team despite his Wessex father. For Wessex, he was one-of-the-other-team, despite his Wessex father.

Anyway, long story short, Mercia unilaterally made Athelstan their king; and with remarkably little bloodshed, given the hostility in Wessex, Athelstan managed to get himself crowned on the Mercia/Wessex border at Kingston-upon-Thames in 925 as King over both kingdoms. With this title: King of the English. The once warring entities had merged.

Interestingly, Athelstan's grandfather, Alfred the Great, had singled out Athelstan for favour when he was aged five, as Alfred had also been five when singled out. I have read niggly motives inferred for this, as if Alfred were tweaking the nose of his son, Edward, by favouring the grandson. That sort of thing does happen. However, Alfred was of regenerate Christian nature and Great, not niggly. It seems far more reasonable to assume Christian prophetic insight. It is as if Alfred knew that Athelstan would be the one to complete what he had started. I don't see why not. It is completely within the envelope of the Christian Bible for a grandfather to know which grandson would have what under God. It is one of the most basic patterns within it, e.g., Jacob knowing the destiny of each grandchild. It would be more characteristic of the Holy Spirit of the Christian God to give the likes of Alfred similar prophetic insight than to withhold it. And here's the point to prove it: Alfred turned out to be right.

King Athelstan – King of the English and Ruler of Britain

King Athelstan was a Christian Warrior, in that order. He was a Christian first and a Warrior second. As a Christian, he dedicated himself to celibacy in his sense of set-apartness for a calling under the Christian God. As a Warrior, he was formidable.

From 927, following events I will set out shortly, he came to style himself "King of the English and Ruler of Britain". The words did not mean then what they mean now. You will note that there is no word "England" in there, either. We had better look at some terminology and then develop Athelstan's career to understand. In Athelstan's time, three concepts were in existence:

i. The Kin of the English, denoted by the word "Angelcynn". The King of the Angelcynn would mean the King of the Kin of the English or "English-Kind".

ii. "Engla-Lond", where "Lond" means Land, and "Engla" is short for Angelcynn. The word designated a fluid territory in which the Angelcynn lived. It later became the formal word for "England", but not yet.

iii. Britain, in various spellings, meaning either the whole island of Britain or people groups now known as Welsh and Scots, i.e. those who were not Angelcynn. It depended on context.

"Angelcynn" – Kin of the English – "English-Kind"

It was Alfred the Great who had brought the word "Angelcynn" into prominence. He became styled as the King of the Angelcynn. However, it would be a stretch to call him the first "King of the English" as a nation. He at first meant Wessex and Western Mercia, united in Christian Identity, and of common Germanic ancestry, but still within the two different senses of Wessex and Mercia Identity, Wessex as overlord. There was also no settled place in Alfred's title for the people in the Danish-controlled territories, many of them Christian of Germanic origin, others Christianising Anglo-Danish.

The people group in the Danish-controlled territories of Eastern Mercia and East Anglia complicated the three concepts so far set out. The Eastern side of England contained controlling pagan Danish settlers and subject Christians of old Anglo-Saxon origin. They were slowly turning into an Anglo-Danish hybrid people group. Part Christian, part pagan. Partly inclined to settle peacefully into the Angelcynn. Partly inclined to break out and conquer the Angelcynn. Therefore, in Athelstan's time, this group could have been seen either as Angelcynn or, like the Welsh and Scots, part of Britain, depending upon context.

There was another ambiguity: Northumbria. That had once been Angle-ish. By Athelstan's time, the old Bernician rump of it was still Angle-ish ethnic ruled. The bulk, old Deira, was Danish ruled from York and Anglo-Danish in nature. The Christian heritage in Bernicia remained but had lost the spark of the golden Christian times. The Anglo-Danish old Deira was Christianising. And both the Bernician rump and the Anglo-Danish Deiran majority saw "The North" as independent from "The South".

So it was complex and muddled. Some Danes in the East – Deira, East Mercia, East Anglia as once it had been – were Christianising. The Danish homeland was Christianising too. There was an epically violent culture to emerge from. But there was also something in common with the Angelcynn that transcended ethnicity: emerging Christian Identity.

Anyway, here's the point. Alfred the Great as "King of the Angelcynn" might have had a vision for the role of a King of the Angelcynn to be wider spread and more inclusive. However, his actual rule was Wessex and Mercia, each still as a distinct polity. It was Athelstan who fulfilled the wider vision as "King of the English (including the Anglo Danes) and Ruler of Britain (or, as I have seen it expressed more fully, "Ruler of the pagans and Champion of the Britons"). He styled himself to rule or overlord the lot, including all ambiguities and differing origins of ethnicity, with emphasis on promoting a commonly held Christian Identity framework. It was from that point on that "England" could emerge.

"Engla-Lond"

"Engla-Lond", i.e. England, was a term existing but not much in use, even in Athelstan's time. There were no set national borders. The centralised political entity was still developing too. The term more applicable was "the English", as a people group, not "England" as a territory.

"Britain"

"Britain", in Athelstan's time, most often meant the Welsh and the Scots as people groups. It might or might not include the Anglo-Danes, depending upon how much they were perceived to be integrating or not into Christian Identity with the Angelcynn. It sometimes meant the geographical island itself.

Got all that?

Phew.

No wonder you could throw bricks by the cartload in any crowded gathering in England today without serious danger of even grazing someone who knows how they first came to be the English and England, let alone that their Identity was Christian through and through.

King Athelstan's Career

Anyway, now to King Athelstan's career.

In 926, Athelstan followed up on the earlier peace feelers from Danish York to Aethelflaed in 918. He came to an agreement with the Danish King of York, Sihtric, not to go to further war. Broadly, the English had recovered all of Mercia, and the Danes kept most of Northumbria.

In 927, however, Sihtric died. There was no settled succession. Whilst a cousin, Guthfrith, mustered forces from Dublin to contest for it, Athelstan slipped forces of his own into York and took it over, and with it, most of Northumbria. You could infer it as a sneaky conquest. But you could also call it safeguarding the infant Christian peace from a new wave of warlike settlers in the North. This is for sure: Athelstan took York peacefully, fulfilling the peace feelers to Aethelflaed in 918. I would infer that the dying Aethelflaed had committed them to her Christian God. I am surprised that the bloodlessness, a hallmark of the Christian God when human beings will let him work that way, goes generally unremarked.

Over the next seven years, Athelstan's concept of himself as "King of the English" and "Ruler of Britain" developed in a fluid way. "English" now broadly included Northumbria as well as Eastern Mercia and East Anglia. It was by now discernibly the English nation that descended to us. It would be an exaggeration, however, to say that Athelstan had won over the hearts and minds in Northumbria.

"Ruler of Britain" meant broadly, as from 927, overlord in what we now call Wales and Scotland. Relations had become quite good with the Welsh. You may recall that his grandfather, Alfred, had made great use of Welsh Christian sources. However, the relations were also forceful: Athelstan took a lot of tribute. Even so, the Welsh rulers had a high place of honour. They either fought on Athelstan's side or at least stood aside from conspiring against him.

Relations with the "Scots" were less stable. "Scotland" did not yet exist, no more than "England" did. What we mean by "Scot" in Athelstan's time is different to what was meant in King Oswald's time. As at 635, "Scot" meant Gaelic Celt or the "Scoti" as the Romans called them. Three hundred years on, Gael and Pict had merged into the Kingdom of Alba. Modern commentators seem to call those people "Scot" already, but I think they run ahead somewhat in doing so. As I understand it, what we now call Scotland emerged once Alba went on to assimilate peacefully the many Angles of the Border regions after Athelstan's time. Victorian history and modern DNA analysis seem to agree on that.

Anyway, Athelstan's relations with the Kingdom of Alba were uneasy. Alba had a preference to ally with the pagan Vikings of Dublin. My enemy's enemy is my friend, and all that; we can agree on opposing the "English". Centuries of hurt had developed since the times of the Synod of Whitby, Bishop Wilfrid and King Ecgfrith of Northumbria.

To continue, the relationship between the "Ruler of Britain" (or Champion of the Britons) and the Kingdom of Alba was very uneasy. From 927 to 934, peace held throughout the north. Athelstan had the reluctant submission of the King of Alba, Constantine II, to his overlordship. However, in 934, Viking Dublin broke the peace and Constantine II seems to have rooted for them. At that time, Athelstan took forces to the very far north of what we now call Scotland to enforce renewed overlordship. Welsh forces were on his side. No battle ensued.

In 937, however, Viking Dublin and Alba forces joined full-on battle with Athelstan, invading English territories. Welsh leaders stood aside. Athelstan emerged as the victor from the bloodiest battle of the age, known as Brunanburh. He was unable to build any form of government structure into Alba, however. It was never a realistic proposition. From then on, Alba changed tack, quietly assimilating the Border Angles, and out of that came Scotland. The process was made much easier for them by the Angles having the legacy Gaelic Martinian Christian spirituality, above all that of St Cuthbert. Centuries of Christian commonality had developed as well as centuries of hurt. Care to guess which element is emphasised in the conventional histories and which is airbrushed out?

Athelstan died two years after Brunanburh in 939. The Viking threat to the English was defeated. The threat from Alba to the English was defeated. Wales was on reasonable terms. What we now call England was fairly secure for the Christian English and their ambiguously viewed Anglo-Danish Christianising settlers. Northumbria remained distinct, sub-nationalistic, and prone to erupt into further conflict internally within the English whole. Force would continue to be needed for a while to keep it on side. But basically, the Kingdom of the English was established firm.

King Athelstan – His Motives

It is important to remember what Athelstan had secured the Kingdom of the English for. He had not secured it for personal aggrandisement. He had not secured it for Imperial glory. He had secured it for Christian Identity. He had a big ego. But within a Christian understanding, that is not the same thing as pride. You can have a big ego but be humble. Or you can be self-effacing but proud – 'umble, like Uriah Heep. It depends whether the Christian God has broken you in or not, rather like a horse. Athelstan had been broken in, I would say. His heart was to serve. A strong king with an ego can be humble, in Christian terms, if he is also a servant king. Paradox upon paradox, but that is the way of things with the Christian God. Jesus Christ, Servant King, had the strongest of strong egos.

There were many things that the modern mind could highlight out of context and condemn in King Athelstan. However, in a culture emerging from fragmentation and existential threat, he was noble, civilising, law-making, a developer of delegating government, and in general a Christian of Integrity. He was Christian first, Warrior second. Even in his "Ruler of Britain" mode, what he wanted above all was high Christian standards. The modern mind might dwell on his tribute taking. Athelstan's mind, for reasons we explored in earlier chapters, would have dwelt on his forbiddance of idolatry – his Christian mission to liberate the peoples from the oppression of it. Athelstan had the ancient Christian understanding: there were hidden courts behind the idols. He wanted his peoples and his tributaries free from them in Christ. Patronising? Or spiritually insighted Christian? Rulership was a means to an end: Christian good. As regards Wales and Scotland, we might note the expanded version which I have read of his title, "Ruler of the pagans and Champion of the Britons". If accurate, that would better summarise Athelstan's inner attitudes. "Champion" means an Advocate for the Celtic Christian peoples. "Ruler" indicates determination to Christianise the pagan.

Now, here's the point: under Athelstan, the "English" did not rally to become "English" in the modern secular sense. "English" was the titling word that emerged during the process. There is no doubt that a distinct sense of ethnicity was a driving force for survival. But the creative force, the restore-and-new-build element, was the uniting sense of Christian Identity. That had drawn upon multiple reconciled, fused and transcended ethnic sources to make a people much more complex than the tribal Germanic original.

Therefore, the thing to remember is this. The Early English did not fight to be English. They fought to be Christian. Then they called themselves English. And in the process became quite inclusive, by the standards of the times.

I would sum it up for King Athelstan like this:

- As to "King of the English", Athelstan fulfilled what King Alfred the Great had begun, bringing the West, the East and the Anglo-Danish into the Christian English whole.

- As to "Ruler of Britain", he was never going to succeed in Alba.

Although the title of "Engla-Lond" had yet to be formalised, by the end of Athelstan's life we can see "England" set to take shape, "Wales" set to take shape, and "Scotland" set to take shape.

A Sense of "Calling"

I would infer from all this the following, out of a Christian understanding. Athelstan had a Calling under the Christian God to secure the Christian Identity of the Angelcynn – Kin of the English – including the Anglo-Danes. In regard to the latter, he completed in Christian peace what Aethelflaed would have committed to the Christian God. As a *sign* that he did indeed have a Calling to do that, York was taken without bloodshed. Seeking to rule beyond this Call, however, he overreached. Brunanburh, 937, was bloodshed followed by stalemate. In a Christian understanding: stick to your Calling, not less, not more.

These days, some might baulk at the use of the word "Calling". However, a sense of Calling is normal in human beings in many walks of life. It is not a uniquely Christian thing. Some people have it in the medical profession, services, teaching or politics. In general, it comes with a spiritual drive to serve. The Christian God harnesses something perfectly normal in many people to impart a sense of Christian Calling. That is how it was it was with King Athelstan.

It imparted to Athelstan a sense of destiny, and he acted out of that. These days, it seems to be fashionable to sneer at the idea of a sense of destiny. But if you have a "Calling", you also have a sense of destiny to fulfil it. The two are symbiotic. It is consistent to reject the idea of "Destiny" if you believe that all things arise from impersonal forces, all patterns in human life imagined. However, if you do not believe that, if you do believe there is meaning in life, then of course people can have a sense of destiny. What could be more rewarding than fulfilling it? And what could be more wholesome than to recognise it?

King Athelstan – Difficult Christian Things

Athelstan's Christian Life had three features that might perturb the modern mind:

- He remained celibate. Did he have guilty secrets?

- He was an avid collector of relics and carried them around with him. Were these superstitious totems for victory?

- He was a Christian Warrior. Surely the Christian God is a pacifist?

As to celibacy, the Christian Bible makes it clear: to be able to fulfil a life of celibacy is a gift of the Christian God to some, not all. No-one should presume upon the gift. If you do not have the gift, do not remain celibate. That is what will lead to guilty secrets. If you do have the gift, it will not lead to guilty secrets. Jesus Christ and the Apostle Paul: celibate. The Apostle Peter: married. To each their Calling. Everything in Athelstan's record indicates integrity in his celibacy: he had the Christian gifting required for it. Just like Jesus Christ.

As to relics, I could think of few things more dismal than relics when I was young. So much corruption and occultism came to surround them. Nowadays, I can find a more tolerant way of seeing them. I would not want them in my world, but I can come to terms with them, as follows:

Alfred the Great set store by Christian relics. He was not corrupt or superstitious. Athelstan had an absolute passion for them. He was not corrupt or superstitious either. That indicates that they were both on the right side of following rule of Christian thumb:

- If you trust in the relic, that equals occultism.

- If the relic prompts you to seek out the Christian God in respect of the Christian example which the relic leads you to value, that could be fine with the Christian God.

Athelstan was a noble-minded man. He wanted the high value that every relic represented to be at work within his times.

As to relics as a totem for victory, of course Athelstan wanted victories. However, within a Christian understanding, it would depend how you relate with the Christian God when seeking war victory. If you try to manipulate the

Christian God, having no relationship with him, the Bible says this: God is not mocked. If you have integrity and humility, however, having a genuine relationship with the Christian God, as many of the Early English rulers did, then a relic would not be a totem; it would be a prompt to relate with the Christian God over the coming battle. He may or may not give you victory. Whichever way it went, you would want to be in the centre of his will. That approach is the normal one for a Christian in any walk of life. I see no reason why it would not have been Athelstan's.

As to "Christian Warrior" and the Christian God as a pacifist, any atheist who reads the Bible will tell you, correctly it seems to me, that the Christian God acknowledges a real world in which rulers sometimes have to fight. We must note a central hero of the Bible, King David. In the Early English times, he would have been the obvious hero figure of the Christian ruler. There is a Commandment to do no murder. It is not to be translated as do not kill. You see that in King David. The Christian God called him to much warfare. David went too far on occasions, but by and large, his God said that he honoured David. However, David also plotted one murder. His God disciplined David very severely for that.

Some might say, well, defensive war is all that would be allowed. However, as any football supporter knows, attack is sometimes the best form of defence. That was the way of King David, for what it is worth. He was less moral than a moralist, but he did have the wisdom of a football supporter. As did many of the Early English Christian Kings.

Am I making an apology for "Holy War"? By no means. King David fought to secure the Messianic Line. Kings Oswald, Anna, Alfred and Athelstan fought to secure Christian Identity. Different framework, same principle, within the envelope of the Christian Bible. Only one rogue king made Holy War, Caedwalla of Wessex, and in doing so cursed the generations after him. Besides, any King could lay down their kingly Calling and die defenceless as a monk, like King Sigeberht of the East Angles. They were free under the Christian God to do that.

So, King Athelstan, Christian Warrior: Christian First, Warrior Second. His great example would have been King David. And he would have homed in on one of the titles of Jesus Christ: Son of David.

Now of course, another title of Jesus Christ is Prince of Peace. The Christian God of the Bible is full of paradoxes like those two titles. They never resolve, running like everlasting parallel railway lines. It follows that Christian history will be full of paradox too. And a great deal of irony.

The Formalisation of "England" – King Canute

Which brings us to a final great irony within the sequence of the history. Very ironic for Alfred the Great. Not what he intended at all. Maybe what his Christian God intended, but not Alfred. And a very humbling irony for English Pride as well. It was not the English who formalised the existence of a nation called England. They invented the name. But it was given to the Danes to institute what we now call England as England.

After Athelstan, and indeed from then to the Norman Conquest in 1066, Christian standards declined within the old Anglo Saxon ethnicity. There was peace between ethnic origin Anglo Saxon and Danish for a while. But from about 980, new waves of Danish forces invaded again. By 1002, there was an English king named Aethelred the Unready. Aethelred means noble counsel. Unready means foolish or ill-counselled. "Aethelred the Unready" means "Wise by name but foolish by nature". He loosed a treacherous massacre on his Anglo-Danish subjects.

In response, forces came out of the Danish homeland and eventually prevailed for the kingship over all the Angelcynn. In 1016 there came to the throne a young King, Canute, who had something in common with Alfred the Great and Sir Winston Churchill: he had been moulded as an infant into a Christian worldview by his mother. Yet another lost-to-history Christian female hand that rocked the cradle that shaped the world. She was named Gunhild, of Polish extraction, and not even accorded the status of marriage.

Canute took "Engla-Lond" as a violent young King. He came under the influence of a gifted and wise Archbishop of York, Wulfstan II. Yet another example of a gifted cleric as the right person in the right place at the right time. Note his Northern base too: a much-overlooked integrator of the uneasy North into the whole.

Canute's behaviour as he went through life indicates to me that he co-operated with the Christian God as the wise Archbishop's guidance touched chords with his earliest upbringing. He was politically astute and, as a Christian, wise. The modern mind puts a wall between the political world and "Religion". With the Christian God, there is no such wall, and neither was there in Canute.

There was to be no Deliverer for the old Anglo Saxon ethnicity this time round. It was the Danish one that had the Christian wisdom, and more integrity with it.

There is an old tale that King Canute tried to order the tide to stop coming in. He sat on a throne to command the incoming waves to recede. But he got his feet wet. From that, he gets called out as vain. If there is any substance at all in the tale, Canute would have been showing his people that the Christian God, not he, is the one who has power over the wind and waves, as Jesus Christ is recorded to have had. And doing so in a way profoundly relevant to his seaborne Danish culture, saying, as it were: "We rule the waves by boat," – as they did – "but there is one whose power over the waves is greater still. Trust in him, not your King." Which would have been as culturally relevant a Biblical message as it is possible to be.

Anyway, the point about King Canute is this. He became wise with discernible Christian wisdom. He reconciled the Angelcynn and Anglo-Danish ethnicities on common Christian foundations and with the governing and legal structures that had arisen from the lineage of Alfred the Great of Wessex. It was a big step forward in the context of his times. It went beyond what Alfred could have imagined or Athelstan achieved. And in token of that, it was in Canute's time that England came customarily to be called "Engla-Lond" to distinguish it from Canute's Danish territories.

More Christian Phenomena, Saint King Oswald's Bones, St Cuthbert's Visitation

It remains for me, in closing this journey from the seed times of the Christian English to the Nation-founding times, to explore these things:

- St Cuthbert appearing to King Alfred in 878.

- Aethelflaed winning the defining battle on Saint King Oswald's Day in 910, after giving a special place to his bones in her new church.

We have King Alfred's testimony for the first event. We have the facts for the second. As to King Alfred's testimony, I won't rehash all the arguments from the chapter about St Martin of Tours. Suffice to say, it would be appropriate to admit it to a court of law.

So, how can we come to terms with the following phenomena?

- St Cuthbert, passed away 687, appearing to King Alfred 878.

- Aethelflaed, Alfred's Genius Daughter, winning the Battle of Tettenhall in 910 on St Oswald's Day. Having laid the bones of Saint King Oswald in her new church at Gloucester not long before. Those bones having been involved in the Northumbria/Mercia peace of 679 and being the long-standing focal point of a cult.

Banana oil? Superstition? Occult? Coincidence?

Well, we should note certain Christian principles.

i.   The Christian God calls himself Father. He enjoys giving gifts to those children he adopts in Christ. He particularly loves to do so in ways that have unique significance for them. These impart delight in the adult Christian like the delight in a child on Christmas morning. They affirm relationship and love. Now, to Aethelflaed for example, what could have been more uniquely significant and affirmatory than winning a defining battle on a day which would have had special meaning for her? In my lifetime, I have heard many a testimony in Protestant Christian churches which could be paraphrased like this: "God heard my prayer in a way which included a sign special to me, like a unique fingerprint of affirmation. I'm full of wonder." After winning at Tettenhall on the set-apart Day of the Saint King who was both her hero and origin-seed godfather, Aethelflaed would have felt like that. It is a normal and frequent testimony of Christians worldwide. So why would the Christian God not give Christian Aethelflaed victory on a day special to her? The Apostle Paul warned against setting apart special days for reasons of religiosity. He did not proscribe the Christian God from developing a relationship with his children.

ii.   There is no problem per se with a departed person of Christian Faith appearing for a purpose after bodily death. Jesus Christ appeared to many after death. And the Christ said that as things had been for him, so they could be for his followers. It would be at the discretion of the Holy Spirit of the Christian God. Jesus Christ said that he was the resurrection and the *life*, meaning that all Christians live in him whatever may have happened to their body and pending their ultimate resurrection. So there is no problem with one of the Christian God's departed ones being delegated to appear for a purpose: Elijah and Moses appeared to Jesus.

As to involving the bones of Saint King Oswald, the modern mind recoils. However, think of Christian bones as a means of Christian grace, relevant within their culture, provided that the one whose bones are honoured had significant Christian Anointing and the one honouring them trusts in the Christian God rather than the bones – has Christian Integrity, in other words. Significant Christian Anointing on Oswald: tick. Significant Christian Integrity in Aethelflaed: tick. The bones were bones. But Oswald's Anointing bridged across them.

The nearest analogy in the Christian Bible is handkerchiefs blessed by the Apostle Paul healing the sick. Handkerchiefs are handkerchiefs. Bones are bones. But Paul had enormous Christian Anointing and his disciples had premier league Christian Integrity. To this day, Protestant small c catholic Christians tend to be just fine with someone blessing a handkerchief. They carry it to the sick to impart the Anointing of the one who has done the blessing.

Paul was alive and Oswald was dead, a big difference. However, Jesus Christ declared that he is the resurrection and the *life*. This means that any Christian remains alive with Christ pending the day of their resurrection. Therefore, if the Holy Spirit of the Christian God so wishes, he can pass on something of what was on Oswald to the living. It would be part of Oswald's reward, very fulfilling to him.

Returning to the bones, they would also be a culturally relevant prompt. To this day, a Protestant small c catholic might watch a film of great Christian teaching of bygone times. Then they would pray that the Christian values which were in the departed teacher would be alive and on them in their times. The film is the culturally acceptable prompt to draw near to the Christian God. Aethelflaed would have prayed in the presence of the bones, broadly, "May what was on Saint King Oswald be on me and in my times." No difference. The bones were the prompt to draw her near to the Christian God.

Bones are a big hang-up these days because much deception, occultism and superstition developed around them as Medieval corruptions matured. But… since when did what was guilty cause the Christian God to reject the innocent? If *you* are Aethelflaed's Christian God, in her times, and she has innocent integrity in her praying, you work with the innocent grain.

I am not saying for a moment that I would want a culture of bones and relics back. I would say that the culture belongs with a world I would not want to live in. And gave rise to dismal things as corruption matured.

Nor am I saying that every vision of a departed Saint is valid. But they can be. There is no reason why the likes of a Cuthbert may not be delegated to appear at the discretion of the Holy Spirit of the Christian God.

However, I am saying that we need open eyes and minds when considering Christian phenomena in our past. Many of them, as we have seen throughout this book, tend to be well within the envelope of the Christian Bible. Just because we fashionably practice cancel culture on them does not mean the Christian God may not have worked them. A cat hides its head behind a curtain, its backside poking out. It thinks you can't see it. To dismiss the Christian phenomena is to think like the cat.

In the cases of Cuthbert and Oswald, much would depend upon whether there was a Christian prophetic element in the phenomena linked with them. And there was. As follows:

- St Cuthbert was a Northumbrian Saint of Angle-ish ethnicity but Gaelic Celtic Martinian Christian spirituality. He embodied a reconciliation. Saint King Oswald embodied the same.

- Saint King Oswald had been the spiritual progenitor of Wessex as it was Oswald who had first sponsored Wessex into Christ. Saint King Oswald was the original or seeding godfather to Alfred's family, in other words. The Biblical analogy would be Abraham and the Christian. In terms of spiritual descent, Abraham can validly be called "father", small f, of the Christian. The first verse and chapter of the New Testament establish that. Now, no Christian prays to Abraham. But they all treasure his example under their God. And ask their God for the faith that had been in Abraham to be alive in them. By extension of the analogy, Aethelflaed would not have prayed to Oswald. But she would have treasured his example under her God and wanted it alive in her.

- St Cuthbert became the highest expression of the Christian spirituality which Oswald had stood for. Oswald had fire-started the process which led to Cuthbert. So Cuthbert was a fitting ambassador to Alfred of what Alfred's seed-godfathering Christian king, Oswald, had started.

- In his lifetime, if you recall, Cuthbert had lived by non-contentious spirit. It seems that the effect of his cult, reconciliation, was consistent after his death with what he had embodied in life. By Athelstan's time, St Cuthbert was becoming a rallying force that transcended ethnic division of Dane and Angle in the North. The transcending of ethnic division was consistent with what Oswald had embodied in life as well.

So then what might they stand for, Oswald and Cuthbert, to a royal Wessex Christian understanding enlightened by the Holy Spirit of the Christian God?

- Saint King Oswald, you could say, would stand for the political union of peoples on Christian foundations. He would also stand for ethnic divisions united in Christian grace. And, although Alfred's ancestral family was a cousin branch of the one godfathered by Oswald in 635, he seems to have been seen as the progenitor godfather in Christ for the whole.

- Saint Cuthbert, you could say, would stand for the highest expression of Christian spirituality within a Christian polity. He would also stand for a uniting force which transcended ethnic divisions.

- Put another way, Oswald and Cuthbert combined would stand for much that Alfred might have seen as seminal within his Christian understanding. He did, after all, take an ethnicity-transcending Christian approach to peace with the Danes. In the end, it worked out beyond his imagining. But think about it: no sooner the visitation of the ethnicity-reconciler, Cuthbert, than the first baby steps to ethnicity-reconciling Christian peace with the Danes.

What better way to encourage Alfred and Aethelflaed, then, than a visitation by Saint Cuthbert and a significant victory on Saint King Oswald's day?

As to the nature of the encouragement to King Alfred before the Battle of Edington, that repays some thinking about. Alfred would have intuited out of the visitation by Cuthbert:

- That he was being confirmed in the Calling which was conferred when he was singled out by the Pope at age five.

- That he was affirmed as being of the spiritual lineage which had brought Christian Wessex into being.

- And that he was to rest assured that his Christian God would be with him to restore what was good in it.

Strengthening, don't you think? Very strengthening. And hardly delusional, given that he did fulfil the Calling, was in the spiritual lineage and did restore what was good in it.

Put another way, the following sense of destiny would be planted into Alfred and develop in Edward the Elder, Aethelflaed and Athelstan: "What Saint King Oswald had stood for, and what Saint Cuthbert had stood for, is alive in you and will be fulfilled in you." All of which turned out to be true.

It would have been out of this, not weird superstition in his misguided-little-ancient-head that Edward the Elder raided for the bones of Oswald in 909.

There is another implication that comes across too. In Alfred the Great's time, the old debates about whether the outward trappings of Christian expression should be Gaelic or Roman had long gone. Roman was the norm. Within Christian Identity, however, the outward trappings tend to be beside the point. They matter to human beings but not to the Christian God. An Old Testament prophet said that human beings look on the outside whereas God looks at the heart. Updated to a New Testament understanding, church forms are one thing, spiritual reality is another.

So what is the *sign* asking to be uncovered, then, in that St Cuthbert was the one delegated from the Christian heaven, apparently, to strengthen Christian King Alfred before the turning point battle of his Christian life and Christian English history? That the Gaelic Martinian Life in the Holy Spirit of old Northumbria, which had been seeded through Oswald and Cuthbert, was in the mix once more in Alfred and his family.

It was not in the original form. The Gaelic Martinian spirituality had fused into the whole with the Romano Martinian and Roman Catholic as long ago as

Theodore's time. And the old Northumbrian expression of it had been overrun and semi-paganised in Northumbria itself. But we've already covered this: Christian spiritualities, once sown, once there has been an Anointed progenitor of them, pop up in later generations, different people groups, and different places. They are not tied to physical lineage. Spiritual lineage works differently.

The *sign*, therefore, is this: Alfred and family inherited, in modified and developed form, the full power of the ancient Fusion Christian Identity which had been conceived in the Early English in 597, born in 635 in Saint King Oswald, and perfected in Saint Cuthbert.

Well, it is harder not to see it than to see it.

Now, you may prefer to apply a more modern understanding to all of this, i.e. "Superstition; coincidence; there are no patterns; all are imagined". That is consistent, providing that you also believe that all things arise out of impersonal blind process, which seems to be the modern English belief system.

However, how is that approach any more reasonable than the Christian understanding I have set out here? It has consistency and integrity with the Christian belief system. And it has consistency and integrity with the facts of the history. The one thing I make allowance for, which is unusual for the modern mind, is that the Christian God might be active in history through Christian people. How is making allowance for that any less valid than assuming that all things are subject to blind process?

Legacies

When it came to the crunch, when all seemed nearly lost, a family arose which took forward the Christian Identity that had first been laid two hundred and fifty years before in times of momentous Christian Awakening. Out of that, in the end, came first the Christian English and then Christian England.

As to "England", that became an Identity which has not passed away from that day to this. The English defined their Identity within England as a Christian Identity for about a thousand years from Alfred's time to the Great War of

1914-18. It came into being upon shared and intertwined Romano Gaelic Martinian Catholic Fusion Christian foundations. These made for Life in the Holy Spirit of the Christian God in the many figures whom I have recovered in this book. That did not express itself on a "religious" side of a great wall dividing it from "reality", as the modern mind would be inclined to see. It intertwined Christian Reality with all other forms of reality.

To me, nothing in the England of today signifies what made England better than Canterbury Cathedral. If you visit a cathedral in, for example, Italy, it is a grand statement of "Church", usually presenting a beautiful face. The Cathedral at Canterbury is a symbiotic interweaving of "Church" with "State" within real and turbulent English history. It presents not a beautiful face but the face as it is. And it is still standing, with an elegant bone structure, through centuries of tumult.

Christian Identity had been conceived in King Ethelbert of Kent in 597; been born in Saint King Oswald of Northumbria in 635; developed like an irresistible tide in the face of the sword of King Penda of Mercia; overwhelmed Mercia; and been planted deep into Wessex.

By 689, Archbishop Theodore of Canterbury had embedded the Christian Fusion Identity into the founding roots of intertwined Church and State. In his times, the Early English went Off to School in it. By 927, they had Graduated. What Theodore first laid down, and Alfred's family restored, endured to the watershed of the Great War, 1914-18.

Norman rule from 1066 swapped out the aristocracy but it did not change the English Christian Identity. The Protestant Reformation did not change it either. Large C Catholic became small c catholic. The monolithic Romanised expression of Christian Identity became diverse. Once English-speaking Protestants were ready to outgrow four hundred years of sectarianism, the ancient Martinian Christian spirituality – which was Life in the Holy Spirit of the Christian God – was released into the wider earth more powerfully than ever before, in myriad new outer casings and labels.

I close with this: King Alfred the Great of Wessex, his genius daughter Aethelflaed and his formidable grandson Athelstan secured this Martinian Christian legacy to descend to countless millions worldwide today. So they secured a good deal more, you might say, than England and the English. Not that they knew it at the time. But they had Christian Anointing, and it is in the nature of Christian Anointing to activate the long-run processes which lead to more than we ask or imagine.

CHAPTER 23.

The Mustard Seed

This book has been for anyone of any background, ethnic English or not, Christian or not, to see how "Christian England" first came to be.

I have sought to be accurate with facts and dates. I have done my best not to mislead as to the facts I interpret. My focus has been on bringing lost and hidden things back to light.

I used many sources but will highlight for you just three if you want to read further:

i.   *The Ecclesiastical History of the English People by Bede*

ii. *They Built on Rock by Diana Leatham (re the Celtic Saints)*

iii. *Martin of Tours by Christopher Donaldson*

Why the stress on "England"?

I suppose that this book has discovered not only the Christian spiritual roots of the English but also, in part, their neighbours in the United Kingdom and any who descend from any part of that.

Therefore, the focus on England-only may surprise. I apply it out of respect, not nationalism. Let me explain.

Whether, from anywhere in the world today, you descend from British ancestry out of any part of the UK or you come today from a part of the UK which is not England, this book is focussed on the English not because I believe in a narrow England but because each component of the UK and of UK descent has a subtly different history of Christian Identity. It would be for a Scot to write up Scotland; Welsh and Northern Irish to write up Wales and Northern Ireland;

American, Australian et al., as descended from any part of the UK, the same. I have dwelt on England out of respect for that, not out of narrow nationalism.

It is impossible, however, to write about the Christian Early English without seeing how they interacted with the Christian Scotic and Britonnic Welsh. Therefore, I have shown you certain Christian roots that became common to the spiritual rootstock in all. And I have left some clues in this book for anyone who wants to follow up elsewhere for other parts of the UK or elsewhere in the world.

If the very words "Christian" and "English" grate on you

If you come from any background, tradition, belief system or sense of ethnicity that causes the words "Christian", "English", "England" and "Christian English" to grate, I see it like this. Things which have brought "Christian England" into disrepute in more recent history have more often arisen when the English have been cut off from what was good in their Christian roots. Things that have been good in the English have arisen when they have acted with integrity out of the good side of their Christian roots. It is in everyone's best interests for the English to rediscover their Christian roots. They draw out the kind side; they draw out the fusion side. Much that is good in English culture to this day descends from Christian values.

So I see it like this: if the English were to recover the good side of their Christian Identity, it would be to the benefit of any and all cultures they engage with. Well, so it seems to me. Found souls are generally more gracious than lost souls.

I see it like this, as well. The modern English want to find something to be proud of. Their Christian heritage is a much-overlooked candidate, and it has the following distinction: the good in it comes from Life in the Holy Spirit of the Christian God, not from humankind's own strength. Therefore, none can boast. That would be the Christian understanding. This distinction has the following effect: the Christian heritage is something good to be proud of without becoming conceited. Put another way, if the English were to celebrate the good side of their Christian history, the collective mental health would improve and the collective national head would still fit through the door.

As to the Christian God, differing ethnicities within human life are practicalities with which he works in a reconciling way. And as to Life in the Holy Spirit of the Christian God, there is no ethnicity in it. Therefore, just as any English belong to England, and any Christian belongs to Christ, so any Christian English belong to Christian England and, with that, to the spiritual heritage whose founding times have been recounted in this book. The Christian Bible puts it like this: *all* the different apostles belong to you. Therefore, for example, Saint King Oswald, Saint Cuthbert and King Alfred the Great belong to anyone in the England of today.

I know they try to tell you otherwise. But the Christian logic is as I have just set out.

If you have Christian Background

If you come to this book from a Christian background, this is not a Christian discipleship or teaching book. I have not done a systematic presentation of the way the Christian God engages. Jesus Christ used this image of the Holy Spirit of the Christian God: he is like the wind. You may see the leaves rustle, but you do not see the wind. For the most part, the Christian God lets principles which he claims to have spoken into everything take their course as human beings activate them, for better or for worse. Therefore, you have to discern the principles which have prevailed in the real history. Those are the leaves that rustle. My focus has been on those.

"Christian Bible" – Why I keep adding "Christian"

The Bible used by Christians comprises two Testaments, Old and New. The Old is derived from the more ancient scriptures of the Jewish peoples. Christians honour the Old as well as the New. When I use the phrase "Christian Bible", it means "both Testaments of the Bible as Christians understand the whole".

Roman Catholic?

This writer is of Protestant catholic background. When I write that, for example, the old Life in the Holy Spirit of Saints Martin and Cuthbert is alive and well in the world today through Protestant Christians since the Reformation, I am not trying to say that the spirituality is not also alive in the Roman Catholic Church. I highlight the Protestant aspect in this book because it may come as a surprise to the Protestant Christian, it being something that many eyes have been closed to. My purpose has been to open eyes to lost and hidden things, remember.

I would hope that a Roman Catholic might rejoice more than take offence.

Personally, I never use the word "Catholic" and not often the word "Protestant". I say either "Roman Catholic" or "Protestant catholic". This is not just a matter of being accurate. All readers might reflect on what healing and wholeness are in this way of saying things rather than the more conventional "Catholic" and "Protestant". Much confusion endures from not understanding the difference between large C and small c as I explained it in writing about St Martin of Tours.

For any Christian reader of any persuasion, this book assumes that what shapes history for the best within Christian Identity is Life in the Holy Spirit of the Christian God. I try not to be bothered what form that takes. When you have that in a Roman Catholic set-up, all well and good to me. If you do not have it in a Protestant catholic set-up, more's the pity.

Not Perfect

The backdrop to this book is warrior culture and much darkness. And not all, in English history, who have taken the name of Christ have belonged to the Christ. For the modern mind, the lack of 100% perfection in Christian history seems always to be a stumbling block. As it was for King Penda of Mercia, so for the modern mind.

However, we should remember what the Christ taught: that the Christian influence would be like, for example, salt in meat or fish. You don't eat pure salt. You eat salted meat or fish. It remains meat and fish. There only needs to be enough salt to make the purifying difference. In English history, until the Great War, there were often enough Anointed Christians at the heart of the culture to do so. There certainly were in the times I have written about.

It is important to remember, too, that the Christian God is not an idealist. Jesus Christ and Paul between them taught that this God has bound the world over, for the time being, to frustration, irony and a mixture of good and bad. Jesus Christ taught that the mixture will only get sorted when he returns, and Paul clarified when this would be: when the Christian God deems the family of Christ to have become complete worldwide. Until then, the light of Christ shines within darkness which tries to put it out.

However, as the Christian would see it, the source of what is dark is never the Christian God. He has bound human beings over to frustrations so that they might come to humility of understanding. Until then, the Christian God, although he engages with a world of much trouble, is not the author of it. He is the Redeemer of it. As to the system of irony into which the Christian God has bound all things over, that prevails as human beings seek to bend all things to self-will and their own control. The Christian scriptures indicate that the period allowed for that, and for the system of irony which results, is temporary.

Things that stood out for me as I researched

I never expected to write such an epic. I set out to develop the charming story of King Ethelbert and Queen Bertha of Kent in 597. I thought the book would be slim and small. Instead, I discovered what I would hold to be the second most transformative Christian Awakening of all history. Only the transformation of the Roman world in the origin Christian times exceeded it. By transformative, I mean a thoroughgoing change to both the cultural and official senses of Identity. "Turned the world upside down" is how some sought to describe it back in the days of the Apostle Paul. Rome became constitutionally Christian.

The same happened to the English. In Queen Elizabeth II, the English part of the United Kingdom may be the last remaining such entity on earth, apart from, I should think, the Vatican City.

I say this because I came to realise that, since the Church of England and the UK state are accountable to the monarchy separately, the monarchy is formally Christian English within the England part of the UK. Therefore, I reflect that this book recounts, for what is now a very confused nation of the English, the origins of what, constitutionally, their head still makes them. When I say in the book that the English departed from Christian Identity after the Great War, I mean that in terms of collective psyche.

I was amazed when I uncovered the Christian spirituality roots of our present Queen of the United Kingdom. It descends from united-into-one Christian Life in the Holy Spirit from the most ancient Scotic, Welsh and Northern Irish sources. If you allow for the Christian understanding that all the generations are one, her godfather was the Angle-ish Saint King Oswald. As for Saint King Oswald himself: epic – Early England's Christ figure. But indebted to St Patrick and the Gaelic Scots. Humbling, I found that.

I was moved, too, when I dug into the lives of the Celtic Saints and their spiritual descent from St Martin of Tours. Take St Patrick, for example. He extended Christian grace to his enslavers: in so doing, he set loose a chain of blessing which descended to the English – who are now known for hurting the Irish whose Patron Saint he is.

As an Englishman, I was also humbled when I came to understand what a debt the English and England owe for their Identity to so many Christian others: Latin, Greek, North African, Frankish and Danish, besides Scotic, Welsh and Irish. Christian Identity from so many sources turned pagan Dark Age Anglo Saxon tribes into the Nation of the English.

Then again, I was taught, like so many, that the Vikings in their boats of war had somehow shaped the English. The Martinian Christian Saints in their boats of peace – *they* shaped the English. The Vikings adopted what had been in them.

Artwork: Denise Critchell

These were the origin seed shapers of the Early English.

Martinian Christian monks.

As to the conventional understanding that Alfred the Great set up secular England: he and his family brought forth the Christian English, Christian and English fused.

As to the Christian God's sevenfold reply to King Penda of Mercia, serial killer of Christian kings, that took my breath away.

I was struck, too, that time after time, a Christian leader with significant Anointing from the Christian God was the right person in the right place at the right time for the Early English.

The Temptation of St Martin

Another thing that stood out for me was the temptation to St Martin of Tours, on the penultimate day of 25 years' service against his will in the Roman Army, to comply with the Emperor and lose his Christian Integrity. Only one day to go. Compromise. Martin would not, so he found himself on the front line for a coming battle without armament. The opposing force stood down on the day, the very last day of his 25 years.

One thing which longer life in the Holy Spirit of the Christian God teaches you is that no-one has enduringly strong Christian Anointing without having been subjected to the most probing tests of their Christian integrity. Some can have Christian Anointing spectacularly for a while without integrity, but sooner or later, they blow up. Some of them can recover it. But none can either recover it or maintain it enduringly without sharp testing. What was in St Martin has blossomed to this day, spiritually, worldwide. That tells its own tale, I think.

Ritual versus Reality

The prevailing modern English cultural picture of their earlier Christian ancestors seems to be a caricature of religious ritual merchants chanting behind closed doors, profiting from superstition, whilst the real world got on with the smiting. However, smiting builds little or nothing. Fighting might secure values and civilisation. But values and civilisation arise out of spirituality. And history tends to be shaped, in the long run, by the spirituality that is the most embraced.

For the English of today, it seems to be a chaotic spirituality that is the most embraced: personal meaning is sought within a system of belief in an impersonal process. For the Early English, however, it was Christian spirituality that was embraced. That came out from multiple sources. The effect of it was that the English matured into Christian Identity on a rootstock of Life in the Holy Spirit of the Christian God. There were three Founder generations from 587 to 689, and three Restorer generations from 878 to 927. Their Christian spirituality first set up, and later rescued, much of what became good within the very turbulent and mixed history of the English.

The Christian Reality, meanwhile – which is Life in the Holy Spirit of the Christian God – is at large in the real and wider world to this day, even if the post-Great War English have decided to caricaturise it as religious ritual.

The Mustard Seeds

Jesus Christ spoke of the mustard seed, the tiny seed which would become the largest plant in the garden. He meant his family of faith. Worldwide today, it has become so.

The original seed was the Christ himself. He pointed out that he must fall to the ground like a seed and die. From that would sprout the crop.

Others following on can also become types of mustard seed, sowing small, reaping large down the generations.

I was in the churchyard of the tiny church of St Martin's in Canterbury and spied the huge cathedral in the distance. I realised that I was looking at a *sign*: the tiny church as the long-term seed of the greater one. However, buildings are not seeds. People are seeds. In this case, the mustard seed was Queen Bertha of Kent. Her grown-up plant is the worldwide Anglican Communion. The Protestant Reformation shaped the plant, but it did not give it origin. Rather, it released the plant to sprout some more.

I soon realised that in Saint King Oswald of Northumbria, I was looking at another mustard seed. Out of him came Christian England.

To my great surprise, I discovered a well-hidden seed: James of York, the Deacon. Out of him came the Christian contents beneath the lid of the tin labelled Christian England.

As for St Martin of Tours, has any human follower of the Christ seeded more? Life in the Holy Spirit of the Christian God comes, in the origin, out of Jesus Christ and the Apostle Paul. But St Martin was the seed of its spiritual descent to the West. Remember the secular understanding that it was outlying monks who saved Western civilisation? They were Martinian monks. And they did not save their civilisation just to illustrate beautiful old books. They saved it for Life in the Holy Spirit of the Christian God. That was their motive for copying the books.

What the World Considers Small

The Apostle Paul taught that the Christian God would make a speciality of impacting the real world through those whom the world would think of no account: small, like the mustard seed that the Christ taught about.

None of these four people I have brought to light for you goes remarked by modern history. Queen Bertha, a footnote; James of York, lost; Saint King Oswald, a footnote. Pseudo figures such as King Arthur are preferred these days to Early England's epic and real-life Christ figure. St Martin of Tours – "Who?" says the worldwide Protestant Body of Christ descended from him. Confused by relabelling and by the inheritance of an indiscriminate loathing of the past, you see.

I have highlighted just these four. You may discern others in the book too.

Thankfully, however, if we are to trust the Christian Bible, then, at the end of all things, the books will be opened to these four and to all of them. Then we shall see. Until then, it has been my privilege and delight – I have had a sense of wonder in compiling this book – to bring these figures back to at least a little bit of the light which I think they deserve.

It would do much good to the Mental Health of the modern English to rediscover and celebrate their founding Christian heroes. Well, I think so, anyway. So, Good Mental Health to you, England. For the most part, it would be a matter of saying "Thank you" to the many Christian ancestors from many cultures. They seeded that element which is good in you.

CHAPTER 24.

Saint King Oswald of Northumbria

Early England's Christ Figure

Artwork: Denise Critchell

The Legacy of Saint King Oswald Down to this Day

When Saint King Oswald of Northumbria sponsored the royal family of Wessex into Christian Identity in 635, he became its godfather. He also mixed his Christian spirituality with that of Bishop Birinus, who administered the teaching and the baptismal sacrament. Oswald: Gaelic Martinian Christian; Birinus: Romano Martinian Catholic Christian. This fusion seed spirituality became the ultimate Fusion Christian Identity of the Early English: they grew up to become Romano Gaelic Martinian Catholic. Even to this day, whether Protestant small c catholic or atheist, that is the ancient cultural and spiritual root of the English.

Interestingly, the present royal family of the United Kingdom descends from King Alfred the Great of Wessex. He was from a cousin branch of the Wessex royal family which Oswald sponsored into Christian Identity in 635. The family of Alfred the Great defined Saint King Oswald as the hero at the heart of their culture and aspirations in the times when they were founding the Nation of the Christian English. They seem to have seen him as their origin-seed godfather in Christ. Once his Christian spirituality had seeded into one branch of the family, it spread out into all.

Now, in a Christian understanding, all the generations are one in Christ. In a sense, therefore, you could see Saint King Oswald as either (i) the godfather of our present Queen Elizabeth II or, if that stretches it too much for you, at the very least (ii) the defining original Christian hero of her English Nation-founding family.

Put another way, what Oswald sowed in Christian faith in Wessex in 635 is with us to this day in the monarchy of the United Kingdom.

Interesting to recall, the Martinian spiritual legacy which descended to Angle-ish Saint King Oswald followed this chain:

St Patrick – North of Ireland and onwards to St Columba via St David – Scotland and Wales

So you could say that the proto-English godfather of the royal family of the United Kingdom took his Christian Identity from the rest of the proto-United Kingdom. And the Christian seed which was in Oswald has descended to this day in a monarchy which unites those nations. And all things in that seed belong to any person with Christian Identity, or English Identity, or other part of the UK Identity, or UK-descended Identity, or any combination of these.

Also interesting to note, the spirituality of St Martin of Tours, seed of the lot of them – Oswald, Patrick, David and Columba – had much in common with that of a modern Protestant small c catholic Christian who also has Life in the Holy Spirit of the Christian God. That remains the most alive section of the church in England down to this day.

Blessings sown in faith descend to a thousand generations… the Second Commandment in the Old Testament of the Bible used by Christians.

I sense enduring and real-world-history-shaping mysteries for meditation.

Index

A

Aethelflaed, Lady of the Mercians, 326, 347, 351

Aethelfrith, King of Northumbria, 46, 47, 48, 50, 52, 53, 54, 55, 61, 69, 73, 79, 80, 95, 97, 289

Aethelwulf, King of Wessex, 323, 324, 328, 337, 338, 339, 340, 341

Aidan, Saint, 17, 22, 90, 93, 94, 100, 101, 106, 110, 111, 113, 114, 117, 118, 123, 124, 125, 129, 130, 132, 133, 135, 136, 139, 144, 161, 163, 164, 181, 182, 188, 193, 197, 198, 200, 212, 213, 214, 215, 218, 223, 224, 232, 255, 265, 267, 270, 282, 298, 299, 308, 332,335, 350

Aldfrith, King of Northumbria, 272, 290, 304, 311, 314, 315, 316, 317, 318, 319, 320

Alfred, the Great, 9, 13, 26, 27, 39, 90, 91, 93, 96, 97, 99, 100, 107, 114, 115, 125, 133, 134, 142, 146, 149, 193, 194, 201, 202, 206, 209, 268, 269, 270, 271, 283, 284, 310, 321, 322, 323, 324, 325, 326, 327, 328, 329, 331, 333, 334, 336, 337, 338, 339, 340, 341, 342, 343, 344, 345, 346, 347, 348, 351, 352, 353, 354, 355, 358, 360, 361, 362, 363, 364, 367, 368, 369, 370, 371, 372, 375, 379, 384

Alhfrith, sub-king of Deira, 230, 231, 278

Anna, King of the East Angles, 18, 20, 113, 127, 128, 137, 138, 139, 141, 142, 144, 174, 181, 187, 189, 190, 193, 197, 198, 208, 232, 234, 254, 266, 268, 361

Arian, 153, 155, 156, 157, 158, 159, 160, 241, 242, 243, 246, 247, 251, 252, 253

Arianism, 153, 154, 155, 157, 158, 159, 161, 240, 241, 266, 267, 283

Athelstan, King of the English, 26, 134, 326, 327, 328, 349, 351, 352, 353, 354, 355, 356, 357, 358, 359, 360, 361, 362, 363, 367, 369, 372

Augustine of Canterbury, Saint, 11, 13, 14, 15, 21, 31, 34, 35, 37, 38, 39, 41, 42, 43, 45, 47, 48, 49, 50, 56, 57, 58, 60, 61, 63, 67, 68, 72, 73, 74, 75, 80, 83, 84, 92, 110, 111, 113, 120, 121, 124, 138, 153, 155, 163, 165, 168, 169, 171, 172, 173, 174, 203, 207, 259, 261, 267, 281,282, 332

B

Bardney, monastery, 296, 298, 349, 350

Becket, Saint Thomas, 130, 131

Bede, Historian, 38, 49, 50, 53, 54, 57, 59, 60, 61, 62, 63, 64, 65, 72, 84, 94, 98, 115, 116, 124, 139, 140, 141, 153, 165, 166, 168, 171, 188, 189, 204, 215, 220, 226, 228, 231, 259, 261, 290, 296, 298, 299, 302, 312, 316, 317, 329, 373

Bertha, Queen of Kent, iv, 13, 14, 28, 29, 30, 31, 33, 36, 41, 42, 43, 45, 49, 56, 57, 58, 80, 83, 102, 117, 147, 167, 177, 188, 195, 207, 208, 229, 230, 251, 254, 257, 377, 381, 382

Birinus, Bishop of Wessex, 16, 17, 89, 90, 91, 92, 93, 101, 103, 106, 110, 111, 118, 121, 122, 140, 144, 164, 165, 178, 200, 234, 254, 266, 267, 282, 285, 384

C

Caedmon, singer, 191, 219, 221

Caedwalla

Caedwalla of Gwynedd, 15, 51, 52, 53, 55, 77, 78, 79, 80, 84, 94, 97, 98, 99, 105, 107, 108, 148, 214, 215, 216, 221, 267, 270, 312
Caedwalla of Wessex, 175, 329, 330, 331, 332, 333, 361
Candida Casa, founded by St Ninian, 102, 148, 257, 260, 265
Canute, 26, 328, 345
Caranoc, Saint, 260
Cathedral, Canterbury, 13, 38, 41, 43, 46, 135, 244, 371
Cedd, Saint, 204, 205, 232
Cenwalh, King of Wessex, 18, 23, 121, 122, 128, 140, 141, 142, 174, 181, 198, 201, 234, 254, 277, 285
Chad, Saint and Bishop of York and Mercia, 23, 204, 230, 232, 235, 278, 283, 295
Churchill, Sir Winston, 342, 343, 362
Clovis 1, King of the Franks, 251, 252, 253, 255, 258
Coifi, pagan priest, Northumbria, 65, 66, 67, 68, 73, 161, 332
Colman, Bishop of Lindisfarne, 223, 224, 226, 227, 235, 278, 299
Columba, Saint, 14, 15, 16, 17, 33, 34, 68, 88, 95, 96, 97, 99, 100, 102, 124, 139, 148, 224, 255, 263, 264, 265, 266, 267, 269, 270, 271, 299, 350, 384, 385
Columbanus, Saint, 15, 16, 68, 69, 88, 89, 92, 93, 124, 128, 155, 158, 161, 255, 264, 265, 266, 267, 268, 282
Cuthbert, Saint, 24, 25, 26, 60, 99, 100, 113, 114, 117, 140, 163, 164, 181, 182, 223, 228, 231, 235, 255, 265, 267, 268, 269, 270, 271, 277, 278, 287, 290, 298, 299, 300, 302, 303, 304, 305, 306, 307, 308, 309, 310, 312, 314, 316, 324, 332, 334, 335, 344, 349, 356, 364, 366, 367, 368, 369, 370, 375, 376
Cynegils, King of Wessex, 17, 18, 103, 121, 140, 339

D

David, King, 26, 91, 96, 97, 112, 148, 149, 252, 253, 342, 344, 361, 362
David, Saint, 265, 384, 385
Deusdedit, Archbishop of Canterbury, 21, 22, 180, 206, 207, 231, 234, 277, 281, 285
Dunwich, seat of Bishop Felix, 269

E

Eadbald, King of Kent, 14, 18, 49, 50, 57, 58, 75, 121, 137, 167, 168, 169, 170, 171, 173, 177, 204
Eanflaed, Queen of Northumbria, 15, 18, 19, 20, 22, 62, 80, 82, 194, 195, 208, 214, 215, 216, 220, 223, 272, 289, 312
Ecgfrith, King of Northumbria, 231, 234, 235, 272, 289, 290, 294, 295, 304, 311, 312, 313, 314, 315, 316, 317, 356
Edington, Battle of, 26, 344, 368
Edward the Elder, King of Wessex, 325, 326, 327, 346, 348, 350, 351, 369
Edwin, King of Northumbria, 14, 15, 18, 46, 47, 50, 51, 52, 53, 54, 55, 56, 57, 58, 59, 61, 62, 63, 64, 65, 66, 67, 68, 69, 75, 76, 77, 79, 80, 81, 82, 83, 84, 90, 94, 95, 98, 103, 104, 121, 126, 128, 141, 161, 167, 174, 186, 187, 190, 197, 198, 207, 214, 221, 289
Elizabeth Everest, 342, 343
Eorcenberht, King of Kent, 18, 19, 50, 113, 137, 138, 177, 180, 195, 208, 231, 254, 281
Eorcengota, daughter of Anna and Seaxburh, 137, 138, 139, 195
Eormenhild, Queen of Mercia, 195, 208, 278
Eorpwald, King of the East Angles, 14, 15, 67, 68, 69, 75, 77, 92, 141, 174
Ethelbert, King of Kent, iv, 11, 13, 14, 18, 28, 29, 30, 34, 35, 36, 37, 38, 39, 40, 41, 43, 44, 45, 46, 47, 48, 49, 50, 56, 57, 58, 61, 65, 67, 70, 72, 75, 76, 83, 92, 117,

121, 137, 138, 167, 168, 169, 170, 171, 173, 174, 177, 203, 207, 371, 377

Ethelburgha, Queen of Northumbria, 14, 15, 18, 56, 57, 58, 59, 62, 79, 80, 83, 167, 173, 188, 195, 207, 208, 214

F

Felix, Bishop, East Anglia, 16, 17, 92, 93, 101, 106, 110, 111, 118, 122, 138, 144, 161, 165, 200, 254, 266, 267, 269, 282

Fina, Princess, 272, 311, 314, 315

Finan, Bishop of Lindisfarne, 223

Fursa, Monk, East Anglia, 93, 165, 166, 167, 282

G

Gregory, the Great, Pope, 30, 31, 35, 36, 39, 42, 45, 49, 57, 58, 72, 84, 111, 113, 153, 154, 155, 158, 165, 169, 170, 171, 172, 203, 285, 286, 292, 343

Guthrum, Danish leader, 270, 324, 344, 345

H

Hadrian, Abbot, Canterbury, 281, 282, 316, 317, 332

Heavenfield, Battle of, 16, 99, 107, 109, 190

I

Iona, monastery, 14, 17, 18, 33, 34, 54, 88, 97, 100, 102, 106, 123, 124, 132, 148, 192, 213, 220, 223, 263, 265, 267, 272, 290, 315

Isle of Wight, 175, 289, 291, 317, 329, 331, 332, 333, 337, 340

J

James, of York, singer, the Deacon, 76, 81, 82, 193, 221, 229, 317, 381, 382

Jaruman, Bishop of Mercia, 196, 232, 233, 234, 278, 295

John, of Beverley, Bishop of York, 288

L

Lerins, monastery, 60, 172, 255, 259, 261, 264

Leuthere, Bishop of Wessex, 142, 282, 284, 285, 286

Liudhard, Chaplain Bishop of Queen Bertha, 29, 30, 36, 58, 254

M

Martin, Saint, 11, 99, 102, 172, 174, 211, 224, 237, 238, 241, 242, 245, 246, 247, 251, 252, 253, 254, 255, 256, 257, 258, 259, 260, 261, 264, 265, 268, 269, 298, 300, 305, 306, 350, 364, 373, 376, 378, 380, 382, 385

Martin's, Saint, church in Canterbury, 30, 249, 381

N

Ninian, Saint, 102, 148, 149, 224, 255, 256, 257, 258, 259, 260, 264, 265, 269, 350

O

Oethelwald, sub-King of Deira, son of Oswald, 145, 146, 187, 189, 190, 215, 223, 312, 313

Osburh, Osburh, of Wessex and Isle of Wight, 209, 323, 328, 337, 339, 343

Osthryth, Queen of Mercia, 296, 298

Oswald, of Northumbria, Prince, King, Saint King, iv, 14, 16, 17, 18, 24, 26, 47, 50, 54, 69, 82, 84, 85, 86, 88, 89, 90, 91, 93, 94, 95, 96, 97, 98, 99, 100, 101, 102, 103, 104, 105, 106, 107, 108, 109, 110, 111, 113, 114, 118, 119, 121, 123, 124, 125, 127, 128, 129, 130, 131, 132, 133, 134, 135, 136, 137, 140, 141, 143, 144, 145, 146, 147, 148, 149, 150, 161, 174, 182, 187, 189, 190, 192, 194, 197, 198,

202, 213, 215, 217, 218, 221, 223, 229,
254, 257, 258, 262, 263, 264, 265, 267,
269, 270, 271, 273, 290, 293, 294, 296,
297, 298, 308, 310, 311, 312, 315, 317,
318, 319, 320, 321, 326, 339, 347, 349,
350, 356, 361, 364, 365, 366, 367, 368,
369, 370, 371, 375, 378, 381, 382, 383,
384, 385
Oswestry, Oswald's Tree, 128
Oswine, King of Deira, 22, 181, 213, 214,
215, 229, 312, 318

P

Patrick, Saint, 60, 95, 102, 136, 172, 173,
174, 192, 218, 224, 255, 256, 258, 259,
260, 261, 262, 263, 264, 265, 266, 293,
299, 313, 315, 350, 378, 384, 385
Peada, sub-King, Mercia, 20, 182, 183, 187,
188, 191, 192, 193, 194, 217, 311
Pelagian, 74, 161, 196
Penda, King of Mercia, 15, 17, 18, 20, 51,
52, 55, 57, 67, 77, 78, 79, 80, 84, 90, 94,
97, 98, 101, 102, 104, 105, 107, 118,
119, 121, 122, 125, 126, 127, 128, 129,
130, 131, 132, 133, 135, 141, 142, 143,
144, 145, 146, 150, 161, 175, 180, 181,
182, 183, 184, 185, 186, 187, 188, 189,
190, 191, 195, 196, 197, 198, 199, 200,
201, 202, 205, 209, 213, 214, 215, 216,
217, 225, 230, 232, 291, 294, 310, 312,
313, 332, 371, 376, 379

R

Raedwald, King of the East Angles, 14, 48,
49, 50, 51, 52, 53, 54, 56, 61, 62, 67, 68,
69, 70, 92, 174, 289, 336
Rhiainfellt, of Rheged, Princess, 102, 132,
182, 188, 190, 214, 223, 272, 311

S

Saxnot, god in London, 204

Seaxburh, Queen of Kent, 18, 19, 113, 137,
138, 177, 180, 195, 208, 254
Sigeberht
Sigeberht of East Angles, 14, 16, 18, 67,
68, 69, 77, 82, 89, 92, 93, 105, 106,
110, 122, 127, 128, 138, 141, 165,
187, 197, 198, 254, 266, 361
Sigeberht of Essex and London, 21, 22,
204, 205, 232

T

Theodore, Archbishop of Canterbury, iv,
24, 25, 27, 125, 195, 206, 222, 236, 277,
280, 281, 282, 283, 284, 285, 286, 287,
289, 290, 292, 293, 294, 295, 298, 304,
305, 309, 310, 311, 312, 314, 316, 317,
321, 325, 332, 335, 349, 370, 371
Trumhere, Bishop of Mercia, 125, 194,
195, 196, 233, 234, 278, 294, 295

W

Whitby, Synod of, 22, 23, 82, 191, 218,
219, 220, 221, 222, 223, 225, 227, 228,
229, 230, 231, 232, 277, 286, 287, 289,
291, 292, 299, 300, 305, 316, 356
Wilfrid, Bishop, 24, 181, 182, 222, 223,
224, 226, 227, 229, 230, 231, 235, 272,
277, 278, 283, 284, 286, 287, 288, 289,
290, 291, 292, 293, 295, 298, 299, 304,
305, 307, 309, 310, 311, 312, 313, 316,
317, 329, 330, 332, 356
Wine, Bishop of Wessex and London, 23,
234, 235, 277, 279, 285
Winwaed, Battle of, 20, 187, 189, 190, 192,
203, 216, 217, 218, 223, 232, 294, 312,
320
Woden, god of the Anglo Saxons, 126,
162, 163, 186, 197, 203
Wulfhere, King of Mercia, 194, 195, 196,
231, 232, 233, 234, 278, 294
Wulfstan II, Archbishop of York, 363

Lightning Source UK Ltd.
Milton Keynes UK
UKHW021302161222
414042UK00012B/373